THE LATE ROMAN WORLD
AND ITS HISTORIAN

Interpreting Ammianus Marcellinus

THE LATE ROMAN WORLD AND ITS HISTORIAN

Interpreting Ammianus Marcellinus

edited by
Jan Willem Drijvers
and David Hunt

London and New York

First published 1999
by Routledge
11 New Fetter Lane, London EC4P 4EE

Simultaneously published in the USA and Canada
by Routledge
29 West 35th Street, New York, NY 10001

Routledge is an imprint of the Taylor & Francis Group

© 1999 Edited by Jan Willem Drijvers and David Hunt

The right of Jan Willem Drijvers and David Hunt to be identified
as the Author of their contributions to this work has been asserted by them
in accordance with the Copyright, Designs and Patents Act 1988

Typeset in Garamond by Graphicraft Limited, Hong Kong
Printed and bound in Great Britain by Biddles, Guildford and King's Lynn

All rights reserved. No part of this book may be reprinted or reproduced
or utilised in any form or by any electronic, mechanical, or other means,
now known or hereafter invented, including photocopying and recording,
or in any information storage or retrieval system, without permission in
writing from the publishers.

British Library Cataloguing in Publication Data
A catalogue record for this book is available from the British Library

Library of Congress Cataloging in Publication Data
The late Roman world and its historian : interpreting Ammianus
Marcellinus / edited by Jan Willem Drijvers and David Hunt.
  p.   cm.
Includes bibliographical references and index.
ISBN 0–415–20271–X
  1. Ammianus Marcellinus—Contributions in history of late Roman
Empire. 2. Historians—Rome—Biography. 3. Greeks—Rome—
Biography. 4. Rome—History—Empire, 284–476—Historiography.
5. Emperors—Rome—History. I. Drijvers, Jan Willem. II. Hunt,
David (Edward David), 1947– .
DG206.A4L37   1999
937'.08'092—dc21   99–18312
                                                                  CIP

ISBN 0–415–20271–X

CONTENTS

Notes on contributors viii
Acknowledgements x
List of abbreviations xi

1 Introduction 1
   DAVID HUNT AND JAN WILLEM DRIJVERS

PART I
Ammianus, soldier and historian 15

2 Ammianus Marcellinus and fourth-century warfare:
   a *protector*'s approach to historical narrative 17
   FRANK TROMBLEY

3 Preparing the reader for war: Ammianus' digression on
   siege engines 29
   DAAN DEN HENGST

4 The Persian invasion of 359: presentation by suppression in
   Ammianus Marcellinus' *Res Gestae* 18.4.1–18.6.7 40
   JOSEPHINA LENSSEN

5 The outsider inside: Ammianus on the rebellion of Silvanus 51
   DAVID HUNT

6 Ammianus and the eunuchs 64
   SHAUN TOUGHER

CONTENTS

PART II
Images of emperors 75

7   Images of Constantius   77
    MICHAEL WHITBY

8   Telling tales: Ammianus' narrative of the Persian expedition of Julian   89
    ROWLAND SMITH

9   Ammianus on Jovian: history and literature   105
    PETER HEATHER

10   *Nec metu nec adulandi foeditate constricta*: the image of Valentinian I from Symmachus to Ammianus   117
    MARK HUMPHRIES

11   Ammianus, Valentinian and the Rhine Germans   127
    JOHN DRINKWATER

PART III
Rome, the historian and his audience 139

12   Ammianus Satiricus   141
    ROGER REES

13   A Persian at Rome: Ammianus and Eunapius, *Frg.* 68   156
    DAVID WOODS

14   Some Constantinian references in Ammianus   166
    BRIAN WARMINGTON

15   *Templum mundi totius*: Ammianus and a religious ideal of Rome   178
    THOMAS HARRISON

PART IV
The world beyond, Persia and Isauria 191

16   Ammianus Marcellinus' image of Arsaces and early Parthian history   193
    JAN WILLEM DRIJVERS

CONTENTS

17 Pure rites: Ammianus Marcellinus on the Magi   207
    JAN DEN BOEFT

18 *Visa vel lecta?* Ammianus on Persia and the Persians   216
    HANS TEITLER

19 Ammianus Marcellinus on Isauria   224
    KEITH HOPWOOD

Select bibliography   236
Index   241

NOTES ON CONTRIBUTORS

Jan den Boeft is Professor of Latin at the Free University, Amsterdam. He is also professor extraordinarius for Hellenistic religions at Utrecht University and editor-in-chief of *Vigiliae Christianae*. He is co-author of the commentaries on Ammianus Marcellinus Books 20–3.

Jan Willem Drijvers is Lecturer in Ancient History at the University of Groningen. He is co-author of the commentaries on Ammianus Marcellinus Books 22–3.

John Drinkwater is Professor of Roman Imperial History in the Department of Classics at the University of Nottingham. He is editor (with H. Elton) of *Fifth-Century Gaul* (1992), and is currently working on a book on Gaul from the third to the fifth century.

Thomas Harrison is a British Academy Postdoctoral Fellow in the Department of History, University College London. He has written a number of articles on Greek historiography and is the author of a forthcoming monograph entitled *Divinity and History: The Religion of Herodotus* (Oxford University Press).

Peter Heather is Reader in Early Medieval History at University College London. He has written extensively on Goths and other barbarians, and is just completing a volume for the Liverpool Translated Texts for Historians series on the fourth-century Greek philosopher and orator, Themistius.

Daan den Hengst is Professor of Latin at the University of Amsterdam. He is co-author of the commentaries on Ammianus Marcellinus Books 20–3.

Keith Hopwood is Lecturer in Classics at the University of Wales, Lampeter. He has compiled a bibliography of ancient history and has edited a volume on *Organised Crime in the Ancient World*. He has contributed articles on classical, Byzantine and Ottoman Asia Minor to classical and oriental periodicals.

Mark Humphries is Lecturer in Classics at the National University of Ireland, Maynooth. He is the author of *Communities of the Blessed: Social Environment and Religious Change in Northern Italy, AD 200–400* (1999), and is a contributor to *The Cambridge Ancient History*.

NOTES ON CONTRIBUTORS

David Hunt is Senior Lecturer in Classics and Ancient History at the University of Durham. He has contributed three chapters on the late Roman empire to the new *Cambridge Ancient History*, and has also written articles on the theme of Christianity in Ammianus Marcellinus.

Josephina Lenssen (Department of Classics, University of Amsterdam) is completing a book on narrative technique and historical credibility in Ammianus Marcellinus. She has taught Latin at the University of Amsterdam and the Free University, Amsterdam.

Roger Rees is Lecturer in Classics at the University of Edinburgh. He has written articles on Latin poetry and prose and is preparing a book on Tetrarchic panegyric.

Rowland Smith is Lecturer in Ancient History at the University of Newcastle-upon-Tyne. He has research interests in late Roman society and culture, and is the author of *Julian's Gods: Philosophy and Religion in the Thought and Action of Julian the Apostate* (Routledge, 1995).

Hans Teitler is Senior Lecturer in Ancient History at the University of Utrecht. He is co-author of the commentaries on Ammianus Marcellinus Books 20–3.

Shaun Tougher is Lecturer in Ancient History in the School of History and Archaeology at the University of Wales, Cardiff. He has written articles on the relations between Julian, Constantius II and the empress Eusebia, and also on eunuchs in the Byzantine world.

Frank Trombley is Senior Lecturer in Religious Studies at the University of Wales, Cardiff. He has written books and articles on late Greek paganism and Christianization, and more recently on war and religion in late Roman and Byzantine society.

Brian Warmington was formerly Reader in Ancient History at the University of Bristol. He is the author of several books, including *The North African Provinces from Diocletian to the Vandal Conquest*, and has written a number of articles on Constantinian topics.

Michael Whitby is Professor of Classics and Ancient History at the University of Warwick. He is co-editor of *Cambridge Ancient History* XIV, and has published on the Greek historiography of the later Roman empire; he is currently working on the late Roman army.

David Woods is Lecturer in Classics at the University College of Cork, Ireland. He has published widely on the military martyrs, the life of Constantine I, and Ammianus Marcellinus. He is currently working on a monograph on the organization, identities and succession of the *magistri militum* during the period *c.* 350–408.

ACKNOWLEDGEMENTS

This book is the result of an international conference held at the University of Durham from 28 to 31 August 1997. The conference was a joint initiative by British and Dutch scholars working on Ammianus, and we are grateful to the Department of Classics in Durham for hosting the occasion and handling the administration. Our thanks go to all the participants, many of whom have contributed to this volume. Van Mildert College provided a congenial environment for our formal sessions, as well as lavish hospitality conducive to friendly conversation at both bar and dinner-table. A welcome feature of the gathering was the presence of a considerable number of postgraduate students, and we are grateful to the Classical Association for the financial support which made this possible; we also benefited from grants provided by the University of Groningen's research centre, COMERS.

January 1999
David Hunt
Jan Willem Drijvers

ABBREVIATIONS

AJAH	American Journal of Ancient History
AJPhil.	American Journal of Philology
ANRW	Aufstieg und Niedergang der römischen Welt
AS	Anatolian Studies
CAH	The Cambridge Ancient History
CHI	The Cambridge History of Iran
CIG	Corpus Inscriptionum Graecarum
CIL	Corpus Inscriptionum Latinarum
CP	Classical Philology
CQ	Classical Quarterly
FGrHist	F. Jacoby, Fragmente der griechischen Historiker (Leiden 1923–)
FHG	C. Müller, Fragmenta Historicorum Graecorum (Berlin 1841–70)
GRBS	Greek, Roman and Byzantine Studies
G&R	Greece and Rome
ILCV	E. Diehl, Inscriptiones Latinae Christianae Veteres (Berlin 1925–31)
ILS	H. Dessau, Inscriptiones Latinae Selectae (Berlin 1892–1916)
JESHO	Journal of Economic and Social History of the Orient
JHS	Journal of Hellenic Studies
JRA	Journal of Roman Archaeology
JRS	Journal of Roman Studies
LCM	Liverpool Classical Monthly
OLD	Oxford Latin Dictionary
PLRE	The Prosopography of the Later Roman Empire (Cambridge 1971–92)
RAC	Reallexikon für Antike und Christentum (Stuttgart 1941–)
RE	Real-Encyclopädie der classischen Altertumswissenschaft (Pauly/Wissowa)
REA	Revue des études anciennes
REL	Revue des études latines
RhM	Rheinisches Museum für Philologie
RIC	The Roman Imperial Coinage

ABBREVIATIONS

RPh	*Revue de philologie*
SEG	*Supplementum Epigraphicum Graecum*
SHA	*Scriptores Historiae Augustae*
TLL	*Thesaurus Linguae Latinae* (Leipzig 1900–)
Vig. Christ.	*Vigiliae Christianae*
ZPE	*Zeitschrift für Papyrologie und Epigraphik*

1

INTRODUCTION

David Hunt and Jan Willem Drijvers

A bibliographical essay, 1947–97

When in late August 1997 the contributors to this volume gathered in Durham, it was fifty years since the publication of E.A. Thompson's pioneering study of the late Roman historian Ammianus Marcellinus.[1] This book had appeared in an age when English-speaking scholarship (at least) had largely ignored Ammianus: in an isolated, but appreciative, essay J.W. Mackail had once remarked of the historian that he 'has in this country long suffered undue and unfortunate neglect'.[2] In Thompson's day, only M.L.W. Laistner accorded him a useful survey.[3] Ammianus fared rather better among French and German scholars, and in 1947 Thompson was able to turn to the still basic work of Gimazane (then nearly sixty years old) and to Ensslin's sharply concise overview of the political and religious outlook of the *Res Gestae*.[4] While acknowledging Ammianus' qualities – rating him a better historian even than Tacitus – Thompson was the first to abandon reverential insistence on the reliability and impartiality (Gibbon's 'accurate and faithful guide') of a narrative earlier applauded by Mackail as that of 'an officer and a gentleman', in favour of more critical analysis of the prejudices and pressures which shaped Ammianus' coverage of contemporary events. Through a lively examination of selected episodes in the narrative, Thompson exposed not only the extent to which the sympathies of the 'middle-class' *curialis* from Antioch (who became a Roman army officer) coloured the substance of what he wrote, but also the political constraints which he believed the coercive regime of the emperor Theodosius I imposed upon the composition of the last part of the work (Thompson regarded Books 26–31 as a later product than the rest). Thompson's approach, which centred upon the engagement between Ammianus' own contemporary experience and the writing of the *Res Gestae*, also led him to question the emphasis which traditional *Quellenforschung* had accorded to identifying the historian's written sources: for him Ammianus' surviving books were not derivative, but – as the historian himself claimed them to be – first-hand history compiled from personal observation and encounter. The debate about Ammianus' source material continues to this day, especially in relation to the narrative of Julian's ill-starred military intervention in Persia, where the opportunities of comparison with other contemporary accounts and fragmentary survivals have generated a series of investigations into the elusive extent of Ammianus' literary dependence for the record of events in which he himself participated.[5] Thompson's stress on the priority of autopsy in the Persian narrative found influential backing from Louis Dillemann in 1961;[6] and more recently thirty years on Charles Fornara has defended the same view against the continuing fascination with Ammianus' sources.[7]

Thompson's exposure of the partiality of Ammianus' narrative was taken up by Andrew Alföldi in respect of the confrontation between the regime of Valentinian I and the senators of Rome: the distortion which Thompson had attributed to constraints imposed by the time of composition was now less charitably denounced as 'incredibly one-sided' and 'wild prejudice'.[8] Alföldi interpreted Ammianus' stance in defence of the supposedly beleaguered senators as a reflection of traditional aristocratic opposition to imperial tyranny, and the historian's own close identification with the interests of the Roman establishment (he was writing and publishing the history in Rome). This was a view of Ammianus which could be traced back via Thompson to Ensslin's 1923 monograph; but it was to be significantly challenged by Alan Cameron, who undermined the historian's traditional association with the Roman élite of the likes of Symmachus and Praetextatus ('as a newcomer in the capital, *miles quondam et Graecus*, he would not have found it easy to break into society'),[9] and pointed the way to the less exalted company of expatriates and retired courtiers in the capital (like the eminent eunuch Eutherius) where it is these days natural to find him. This distancing from the Roman establishment also freed Ammianus from the expectation of traditional stereotypes: it became less easy to take his work for granted as one which displayed an 'identikit' Roman outlook and matching attitudes. Demandt's 1965 dissertation revealed the diversity of viewpoints reflected in the *Res Gestae*, both on contemporary affairs (barbarians, Christianity, Roman society) and on matters of religion and theology (fate, fortune, nemesis, etc.): Ammianus emerged here as something of an unsystematic pragmatist who defied tidy labelling.[10] The view of barbarians, for example, was far from the unqualified hostility of Roman tradition (Ensslin's 'römischer Patriotismus'); equally the work's religious standpoint, though clearly 'pagan', was not uniformly averse to Christianity.

As an indication of Thompson's success in stimulating scholarly interest in Ammianus on this side of the English Channel, Demandt's work was honoured with a considerable review-discussion by Ronald Syme, and the observation that 'nobody can resist Ammianus Marcellinus'.[11] Syme's own failure to resist was fuelled by his investigations into the composition of the *Historia Augusta*, which he held to display evidence of literary dependence on Ammianus (although not all were convinced by the parallel passages which

Syme adduced to support his contention).[12] None the less Syme's sensitivity to the question of literary dependence marked an important development in the understanding of Ammianus' 'views': in reviewing Demandt Syme noted his neglect of the 'bookish' dimension of the historian's writing – obviously integral to any conclusions about what he actually thought – and called for more attention to be paid to Ammianus' 'reading-matter'. It was a call which had already been heeded by P.M. Camus, whose work explored Ammianus' eclectic cultural background in both Greek and Latin learning (an aspect generally missing from previous studies), and its impact on the religious attitudes displayed in the *Res Gestae*.[13] Despite Camus' more 'literary' approach, the conclusions which emerged were not in the end substantially different from those of Demandt: Ammianus represented an empiricist medley of views which did not sustain a coherent ideology ('son credo païen est inorganique'). In one respect at least Camus did identify a more consistent strain in the historian's position, in his lofty conception of the emperor's role in the world as a divinely inspired phenomenon, and thus pointed the way to a number of later studies which would preoccupy themselves with Ammianus' contemporary perspective on imperial power.

A shift of emphasis towards the literary influences and techniques conditioning the nature of Ammianus' work produced its most sceptical outcome in the pages of Klaus Rosen.[14] Again the veracity and objectivity of the narrative were impugned, but the distortions which Thompson had blamed on partiality or political constraint were now presented as endemic features of Ammianus' historiography: for Rosen this was an amalgam of Hellenistic artistry and Roman moralizing, which combined to the detriment of historical accuracy and called into question the reality of the historian's record of events. Most, if not all, subsequent study of Ammianus has focused, directly or indirectly, on addressing this balance of objective reality and literary invention. Soon after the publication of Rosen's thesis Jacques Fontaine was already dubbing Ammianus 'historien romantique', and Wolfgang Seyfarth was writing of the hostile portrayal of Petronius Probus under the title 'Legende und Wirklichkeit';[15] Hans Drexler emphasized again the stylized characterization and moralizing;[16] to be followed by Norbert Bitter's thoroughgoing exposé of the rhetorical artifice and literary derivativeness of the battle descriptions, which left the officer-historian seemingly devoid of any claim to objective accuracy in military matters (although reviewers were quick to protest that rhetoric and reality are not mutually exclusive).[17] Ammianus had in fact already found a champion of his credentials as a 'military historian' in G.A. Crump, who, while not ignoring the literary features, none the less sounded a positive note on the historical value of Ammianus' treatment of military matters, and on his contribution to our knowledge of the late Roman army.[18] Crump's confidence in the historian's reliability, in reaction to the more 'literary' readings in the tradition of Rosen, was later given more detailed and specific direction by N.J.E. Austin, who proclaimed of Ammianus that he was the 'most important military writer since Caesar'.[19] Paying closer attention to the text than Crump, Austin detected in its choice of content and emphasis a perspective derived from the real world of Ammianus' own military experience, i.e. that of a staff-officer closely involved in the transmission of intelligence, information and orders.

R.C. Blockley's 1975 monograph on Ammianus had derived from a doctoral thesis supervised by Thompson, and it duly recognized that the historian's repeated profession of truth and accuracy was a literary refrain which deserved to be met with caution.[20] This 'study of his historiography and political thought' in fact amounted to a collection of discussions of different episodes and themes from Ammianus (on the Thompson model), from which certain dominant and related ideas emerged: the construction of the narrative around the characterization of individuals, especially of the emperors, who were designed to conform to traditional moral types of virtue (Julian) and vice (almost all the rest); the significant influence of Hellenistic models of the good ruler; and Ammianus' extensive deployment (notably more so than in other ancient historians) of *exempla* from the Greek and Roman past, mostly to reinforce the pervasive moralizing tone. Blockley demonstrated the extent to which Ammianus' (real) perception of his contemporary world revolved around the person of the emperor and the manifestations of his rule, even if this was voiced through moral stereotypes derived from his literary heritage. If this presented Ammianus as a rather conventional purveyor of hackneyed notions of right and wrong behaviour, the same could hardly be said of Guy Sabbah's massive study of his historical technique.[21] Sabbah focused closely and in attentive detail, not on rehearsing Ammianus' dependence on older sources and traditional models, but on investigating his use of all manner of contemporary material – eyewitness accounts, official reports and documents (Sabbah attempted to demonstrate that the bulk of the history was based upon access to such information), and awareness of other current literature, Greek and Latin, pagan and Christian. Although Sabbah's approach begged the question of the earlier books of Ammianus (which cannot have shared this first-hand methodology), it was at least a timely reassertion of the qualities of immediacy and directness which characterize the surviving contemporary section of Ammianus' work, in contrast to those who would dilute this into a derivative patchwork of clichés from the past.

By 1982 Rosen was able to list 384 items in his bibliographical survey on Ammianus,[22] a statistic which strikingly confirms Syme's judgement of his irresistibility (and makes it difficult to credit Blockley's lament in his preface that the historian was still 'sadly underinvestigated'). Moreover, issues long dormant or uncontested were being reactivated. Discussions of Ammianus' religious views, for example, while differing on the degree of coherence to be found in the divine scheme of the *Res Gestae*, had thus far shared the premise that he was dispassionate about the 'divide' between paganism and

Christianity: Ammianus was routinely characterized as a pluralist, undogmatic and tolerant of religious diversity. His mentions of Christianity were, in any case, to be treated with reserve, since it had been demonstrated in an article which had appeared as early as 1964 that they were often couched in terms which owed more to literary convention than to contemporary reality (a familiar dichotomy).[23] This consensus was sharply interrupted by T.G. Elliott, who, in expressing yet again the intent to 'examine the credibility of Ammianus as a historical source', attempted to destroy the historian's reputation by detecting hitherto unrecognized pagan bias at every turn.[24] Although a disproportionate overstatement of the case, Elliott's effort to discover in Ammianus a polemical anti-Christian has focused much recent attention on this issue: R.L. Rike confidently traced a consistent religious message running through the pages of the *Res Gestae* based in the defence of traditional pagan cult (yet failed to heed Syme's warning of Ammianus' 'bookishness' in relation to many of the passages concerned);[25] while T.D. Barnes diagnosed a pointed significance in Ammianus' silences about Christianity on those occasions when it deserved to be at the centre of the narrative.[26] David Hunt, meanwhile, restated the traditional view of Ammianus' indifference to religious controversy in a history which was self-consciously 'secular' in design.[27]

Previous studies, as we have seen, had already begun to identify an interest in the ideology and function of the Roman emperor as a central preoccupation of Ammianus' history. Where Blockley had pointed to the legacy of Hellenistic political philosophy, now Valerio Neri turned to more specifically Roman notions of *civilitas* to explain the historian's idealized conception of Julian and its antithesis in the countervailing portrayal of Constantius;[28] while Giovanni De Bonfils concentrated on Ammianus' strong concern with the legitimacy of imperial power, from the manner of the emperor's accession to his responsibility for law and justice.[29] That 'Ammianus is the only writer to present anything like a full analysis of the nature and the duties of imperial power' was also a conclusion of Robin Seager's close analysis of his favoured language and terminology, in comparison with that of other Latin historical writers.[30] While in this instance linguistic study may be said to have illuminated important aspects of Ammianus' thinking, much else that emerged from Seager's analysis was perhaps predictable and unsurprising: it is unremarkable, for example, that a historian whom scholars had long identified as much given to moralizing about people and events should have a *penchant* for the language of moderation and excess.

In reducing the *Res Gestae* to a dictionary of significant terms and linguistic parallels, Seager's work was in danger — as other previous discussions which had focused on 'literary' features — of isolating the historian from his contemporary surroundings. By contrast, Ammianus' engagement with present events had been at the centre of Thompson's approach; and it would now provide the rationale for John Matthews' major study, which presented, on a grand scale, an integrated view of the historian and the fourth-century world in which he lived, as observed through Ammianus' own record.[31] Although not on the surface addressing the varied and complex issues of interpretation which had already exercised the scholarly tradition on Ammianus, Matthews' book (as is evident from the learned depths of its notes and bibliography) represented a comprehensive sifting and summing-up of previous work, while still managing to let the historian speak for himself. The first part of the book, anchored in the context of Ammianus' life and career, retells the contents of his history in a manner illuminated throughout by Matthews' own discussion; in the second part some of the work's principal preoccupations are subjected to more thematic treatment, but again Matthews is careful to allow Ammianus his own say, balanced and supplemented by much comparative material and the fruit of recent scholarship. Of these chosen themes some imposed themselves because of their obvious central importance in the *Res Gestae*, and had already emerged in earlier work on Ammianus (so, for instance, emperors, government, warfare, religion); others represented new directions more distinctive to Matthews himself – there was a pronounced emphasis on the physical and social environment reflected in Ammianus' pages, for example, both within and beyond the bounds of the Roman empire (be it the geography of Julian's Persian campaign, the urban society of Rome and Antioch, or the excursuses on barbarian peoples). In a final chapter entitled 'The Roman and the Greek' Matthews weaves together the man and his material by exploring the combination of personal experience and cultural inheritance which shaped the character of Ammianus' work.

In the course of a large volume Matthews inevitably called into question some of the traditional assumptions which had been commonplace since Thompson. On the composition of the *Res Gestae*, for instance, he challenged the standard view (central to Thompson's contentions about Theodosian coercion) that the last six books were completed later than the rest (in fact reviving an argument mooted long before by Alan Cameron[32]). Where Thompson and others had taken it for granted that Ammianus' principal model was Tacitus, his work starting at the point where Tacitus had ended, Matthews found his literary affinities to lie closer to Greek historiography than to his Latin predecessors (Blockley, too, had adopted a minimal view of Tacitus' influence on Ammianus). Fornara, by contrast, has subsequently argued for the primacy of Latin over Greek historical authors in their impact on Ammianus' narrative, and by his close analysis of relevant passages of the text has by implication shared the complaints of those of Matthews' reviewers who lamented his neglect of the historian's Latinity.[33] Fornara was in similar company in challenging Matthews on the subject of Ammianus' presumed Antiochene origins: Matthews had here aligned himself with the traditional position (based on correspondence of Libanius addressed to a 'Marcellinus' in Rome), and recently returned to print in defence of the view that the *miles quondam et Graecus* did indeed come from Antioch.[34]

INTRODUCTION

Among the broader issues to emerge from Matthews' book, the balance of 'Greekness' and 'Romanness' which contributed to Ammianus' cultural identity was one which has continued to dominate scholarly interest. It was, for instance, a principal concern of the international group of scholars (including Matthews) who gathered for a small conference in Amsterdam in August 1991. The published collection of the papers given on this occasion provides a varied insight into recent preoccupations among Ammianus devotees.[35] It reflects, for example, growing interest in the nature and purpose of the extensive digressions which punctuate Ammianus' narrative: these tableaux of ethnographic, geographical and scientific material are coming to be seen as integral components of the historian's contemporary perspective, and not just as detached displays of derivative learning in a Herodotean tradition. That contemporary perspective was partially conditioned by the nature of the Roman audience for which Ammianus designed his history, another area of modern investigation (what, for instance, does the perceived character of the audience contribute to our understanding of the religious stance of Ammianus' work?). Whatever 'new' questions may have been stirred in the wake of Matthews' volume, however, the Amsterdam contributors were still exercised above all by the familiar tension between, on the one hand, Ammianus' observation and experience of his real world (whether it be the Roman emperor in government and at war, or habits of life both at Rome and among distant peoples), and on the other, the demands imposed by an inherited rhetorical tradition and the literary artifice which accompanied it: theirs was still the same quest for Ammianus' 'historical credibility' which Thompson had addressed in 1947.

At the very time when the contributions assembled in the following pages were first being delivered in Durham, Timothy Barnes was completing the preface to his new volume on Ammianus, based on the Townsend Lectures which he had delivered at Cornell University in 1994.[36] The published work appeared too late to be taken account of here, but is clear testimony to the liveliness of current debate over the interpretation of Ammianus Marcellinus, largely in reaction to John Matthews' book. While the broad issue of literary technique confronting historical substance is shared with many of our contributors, Barnes' unrelenting eye for the significant detail often leads him to conclusions which differ sharply from the standard ('post-Matthews') consensus: he has novel claims, for instance, about the structure of the *Res Gestae* and about Ammianus' origins and social standing. On the other hand, he makes common cause with Matthews in emphasizing the prime influence of Greek culture on Ammianus' historical outlook. Above all, Barnes' Ammianus is permeated by the distorting impact of a pessimistic, Eunapian-style pagan polemic, which places Constantine and Christianity firmly at the root of the Roman world's contemporary ills. It remains to be seen whether this reading of the text, grounded in the judicious selection of key passages, will establish itself as the new orthodoxy.

Text, commentaries and translations

The *Res Gestae* does not have a complex manuscript tradition.[37] Of the sixteen manuscripts in total, fourteen date from the fifteenth century and are of minor importance, since they are all copied directly or indirectly from one of the two older manuscripts, the Codex Fuldensis (Vaticanus Latinus 1873). The Fuldensis, dating from the ninth or tenth century, was discovered by Poggio Bracciolini in 1417, and is the most original and important manuscript of Ammianus' text to have come down to us. Of slightly earlier date is the Codex Hersfeldensis, of which the Fuldensis is now considered to be a transcript. Although Poggio knew of the existence of the Hersfeldensis, he was unable to obtain this manuscript. Where he failed, however, the humanist scholar Sigismund Gelenius succeeded in laying hands on it, and in 1533 he published an edition of the *Res Gestae* based on the Hersfeldensis. Because the Hersfeldensis was again lost soon after this publication, Gelenius' edition is still important for reconstructing Ammianus' text, but needs to be used carefully since it is evidently not a straight copy of the original manuscript: Gelenius adapted the text, made alterations of his own and filled in the lacunae. Part of the Hersfeldensis has subsequently been rediscovered: six pages came to light in Marburg in 1875, and three other fragments in Kassel as recently as 1986.[38]

Gelenius' edition of the text was not the first to be published. The *editio princeps* of Ammianus' *Res Gestae* had appeared in 1474, and many were to follow: by 1693 fifteen editions had already been published,[39] and the eighteenth century saw the appearance of two more. A milestone was reached in 1808, with the publication of the edition by Wagner and Erfurdt, which remained unsurpassed during the nineteenth century.[40] Another milestone came early in this century, with the appearance of C.U. Clark's edition[41] which, although it soon went out of print,[42] remained the standard work until the new Teubner text by W. Seyfarth was published in 1978.[43] The present generation in France has also seen the appearance in instalments of the Budé edition, begun in the 1960s: six volumes have so far seen the light of day, covering Books 14–28; the remainder is still awaited.[44] Two Italian editons also deserve mention, by Antonio Selem (1965) and Anna Resta Barrile (1973–4).[45]

Some fifty years ago Thompson observed that for commentary on Ammianus it was still necessary to have recourse to the notes of Henri de Valois (1603–76), usually known as Valesius, which had been added to the edition of Wagner–Erfurdt; superb though they are, these notes were largely outdated by the twentieth century.[46] Since Thompson the supply of commentaries has much improved. The 1930s saw the Dutchman Pieter de Jonge begin working on his *Philological and Historical Commentaries on Ammianus Marcellinus*. The commentary on Book 14, 1–7, was first published as a Groningen doctoral dissertation in 1935, and he was able to continue his work up to and including Book 19, which appeared in 1982.[47] De Jonge's impressive undertaking, of which the philological aspect was more profound than the historical, has in recent years been continued by a team of at first three and later four Dutch scholars — two Latinists and two ancient historians — who have to date published commentaries on Books 20–3.[48] Like de Jonge they aim for a commentary which integrates notes on historical, philological, linguistic and literary matters, believing that the contents and form of Ammianus' work cannot be separated. M.F.A. Brok's Leiden Ph.D. thesis, published in 1959, provides detailed and still valuable commentary on the description of Julian's Persian campaign in Books 23–5.[49] For Books 20–1, the account of the first phase of Julian's imperial rule, we have a three-volume historical commentary by Joachim Szidat;[50] and another commentary on a significant part of the *Res Gestae* is provided by Pia van der Wiel's Amsterdam Ph.D. thesis on Ammianus' Roman chapters.[51] In addition, the Budé volumes of Ammianus' text include elaborate explanatory notes. Yet, despite the progress of the last half-century, there is still no complete philological and historical commentary on the *Res Gestae* in existence.

Nor, until recently, were there any concordances of Ammianus available. This lack has now been remedied in the last two decades with the appearance of no less than three indices, two of them (Archbold and Chiabò) based on Clark's edition of the text, and one (Viansino) based on the Teubner edition by Seyfarth.[52]

With the appearance of several translations of the *Res Gestae*, Ammianus' work is these days accessible to an audience far wider than Latin specialists. Not to mention various versions of selected extracts, there is a range of translations of the complete work in each of the more important European languages. J.C. Rolfe's English translation in his Loeb edition, which was based on C.U. Clark, is still much used, but needs to be approached with caution: not only is his rendering of the Latin in places inaccurate, but he sometimes deviated from Clark's text for not always sound reasons. For Ammianus' Latinless audience the recent Penguin Classics translation by Walter Hamilton is often to be preferred, despite its regrettable omission of many of the digressions contained in the *Res Gestae*.[53] In German there is both the bilingual edition by Wolfgang Seyfarth and that of Otto Veh,[54] while French readers have the translation included in the Budé edition. Italian translations are to be found in the bilingual editions by Antonio Selem and Anna Resta Barrile, and by Matilde Caltabiano.[55]

* * *

The chapters which follow continue the process of examining Ammianus' work in relation both to its contemporary surroundings and to its literary antecedents. Across a variety of aspects, they address the tension of the author's dual role as both external narrator of events, composing a traditional history of Roman times, and yet himself either party to, or close observer of, that same record of events. The first group of chapters focuses attention on Ammianus' period of military service as a staff-officer (*protector domesticus*) during the reigns of Constantius II and Julian. With particular attention to the near-autobiographical narrative of affairs on the eastern front in 359, Frank Trombley demonstrates the impact of the historian's own 'workplace', the priorities and preoccupations inherent in his functions as a *protector*, on his historical method and chosen subject-matter. The fact that Ammianus' military position placed him among those charged with organizing the defences of Amida against the Persians would, on the other hand, hardly be apparent from the digression on siege engines with which his history heralds Julian's later advance down the Euphrates: this, as Daan den Hengst establishes, owes far more to books than to military practicalities. Josephina Lenssen's detailed attention to a small part of the narrative of toings and froings in 359 reveals again, as does Trombley, the historian's closeness to the centre of events (and to his commander Ursicinus), but this time Ammianus' proximity results in a distorted perspective on decision-making at Constantius' court. David Hunt's contribution on the rebellion of Silvanus investigates a similar theme in relation to the other central episode in which Ammianus as at once *protector* and historian confronts the political manoeuvring of imperial government; while a distinctive component of the historian's denunciation of the court which he had served is explored in Shaun Tougher's discussion of eunuchs.

Ammianus' image of Constantius was forged not only out of his own experience in the service of the empire but also, as Michael Whitby illustrates, in reaction to the parade of official virtues displayed by contemporary panegyrics. The chapters in Part II serve to illuminate this dialogue between Ammianus' imperial portrayals and the models of panegyric. In the case of Julian, the historian was himself the encomiast, even if, as Rowland Smith's exposition of the subtleties of the Persian campaign narrative makes clear, Ammianus undercut his own eulogy of the heroic emperor with an alternative, darker presentation. But any dimming of Julian's glory was not enough to rescue the reputation of Jovian, whose brief appearance in Ammianus' pages (as Peter Heather reveals in his comparison with the more positive Themistian portrait) functions only to safeguard the praises of his predecessor. Two contributions consider Ammianus' Valentinian I in relation to the official speeches of Symmachus: Mark Humphries shows the author modifying the picture of the emperor to appeal to the Roman audience for his work; while John Drinkwater exploits the comparison with Symmachus to minimize not only the significance of Valentinian's defence of the Rhine frontier but also Ammianus' own estimation of his military achievement (it was, rather, the eastern narrative and the fate of Valens, Drinkwater argues, which provided the real inspiration for the last books of the *Res Gestae*).

The opposing strains of contemporary reality and literary composition (and of Ammianus as both 'internal' and 'external' to his narrative) are nowhere more apparent than when he is writing about Rome, in a work of history being published to a contemporary Roman audience. In this context, as Roger Rees demonstrates in his study of the historian's evocation of the satirist, Ammianus the Roman 'outsider' owed a literary debt to Juvenal for many of the motifs which comprise his critical observation of the capital's society. Yet the *Res Gestae* also subscribed to traditional, nostalgic Roman notions of the city's primacy and permanence, as reflected (for example) in the celebrated description of Constantius' ceremonial *adventus* in 357. Here David Woods' new elucidation of a fragment of Eunapius in connection with this episode reinforces the anachronistic atmosphere of nostalgia by emphasizing that Ammianus has ignored the Christian symbolism which would in reality have marked the occasion. The religious tone of Ammianus' adopted 'Romanness' is also reflected in Brian Warmington's discussion of Constantine's occasional appearances in the surviving books, which, although given to criticism, are notably unpartisan by comparison with the anti-Christian venom to be found in certain of Ammianus' contemporaries; and above all in Thomas Harrison's panoramic overview of Ammianus' divine scheme of things, embracing Rome, emperors and empire in an amalgam of traditional belief capable of embracing both literary derivation and genuine assent.

Harrison's general picture finds confirmation in a specific instance from Jan den Boeft's treatment of the short excursus on Persian Magi, in which Ammianus' positive tone represents something of his own convictions about the practice of true religion. Here, as elsewhere in this extensive Persian digression, the interest lies in what Ammianus as contemporary historian has made of his book-learning. On Arsaces and Parthian beginnings Jan Willem Drijvers concludes that he has added nothing to the traditional pickings of classical historiography; whereas Hans Teitler finds the predominantly Herodotean discussion of Persian *mores* significantly adapted in the light of the historian's own experience. A similar willingness to modify barbarian stereotypes emerges from Keith Hopwood's survey of Ammianus' Isaurian passages, where specific and distinctive historical details are found keeping company with the traditional rhetoric of banditry and disorder.

Notes

1 E.A. Thompson, *The Historical Work of Ammianus Marcellinus*, Cambridge 1947 (repr. Groningen 1969).
2 J.W. Mackail, 'Ammianus Marcellinus', *JRS* 10 (1920), 103–18; repr. in his *Classical Studies*, London 1925, 159–87.
3 M.L.W. Laistner, *The Greater Roman Historians* (Sather Classical Lectures 21), Berkeley 1947, 141–61.
4 J. Gimazane, *Ammien Marcellin, sa vie et son œuvre*, Toulouse 1889; W. Ensslin, *Zur Geschichtsschreibung und Weltanschauung des Ammianus Marcellinus* (Klio Beiheft 16), Leipzig 1923.

5 A.F. Norman, 'Magnus in Ammianus, Eunapius and Zosimus: New Evidence', *CQ* 7 (1957), 129–33; W.R. Chalmers, 'Eunapius, Ammianus Marcellinus and Zosimus on Julian's Persian Expedition', *CQ* 10 (1960), 152–60; F. Paschoud (ed.), *Zosime: Histoire nouvelle, I–II*, Paris 1971, xliii–lvii; ibid. *III* (1979), xii–xix; T.D. Barnes, *The Sources of the Historia Augusta* (Collection Latomus 155), Brussels 1978, 114–23; J.F. Matthews, *The Roman Empire of Ammianus*, London 1989, 161–79.
6 L. Dillemann, 'Ammien Marcellin et le pays de l'Euphrate et du Tigre', *Syria. Revue d'art oriental et d'archéologie* 38 (1961), 87–158.
7 C.W. Fornara, 'Julian's Persian Expedition in Ammianus and Zosimus', *JHS* 111 (1991), 1–15.
8 A. Alföldi, *A Conflict of Ideas in the Late Roman Empire*, Oxford 1952, 3–5, 65ff.
9 A. Cameron, 'The Roman Friends of Ammianus', *JRS* 54 (1964), 15–28.
10 A. Demandt, *Zeitkritik und Geschichtsbild im Werk Ammians* (diss. Marburg), Bonn 1965.
11 R. Syme, *JRS* 58 (1968), 215–18.
12 R. Syme, *Ammianus and the Historia Augusta*, Oxford 1968, with review by A. Cameron, *JRS* 61 (1971), 255ff.
13 P.M. Camus, *Ammien Marcellin, témoin des courants culturels et religieux à la fin du IVe siècle*, Paris 1967.
14 K. Rosen, *Studien zur Darstellungskunst und Glaubwürdigkeit des Ammianus Marcellinus*, Heidelberg 1968 (repr. 1970).
15 J. Fontaine, 'Ammien Marcellin, historien romantique', *Bulletin de l'Association Guillaume Budé* 28 (1969), 417–35; W. Seyfarth, 'Petronius Probus, Legende und Wirklichkeit', *Klio* 52 (1970), 411–25.
16 H. Drexler, *Ammianstudien* (Spudasmata 31), Hildesheim 1974.
17 N. Bitter, *Kampfschilderungen bei Ammianus Marcellinus*, Bonn 1976, with review by G. Sabbah, *Latomus* 36 (1977), 822–4.
18 G.A. Crump, *Ammianus Marcellinus as a Military Historian* (Historia Einzelschriften 27), Wiesbaden 1975.
19 N.J.E. Austin, *Ammianus on Warfare. An Investigation into Ammianus' Military Knowledge* (Collection Latomus 165), Brussels 1979; cf. idem, 'In Support of Ammianus' Veracity', *Historia* 22 (1973), 331–5.
20 R.C. Blockley, *Ammianus Marcellinus. A Study of his Historiography and Political Thought* (Collection Latomus 141), Brussels 1975.
21 G. Sabbah, *La méthode d'Ammien Marcellin. Recherches sur la construction du discours historique dans les Res Gestae*, Paris 1978.
22 K. Rosen, *Ammianus Marcellinus* (Erträge der Forschung 183), Darmstadt 1982.
23 A. Cameron and A. Cameron, 'Christianity and Tradition in the Historiography of the Late Empire', *CQ* 14 (1964), 316–28.
24 T.G. Elliott, *Ammianus Marcellinus and Fourth-Century History*, Sarasota 1983.
25 R.L. Rike, *Apex Omnium. Religion in the Res Gestae of Ammianus*, Berkeley 1987.
26 T.D. Barnes, 'Literary Convention, Nostalgia and Reality in Ammianus Marcellinus', in G.W. Clarke et al. (ed.), *Reading the Past in Late Antiquity*, Rushcutters Bay 1990, 59–92; idem, 'Ammianus Marcellinus and his World', *CP* 88 (1993), 55–70, 67–70.
27 E.D. Hunt, 'Christians and Christianity in Ammianus Marcellinus', *CQ* 35 (1985), 186–200; idem, 'Christianity in Ammianus Marcellinus Revisited', *Studia Patristica* 24 (1993), 108–13. The series of discursive discussions by V. Neri, *Ammiano e il cristianesimo. Religione e politica nelle 'Res Gestae' di Ammiano Marcellino* (Studi di Storia Antica 11), Bologna 1985, did not, despite the book's title, bring anything new to this debate.
28 V. Neri, *Costanzo, Giuliano e l'ideale del Civilis Princeps nelle storie di Ammiano Marcellino* (Studi Bizantini e Slavi 1), Rome 1984.
29 G. De Bonfils, *Ammiano Marcellino e l'imperatore*, Bari 1986.
30 R. Seager, *Ammianus Marcellinus. Seven Studies in his Language and Thought*, Columbia 1986, 130.
31 Matthews, *The Roman Empire of Ammianus*.

32 In a review of Syme, *Ammianus and the Historia Augusta*, in *JRS* 61 (1971), 259–62.
33 C.W. Fornara, 'Studies in Ammianus Marcellinus II: Ammianus' Knowledge and Use of Greek and Latin Literature', *Historia* 41 (1992), 420–38; cf. reviews by G.W. Bowersock, *JRS* 80 (1990), 244–50, and Barnes, 'Ammianus Marcellinus and his World'. On Ammianus and Tacitus, see K.-G. Neumann, *Taciteisches im Werk des Ammianus Marcellinus*, Munich 1991.
34 C.W. Fornara, 'Studies in Ammianus Marcellinus I: The Letter of Libanius and Ammianus' Connection with Antioch', *Historia* 41 (1992), 328–44; J.F. Matthews, 'The Origin of Ammianus', *CQ* 45 (1994), 252–69.
35 J. den Boeft, D. den Hengst and H.C. Teitler (eds), *Cognitio Gestorum. The Historiographic Art of Ammianus Marcellinus*, Amsterdam 1992.
36 T.D. Barnes, *Ammianus Marcellinus and the Representation of Historical Reality* (Cornell Studies in Classical Philology 56), Ithaca and London 1998.
37 The following does not pretend to be a complete discussion of manuscripts, editions, translations and commentaries on Ammianus' text, for which we refer to the introductions of the various editions as well as to the literature mentioned in the following notes. We have laid emphasis on developments in recent years, especially since the appearance of Rosen, *Ammianus Marcellinus*, which includes a 'Stand der Ammianforschung'.
38 H. Broszinski and H.C. Teitler, 'Einige neuerdings entdeckten Fragmente der Hersfelder Handschrift des Ammianus Marcellinus', *Mnemosyne* 43 (1990), 408–23; this article refers to the earlier, more important views and publications on the manuscript tradition of the *Res Gestae*, on which see also W. Seyfarth, 'Der Codex Fuldensis und der Codex E des Ammianus Marcellinus', *Abhandlungen der Deutschen Akademie der Wissenschaften*, Klasse für Sprachen, Literatur und Kunst, 1962.2, Berlin 1962, and now Barnes, *Ammianus Marcellinus*, Appendix 1 ('The Text of Ammianus'). Barnes is unnecessarily preoccupied with the 'poor state' (p. 204; cf. p. 111 'poorly transmitted') of the text, which is in fact no worse than many other texts surviving from antiquity. For the transmission of Ammianus' text, see also the clear summary of L.D. Reynolds, Texts and Transmission. A Survey of the Latin Classics, Oxford 1983.
39 For an overview of all editions, see W. Seyfarth, *Ammiani Marcellini Rerum Gestarum libri qui supersunt*, 2 vols, Berlin 1978, vol. 1, xxv–xxvi.
40 J.A. Wagner, *Ammiani Marcellini quae supersunt*, cum notis integris Frid. Lindenbrogii, Henr. et Hadr. Valesiorum et Iac. Gronovii, quibus Thom. Reinesii quasdam et suas adiecit, editionem absolvit Car. Gottl. Aug. Erfurdt, 3 vols, Leipzig 1808 (photomech. repr. in 2 vols, Hildesheim and New York 1975).
41 *Ammiani Marcellini, Rerum Gestarum libri qui supersunt*, Recensuit rhythmiceque distinxit C.U. Clark, 2 vols, Berlin 1910–15 (repr. 1963). Clark had earlier completed a doctoral thesis entitled 'The Text Tradition of Ammianus Marcellinus', Diss. Yale 1904.
42 Thompson, *The Historical Work of Ammianus Marcellinus*, xi complained that 'the excellent standard edition of the American scholar C.U. Clark . . . is also out of print and is exceedingly difficult to obtain'.
43 See n. 39 above.
44 *Ammien Marcellin, Histoire*, Texte établi, traduit et annoté par J. Fontaine, E. Galletier, G. Sabbah, M.-A. Marié, vols 1–5, Collection des universités de France publiée sous le patronage de l'Association Guillaume Budé, Paris 1968–96.
45 A. Selem, *Le Storie di Ammiano Marcellino. Testo e Traduzione*, Turin 1965 (repr. 1973); A. Resta Barrile, *Ammiano Marcellino, istorie, testo latino, traduzzione e note*, 4 vols, Bologna 1973–6.
46 Thompson, *The Historical Work of Ammianus Marcellinus*, xi.
47 Thesis: P. de Jonge, *Sprachlicher und Historischer Kommentar zu Ammianus Marcellinus XIV 1–7*, Groningen 1935. The second part of the commentary on Book 14 was published in 1939, and the commentaries (in English) on Books 15–19 appeared between 1948 and 1982.

48 J. den Boeft, D. den Hengst, H.C. Teitler, *Philological and Historical Commentaries on Ammianus Marcellinus XX–XXI*, Groningen 1987–91; J. den Boeft, J.W. Drijvers, D. den Hengst and H.C. Teitler, *Philological and Historical Commentaries on Ammianus Marcellinus XXII-XXIII*, Groningen 1995–8.
49 M.F.A. Brok, *De Perzische expeditie van keizer Julianus volgens Ammianus Marcellinus*, Groningen 1959.
50 J. Szidat, *Historischer Kommentar zu Ammianus Marcellinus Buch XX–XXI* (Historia Einzelschriften 31, 38, 39), Wiesbaden and Stuttgart 1977–96.
51 P. van der Wiel, 'Hoofdstukken uit de Geschiedenis van Rome in Ammianus Marcellinus *Res Gestae*', Amsterdam 1989 (Ph.D. thesis).
52 G. Archbold, 'Concordance to the Works of Ammianus Marcellinus', *Phoenix Supplementary Volume*, Toronto 1979 (on microfiche: University of Toronto Press, 1980); M. Chiabò, *Index verborum Ammiani Marcellini*, 2 vols, Hildesheim, Zurich and New York 1983; I. Viansino, *Ammiani Marcellini Rerum Gestarum Lexicon*, 2 vols, Hildesheim, Zurich and New York 1985.
53 J.C. Rolfe, *Ammianus Marcellinus*, with an English translation, Loeb Classical Library, 3 vols, London and Cambridge (Mass.) 1935–9 (various reprints); W. Hamilton and A. Wallace-Hadrill, *Ammianus Marcellinus. The Later Roman Empire (A.D. 354–378)*, Harmondsworth 1986. An older English translation still occasionally referred to is that of C.D. Yonge, *Ammianus Marcellinus. The Roman History*, London 1862.
54 W. Seyfarth, *Ammianus Marcellinus, Römische Geschichte. Lateinisch und Deutsch und mit einem Kommentar versehen*, 4 vols, Berlin 1968–70/1 (various reprints); O. Veh, *Ammianus Marcellinus. Das römische Weltreich vor dem Untergang*, übersetzt von O. Veh, eingeleitet und erläutert von G. Wirth, Zurich and Munich 1974.
55 For Selem and Resta Barrile, see n. 45 above; M. Caltabiano, *Ammiano Marcellino. Storie*, Milan 1989.

Part I

AMMIANUS, SOLDIER
AND HISTORIAN

2

AMMIANUS MARCELLINUS AND FOURTH-CENTURY WARFARE

A *protector*'s approach to historical narrative

Frank Trombley

Ammianus Marcellinus is usually studied as the mature author who completed the *Res Gestae* in the mid-390s, whose reporting on political and military affairs is subjected to all the usual tests for historical accuracy and literary influences. Less has been said, however, about the formative background and military experience upon which Ammianus drew: in other words, what effect did his career as a *protector* between 354 and 363, when he was perhaps 25–35 years of age, have on his approach to interpreting historical phenomena? To put it another way, Ammianus' professional socialization in the *schola* of *protectores domestici* is certain to have given him a methodology for understanding political events at the imperial court and military operations on the Rhine and eastern frontiers different from that of a purely literary man. Along with his presumed early education in Latin and Greek rhetoric, this 'staff work' he carried out in the *protectores* was an important formative influence. It is possible that the tasks given *protectores*, everything from inspecting ships' manifests to siting siege artillery, lay behind the criteria of relevance he used in deciding what belonged in a historical narrative. His reports reveal a rather unique preoccupation with the operational side of war-making, including such matter-of-fact issues as supply, bridging trains and reconnaissance. This applies particularly to the campaigns in which he took part and on which he gives eyewitness testimony.

The following discussion will first look at the professional tasks assigned to the *protectores* mentioned in the epigraphy, papyri and imperial edicts. Thereafter it will consider what Ammianus, our most important witness, has to say about the same matters. Finally his handling of the operational side of the Mesopotamian campaigns of 359 will be looked at. In them, traces can be found of a '*protector* at work'.[1]

It is important to keep Ammianus' historical epistemology in view. In other words, what could he know by virtue of his professional competence?

How would he have described what he knew in reporting to men like Aelianus, *dux Mesopotamiae* during the siege of Amida in 359, or to his superior officer and patron Ursicinus, *magister equitum per Orientem* between c. 349 and 359? What aspects of his professional attitude would have prevented him from describing an incident with complete candour? In 359, the results of Ammianus' and his colleagues' daily work, including all intelligence that came to light, will have helped his superior officers to dispose the forces under their command, shift supplies to vital fortresses, and govern their own movements to the points of greatest danger. Fact-gathering skills were certainly a requirement in Ammianus' professional environment. The *Res Gestae* are in part the rare literary product of such working methods, which can best be studied by scrutinizing Ammianus' eyewitness reports. In practice, this means looking closely at his movements in 359 that led him to Amida in time for the siege by Shapur II's army.

Previous scholarship has outlined most of the main issues about the activities of the *protectores*.[2] Less has been said, however, about how they learned to approach their tasks intellectually. For example, if a *protector* was called upon to report on an engagement with a limitrophic enemy, what sort of Latinity would he have employed and what aspects of the incident would he have regarded as most worthy of inclusion in the report? For reasons that will be seen, I suspect such documents, if any had survived, would have had much in common with Ammianus' descriptions.

There were two types of *protector* in the mid-fourth century when Ammianus took up his appointment, still a young man, an *adulescens* in his twenties. The first and earlier form of appointment, which probably went back as far as the reigns of Philip the Arab or Decius in the third century, was that of men who had risen through the ranks by distinguished service. One of them, named in an inscription of 267, L. Petronius Taurus Volusianus, had gone from *primipilaris* of the III Ulpia legion, and later *praepositus* of a formation of *equites singulares Augustorum*, to tribunates in three legions, ending with an appointment as tribune of the First Praetorian Cohort and *protector Augustorum* (*ILS* 1332). There are numerous examples of the continuation of this system in the fourth century, and the details of the men's promotion through the ranks, discussed elsewhere by A.H.M. Jones, need not detain us here.[3]

The main question for our discussion is what assignments *protectores* got at the time of their promotion. They seem usually to have been given command of medium-size formations. Funerary inscriptions provide corroboration for this. Among the *protectores* named with their units are a Viatorinus of the *numerus Divitensium* stationed at or near Cologne, a Martinus in a *numerus lanciariorum* (*ob.* Rome), a formation of *comitatenses*, and a Valerius Thiumpus who became *praefectus* of the II Herculiana legion (*ob.* Troesmsis in Scythia Minor).[4] These tasks are known in greater detail from the papyrus archive of Flavius Abinnaeus, who was promoted to *protector* after 33 years' military service when he delivered the envoys of the Blemmyes, a Nubian people, to

Constantinople. Three years later, he became prefect of the Roman garrison at Dionysias in Upper Egypt and completed his military service there.[5] His story, known in some detail, is probably not much different from that of the others.

Regular *protectores* handled all kinds of mundane tasks. By virtue of their military rank regular *protectores* had implied policing powers, thanks to the immediate presence of the armed men under their orders. Several cases given in the *Theodosian Code* corroborate this view.[6] For example, records of the destination and nature of goods on ships going by river or sea into the *barbaricum* had to be completed before sailing in the presence either of the local *protector* or officers of the *dux*.[7] The *magistri peditum* and *equitum* were given the responsibility of dispatching *protectores* with troops to the *mansiones* on the post roads to check wagons and post horses for overloading. Specific weights are given.[8] They had the regular task of searching out sons of veterans, *vagi* and *fugientes* who had left their *origo* or place of legal residence to escape military service.[9] On one occasion the *protectores* were given the task of escorting the former *dux* of Sardinia back to the island to enforce repayment fourfold of the monies that he and his *officium* had extorted from the provincials.[10] *Protectores* also supervised the construction of essential public works when necessary. At Basienis (present-day Qasr al-Azraq), about 90 km south-east of Bostra in the provincia Arabia, the *protector* Vincentius fortified a spring or water catchment (AD 334). An inscription reads:

> Vincentius the *protector*, while on duty at Basia, when he realized that very many of the agriculturalists died after being ambushed by the Saracens while carrying water for their own use, built this water reservoir from the foundations up when the senators Optatus and Paulinus served as consuls.[11]

Other inscriptions refer to works supervised by *protectores*. These include statues in honour of emperors[12] and temples of the imperial cult.[13] These were undoubtedly *ex officio* tasks. During the reign of Gallienus, two *protectores* are known to have erected temples in consequence of dream visions of gods.[14] It can be seen from these examples that formerly rough soldiers who distinguished themselves and developed sound literacy became *protectores*, working thereafter with the documents and receipts connected with the movement of strategic materials and personnel, fortifications and other public buildings.

Around 350, young men without military experience were allowed to join the *protectores*, which by this time were being organized as a 'school' or *schola* under the command of an imperial count with the title of *comes domesticorum*. These young men, who in effect became trainees for future military commands, were referred to as '*protectores* of the imperial household', *protectores domestici*, and at times *protectores dominici*, '*protectores* of the *domini*', their lords the emperors (*ILCV* 469). These men seem often to have come from families where the father had achieved high civil or military rank, thus getting a head start in their careers. Ammianus' upbringing gives the impression of his having been raised and educated in a family of curial rank. The *domestici* were divided into four schools of *seniores* and *iuniores* in both the infantry and cavalry. If some served in the imperial *comitatus*, others were assigned to the masters of soldiers to perform what today would be called 'staff' functions. For example, Ursicinus took ten *protectores* with him to Gaul *ad iuvandas necessitates publicas* when Constantius II asked him to suppress Silvanus' rebellion (Amm. Marc. 15.5.22). From a bureaucratic point of view, their tasks did not differ much from the extraordinary tasks assigned ordinary *protectores* mentioned in the *Theodosian Code* and Abinnaeus archive; but the *domestici* were not attached permanently as prefects of a single formation of *comitatenses* or *limitanei*, operating instead like *tribuni vacantes*, being directly at the disposal of their commanders for special assignments.

The *domestici* and ordinary *protectores* who rose through the ranks in theory enjoyed equality, but in practical terms and preferment the *domestici* enjoyed better prospects, not least because of the political connections that got them their assignments at an early age. The only career in the epigraphic record deserving mention is that of a Flavius Memorius who served in a formation of *comitatenses* for twenty-eight years before his promotion to *protector domesticus*. Unlike Ammianus, who seems never to have got a field command of his own, Memorius eventually rose to the rank of *dux* of Mauretania Tingitana and seems to have retired in his early sixties (*ILCV* 295a).

Ammianus mentions the promotion of several *protectores* who were probably among the ten Ursicinus brought to Gaul in 355. When Ursicinus returned to Oriens to take charge of the defence against Shapur II's threatening moves, 'the senior members of our band were promoted to command soldiers, while we young men were ordered to attend him on whatever he ordered to be done on behalf of the republic'. The status of at least a few *protectores* is in question here, including Verinianus, another member of Ursicinus' staff, who, like Ammianus, was *not* promoted with the others at this time and later went missing while still a *protector* outside the walls of Amida in 359 (16.10.21). A salary schedule survives from the reign of Anastasius I (491–518). It is an imperial directive to Daniel, *dux* of Libya. The annual pay of the *protector* assigned to him was 126 *solidi*, over ten times the wages of an ordinary workman.[15] The mid-fourth-century pay schedule is unknown.

There is no explicit evidence for supposing that Ammianus left the *protectores* at the time of Ursicinus' dismissal after the destruction of Amida in 359 or indeed after the failure of Julian's expedition against Ctesiphon in 363. If his reports on operations between 360 and early 363 do not reflect eyewitness participation, it could merely be a consequence of Ammianus' adaptation to new circumstances and search for a new patron, or duties that kept him away from the zone of operations.

Leaving the *protectores* while still a young man in his early thirties is not consistent with what is known of them either from Ammianus or the inscriptions. An epigraphic sample of twenty-eight known *domestici* and ordinary *protectores* gives some demographic indicators.[16] From the twenty-five inscriptions that give the age of these men at death, the average lifespan is 44.5 years. The eight inscriptions giving the length of military service put it at an average of 28.8 years. Neither of these figures is necessarily untypical of the career of a *protector* who avoided death in battle. But the inscriptions of men who died young usually lack information on the length of their military service. If this were known, it would bring the latter figure down considerably. A relatively large number were killed in battle, two out of twenty-eight. Viatorinus, a *protector* in the *numerus Divitensium*, died in barbarian territory near Cologne at the age of 30 (*occisus in barbarico iuxta Divitia*; *ILS* 2784). The other, Valerius Valens, who was interred in Dalmatia, apparently fell during the civil war between Constantine and Maxentius (*defu[ncto] bello civile in [It]alia*). He was at least 50 years of age (*ILS* 2776, AD 312?). Ammianus came close to death in battle twice in 359, once at the hands of Persian cavalry during his escape from Nisibis, and again during the fighting inside the walls of Amida on the day the city fell. Furthermore, his colleague Verinianus was wounded and went missing in battle (18.8.11), and a number of *protectores* went into captivity after the siege. Aelianus, *dux* of Mesopotamia and a former *protector*, was hanged on the same occasion (19.9.2). Ammianus' testimony corroborates the view that *protectores* who carried out their duties conscientiously were not likely to live long. Ammianus must have lived well beyond the age of 44.5 years to judge from the chronological scope of the *Res Gestae*.[17]

Ammianus' descriptions based on his 'travels' between *c.* 363 and 383 are not at all inconsistent with the kinds of discoveries a *protector* might have made in the course of carrying out his duties in several provinces.[18] So, for example, he may have got a 'touristic' knowledge of Pharaonic Egypt during supervisory tasks related to the shipment of the *annona* of Aegyptus, Arcadia, and Thebais I and II to the Mediterranean ports that did not seem particularly newsworthy for the theme of his history. With this in view, it is not at all impossible that Ammianus' had a 'typical' career of 28.8 years, a longer interval than the length of his narrative from Caesar Gallus' cruelties in 353/4 to the battle of Adrianople in 378. His possible expulsion from Rome *c.* 383–4 as a *peregrinus* and scholar in the liberal arts does not affect this hypothesis.[19] This would suppose, however, that Ammianus survived Ursicinus' dismissal in 359 and Julian's purge of the school of *domestici* in 362 which brought its numbers down to 200, and remained in service under Valens.

Ammianus met other men of his own class and educational background among the *notarii* and other *domestici*. What was the cultural make-up of these people? Ammianus gives the barest of hints in his discussion of the months before the siege of Amida in 359. The first was a message sent by the *notarius* Procopius, who with the count Lucillianus had been at the court of the Sasanid monarch Shapur II, in deliberate cipher in case of its capture.

'Cipher' in this instance meant all sorts of obscure allusions relating to classical historical literature that only a well-educated person could resolve. The later Roman Empire is called *Graecia* and the *protector* Antoninus who defected to the Persians is referred to as the 'successor of emperor Hadrian' by virtue of the latter's *nomen* 'Antoninus'. This may already have been an inside joke among the *protectores* and *notarii*. The reference to the bridges on the Granicus and Rhyndacus, known respectively from the wars of Alexander the Great and the proconsul Lucullus, was taken to mean that Shapur had already crossed the Zab and Tigris rivers *en route* to Roman Mesopotamia. Ammianus and his colleagues worked out this interpretation only with the greatest difficulty (*his ob perplexitatem nimiam aegerrime lectis*; 18.6.17–19). It is evident from this that the business of thinking up classical allusions came easily to some adepts and served a useful function.

The second example concerns the practical linguistic skills of Antoninus who defected to the Persians in 359. He was an ex-merchant, allegedly hounded by debt, who had served in the *officium* of the *dux* of Mesopotamia and was later admitted to the *protectores*. His asylum and employment in Persia was purchased by providing the enemy with intelligence:

> He covertly pried into all parts of the empire, and being versed in the language of both tongues, busied himself with calculations, making record of what troops were serving anywhere or of what strength, or at what time expeditions would be made, inquiring also by tireless questioning whether supplies of arms, provisions and other things that would be useful in war were at hand in abundance. And when he had learned the internal affairs of all Oriens, since the greater part of the troops and the money for their pay were distributed through Illyricum, where the emperor was distracted by serious affairs . . . he made a great effort to flee to the Persians . . .
> (18.5.1–2)

Knowledge of both Greek *and* Latin enabled Antoninus to read action reports, transfer orders, unit rosters and dispositions, deliveries of weapons and armour from the imperial *fabricae*, and supply shipments (particularly those going to troops billeted in the riverine towns of the Euphrates). His success makes us think that any *protector*, even Ammianus himself, could have apprised himself of this privileged information by going through normal channels at the ducal *officium* in Amida, Edessa, or even Antioch. Antoninus' inquiries remind us very much of a late fourth-century historian at work, but only because the kind of information he sought also happens to fill the pages of Ammianus' history where military operations come into play. It also reflects the kinds of tasks given to *protectores* in the *Theodosian Code*. Knowledge of this, coupled with a good Latinity and a flair for finding suitable analogues in Greek and Latin literature, were all one needed to write recent and contemporary history, especially as patrons and listeners were potentially ex-soldiers and civil governors of provinces, from ordinary *notarii* and *protectores* straight up to praetorian prefects and masters of soldiers.

In short, Ammianus' history may owe more than a little to the ethos of the workplace. He had particular need of this connection, seeking as he did to establish his authority as a well-informed, occasionally eyewitness observer of politics and military affairs. He could thereby corroborate the arguments advanced to rehabilitate Ursicinus' reputation, refuting the battlefield 'rumours' in circulation about Ursicinus' supposed failure to conduct a mobile defence against the Sassanid army besieging Amida. When he was not present, as for example at the battle of Strasbourg in 357, his close questioning of participants or the use of vivid battle reports almost gives the impression of an eyewitness account. Only Ammianus' personal statement of his whereabouts elsewhere, *en route* to Oriens with Ursicinus, makes his absence from the battle a certainty.

In the space remaining, I shall concentrate on aspects of Ammianus that reflect preoccupations of the workplace during his service in Syria, from Shapur II's march against Amida in 359 to Constantius II's death in November 361.

One of the more certain indications of Ammianus' professional concerns is the constant reference to supply and transport. The importance of this can be seen in the fact that the defector Antoninus' survey of the military resources of Oriens included 'supplies of arms, provisions and other things that would be useful in war' (*armorum et commeatuum copiae, aliaque usui bello futura*; 18.5.1), as these stocks will have affected the battle-worthiness of the Roman forces and, if captured, could have aided the Persians in the arid summer of the Syrian steppe and Taurus highlands. After the sack of Amida, in the winter of 359/60, Constantius poured supplies into Oriens in preparation for a defensive war the following spring. Cavalry equipment (*arma clibanaria*) from *fabricae* as far away as Caesarea in Cappadocia and Nicomedia will have supplemented that produced at Antioch, Damascus, Edessa and Irenopolis in Cilicia.[20] It is probable that much of the equipment was collected along the route of the *comitatenses* being transferred from Illyricum, as they passed through Caesarea and concentrated at Edessa where great food supplies had been dumped (*rei cibariae abundantes copias*; 20.11.4). Much of this was probably *bucellum* or soldier's bread. The supervision of these movements on the post roads and river system must have been handled in part by the *protectores* along the routes, as also was the transfer of new recruits (*tirocinia*) there (20.8.1, 21.7.6–7). This high level of preparation may explain why Shapur II hesitated to cross the Tigris in 361, his receiving of unfavourable omens being a useful dodge when he came up against the Roman cavalry screen (21.13.1–4).

The status of bridges is another detail that turns up frequently. These were of two kinds: bridges built of masonry and mortar, and temporary bridges constructed by tying boats together and laying planks across them.

It is quite likely that *protectores* had supervision over the latter, because the bridging train was carried by wagon transport. If Ammianus' movements between Nisibis and Amida during the campaign of 359 were typical – and he was admittedly travelling in Ursicinus' praetorian band much of the way – he would have possessed clear knowledge of the state of the permanent bridges (e.g. 18.5.7, 6.19). Ammianus' mission to collect information from the Hellenized Armenian satrap Iovinianus enabled him to report from direct observation that the Persians had crossed the Tigris on a single bridge of boats and were moving in the direction of Osrhoene, so that towns with broken fortifications like Carrhae-Harran could be evacuated and the summer crops burnt throughout the province.[21] As it turned out, the Persian plan of campaign involved crossing the Euphrates and entering Euphratesia to sack the cities there (18.6.3). When melting snows made the fords of the middle Euphrates impassable, in consequence of this and the scorched earth, Shapur took the army across the foothills south of Tur Abdin where water and pasturage could still be found, aiming to reach the fords on the upper Euphrates west of Amida. The task of organizing the defence of the fords was given to the *tribuni*, who were evidently the commanders of the various cavalry formations under the orders of the *dux* of Mesopotamia, who put together small *castella*, emplanted sharpened stakes (*praeacuae sudes*) in the fords, and positioned light artillery devices (*tormenta*). Ammianus indicates that the *protectores* accompanied them (*cum protectoribus missi*; 18.7.6). The *protectores* were most probably men who, unlike Ammianus, had risen through the ranks and knew the techniques of improvising field fortifications. While this was being done, Ammianus was riding with Ursicinus' band toward Samosata, where they planned to cut away the joins of the bridges at Zeugma and Capersana. These may have been permanent bridges. If so, their blocks would have required lifting from the arches after cutting away the clamps (*pontiumque apud Zeugma et Capersana iuncturis abscisis*).[22] A bridge of boats was there two years later during Constantius' defensive campaign in 361. It is probable once again that there were several long-serving *protectores* to take the task in hand. Unfortunately nothing is known of the background of Verinianus the *domesticus protector* who was later wounded and went missing (18.8.11). The ride to Samosata was interrupted when Ursicinus' band stumbled across the Persian main body and was scattered in the resulting mêlée.[23]

The third category of the *protectores*' activity is the direction of artillery during sieges. It figures prominently in the unsuccessful defence of Amida in 359 and in all subsequent sieges down to Julian's retirement from Ctesiphon in 363. Amida had been specially equipped with stone- and bolt-firing *ballistae* and *scorpiones* (also called *onagri*) as well as specialist operators[24] at the express order of Caesar Constantius II when he first fortified Amida (*ante* 337). Their massed fire must have accounted for a high proportion of the Persians killed in the siege of 359, which Diskenes the *notarius* put (probably spuriously) at 30,000 when he inspected the site afterwards (19.9.9).

There are frequent 'we' (*nos*) passages which reflect the execution of the orders of Aelianus, *dux Mesopotamiae* and garrison commander. These seem to be tasks given to the *protectores* and other officers, including the massing of artillery during emergencies, concentration of troops in particular sectors, and direction of sorties against particular points of the Persian lines.[25] This is revealed, for example, in the report about the Persians' temporary seizure of one of the towers and simultaneous escalade:

> We were perplexed and uncertain where first to offer resistance, whether to those who stood [in the third storey of the tower] above us [on the wall] or to the crowd climbing the scaling ladders and already grasping the battlements; so the tasks [*opera*] were divided among us, and five lighter *ballistae* were moved and placed in the direction of the tower, rapidly firing wooden shafts which sometimes pierced two men at once. Some fell seriously wounded but others, fearful of the creaking machines, leapt away and died when their bodies were crushed. When this was quickly accomplished and the machines were restored to their usual positions, all ran to the walls with greater confidence.
>
> (19.5.6–7)

The execution of the task required men directing it who could demand the immediate transfer of the weapons from artillerists preoccupied with their own sectors. The bolt and shaft-firing *ballistae* were evidently taken from and carried through the other towers, positioned on the curtain, and fired in an upward direction against the enemy on the captured tower. Ammianus and the others will have done little more than tell the specialists at what targets to shoot after some moments of indecision about which enemy posed the greater threat. Another passage reflects Aelianus' 'staff at work' on the day the city fell:

> And finally after we had turned over many schemes [in our minds] (*multa versantibus nobis*) a plan was resolved (*sedit consilium*) which quick action made safe, to oppose four *scorpiones* to the [enemy's] *ballistae*. But while they were being moved exactly opposite and cautiously emplaced – a task requiring technique of a difficult nature (*quod artis est difficillimae*) – [the defence collapsed].
>
> (19.6.1)

Another element in 'staff work' was selecting the right moment to put certain forces into the battle. The formations present at Amida in 359 included the *legio V Parthica* that was regularly billeted there. Six others had got there ahead of the Persians by forced marches: *legiones XXX Ulpia*, *X Fortenses*, two formations formerly loyal to the usurper Magnentius, the so-called *Magnentiani* and *Decentiani*, and the *Superventores* and *Praeventores*, both light cavalry. The greater part of a *turma* of *comites sagittarii* was also present. The two Gallic legions were full of aggressive but undisciplined fighters. In discussing their performance, Ammianus lapses into the first person, his staff-work '*nos*':

> There were with us two Magnentian legions recently withdrawn from Gaul . . . brave and active men skilled in open-field fighting but in no way useful for the methods of warfare to which we were restricted; on the contrary they were terrible troublemakers (*turbatores*) who, while they could not help either with the artillery or in the construction of [defensive] works, on several occasions made senseless sorties but would return in small numbers after fighting bravely. Ultimately, when the gates were bolted as a precaution and their *tribuni* refused to let them make sorties, they gnashed their teeth like wild beasts. But in the days that followed their effectiveness was prominent.
> (19.5.2–3)

Ammianus returns to the Gauls' furious desire to enter the fight once again shortly thereafter, observing that they had begun to hack at the gates with their swords, threatening their *tribuni* and certain 'higher officers' (*primi ordines*) with death (19.6.3), and telling of the plans being made in the ducal *comitatus*:

> We were without a plan and in doubt as to what argument to use against the furious men, but at last chose this plan as the most practicable, to which they reluctantly assented: since they could bear [inactivity] no longer, they should delay for a while and then be allowed to attack the enemy pickets which were located not far from the missiles [of the Roman artillery], so that if the enemy broke the [Gauls] should push on. For it was obvious that they would mete out terrible slaughter if they got their way.
> (19.6.5)

The decision proved the right one in view of the slaughter done to the besieging army, but the Gauls lost 400 men killed and injured from the two legions that were altogether perhaps 1,500–2,000 strong.

I have endeavoured to show that Ammianus' activities in the campaign of 359 were typical of the tasks given to other *protectores*. He seems to have enjoyed some input in tactical matters such as the siting of artillery and deployment of troops in sieges. At other times his tasks were more in the order of 'operational planning' in the modern sense of the word, as for example mapping out the march route of the army with a view to directing it to the proper bridges, river crossings and supply centres. This is not to suggest that Ammianus was some sort of military 'genius', for these activities were as a rule carried out collegially by the *protectores* and *tribuni vacantes* in Ursicinus' retinue. In comparison with other writers, Ammianus' repeated references to bridges and supplies, exact terminology for officers' ranks, and vivid topographical description seem a little out of place amidst the literary allusions and digressions that accompany the narrative. Although he enjoyed access to many sources of information at the time he was writing the *Res Gestae*, Ammianus demonstrates an organic understanding of 'operations' in the modern sense of the term, with attention to personnel, intelligence, and timely movement of supplies and troops. Thus, when Ammianus describes a campaign, he draws not only on a chronological recollection of events, but on a professional consciousness that saw fortresses, roads, rivers, bridges, billets and particular bodies of troops as part of an organic whole. He and his audience were agreed that 'good history-writing' left scope for such an approach.

Notes

1 The following discussion owes much to John Matthews, *The Roman Empire of Ammianus*, London 1989. Its aim is to bring Ammianus' career as *protector domesticus* into sharper focus, and is as such merely an attempt to build on the existing scholarship. Translations of Ammianus' Latin (with occasional modifications) are from J.C. Rolfe's Loeb edition.
2 H.-J. Diesner, 'Protectores (Domestici),' *RE*, Suppl. XI (1968), 1113–23; Th. Mommsen, 'Protectores Augusti', *Gesammelte Schriften* 8 (Berlin 1913), 419–46; Matthews, *The Roman Empire of Ammianus*, 74–9.
3 See the full discussion in A.H.M Jones, *The Later Roman Empire 284–602. A Social, Economic and Administrative Survey*, Oxford 1964, 636ff.
4 *ILS* 2781, 2784; *ILCV* 532.
5 Matthews, *The Roman Empire of Ammianus*, 75. Cf. H.I. Bell, V. Martin, E.G. Turner and D. Van Berchem (eds), *The Abinnaeus Archive: Papers of a Roman Soldier in the Reign of Constantius II*, Oxford 1962 (*non vidi*).
6 Mommsen, 'Protectores Augusti', 434 n. 1.
7 *Cod. Theod.* 7.16.3 (18 Sept. 420).
8 *Cod. Theod.* 8.5.30 (23 Sept. 368).
9 *Cod. Theod.* 7.18.10 (17 May 400). We know this only because, as the law stipulates, some *protectores* were guilty of overzealousness and rounded up agricultural labourers working on the estates of landed magnates without just cause.
10 *Cod. Theod.* 9.27.3 (12 June 382).
11 M. Speidel, 'The Roman Road to Dumata (Jawf in Saudi Arabia) and the Frontier Strategy of *Praetensione Colligare*', *Historia* 36 (1987), 213–21, at 217. Cf. D. Kennedy and H.I. MacAdam, 'Latin Inscriptions from Jordan, 1985', *ZPE* 65 (1986), 231–6, no. 1.
12 *ILS* 569 (Gratianopolis, Viennensis, AD 269).
13 *ILS* 545 (Aquincum, Valeria, AD 267).
14 *ILS* 546 (Vitalianus to Iuppiter Monitor after being warned in his sleep, [*somno mon*]*itus*, Sirmium) and 4002 (Aurelius Faustus to the goddess Valentia, *ex visu deae Valentiae*, Ocriculum, Umbria).
15 *SEG* 9.356 (Ptolemais), lines 60–5. Cf. *SEG* 9.414 (Teucheira) and 17.1139 (Apollonia).
16 *ILCV* 44, 295a, 296, 467, 468, 469, 471, 477, 480, 481, 532, 539, 811; *ILS* 2775, 2776, 2777, 2781, 2783, 2784, 9205; *CIL* III 387, 3335, 8741, V 8282, XIV 918. *Publications of the Princeton University Archaeological Expeditions to Syria in 1904–05 and 1909, Division III: Greek and Latin Inscriptions, Section A: Southern Syria*, ed. by E. Littmann,

D. Magie, D.R. Stuart (Leiden 1921), no. 213. M. Speidel, 'The Army at Aquileia, the Moesiaci Legion, and the Shield Emblems in the Notitia Dignitatum,' *Roman Army Studies* 2 (Stuttgart 1992), 414–18. Hereinafter abbreviated as *RAS*. M. Speidel, 'Maxentius' Praetorians,' *RAS* 2, 388f.

17 A larger, still growing sample of 167 inscriptions reveals an average lifespan of 46.6 years for soldiers, many of them cavalrymen, between *c.* 260 and 600, and an average length of service of 21.3 years. It is quite probable that *protectores* enjoyed somewhat longer careers thanks to their particular skills. It should be remembered, however, that the lower ranks and men with shorter careers are under-represented in the epigraphy, as are the men killed in battle. See F. Trombley, 'Herakleios' First Campaign against Rahzadh in 613', *Byzantine and Modern Greek Studies* 25 (forthcoming).

18 Discussed in Matthews, *The Roman Empire of Ammianus*, 13–15.

19 I.e. it comes after the *terminus post quem* suggested here.

20 *Notitia Dignitatum. Or. XI Mag. Offic.* 18–28, ed. O. Seeck, 1876 (repr. Frankfurt 1962).

21 Amm. Marc. 18.7.1–6. Ammianus calls Cassianus the *dux Mesopotamiae*, but the context suggests that he was either the *dux Osrhoenae* or else exercised a special command over the troops of both provinces. The *dux Mesopotamiae* was in fact the *protector* Aelianus who directed the defence of Amida.

22 Amm. Marc. 18.8.1. A bridge of boats was there two years later during Constantius II's defensive campaign of 361. It is possible that it replaced the original bridge, as Ursicinus will doubtless have ordered any permanent structure to be taken down after he escaped. Ammianus (21.7.7) uses the term *navalis pons* in the latter case.

23 Ammianus devotes much attention to the construction of boat bridges on Julian's campaign against Ctesiphon in 363; e.g. 23.5.4, 24.3.8–11, 24.6.2.

24 This can at best be inferred from Amm. Marc. 19.1.7, where a 'skilled aimer' or 'observer' (*contemplator peritissimus*) directing a stone-firing *ballista* succeeded in hitting and killing the son of the Chionite king Grumbates. See also the contribution of den Hengst in this volume (chapter 3).

25 What follows here has a somewhat different 'spin' from Matthews, *The Roman Empire of Ammianus*, 64f.

3

PREPARING THE READER FOR WAR

Ammianus' digression on siege engines

Daan den Hengst

In studies on Roman warfare Ammianus figures prominently. As a former army officer, he shows a lively interest in and a detailed knowledge of military matters. His digression about siege engines (23.4) serves to provide the necessary background information for the account of Julian's Persian campaign. Military conflicts between Romans and Persians in Mesopotamia invariably took on the character of siege wars, in which siege engines played a crucial role. That explains why Ammianus places his digression in the overture to the Persian campaign, although in his accounts of the sieges of Amida (19.7), Bezabde (20.11) and Aquileia (21.12) they had been mentioned several times already. The immediate cause for the digression is the remark about the large number of siege engines that Julian had shipped along the Euphrates to Callinicum (23.3.9).

Earlier descriptions of these engines in Greek and Latin are of two kinds. There are technical treatises in which their construction is explained in great detail with exact measures for their component parts. Such treatises, by Greek authors like Heron, Philon and Biton and in Latin by Vitruvius in the tenth book of his *De Architectura*, which date from the second century BC to the first century AD, are collected, translated and expertly commented upon by E.W. Marsden.[1] On the other hand we find less technical descriptions of siege engines in the works of historians like Josephus, Procopius, Eusebius (*FGrHist* 101) and military authors like Vegetius and the Anonymus *De Rebus Bellicis*. The similarities between the descriptions in the Greek historians and in Ammianus at times suggest a common model, which, however, it is impossible to identify.

In this chapter I shall not comment on every detail of this digression,[2] but focus on its technical quality, both intrinsically and in comparison with other descriptions. Ammianus treats successively the *ballista* (§ 2–3), the *scorpio* or *onager* (§ 4–7), the *aries* (§ 8–9), the *helepolis* (§ 10–13) and the *malleolus*

(§ 14–15). Strictly speaking, the last item does not belong in the series, because, as Ammianus tells us himself, the *malleolus* is a kind of missile (*teli genus*), not a siege engine.[3] What the descriptions have in common is that the author begins with the material from which the engines are made. Next, he describes them not as finished products, but as they are put together: 'an iron strut is fixed firmly', 'two beams of oak are fashioned', 'a tall fir is selected . . . , to the end of which is fastened a long, hard iron', 'it is built . . . in the following manner', 'the shaft . . . is hollowed out'.[4] In this respect the digression resembles the technical treatises of Philon, Biton and Vitruvius. It would be as difficult, however, to construct these engines following Ammianus' instructions as to make a living as a farmer using only Virgil's *Georgics* for one's manual. In comparison to the technical treatises mentioned above Ammianus' description is lacking in precision and unsatisfactory even with regard to essential parts of the engines. It would, however, be unfair to condemn this digression because it is technically inferior to these specialized treatises. Ammianus clearly supposed his readers to have some idea of how these engines looked and worked, and his aim differs completely from that of the technical authors. His digression is first of all a literary *tour de force*. This is evident not only from the descriptions of the engines themselves, but also from the vividness with which, at the end of each description, he relates the machine's deadly effects. The flowery style Ammianus favours for his digressions makes the interpretation of this chapter especially difficult.

First the *ballista*. The essential parts of this arrow-shooting engine, Vitruvius' *catapulta*,[5] are the bow, the stock and the slider.[6] The bow is mounted on the stock, which is a long beam sticking out in front of and behind the bow. In front, the arms of the bow are stuck into vertical cylinders holding the sinew-springs, which provide the motive power for this torsion engine. The other end of the arms is attached by the bow-strings to the slider, which moves forward and backward along a groove in the stock, into which it is dovetailed. An arrow is placed in a channel in the slider. When the slider is drawn backward the bow is bent. When the slider is released, it is shot forward and the arrow flies off. These component parts are described by Ammianus as follows:

> an iron strut is fixed firmly between two little posts; it is sizeable and stretches out like a rather large ruler. From a well-finished joint in this which a smooth portion in the middle forms, a rectangular beam emerges rather a long way, fitted with a straight narrow-channelled groove, and bound in the complex chordage of twisted sinews.[7]

A comparison with Procopius' description of the βαλλίστρα in his account of the siege of Rome by Belisarius is instructive in more ways than one:

> But Belisarius placed upon the towers engines which they call 'ballistae'. Now these engines have the form of a bow, but on the under side of them

a grooved wooden shaft projects; this shaft is so fitted to the bow that it is free to move, and rests on a straight iron bed.[8]

Procopius mentions the bow first, whereas Ammianus refers to it only implicitly. Moreover, Procopius makes a clear distinction between the slider, the ξυλίνη κεραία, moving freely on top of the stock, and the stock itself, the σιδηρᾶ εὐθεῖα (sc. κεραία), which makes his description distinctly superior to that of Ammianus. The term used by Procopius for the stock, σιδηρᾶ εὐθεῖα, makes it practically certain that in Ammianus too the *ferrum* indicates the stock of the *ballista*, *pace* Marsden, who gives it a totally different interpretation on p. 238 note 1. Strange though the choice of *stilus* ('spike') for the slider may seem, it corresponds exactly to Procopius' κεραία, just as προύχει matches *eminet*.

Ammianus' description of the way in which the slider is fastened to the stock is baffling. The slider sticks out, he tells us, from a *volumen teres*, which can only be understood as a semicylindrical groove in the stock, into which it is dovetailed. The reading *pars*, quoted above, was conjectured by Wagner for the manuscript's *ars*. As it seems a priori unlikely that, in a technical description like this, *politus* should have any but its literal meaning 'polished', 'finished', Fontaine's defence of *ars polita* as meaning 'une technique raffinée' is unconvincing.[9] The question is then what is meant by this exasperatingly vague phrase, a perfect illustration of Horace's *brevis esse laboro, obscurus fio*. If *componere* is taken in its literal meaning 'to put together', the phrase could mean that the semicylindrical groove within which the slider moves is part of a well-polished central component of the stock, stuck between two other components to its right and left, which, incidentally, would simplify the construction of such a groove considerably. It is to be noted that in Vitruvius' description of the arrow-shooting *catapulta* (10.10.4), the groove for the slider is constructed by fastening two strips (the *regulae*) to the right and left of the case, leaving room in between serving as the female dovetail into which the male dovetail of the slider is inserted. If this interpretation of *componere* is correct, *pars polita* refers to the polished central part of the stock.

The connection between the slider and the bow is not described with any precision either. Ammianus just says that the two are fastened by 'this complex chordage of twisted sinews',[10] without explaining whether he means the sinews in the sinew-springs, the bowstrings or both. His description of the way in which the engine is operated is much better. The marksman, carefully fitting the arrow in its groove,[11] and the young men turning the winches drawing back the slider[12] are sketched with attention to detail, and the deadly effect of the weapon is brought out vividly by the personification of the pain inflicted: 'it quite often happens that, before the missile is seen, pain indicates a mortal wound'.[13]

The *scorpio* or *onager* is described much more clearly than the *ballista*.[14] Still, here too some phrases are difficult to explain. The essential parts of the *scorpio/onager* are the ground frame, consisting of two side beams joined together at both ends by cross-beams. In the middle of the side beams spring-holes are drilled, through which powerful ropes are tied which serve as the sinew-springs that give the engine its motive power. A wooden arm, the *stilus*, is stuck into these ropes. At the end of the arm there are iron hooks to which the sling holding a heavy stone is fitted. The arm is first drawn downwards and then released; it shoots forward and, when it strikes the buffer, hurls the stone away. In Ammianus' words:

> Two beams are fashioned... and the beams are connected as in a frame-saw... between them, through the holes, powerful ropes are stretched, preventing the structure from falling apart. From the middle of the cords a wooden arm rises at an angle and, being set upright in the manner of a yoke-pole, is so inserted in the twists of sinew that it can be raised higher and lowered; to its tip iron hooks are fastened, from which hangs a sling of tow or iron. A huge buffer is placed in front of this arm.[15]

The two main problems here are the comparison to the frame-saw (*serratoria machina*) and the position of the buffer (*fulmentum*). Marsden has provided an ingenious explanation of the comparison.[16] He starts from a very common type of frame-saw, consisting of two sides, held together in the middle by a strut. At one end of the sides the saw-blade is inserted, at the other end they are held together by a tightening rope that at the same time stretches the blade. If we imagine that the tightening rope is placed in the middle and that the saw-blade and the strut are replaced by cross-beams at either end of the sides, we have, according to Marsden, the ground frame of the *scorpio*. That would also explain the enigmatic phrase 'preventing the structure from falling apart'. Here the comparison of the frame of the onager to a frame-saw may have led Ammianus astray. In a saw of the type described above the ropes can be said to hold the saw together. In the *scorpio* it is the cross-beams, not the ropes, that prevent the structure from falling apart.

A second problem is posed by the verb *prosternere* in the phrase *cui ligno fulmentum prosternitur ingens*, which must mean that the buffer is spread out on the ground (as in Fontaine's fig. 2).[17] The next section, however, states that the shot is projected from the sling when the arm hits the buffer,[18] which, of course, should happen well before the arm hits the ground. Experiments carried out by Schramm and Marsden have shown that the best results are obtained when the buffer is placed in an upright position.[19] In other words the buffer must be above the horizontal frame of the *scorpio*. *Prosternitur*, therefore, is probably corrupt and a verb meaning 'to stop' or 'to block' should be substituted for it. *Obtendere* (sometimes written *obstendere*, TLL IX 2.273.72–3), 'i.q. tendendo obicere, opponere' (*TLL*), would suit the meaning well. It is found in combination with *cilicium* also in 20.11.9 *sub obtentis ciliciis*.

The description of the *scorpio/onager* ends with a vivid picture of the artillery officer bringing down his hammer to release the *stilus* and of the devastating effect of the machine. The climax is introduced by *itaque demum sublimis astans magister claustrum . . . reserat*. Matthews rightly rejects Marsden's interpretation of *sublimis* as referring to the rank of the officer.[20] He himself supposes that the operator 'had in some way to stand "above" the mechanism'. It seems preferable, however, to take *sublimis* in its meaning 'drawing himself up to his full height' (*OLD sublimis* 6b). Again, there may be an echo of Virgil here, cf. *Aen.* 12.788 *olli sublimes armis animisque refecti*. The enormous power of the *onager* is demonstrated by the anecdote about the engineer who was killed by his own engine:

> a builder on our side . . . happened to be standing behind a scorpion, when a stone which one of the gunners had fitted insecurely to the sling was hurled backward. The unfortunate man was thrown on his back with his breast crushed, and killed; and his limbs were so torn asunder that not even parts of his body could be identified.[21]

The *aries* was already shown in action in the account of the siege of Bezabde (20.11.11–15). Two details of that description are repeated here. *Prominentem eius ferream frontem* (20.11.15) matches *arietis efficiens prominulam speciem* and *quae re vera formam effingit arietis* (ibid.) has its counterpart in *quae forma huic machinamento vocabulum indidit*. Equally detailed descriptions of the battering ram are to be found in Vitruvius (*De Arch.* 10.13.1–3), Flavius Josephus (*BJ* 3.214–17) and Procopius (*Goth.* 1.21.5–12). The resemblance between the passages in Josephus and Ammianus is especially striking. Compare Ammianus' opening phrase 'a tall fir or mountain ash is selected, to the end of which is fastened a long, hard iron; this has the appearance of a projecting ram's head'[22] with Josephus *BJ* 3.214 '[the ram] is reinforced at its extremity with a mass of iron in the form of a ram's head, whence the machine takes its name'.[23] The type of ram described by Josephus is less complicated than the *aries* in Vitruvius and Procopius. In Josephus the *aries* is suspended from a beam that rests upon two posts fixed in the ground.[24] The construction described in the other two authors consists of a four-sided building, with four upright posts and four horizontal timbers in the middle of which the ram is suspended. From the fact that Ammianus mentions two horizontal beams at either side of the ram it follows that his engine belongs to the second, more sophisticated type.[25]

One would expect the operation of the *aries* to be compared to the attack of a ram, but the main manuscript (V) has *instar assurgentis et cedentis armati*, 'charging and retreating like a soldier'. *Pace* Fontaine, V's *armati* seems untenable, since Ammianus never uses *armatus* in the singular for *miles*. For the whole phrase compare the description of counter-measures against a battering ram during the siege of Bezabde: 'that it [the ram] might not move back and gather new strength, nor be able with good aim to batter the walls with repeated lunges'.[26] Valesius' simple correction *arietis* seems perfectly acceptable and is palaeographically much closer to *armati* than Clark's *cornuti*. Cf. Veg. Mil. 4.14 *et appellatur aries* . . . , *quod more arietum retrocedit ut cum impetu vehementius feriat* ('and it is called a ram, because it retreats like rams do in order to charge and strike with greater force'). The following words, *qua crebritate velut reciproci fulminis impetu aedificiis scissis* ('as this is renewed with the force of a repeated stroke of lightning') are inspired by Virgil, *Aen.* 2.492–3 *labat ariete crebro / ianua*. The idea that the lightning bounces back after touching the earth is illustrated by Bailey ad Lucr. 6.86–9 and Beaujeu ad Pliny, *NH* 2.43.[27] There is, therefore, at first sight no reason to read *fluminis* with Petschenig, although it must be admitted that *reciprocus* is not found as an attribute with *fulmen*, whereas it is the normal adjective for tidal movements, and, moreover, that the notion of repetition (*crebritas*) is brought out more naturally by a comparison with the recurrence of the tides, which would also tally with the preceding words *assurgentis et cedentis*. Ultimately, however, the fierceness of the attacks of the ram favours a comparison with a shaft of lightning.

The description of the *helepolis*[28] has been called a 'phantasievolle Darstellung', which cannot be used as a source.[29] Southern and Dixon are of the opinion that the machine of Ammianus should not be confused with the *helepolis* of the Hellenistic period.[30] And indeed, there are indications that the word *helepolis* was used in later times with a less restricted meaning to indicate different types of siege-towers. Hesychius *s.v.* defines *helepoleis* as 'machines, like rams or whatever engines with which cities are destroyed',[31] that is to say he does not distinguish them from battering rams and other siege engines. The same seems to be the case in Josephus. In his account of the siege of Iotapata he mentions the heroic deeds of one Eleasar, who succeeded in putting the *helepolis* of the Romans out of action: 'lifting an enormous stone, he hurled it from the wall at the *helepolis* with such force that he broke off the head of the engine'.[32] His death is described by Josephus with the words 'he fell headlong with the ram's head in his arms'.[33]

The first part of Ammianus' description (§ 11) is conventional. It closely resembles a passage in Caesar:

> and on the top of this flooring they made a layer of bricks and clay so that the firebrands of the enemy might do no harm. And they further laid thereon mattresses, that missiles hurled by engines might not crash through the flooring or stones from catapults dislodge the brickwork.[34]

The problems really start in the next section: 'on its front side are set very sharp, three-pronged spear-points made heavy with iron weights'.[35] Now the Hellenistic *helepolis* had several storeys, no less than twenty in the tower built (or designed) by Diades, the engineer of Alexander the Great, according to Vitruvius (*De Arch.* 10.13.3), which carried artillery, drawbridges and sometimes battering rams.[36] Ammianus, however, does not mention any storeys here and he depicts the front of the tower as closed with the *trisulcae cuspides* somehow fastened to it. Unfortunately, it is impossible to imagine how these *cuspides* could be put to any use if they were fixed onto such an unwieldy contraption. The function of the *trisulcae cuspides* being to tear down the wall, they must be compared to the siege hook (*falx muralis*) described by Vegetius in the following terms: 'Inside the tower there is a beam, fitted with a curved iron hook and called a sickle because of its form, for pulling stones out of the wall.'[37] Presumably these sickles were swung against the wall, which is the only way in which the detail about the iron weights makes sense. It was precisely the incongruity of the *trisulcae cuspides* in the description of the *helepolis* that led Brok to believe that Ammianus was thinking of the *tichodifros*, a siege engine mentioned by the Anonymus *De Rebus Bellicis*. Indeed this engine was fitted with tridents and spears.[38] Still, the short passage in the Anonymus evokes a small wheeled vehicle serving exclusively to protect *ballistae* approaching a wall. We must conclude that the *helepolis* described by Ammianus is a hybrid.

With regard to the effect of the real *helepolis*, Ammianus reports that the defenders of Pirisabora surrendered at the mere sight of one being put together by the Romans: 'to this huge mass, which would rise above the battlements of the lofty towers, the defenders turned an attentive eye . . . and they fell to their prayers'.[39] As Vegetius says at the conclusion of his discussion of the engine itself and the possible counter-measures to be taken against it: 'What help is left, when those who placed their hope in the height of the walls suddenly see a higher wall of the enemy above them?'[40]

Finally, the *malleolus*. The 'little hammer' derives its name from its form. It is basically a stick with at its end a round thickening consisting of or filled with incendiary material, which makes it resemble a mallet or a club. The *malleolus* or fire-dart is mentioned for the first time in Latin literature by Sisenna (*Hist.* 83), so that it may safely be assumed that this weapon, like the engines mentioned earlier in this digression, dates back to at least Hellenistic times. Apart from the brief mention in Vegetius (*Mil.* 4.18), this is the only description of the fire-dart in Latin. Ammianus mentions *malleoli* in his descriptions of the sieges of Singara (20.6.6) Bezabde (20.7.10 and 20.11.13) and Maiozamalcha (24.4.16), and in his account of the riots in Rome against the urban prefect Lampadius (27.3.8).

The construction of the *malleolus* is described as follows (§ 14): *sagitta est cannea inter spiculum et harundinem multifido ferro coagmentata*. The *sagitta* is the fire-dart as a whole, of which the *spiculum* ('point') and the *harundo* ('shaft') are the component parts. Between the point and the shaft is the *multifidum ferrum*. The first satisfactory explanation of this puzzling phrase has again been given by Brok.[41] He compared the present description with the following passage from the Greek historian or poliorcetician Eusebius:

these fire-darts were as follows: instead of the point at the end of the arrow it had a part that was constructed with a view to carrying fire. It was made of iron and had strips diverging below from the shaft. These diverging strips then bent back and met at the top. Where they were joined together at the top, a straight and very sharp point projected from all of them. The effect of this construction was that it remained fixed in whatever object it was shot into.[42]

The part of the *malleolus* that carried the fire is described by Eusebius as follows: 'these bending iron strips formed a hollow bosom by the distances between them, like the distaffs of women spinning wool, around which wool is wound and from which they draw the thread'.[43] The comparison with the distaff in both authors proves beyond reasonable doubt that they are describing the same weapon, so that Eusebius' text may be used to interpret Ammianus' vague phrase *multifido ferro*, which turns out to refer to an iron container between the point and the shaft.

About the incendiary material inside the *malleolus* Eusebius is more specific than Ammianus: 'within this cavity they put hemp ... smeared with sulphur or rubbed with what is called Medic oil'.[44] What makes the *malleolus* so effective is the fact that its fire cannot be extinguished by water. As Ammianus tells us: 'water poured upon it rouses the fire to a still greater heat'.[45] Why this is the case he does not explain. We have to turn to Eusebius and to the parallel passage in 23.6.37 to find the answer. Sulphur and Medic oil burn even more hotly when they come into contact with water. It is an old trick, already described by Livy in his account of the Bacchanalia: 'matrons in the dress of Bacchantes, with dishevelled hair and carrying blazing torches, would run to the Tiber, and plunging their torches in the water (because they contained live sulphur mixed with calcium) would bring them out still burning'.[46] As Ammianus tells us, the flames can only be put out by sand: *nec remedio ullo quam superiacto pulvere consopitur*. In this way, he ends his literary *tour de force* in style, with an allusion to Virgil's famous verses about ending a war between bees: 'these storms of passion, these conflicts so fierce, by the tossing of a little dust are quelled and laid to rest'.[47]

From a military man like Ammianus, one would have expected a description based on personal observation, but, as in his digressions on countries he had visited himself, both the vagueness of his account and the similarities in the descriptions found in other historians suggest that his knowledge, or at least the way in which he presents his material, stems primarily from book-learning. The power of the literary tradition and the demands it imposed on the style of presentation produced this curious mixture of imprecision in the description of the technical aspects of the siege engines and vividness in the representation of the effects of these weapons.

Notes

1 E.W. Marsden, *Greek and Roman Artillery*, Oxford 1971. The English translations of passages in the digression are based partly on Marsden (pp. 238 and 251), partly on Rolfe's translation in the Loeb edition.
2 A detailed discussion of the digression is given in the commentary by J. den Boeft, J.W. Drijvers, D. den Hengst and H.C. Teitler, *Philological and Historical Commentary on Ammianus Marcellinus XXIII*, Groningen 1998.
3 Still, firebrands were a regular feature in sieges; cf. e.g. Tacitus, *Ann.* 2.81.2 *tormentis hastas, saxa et faces ingerere* and the battle scenes in Amm. Marc. 20.11.13 (*adsidue malleolos atque incendiaria tela torquentes laborabant*), 21.12.10, 24.4.16, 27.3.8.
4 *ferrum ... compaginatur* (§ 2), *dolantur axes duo quernei* (§ 4), *eligitur abies ... cuius summitas duro ferro concluditur* (§ 8), *aedificatur ... hoc modo* (§ 11), *sagitta ... concavatur* (§ 14).
5 For an explanation of the terminological change from *catapulta* to *ballista* and from *ballista* to *scorpio* or *onager* see Ph. Fleury, *La mécanique de Vitruve*, Caen 1993, 226–39. Ammianus distinguishes clearly between them in 20.7.10: *nec ballistae tamen cessavere nec scorpiones, illae tela torquentes, hi lapides crebros*.
6 The drawings in Fontaine's commentary volume of *Ammien Marcellin. Histoire* (Livres XXIII–XXV), 2 vols, Paris 1977, are most helpful, although, in my opinion, they are not completely correct and at times are at variance with the notes in his commentary.
7 *ferrum inter axiculos duo firmum compaginatur et vastum in modum regulae maioris extentum, cuius ex volumine tereti, quod in medio pars polita componit, quadratus eminet stilus extentius recto canalis angusti meatu cavatus et hac multiplici chorda nervorum tortilium illigatus* (23.4.2).
8 Procopius, *Goth.* 1.21.14: Βελισάριος δὲ μηχανὰς μὲν ἐς τοὺς πύργους ἐτίθετο, ἃς καλοῦσι βαλλίστρας. τόξου δὲ σχῆμα ἔχουσιν αἱ μηχαναὶ αὗται, ἔνερθέν τε αὐτοῦ κοίλη τις ξυλίνη κεραία προὔχει, αὐτὴ μὲν χαλαρὰ ἠρτημένη, σιδηρᾷ δὲ εὐθείᾳ τινὶ ἐπικειμένη. The parallel passage in Procopius was pointed out by M.F.A. Brok, 'Bombast oder Kunstfertigkeit? Ammians Beschreibung der *ballista*, 23,4,1–3', *RhM* 120 (1977), 331–45.
9 *Pars polita*, moreover, may well be a snippet from Virgil, *Aen.* 8.426–8: *iam parte polita ... pars imperfecta manebat*.
10 In Marsden's translation, quoted on p. 30, the pronoun *hac* is neglected. It is not immediately clear what it refers to. For that reason Brok conjectured *arcu*, which certainly would be a great improvement. However, Ammianus is very free in his use of anaphoric pronouns. Cf. e.g. *hac medietate restium* in § 5, and *hac fiducia spei maioris animatus* (20.5.8). *Hac* may be paraphrased as '[the chordage] that is a part of this engine'.
11 *assistit artifex contemplabilis et subtiliter apponit in temonis cavamine sagittam* (23.4.2).
12 *hinc inde validi iuvenes versant agiliter rotabilem flexum* (23.4.2). Cf. Procopius, *Goth.* 1.12.17: σφίγγουσι τε σθένει πολλῷ οἱ ἀμφοτέρωθεν μηχαναῖς τισί.
13 *evenit saepius, ut, antequam telum cernatur, dolor letale vulnus agnoscat* (23.4.3).
14 The term *onager* seems to be more modern and less dignified, cf. 23.4.7: *cui etiam onagri vocabulum indidit aetas novella* and 31.15.12: *quem onagrum sermo vulgaris appellat*.
15   dolantur axes duo ... hique in modum serratoriae machinae conectuntur ... quos inter per cavernas funes colligantur robusti compagem, ne dissiliat, continentes. ab hac medietate restium ligneus stilus exsurgens obliquus et in modum iugalis temonis erectus ita nervorum nodulis implicatur, ut altius tolli possit et inclinari, summitatique eius unci ferrei copulantur, e quibus pendet ... funda, cui ligno fulmentum prosternitur ingens.

(23.4.4–5)

16 Marsden, *Greek and Roman Artillery*, 251–2.
17 Marsden has glossed over this problem in his translation. For *prosternere* in Ammianus cf. 17.8.5: *quorum legatis paulo postea missis precatum consultumque rebus suis **humi prostratis** ...*

pacem... tribuit; 17.13.21: *territi **subactorum** exemplis et **prostratorum***; 22.1.2: *lapso milite qui se insessurum equo dextra manu erexit **humique prostrato***; 22.14.4: *conspexit quendam **humi prostratum***; 29.1.34: *Theodorus... **in precem venialem prostratus***; 30.5.1: ***pedibusque eius prostrata** orabat*; 31.13.13: *Decium equi **lapsu prostratum**.*

18 *stilus... mollitudini offensus cilicii saxum contorquet* (23.4.6).

19 See the reconstructions by Schramm and Marsden in Marsden, *Greek and Roman Artillery*, 263.

20 J.F. Matthews, *The Roman Empire of Ammianus*, London 1989, 293 n. 17.

21 *nostrae partis architectus... post machinam scorpionis forte assistens reverberato lapide, quem artifex titubanter aptaverat fundae, obliso pectore supinatus profudit animam disiecta compage membrorum adeo, ut ne signa quidem totius corporis noscerentur* (24.4.28).

22 *eligitur abies vel ornus excelsa, cuius summitas duro ferro concluditur et prolixo, arietis efficiens prominulam speciem* (23.4.8).

23 ἐστόμωται δὲ παχεῖ σιδήρῳ κατ' ἄκρον εἰς κριοῦ προτομήν, ἀφ' οὗ καὶ καλεῖται, τετυπωμένῳ (*Bell. Jud.* 3.214).

24 καταιωρεῖται δὲ κάλοις μέσος... ἑτέρας δοκοῦ σταυροῖς ἑκατέρωθεν ἑδραίοις ὑπεστηριγμένης (*Bell. Jud.* 3.215).

25 *suspensa utrimque transversis asseribus* (23.4.8).

26 *ne retrogradiens resumeret vires neve ferire muros assultibus densis contemplabiliter posset* (20.11.15).

27 The idea is found also in Cicero, *Div.* 2.42–5; Seneca, *Nat.* 2.57.4; and Lucan 1.156.

28 Ammianus has the Greek term again in 24.2.18 *machinam, quae cognominatur helepolis, iussit expeditius fabricari*. It is used also by Vitruvius in his detailed description of the siege-tower (*De Arch.* 10.16). The Latin equivalent of the term is *turris ambulatoria* (*B. Alex.* 2.5; Vitruvius, *De Arch.* 10.13.3; Vegetius, *Mil.* 4.16), *turris mobilis* (Livy 21.11.07; Curtius 8.10.32) or simply *turris*.

29 O. Lendle, *Texte und Untersuchungen zum technischen Bereich der Poliorketik*, Wiesbaden 1983, 58 n. 71.

30 P. Southern and K.R. Dixon, *The Late Roman Army*, London 1996, 161.

31 μηχανήματα, οἱ κριοὶ ἢ οἱαδήποτε δι' ὧν αἱ πόλεις καθαιροῦνται.

32 ὑπερμεγέθη πέτραν ἀράμενος ἀφίησιν ἀπὸ τοῦ τείχους ἐπὶ τὴν ἑλέπολιν μετὰ τοσαύτης βίας, ὥστε ἀπορρῆξαι τὴν κεφαλὴν τοῦ μηχανήματος (*Bell. Jud.* 3.230).

33 μετὰ τοῦ κρίου κατέπεσεν (*Bell. Jud.* 3.232).

34 *eamque contabulationem summam lateribus lutoque constraverunt, ne quid ignis hostium nocere posset, centonesque insuper iniecerunt, ne aut tela tormentis missa tabulationem perfringerent aut saxa ex catapultis latericium discuterent* (Caesar, *Bell. Civ.* 2.9.4).

35 *conseruntur... eius frontalibus trisulcae cuspides praeacutae ponderibus ferreis graves* (23.4.12).

36 In order to be able to use these, the walls had to have openings and indeed Vitruvius, *De Arch.* 10.13.4 tells us that these towers had openings like windows on each side (*singulis partibus in ea* (sc. *turri*) *fenestratis*). The same detail is to be found in Plutarch, *Demetr.* 21.2 and Vegetius, *Mil.* 4.17.

37 *Haec* (sc. *turris*) *intrinsecus accipit trabem, quae... adunco praefigitur ferro et falx vocatur ab eo, quod incurva est, ut de muro extrahat lapides* (*Mil.* 4.14).

38 *cuius axium extremitates et frons nec non et superior latitudo fuscinis et lanceis armatur* (*De Rebus Bell.* 8.4).

39 *ad hanc molem ingentem superaturam celsarum turrium minas prohibitores oculorum aciem intentius conferentes... vitam cum venia postulabant* (24.2.19).

40 *Quid enim auxilii superest, cum hi, qui de murorum altitudine sperabant, repente supra se aspiciunt altiorem hostium murum?* (*Mil.* 4.17).

41 M.F.A. Brok, 'Ein spätrömischer Brandpfeil nach Ammianus', *Saalburg-Jahrbuch* 35 (1978), 57–61.

42 τὰ δὲ πυρφόρα ταῦτα βέλεα ἦν τοιάδε. ἀντὶ τῆς ἄρδιος τῆς πρὸς τῷ ἄκρῳ τοῦ οἰστοῦ εἶχε ταῦτα τάπερ μεμηχάνητο ὥστε τὸ πῦρ αὐτὸ ἐπιφέρειν· ταῦτα δὲ

ἦν σιδήρεα, ἔχοντα ἔνερθεν ἐκ τοῦ πυθμένος κεραίας ἐπεκκεκλιμένας. αἱ δὲ κεραῖαι χωρὶς ἐπ' ἑωυτέων ἐλαυνόμεναι, ἔπειτα καμπτόμεναι κατὰ κορυφὴν πρὸς ἀλλήλας ξυνήγοντο. συναφθεισέων δὲ τούτων ἐς ἄκρον ἀκὶς ἰθείη καὶ ὀξυτάτη ἀπὸ πασέων ἐξήιε. τῆς δὲ δὴ μεμηχανημένης οὕτως ἔργον ἦν, κατ' ὅτεω ἂν ἐνεχθείη, προσπερονημένην μιν ἐνεστάναι.
(*FGrHist* 101, p. 481.9–21)

43 καμπτόμεναι αἱ κεραῖαι κόλπον κοῖλον, κατὰ τὸν διεστεῶσαι ἦσαν ἀπ' ἀλληλέων, ἐποίεον, οἷον δὴ καὶ τῶν ἐριουργουσέων γυναίκων ἡλακάται, περὶ ἃς δὴ στρέφεται τὸ εἴριον ἔξωθεν περιβαλλόμενον, ἀπ' ὧν δὴ τὸν στήμονα κατάγουσι.

44 μεταξὺ τούτου τοῦ κόλπου εἴσω στυππίον ἢ καὶ ξύλα λεπτά, θείου αὐτοῖσι προσπλασσαμένου ἢ καὶ τῷ Μηδείης ἐλαίῳ καλεομένῳ αὐτὰ χρίσαντες, ἐνετίθεσαν.

45 *aquisque conspersa acriores excitat aestus incendiorum* (23.4.15).

46 *matronas Baccharum habitu crinibus sparsis cum ardentibus facibus decurrere ad Tiberim demissasque in aquam faces, quia vivum sulphur cum calce insit, integra flamma efferre* (39.13.12).

47 *hi motus animorum atque haec certamina tanta / pulveris exigui iactu compressa quiescent* (Virgil, *Georg.* 4.86–7).

4

THE PERSIAN INVASION OF 359

Presentation by suppression in Ammianus
Marcellinus' *Res Gestae* 18.4.1–18.6.7

Josephina Lenssen

Introduction[1]

Chapters 4.1–6.7 of Book 18 of the *Res Gestae* have been aptly called the 'preface' to Ammianus' account of the Persian invasion of 359.[2] With these chapters Ammianus sets the scene for the actual invasion, which reaches its climax in the siege and destruction of Amida. In short, the events are as follows. Shapur, the king of the Persians, is preparing for a major campaign against the Romans (18.4). Antoninus, a Roman, defects to the Persians with detailed intelligence on the Roman defences in the East and encourages Shapur to attack the Roman provinces (18.5). Ursicinus, serving as *magister equitum* in the East, receives an order to yield his position to Sabinianus and return to the court in Sirmium. He is to succeed Barbatio, the *magister peditum* at court, who has been executed for treason. However, on his way to Sirmium Ursicinus receives new orders, instructing him to return and to conduct the defence of the eastern border, yet without being restored to his former rank (18.6).

A recurrent theme within the description of these events is the activity of the courtiers, presented by Ammianus as constantly plotting to discredit Ursicinus, with the final aim of destroying him. They convince Constantius that Ursicinus is aiming at imperial power for himself, and is therefore a danger to the emperor's authority in the East. They are said to have instigated not only Ursicinus' recall to court (18.5.5), but also the decision to reassign him to the East without giving him back his original rank, which is now being held by the incompetent Sabinianus. This was allegedly done with the intent that in the case of a successful campaign against the Persians Sabinianus would receive all the military credit, whereas in the case of defeat Ursicinus could be arraigned for high treason (18.6.6).

The credibility of this version was greatly doubted by E.A. Thompson. He argued that Ursicinus' appointment as successor of Barbatio was a promotion, and that the sudden order to return to the eastern frontier should be explained by the fact that Constantius had not realized previously how dangerous the situation in the East was and how badly Ursicinus' presence was needed there.[3] J.F. Matthews agrees with Thompson and develops his thesis further. He explains Constantius' behaviour by the considerable distance – over 1,500 miles – that separated the government from the scene of action. He argues as follows:

> It was the intensification of Sapor's preparations in the light of the intelligence brought by Antoninus that prompted Ursicinus' re-assignment to the Mesopotamian theatre of war. That he should have received notice of this re-assignment in what were to him such puzzling circumstances is a measure of the time needed by a government in the west to receive information from the eastern frontier and to react to it by sending instructions to participants who were nearer the sources of information than was the emperor himself.[4]

These historical reconstructions differ from Ammianus' version, in that they argue that there was no ill-will toward Ursicinus on Constantius' part, assuming that when he recalled Ursicinus he was simply not aware as yet of the actual danger threatening the eastern border. As soon as he realized the real extent of the danger he sent Ursicinus back. Thus, they introduce an element which seems to be absent from Ammianus' version of the events: they imply an exchange of information between the court and the East which inspired the successive decisions with regard to Ursicinus.

If this is right the question arises how this factor is dealt with by Ammianus. Are there any signs indicating that such exchange of information may indeed have played a part? This question is interesting for several reasons.

It has been long recognized that one of the purposes of the 'preface' is to make it clear right from the start that Ursicinus, on whose staff Ammianus served as an officer, should not be held responsible for the Roman defeat and the loss of Amida.[5] Literary presentation plays an important role in this regard. Guy Sabbah has argued that the main effect of Ammianus' way of presenting the events is contrastive.[6] Instead of giving two full accounts following each other, i.e. one of the Persian war preparations and one of the intrigues at court, Ammianus interweaves these two narrative sequences by alternating Roman sections with Persian sections. Switching repeatedly from one scene of action to the other, he creates a sharp contrast between the corrupt activities of the court clique and the growing danger in the East. In doing so he not only emphasizes the irresponsible character of the decisions taken at court, but also, implicitly, lays the responsibility for the ensuing disaster at the courtiers' door. Sabbah's observations provide us with some insights into the strategies Ammianus adopts to impose on the reader his view of the events. But there is more to it than his analysis shows.

In answering the question of how Ammianus tries to present his view as convincingly as possible, we also have to address the question of which strategies he applies to rule out other interpretations as much as possible – strategies aiming not so much to emphasize certain aspects, but to suppress things that do not fit his view. For this episode, Thompson and Matthews offer just that, an alternative interpretation. This interpretation supposes an exchange of information between the court and the East. So we should ask ourselves what clues we are given about the availability of information at court at different stages in the story. How much does Ammianus tell us about 'who knew what at which point'? If we were to find that Ammianus' own presentation yields indications that he is holding back information on this point, this would provide us with additional, text-internal arguments in support of Thompson's and Matthews' reconstructions. But it would also tell us something about Ammianus himself and how he goes about writing his history. How straightforward is he? Does he hold back information, or manipulate the facts so as to make them fit his own view? Or does he really think that Ursicinus was the victim of intrigues at court, and does he really not understand why Constantius acted as he did? Both Thompson and Matthews seem to take the latter position. They take Ammianus' wrong perception of the situation as an explanation for his incorrect, or at least incomplete, presentation of the facts.

Analysis

The order in which Ammianus presents the events is as follows:

- Shapur is preparing for war (4.1)
- news about these preparations reaches court (4.2)
- the court clique wages a slanderous campaign against Ursicinus (4.2–6)
- at Samosata Ursicinus and his staff (which included Ammianus, hence *nos*) receive news concerning Antoninus' defection (4.7)
- Antoninus' defection (5.1–3)
- the court decides to have Ursicinus recalled (5.4–5)
- the Persian court receives Antoninus, who encourages Shapur to attack (5.6–8)
- Sabinianus arrives in Cilicia and hands Ursicinus the imperial letter ordering him to return to court (6.1)
- protests in the provinces against Ursicinus' recall (6.2)
- rumours about Ursicinus' departure reach the Persians (6.3)
- on the advice of Antoninus, the Persians decide to cross the Euphrates and strike straight at the provinces beyond; continued war preparations (6.3–4)
- Ursicinus receives a new letter ordering him to return to Mesopotamia (6.5–6)

- Ursicinus returns to the East, only to find that the Persians have already arrived (6.7)

Although Ammianus gives no absolute indications of time, it is possible to reconstruct a relative chronology indicating what happened more or less simultaneously and what successively according to Ammianus. This may be represented graphically in an outline of events, as is found in figure 1. The first thing that must be noted (and is represented in the outline) is that it is not enough to distinguish between events on the Roman and on the Persian side, as does Sabbah. In fact, we are dealing with three sequences of events developing at at least three different locations concerning three different parties: the court, Ursicinus and his staff, the Persians.[7] This additional distinction shows something else as well: in the course of the presentation a shift occurs in 18.6. As we can see from the outline, in 18.4–5 the Roman sections (columns 1 and 2, upper half) primarily deal with the activities at court, but in 18.6 the focus shifts to Ursicinus. Although here also we are told about decisions taken at court, nevertheless they are expressly presented from the perspective of Ursicinus: they are introduced in the context of the moment at which he receives the imperial letters containing the new instructions. This shift of perspective conceals at least one important missing link in the narrative that could point to a manipulation of the facts. I shall return to this point later.

Another point which becomes clear from the outline is that the availability at court of information concerning the developments indeed hardly plays a part in Ammianus' version. At two points in the story mention is made of rumours or messages reaching the Roman side with news of developments on the Persian side (marked A and B).

18.4.2 (A)
et cum haec primo rumores, dein nuntii certi perferrent omnesque suspensos adventantium calamitatum complicaret magna formido . . .
When the first rumours of this were confirmed by reliable reports, overwhelming fear of imminent disaster kept everyone in suspense.[8]

18.4.7 (B)
haec operientibus illis et ancipiti cogitatione districtis nobis apud Samosatam . . . parumper morantibus repente novi motus rumoribus densis audiuntur et certis.
While Ursicinus' enemies, a prey to anxiety, were playing a waiting game, we were making a short stay at Samosata . . . There we suddenly received repeated and consistent reports of a new commotion.

Of these two only 18.4.2 (A) tells us something about information reaching court. *Haec* refers back to 18.4.1: Shapur is planning a major attack on Roman territory. The other passage (18.4.7; B) deals with news that reaches Ursicinus and his staff in Samosata. Although the Latin is ambiguous,[9]

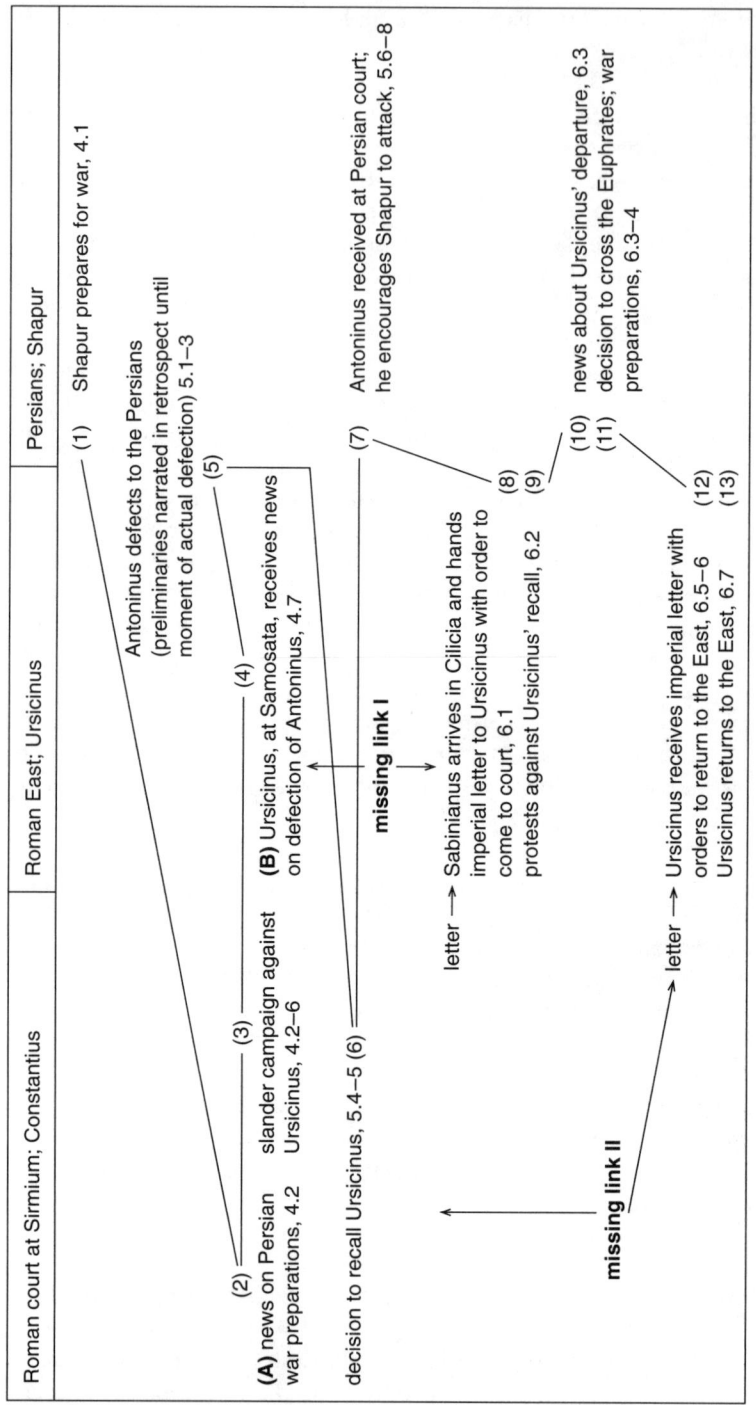

Roman court at Sirmium; Constantius	Roman East; Ursicinus	Persians; Shapur
		(1) Shapur prepares for war, 4.1
	Antoninus defects to the Persians (preliminaries narrated in retrospect until moment of actual defection) 5.1–3	
(2)		
(A) news on Persian war preparations, 4.2		
(3)		
slander campaign against Ursicinus, 4.2–6		
	(4)	
	(B) Ursicinus, at Samosata, receives news on defection of Antoninus, 4.7	
decision to recall Ursicinus, 5.4–5 (6)		
	(5)	
	missing link I	
		(7) Antoninus received at Persian court; he encourages Shapur to attack, 5.6–8
	letter → Sabinianus arrives in Cilicia and hands imperial letter to Ursicinus with order to come to court, 6.1 (8)	
	protests against Ursicinus' recall, 6.2 (9)	
		(10) news about Ursicinus' departure, 6.3
		(11) decision to cross the Euphrates; war preparations, 6.3–4
	letter → Ursicinus receives imperial letter with orders to return to the East, 6.5–6 (12)	
	Ursicinus returns to the East, 6.7 (13)	
missing link II		

Figure 1 Outline of chapters 18.4.1–18.6.7

three columns: three parties/scenes of action horizontally on the same level: simultaneous events vertically from top to bottom: successive events (1)–(2) etc.: order of presentation in Ammianus

I think the gist of this passage is clear and well expressed by Hamilton's translation. There is a clear contrast between *illis* and *nobis*: while *they* were concocting these things, *we* (who were not at court, but at Samosata) heard the following. The information involved is recounted in 18.5: the *protector* Antoninus defects to the Persians with important military intelligence.

This means that at one point only in 18.4.1–18.6.7 explicit mention is made of news reaching the court, and this only amounts to the general, initial information that Shapur was preparing for war. It is nowhere made clear when and how the court became informed of subsequent developments, especially Antoninus' defection. Ammianus leaves us in the dark on this point. The question is why.

Of course, the real issue is whether information about Antoninus' defection and its sequel was already available at court when it was decided to recall Ursicinus from the East and replace him with Sabinianus. If so, this would have fitted the picture Ammianus is trying to draw perfectly and there would have been no reason for vagueness. He could have simply argued as follows: although the court was perfectly aware of the increasingly dangerous situation in the East, those responsible nevertheless decided to recall Ursicinus, a decision which was evidently against the interests of the state.[10] The fact that he does not is an indication that, at least in Ammianus' eyes, the court was not yet aware of Antoninus' defection. But the fact remains that he does not indicate if and when this information did reach court.

Admittedly, it cannot be ruled out completely that Ammianus refrains from giving information on this issue simply because in his opinion this was not a factor of importance in the development of the events. Nevertheless, I believe there are strong indications that Ammianus is holding back information here. This brings me to the element of suppression mentioned in the title of this chapter. There are missing links in Ammianus' narrative that suggest manipulation of the facts.

These missing links occur at two points (cf. outline):

I In 18.4.7 we were told that Ursicinus was in Samosata. In 18.6.1 we are told that Sabinianus arrives in Cilicia and delivers to his predecessor the imperial letter instructing him to return to Sirmium. We must assume that, in the meantime, Ursicinus has travelled to Cilicia.[11]

II In 18.6.5 Ursicinus receives an imperial letter containing new orders. We must assume that the court has changed its plans and decided on a new strategy.

As for the first, it is in itself easy to conclude from 18.6.1 that, apparently, Ursicinus has left Samosata and travelled to Cilicia. But in the light of the dangerous situation at the eastern border it is far from self-evident why Ursicinus should have left the border area and travelled to Cilicia (at least 150 miles to the west).[12]

As for the second missing link, similarly, it is easy to conclude from 18.6.5 that the court has decided to send Ursicinus back to the East, but the question why and when they changed their strategy remains unanswered. Admittedly, Ammianus does give a description of the malicious intentions of the courtiers that allegedly lay behind this decision: in case of a successful campaign against the Persians the credit would go to Sabinianus (who was now in command), while in case of a defeat, Ursicinus could be arraigned for high treason (18.6.6). These malicious intentions, at first sight, seem to give the reason for sending Ursicinus back to the East. However, they only explain the one thing that does not change, viz. the fact that Ursicinus is not being reassigned to the high command, while Sabinianus, the new *magister equitum*, remains in this position. What is not explained are the considerations that led to the decision to send Ursicinus back in the first place, and when this decision was taken.

This means that in both cases not only events that are directly deducible from the context are left out, but also the factors that lay behind them and led to these events. In other words, what we are dealing with here cannot be simply explained by narrative economy, i.e. the leaving-out of easily deducible links just for the sake of narrative flow.

As for Ursicinus' presence in Cilicia, Sabbah suggested that this could be explained by assuming that he travelled westward to meet his successor Sabinianus on his way to the East.[13] If Sabbah is right, this implies that Ursicinus knew Sabinianus was coming even before the latter arrived. And this implies Ursicinus had received information from the court (or from Sabinianus)[14] informing him about the decisions (or at least about Sabinianus' coming). If this is true this exchange of information is the real link left out by Ammianus. The fact that Ursicinus had travelled to Cilicia is deducible from the context. The fact that the reason for this lay in certain information he had received is left out by Ammianus.

As for the change of strategy at court, this was explained by Matthews in a way that has been mentioned earlier: the decision to reassign Ursicinus to the East, only shortly after he had been ordered to come to court, was inspired by the intensification of military activity on the part of the Persians, which in itself resulted from the defection of Antoninus. Because of the large distance between the court at Sirmium and the eastern frontier it took some time for information on this point actually to reach Constantius. If this interpretation is right, this means that in this case also the real link left out by Ammianus is that of the exchange of information between the court and the East. The fact that Constantius has changed his plans is easily deducible from the context. That he was inspired to do so by information he received on the situation in the East remains in the dark in Ammianus' version of the events.[15]

It is not difficult to see what Ammianus gains by leaving this out. A Constantius sending back Ursicinus because his presence was badly needed in the East does not fit very well Ammianus' picture, in which everything that happens to Ursicinus was instigated by his enemies at court trying to undermine his position. At the same time, the change of strategy itself could not be left out, since it is essential for the subsequent development of the story. Ammianus solves this problem by presenting the change of strategy solely in the form of the letter to Ursicinus and by doing so at the moment Ursicinus received this letter. In this way he avoids giving an account of the deliberations at court which must have preceded it and of the factors which led to the new deliberations.

This brings us back to the shift in focus in 18.6. It now becomes clear that this shift in fact serves to camouflage the suppression of developments at court that do not fit the picture Ammianus is trying to draw.

Of course, strictly speaking, it is impossible to prove that this is what Ammianus left out. But it is striking, to say the least, that both missing links can be filled in completely and plausibly if we assume a connection with Ammianus' vagueness concerning the exchange of information between the court and the East.

Interpreted in that context, furthermore, the first missing link (of Ursicinus' departure to Cilicia) might well prove less innocent than Sabbah's explanation suggests it is. It is remarkable enough in itself that Ammianus fails to inform us of the movements of Ursicinus, about whose whereabouts he is quite explicit in the rest of the episode. But if all this conceals is that Ursicinus received news beforehand informing him that Sabinianus was on his way to the East, it may not appear very problematic. However there may be more to it than that. If information from court found its way to the East, the question arises whether information from the East went to the court as well. What is more, would not Ursicinus, as the *magister equitum* in the East, be the first and most appropriate person to inform Constantius of the increasingly dangerous situation and especially of Antoninus' defection (a fact he had learned not too long ago himself; 18.4.7)? If Ammianus wants to prevent the reader from thinking that this kind of information inspired Constantius' change of strategy in 18.6.5, he will definitely want to prevent the reader from thinking that Ursicinus provided the emperor with this information himself. Which would render this missing link far more important than it appears to be at first sight. It would not only be connected to the one in 18.6.5, but it would also become perfectly understandable within the context of Ammianus' strategy to present his version of the events as convincingly as possible and to suppress other possible interpretations.

Conclusions

Strictly speaking, to exonerate Ursicinus from the responsibility of the failure of the Persian campaign, it would not have been necessary to conceal the real reason why Constantius first recalled Ursicinus, then suddenly sent him back. Not concealing it would have exonerated both Constantius and Ursicinus: the former, because he was initially not aware of the real danger in the East; the latter, because he had no part in the decisions at court. But it would also have neutralized the contrastive effect as described by Sabbah, since the corrupt courtiers would no longer be the main factor influencing Constantius' decisions. In this respect Ammianus' vagueness on the exchange of information forms an integral part of his strategy of contrasting the ongoing intrigues at court with the increasingly dangerous situation in the East. Ammianus chooses to exonerate Ursicinus by presenting the decisions at court as negatively as possible. This includes being extremely vague about what was or was not known at court at different stages of the developments. The overall effect is that Constantius receives more blame than he probably deserved, while Ursicinus is further exonerated by being presented as a victim of his enemies at court, who deliberately instigated Constantius to make one wrong decision after another.

In general we may conclude that the above analysis provides us with additional, text-internal arguments to support the historical reconstructions of Thompson and Matthews. It shows that Ammianus not only emphasizes the irresponsible behaviour of the court clique, but also suppresses certain factors that may lead to a different interpretation of the events. At least as important is what this tells us about Ammianus himself and his position with regard to the events. Thompson and Matthews seem to suggest that Ammianus' version represents Ammianus' (and Ursicinus') perception of things at the time itself. The fact that the circumstances under which Ursicinus was first deprived of his rank and recalled, then suddenly reassigned to the East, were 'puzzling' to them, Matthews argues, is simply the result of the fact that they were better and more quickly informed on the developments in the East than was the emperor. They judged Constantius' orders from their own knowledge of the situation which made his instructions look irresponsible and unfair.

This is indeed the impression one gets from Ammianus, which has everything to do with the way in which he presents these orders: in the form of the letters for Ursicinus, and at the moment when he receives them. But looking at the narrative in this way does not take into account the fact that Ammianus is narrating the events in retrospect after they occurred. Such a view implies that not only the character Ammianus at the time, but also the historian Ammianus while looking back, did not realize that what might have been 'puzzling' when it happened could easily be understood in retrospect if the (non-)availability of information at court were taken into account. I find this hard to believe and do not think it is a valid explanation for the way in which Ammianus presents the events. What is more, there is at least one example which shows that Ammianus was fully aware of this factor and its liability to influence developments in a decisive way. In the Silvanus episode (15.5–6), in order to heighten the tension of his story, he actually exploits the fact that it took some time for the court to get information on what was happening in Gaul as well as for Silvanus to learn about developments at court. In particular the fact that Silvanus did not learn (in time) about the exposure of the plot that had been devised against him at court is exploited to add to the tragedy of his (unnecessary) usurpation and subsequent death. In Book 15, then, the exchange of information and the time involved in the process is a leading motif, while it is suppressed systematically in Book 18. This, in combination with the above analysis, strongly suggests that we are dealing with conscious suppression rather than innocent ignorance on Ammianus' part.

Notes

1 The analysis presented in this chapter is part of a larger project on narrative technique in Ammianus Marcellinus. I wish to thank Jaap Wisse for various improvements in both content and form of this chapter.
2 R.C. Blockley, 'Ammianus Marcellinus on the Persian Invasion of A.D. 359', *Phoenix* 42 (1988), 244–60, at 247.
3 E.A. Thompson, *The Historical Work of Ammianus Marcellinus*, Cambridge 1947 (repr. Groningen 1969), 49–50.
4 J.F. Matthews, *The Roman Empire of Ammianus*, London 1989, 41; cf. J.F. Matthews, 'Ammianus and the Eastern Frontier: A Participant's View', in P. Freeman and D. Kennedy (eds), *The Defence of the Roman and Byzantine East. Proceedings of a Colloquium Held at the University of Sheffield in April 1986*, Oxford 1986, vol. 1, 549–64.
5 The loss of Amida ended the military career of Ursicinus, who was fired afterwards by Constantius (Amm. Marc. 20.2).
6 G. Sabbah, *La méthode d'Ammien Marcellin. Recherches sur la construction du discours historique dans les Res Gestae*, Paris 1978, 472–3; cf. especially Blockley, 'Ammianus Marcellinus on the Persian Invasion', 247–8; also K. Rosen, *Studien zur Darstellungskunst und Glaubwürdigkeit des Ammianus Marcellinus*, Heidelberg 1970, 10–31.
7 Rosen, *Studien zur Darstellungskunst*, 31 describes this as 'der dreigliederige Gegensatz Persien-Kaiserhof-Ursicinus'.
8 The translations are taken from W. Hamilton, *Ammianus Marcellinus. The Later Roman Empire (A.D. 354–378)*, Harmondsworth 1986.
9 I interpret both participle constructions (*haec operientibus illis... districtis* and *nobis... morantibus*) as ablative absolutes. The first summarizes the preceding section (the activities of the courtiers: *illis*), after which the second introduces a change in the scene of action from court to the East (*nobis*). Both the order and the contrast between *illis* and *nobis* suggest that *nobis... morantibus* is to be closely connected with *repente novi motus... audiuntur*, whereas the first ablative absolute provides the background for the whole of *nobis... certis*: while they (the courtiers) were concocting these things, we were staying for a short while at Samosata, when suddenly rumours were heard (there, by us) about new events. This seems more natural than taking *nobis* as a dative of the agent with *audiuntur*, as does P. de Jonge, *Philological and Historical Commentary on Ammianus Marcellinus XVIII*, Groningen 1980, 107–8. Either way, the gist of the sentence remains the same.
10 Cf. 19.3.2, where Sabinianus is said to be acting according to the advice of the court clique, who wanted to deprive Ursicinus of any opportunity to achieve success in the East, even if such success would benefit the state (*etiam ex re publica processuram*).
11 *Sabinianus... Ciliciae fines ingressus decessori suo principis litteras dedit...* (18.6.1). De Jonge (*Commentary on Ammianus Marcellinus XVIII*, 152), assuming that Ursicinus is not in

Cilicia, argues that this means that Sabinianus handed the letter to a messenger for delivery to Ursicinus. The Latin does not allow this interpretation. *Litteras dare alicui* normally means 'to give/hand someone a letter'. If this someone is an intermediary who is to deliver the letter, the addressee may be added by means of the preposition *ad*: 'to give someone *(alicui)* a letter for someone *(ad aliquem)*'. 'To send someone a letter' would be *litteras dare ad aliquem*, with the intermediary left implicit (cf. *TLL, do* 1665, 56ff.). Ammianus does not deviate from this pattern. In our case *decessori suo* is Ursicinus, and the sentence must be interpreted as 'Sabinianus gave/handed the emperor's letter to his predecessor'.

12 Admittedly, *parumper* (18.4.7) already suggests that Ursicinus does not intend to stay in Samosata; being the *magister equitum*, he will be travelling around inspecting troops and visiting border strongholds. What is remarkable is that he has left the border area altogether and travelled away to the west.

13 G. Sabbah, *Ammien Marcellin, Histoire II (livres XVII–XIX)*, Paris 1970, 102, with n. 180.

14 When I presented this paper in Durham, John Matthews drew my attention to Ulpian, *Dig.* 1.16.4, which deals with (among other things) the formalities that are to be observed when a new proconsul enters the province assigned to him. With regard to the date of entering, it states: *recte autem et ordine faciet, si edictum decessori suo miserit significetque, qua die fines sit ingressurus* (1.16.4.4). In other words, it is considered proper conduct for a new proconsul to send his predecessor a formal notification stating in advance the day on which he will enter the province. This text may support the suggestion that Ursicinus knew in advance about Sabinianus' coming. If a notification in advance was expected from a proconsul, it is not unthinkable that the same kind of procedure was expected from one *magister equitum* when entering the territory of another, whom he was to succeed.

15 It could be argued that the order of presentation in itself suggests that Antoninus' defection instigated the change of strategy: the letter ordering Ursicinus to go back is introduced directly after the description of the intensification of the Persian war preparations as a result of Antoninus' advice to attack the provinces beyond the Euphrates. What matters is that this remains implicit and that Ammianus' presentation aims at leaving this implicit by suppressing the deliberations at court.

5

THE OUTSIDER INSIDE

Ammianus on the rebellion of Silvanus

David Hunt

After a successful summer campaign in 355 in the southern Alamannic canton of the Lentienses, Constantius II returned in triumph to headquarters in Milan (Amm. Marc. 15.4.13). But joy was misplaced, implies Ammianus, in the light of what was to follow. The historian's next section opens with a typically extravagant flourish: 'there arose a whirlwind of new disasters threatening similar ills for the provinces, which would have destroyed everything at once, had not Fortune, which governs the fate of men, brought a rapid end to a very fearful enterprise (*motum*)' (15.5.1). The 'new disasters' and the 'fearful enterprise' are subsequently revealed to be the events surrounding the short-lived rebellion of Constantius' *magister peditum* in Gaul, Silvanus, and its dramatic suppression by the cloak-and-dagger intervention of another of Constantius' senior generals, the *magister equitum* Ursicinus, supported in his task by a small troop of loyal officers of whom Ammianus himself was one. Those familiar with this famous episode from the *History* will recognize that the narrative which unfolds is far from the uncomplicated triumph of good over ill, of the legitimate order over the forces of disaffection, which the opening sentence might lead us to expect. On the contrary, a close examination of Ammianus' text will, I believe, entitle us to read a measure of ambiguity into the phrase '*calamitatum turbo novarum*': Was Silvanus villain or victim? Who had most cause to fear? Were the 'disasters' provoked by an illicit seizure of power in the provinces, or by the actions of an imperial government so riddled with suspicion and terror that it drove Silvanus into a desperate act of self-preservation?

The double-edged, not to say self-contradictory, nature of Ammianus' Silvanus episode has not escaped notice in the past.[1] Even the actual events of late summer 355 have recently been called into question: on the basis of implausibilities in Ammianus' account of Ursicinus' commando mission into the supposedly rebel camp at Cologne John Drinkwater has challenged the historicity of the whole 'scenario' which constructs Silvanus as a conventional usurper illegally assuming the purple, suggesting instead that

Ammianus may be covering up some failed manoeuvre on the part of Constantius to swap his top commanders around.[2] While there can be no question that the central role of Ursicinus in this episode, and Ammianus' own proximity to the events, has distorted the historian's presentation of the facts (and not only here, for whenever it came to his boss' dealings with the government of Constantius Ammianus suffered a damaging failure of perspective), it seems to me more doubtful that the usurpation of Silvanus is mere invention. This is not to deny the inventiveness of the writing, which in places has all the knife-edge drama and excitement of a modern spy novel.[3] But if the whole episode were a piece of fiction, it would presuppose an extraordinarily rapid process of historical falsification: for within a year or two of the event Silvanus' brief seizure of power had already become a vehicle for Julian's rhetoric in praise of Constantius, providing opportunities for displays of imperial clemency towards the usurper's followers (notably his son), and it earned a notice in Aurelius Victor's *Caesars* (completed before Constantius' death in 361).[4] That Silvanus' uprising has yielded no coins (in contrast to the equally short-lived Roman regime of Nepotianus) may be a product of its peculiarly local character, and a failure to gain control of the nearest mint at Trier (if in any case that was still in operation in August 355[5]). Based on the support of troops at Cologne, the rebellion was extinguished before it could catch fire further afield (such 'one-stop' uprisings are not unheard-of in this period: Trier had rebelled against the regime of the Caesar Decentius, while Aquileia and its neighbourhood would later stand against Julian – both in the name of Constantius[6]). Ammianus had his reasons, as will become clear, for magnifying the localized scale of the threat from Silvanus, exaggerating the extent of the danger which greeted Ursicinus and his coterie, and even raising fears of an imminent invasion across the Alps into Italy.

Even without the ultra-scepticism of denying Silvanus' rebellion, John Drinkwater's call for a 'more far-reaching investigation of Ammianus' historiography' deserves to be heeded.[7] The fact has to be faced that there are serious difficulties about Ammianus' coverage of the whole episode. Nor is it only Ursicinus who has clouded the truth. The imminent entry onto the Gallic stage of a heroic new Caesar has also served to condition the historian's narrative. Julian's mission was proclaimed aloud as destined to rescue a Gaul in the grip of the twin perils of barbarian devastation and 'commanders sent there who aimed higher than they should';[8] and Julian's own version of his call to imperial service attributed it to the reaction of Constantius' court ('fear and terror') at the news of Silvanus' rebellion.[9] In any event, the parlous and unsettled condition of Gaul prior to his glorious advent was a standard concomitant of the praises delivered by Julian's panegyrists.[10] Ammianus, of course, belongs in the same tradition. In his account Julian's elevation to the position of Caesar is grounded in Constantius' reported anxiety at the barbarians' continuing unchecked devastation of Gaul (15.8.1);

while the speech he places in the emperor's mouth commending Julian to the assembled troops in Milan sees this disturbed state of Gaul as the product of 'those rebel usurpers whose designs were inspired by mad frenzy' (15.8.6). Silvanus was the most recent of these, and not the least of his functions in the preceding portion of Ammianus' narrative has been to reinforce this view of Gaul as standing in need of a decisive saviour, and one who is the antithesis of a 'rebel usurper' – i.e. the rightful Caesar, Julian. Even the fact that Silvanus was apparently making a success of driving the barbarians out of Gaul (15.5.4, 16.2.4) was not allowed to overshadow these 'Julianic' expectations.

Besides serving the needs of the heroization of Julian, the episode is prominent among those sections of the *History* which contribute to Ammianus' sweeping denunciation of the methods of Constantius' government.[11] We first meet this, *in medias res*, as the imperial court is wintering at Arles after the final defeat of Magnentius in 353, and reprisals against his erstwhile supporters are in full swing. It was a 'victory made grievous by the murder of innocent men' (14.5.2), as the emperor's fawning courtiers encouraged his pathological suspicions with a flood of accusations, and he responded with indiscriminate savagery. Ammianus' Constantius has ears 'wide open' to false charges (a favourite notion), but a mind closed to anything but perceived threats to his safety,[12] a combination of features on which his subordinates are represented as playing with remorseless effectiveness, 'magnifying every incident and pretending to feel unbounded grief at the dangers threatening the safety of a sovereign (*princeps*) on the thread of whose life, as they hypocritically (*fictis verbis*) declared, the fate of the whole world hung' (14.5.4). This characterization of the court of Constantius, the stereotypical tyrant fearful for his survival, is too well known to need further illustration. Beneath it lurks the real nature of the imperial office in late Roman times, with its heightened sense of self-importance cocooned in an exaggerated language and ceremonial of majestic isolation, protected at close quarters by serried ranks of flattering courtiers, and further afield by a comprehensive network of state security.[13] The caricature of it as some peculiar aberration of Constantius' regime does little for Ammianus' credit as a balanced chronicler of his age.

Yet Ammianus' dismissal of the courtiers' sentiments as merely 'hypocritical', *fictis verbis*, perhaps enshrines a significant perception: that these officials were in some recognizable sense *actors* adept at uttering the right lines and playing their part in the extravagant theatrical drama which constituted the life of the imperial court in the fourth century.[14] The troupe of flatterers are similarly portrayed 'fabricating' (*confingens*) their litany of the emperor's invincibility in the aftermath of the Scythopolis trials in 359 (19.12.16; cf. 15.8.2); while the emperor, most famously, acted out his own role immaculately, a *figmentum hominis*, exuding rigid dignity at the centre of the majestic procession which accompanied him into Rome on his ceremonial visit in the spring of 357 (16.10.10). Such an expression of the fixed impregnability of the imperial office was taken for granted by Ammianus (this was the way the emperor was customarily seen 'in his provinces'), and later endorsed in the obituary section concluding the Constantius books: it counted foremost among his *virtues* that he 'everywhere upheld the solemnity [again the relic of a theatrical metaphor in the use of the term *cothurnus*] of the emperor's majesty and with his great and lofty spirit he disdained popular favour' (21.16.1).[15] But the compartmentalizing of virtues and vices conventional to the literary medium prevented Ammianus from expounding the essential inseparability of the (to him praiseworthy) preservation of the dignity necessary to the imperial office and the court machinery of protection and adulation which surrounded it (and which he repeatedly castigated): in reality both were two sides of the same coin, and majestic emperor and the coterie of loyal underlings players in the same drama at the heart of the late Roman state.

Ammianus' negative vision of the court of Constantius, the emperor helpless in the face of intrigue and flattery, has left its impact pervasively throughout his Silvanus narrative. From the start (15.5.2) the general's command in Gaul is presented as under threat from the damaging rivalry of the long-serving *magister equitum* at court, Flavius Arbitio, military strong man of Constantius' government and seen by Ammianus as the principal power behind the throne.[16] Arbitio now directs against Silvanus the same insidious manoeuvres which he has previously been seen to instigate against another rival commander, Ursicinus: for it is to Arbitio that Ammianus gave the role of chief plotter in the recent intrigues which had almost brought down his superior (15.2.4), and which would have seen Ursicinus suffering the fate of Domitius Corbulo at the hands of Constantius' Nero (Ammianus' *exempla*, not mine). The fact that Ammianus had seen Arbitio behind these earlier allegations of treason against Ursicinus (of which he chooses to remind his readers precisely at this point) makes it very likely that, although he is not named in the immediate context, Arbitio's influence in the consistory is to be seen lurking in the historian's allegation of 'underhand methods' (*insidiosis rationibus*) by which, in dispatching Ursicinus to Gaul to bring down Silvanus, he also aimed at Ursicinus' own destruction (15.5.19). The scheming of Arbitio is part of the stock-in-trade of Ammianus' depiction of Constantius' court (cf. 18.3.3–4). It is explicitly on his initiative that the courier Apodemius ('bitter and inveterate enemy of all good men') is first sent across the Alps with letters of recall for Silvanus, and proceeds to 'disturb the peace' in Gaul by harassing the general's dependants (8–9, cf. 28 *quaestiones familiarium*). The true facts of Apodemius' activity (presumably gaining intelligence about the moves of Silvanus and his supporters) are obscured from view by the role in which Ammianus casts him as one of the principal perpetrators of Silvanus' destruction – had he been successful in this, he would surely have been represented bringing the news back to Milan with the same alacrity and enthusiasm with which he had recently reported the execution of Gallus, throwing the dead Caesar's shoes at Constantius' feet 'as if they were the spoils of the slain Persian king', and then unleashing the customary tide of court flattery extolling the emperor's blessings (15.1.2).[17] Another regular in Ammianus' cast of nasty characters in Constantius' retinue is, of course, the infamous *notarius* Paul, nicknamed the 'Chain' because of the unbreakable bonds of calumny in which he contrived to ensnare those accused of treason:[18] now, true to form, it is Paul who turns up to lead the inquisition into Silvanus' followers after his overthrow, and is seen to relish the task 'with undisguised joy' (15.6.1 *effervens laetitia*).

It is more than just these *dramatis personae* – Arbitio, Apodemius and Paul – who serve to colour Ammianus' Silvanus narrative with his jaundiced view of the ways of Constantius' court. Other details, too, contribute to the same portrayal. The initial evidence against Silvanus – forged, as it transpired – was presented to the emperor in person by the praetorian prefect Lampadius. Ammianus characterizes the prefect as an experienced operator in handling the emperor: he knew his chronic receptiveness to treason allegations, and the rewards which came from being seen as a vigilant defender of imperial safety (15.5.5). It was this same menacing combination around the emperor of accusation and adulation, and Constantius' alleged feebleness in resisting it, which would drive the hapless Silvanus to his desperate effort of survival (15.5.15, 32–3). When the news of his downfall eventually reached Milan, the chorus of flattery was again set in motion, lauding the emperor as one who 'reached to the skies (*caelo contiguus*) and who would control the fates of men' (15.5.37). Ammianus' final perceptions of the episode are reinforced by resort to his stock of historical *exempla* to condemn Constantius' behaviour – his glorying in the defeat of brave men was the equal of Domitian's (15.5.35), while his craving for adulation had its precedents in Croesus and Dionysius (15.5.37) – and by a concluding piece of commonplace wisdom: praise is only worth having where there is also room for criticism of faults (15.5.38).[19]

Ammianus' narrative of the Silvanus affair thus far presented does not inspire historical confidence: the reality of events in Gaul and the mechanisms of government deployed in response to them seem lost in the stereotypes of suspicious tyrant and grovelling courtiers which everywhere characterize the historian's view of Constantius. Features which, seen from a different perspective, might be correctly understood as the necessary concomitants of the imperial office in the late Roman world are projected by Ammianus as no more than the failings of (at best) an indifferent ruler, a *medius princeps*.[20] But in contrast to other comparable episodes in the *History* which focus on treason investigations by Constantius' government, the Silvanus narrative can be shown on occasions to lift the conventional façade, and to peer more closely into the realities of what was going on: perhaps not surprisingly the incident which, more than any other, brought Ammianus (for a brief spell) close to the heart of imperial history is recorded with a degree of attention to the 'internal' details missing from other passages. Take, for example, the formalities and protocol of court procedure, as witnessed by the mention of Ursicinus' admission to the consistory which would decide on sending him to Gaul. Ammianus' words are a stage-by-stage description of the unfolding ceremonial: the general is 'honourably' introduced into the imperial presence by the services of the *magister admissionum*, after which he is invited to kiss the emperor's purple offered him 'more graciously (*placidius*) than before' (15.5.18). The scene details a regular ceremonial of imperial audience familiar to Ursicinus, as a senior commander, from previous occasions, and one likely to have been known to Ammianus himself from the time of his appointment to the rank of *protector domesticus*.[21] The imperial purple here carries a more benign symbolism deriving from this courtly routine of conferring favour and privilege on those permitted contact with it, unlike the associations of state terror and treason charges which Ammianus usually attaches to it (one thinks of the man whose taste for purple decor and clothing 'was the ruin of his rich estate').[22] Admittedly the fact that here and here alone in his narrative Ammianus should choose to highlight these formalities of imperial ceremonial (reinforced by the mention of their introduction by Diocletian) is no mere coincidence or disinterested detail, but one calculated to point up the court's shifty and untrustworthy treatment of his general; none the less it is an observation of the realities of court life and procedure which penetrates the historian's customary veneer of criticism. In contrast, too, to the prevailing image of Constantius as the isolated potentate at the beck-and-call of his scheming entourage, the Silvanus narrative is allowed to expose a process of collective deliberation still at work in the successive meetings of the consistory:[23] both in the matter of investigating the supposedly treasonable correspondence, in which civilian and military officials together participated (15.5.12), and in the urgent night-time meeting summoned to the palace on the news of events at Cologne, where the decision to entrust the mission to Ursicinus and the plan of action to be followed are represented as the outcome of 'many-sided debate' among the emperor's advisers (15.5.21), who had first been at a loss about what to do (15.5.18). Not all of those present, at least according to this strand of the narrative, were malevolent courtiers aiming to encompass Ursicinus' destruction.

This impression of openness surrounding the decision-making process of Constantius' government in Milan is also confirmed by the high profile which Ammianus accords to the coterie of Frankish officers of the guard, and their intervention to protect their compatriot Silvanus from false accusations: it is down to their initiative and plain speaking that the fraudulent letters are exposed (15.5.11), and it is their leader Malarichus, commander of the regiment of *gentiles*, who is the principal spokesman in Silvanus' defence (15.5.6–7).[24] Ammianus singles out the Franks as the voice of opposition at court to the customary wiles of Constantius' ministers, and as the representatives of a genuine and unqualified loyalty to the Roman government.

We are surely meant to detect a significant irony in the contrast between these bold and free-speaking *homines dicatos imperii* (15.5.6) of barbarian stock and those practised exponents of imperial protocol whose professed concern for the ruler's safety was nothing but empty adulation (*fictis verbis*, see p. 53). The point is stressed again in relation to Silvanus himself, when he is reminded that his record of loyal service to the empire of Rome precluded his taking refuge in his own people's *barbarica fides* (15.5.15–16). It is not simply the conventional portrayal of the ills of Constantius' regime (and Silvanus as its victim) which evokes from Ammianus what is his most unequivocal endorsement of the loyalty of barbarian officers – it is more usual to find him hinting at the taint of treachery[25]– but, I suggest, the historian's actual experience in the course of his military service of encounters with officers like Silvanus and Malarichus, and of the particular kind of devotion to the empire which their barbarian background imposed upon them, once committed. Another such was the tribune Laniogaesus, who impressed upon Silvanus the impossibility of flight to the Franks. Laniogaesus had been mentioned by Ammianus, he tells us, earlier in his history (in a lost book) as the only member of the bodyguard to remain at Constans' side right up to the point of his death. He must somehow have escaped the fate of his imperial master and survived to receive a command with the field army in Gaul – did his loyalty to the memory of Constans, and to the house of Constantine, extend to his being party to Silvanus' celebrated desertion of Magnentius on the eve of the conflict at Mursa?[26] At any event Laniogaesus' recent career must have offered a lesson or two in the tortuous practicalities of imperial loyalty (to which Silvanus could add the example of his own father's service in the armies of Constantine at war with Licinius). Ammianus will have known Laniogaesus as his principal informant on the demise of Constans,[27] and perhaps discovered in him the kind of committed service to the Roman empire which he applauds in Silvanus and the other Frankish officers in this chapter.

With Ammianus' glimpses into the ceremony and deliberations of the consistory, and his stress on the interventions of the Franks, his narrative moves closer to the centre of events; yet the perspective remains still predominantly that of the external commentator, given to passing critical judgement on the affairs of the court – what happened in the case of Silvanus might thus far be any other of the episodes of suspicion, palace intrigue and terror which regularly disfigure the history of the reign of Constantius in his pages. What sharply distinguishes it from these, however, is Ammianus' dramatic introduction of himself into the midst of the narrative as one of the close group of officers, tribunes and *protectores domestici* who accompanied Ursicinus on his mission to suppress the reported rebellion at Cologne (15.5.22). The historian suddenly abandons his pose as judgemental observer to join the cast of the drama, and becomes a chief player in the selfsame network of state security and imperial protection which he has been so ready to denounce from the sidelines.[28] The open admission of participation in the official manoeuvres which undermined Silvanus stands in marked contrast to Ammianus' reticence about the treason trials the previous year in Antioch, over which Ursicinus had been summoned to preside on the orders of the Caesar Gallus: although alluding to his presence in the general's entourage (14.9.1), the historian stays silent about his own part, if any, in furthering the prosecutions (he is almost as mute on the involvement of Ursicinus).[29] In the light of Gallus' eventual fate it was doubtless an embarrassment, as Ursicinus was to discover, to have been caught doing the Caesar's dirty work for him. No such feelings restrained Ammianus' recollection of events at Cologne: the whole 'sordid story'[30] of deceit, corruption and treachery is allowed to unfold without the least hint of disapproval or consciousness of the moral contradictions which it poses.

Loyalty to Ursicinus has produced from Ammianus what amounts to an apologia for the underhand tactics of their mission and his own part in it (Arbitio, it seems, had no monopoly on *insidiosis rationibus*; cf. p. 54): indeed the historian's stress on the supposed extent of the danger encountered on the ground, and the skill and effort (15.5.30, *magna industria*; 15.5.36, *industrie gesta*) shown by Ursicinus and his squad in achieving the desired outcome, may well derive from the official communiqué submitted to the emperor in Milan.[31] This called for the recasting of Silvanus no longer as wronged victim of a squalid palace plot, but as rebel and pretender against the legitimate forces of the state. The character change is complete by the time the narrative finds Ammianus and his colleagues accompanying Ursicinus into Gaul, each in fear for their safety like gladiators about to be 'cast before ravening wild beasts' (15.5.23), but at least consoled (he would have us believe) by a Ciceronian *sententia* to the effect that the greatest satisfaction in life comes when disaster gives way to better fortune (an afterthought of the historian's, we may presume, rather than a serious reflection in the heat of the moment). The gathering rebellion among Silvanus' troops threatened them all, he is at pains to point out, with instant death (15.5.26). The regime newly established in Cologne was a *tyrannis* (15.5.24), and Silvanus himself a *perduellis* (15.5.19), both terms which Ammianus employs to discredit usurpation, and which recall the language he elsewhere gives to Constantius himself in contexts of self-congratulation applauding his own success against would-be rivals for power.[32] Ammianus' Silvanus is here virtually indistinguishable from the hopeless rebel of official propaganda.[33] The historian's identification with the interests of law and order is complete: it was to 'assist the public need' (15.5.22) that he accompanied Ursicinus against a usurper, and there is no further call to account for the dubious methods used to overthrow him. This redefinition of Silvanus as beyond the pale damned him even on Ammianus' own terms, regardless of how the official 'media' might outlaw him: for even on occasions when the historian was not faced with the need to defend his own conduct or that of Ursicinus, and however much he denounced the character of the government, he did not waver from recognition of Constantius' rightful claim to empire and of the need for vigilant means of protection[34] – once Silvanus had been transformed from victim to villain, his destruction was given its legal and moral authorization. This image of Silvanus as rival and rebel is reinforced by Ammianus' representation of him playing at being an emperor, holding court at Cologne surrounded by a replica of the protocol accorded the legitimate ruler in Milan, with Ursicinus now acting the part of the deferential subordinate flattering the 'upstart emperor' (*imperator novellus*) with sentiments he wished to hear (15.5.25), and dutifully reverencing the purple-clad figure of one 'aspiring higher than he should' (*anhelantem celsius*; 15.5.27). Here is a foretaste of the mockery which Ammianus would direct more savagely and extensively against the pretensions of another usurper who 'aspired too high' (*altius anhelabat*), Procopius.[35]

So the relabelling of Silvanus as a straightforward usurper banishes scruples about the treacherous methods used to undermine him, and his brutal end: Ammianus, in the service of Ursicinus, confesses himself a dedicated agent of state security. It is an episode of surprising candour, even from the historian who displays, in Momigliano's famous phrase, 'an almost indecent readiness to speak about himself'.[36] Elsewhere, as we have seen, he prefers to draw a veil over such doubtful moments in his career; and even here the government 'insider' is quick to abandon the pose – no sooner is the dirty work done and Silvanus dead than Ammianus steps back from his internal involvement in imperial protection duties to resume the familiar stance of arch-critic of those very same methods of state. Silvanus returns to type as the loyal and deserving general whose career of service to Constantius was unjustly ruined by the pack of schemers and flatterers at court (15.5.32–3), who in their turn are now given renewed opportunity to exalt the emperor's ego 'to the skies' (15.5.37). The court gossip against Ursicinus is also allowed to resurface, in the allegation (flatly denied by Ammianus) that he or his staff were engaged in financial embezzlement in Gaul (15.5.36).

Ammianus' exit from the Silvanus narrative is as sudden as his entry into it. Nothing further is said of these mysterious suggestions of 'sleaze', and, but for two isolated sentences in later sections of the *History*, we would never know that Ursicinus actually remained at his post in Gaul for nearly two years after Silvanus' death and Ammianus, it must be presumed, stayed with him: certainly he was still in the general's retinue when Ursicinus was recalled by Constantius in the summer of 357 and sent back to the East (16.10.21).[37] Given the apparent relish with which he has openly recounted their active contribution to the overthrow of Silvanus, Ammianus' abrupt silence about what followed has attracted considerable discussion: it has been concluded, for example, that he is covering up for failures in Ursicinus' military stewardship of the Rhine frontier and/or his inability to impose order upon a still fractious army.[38] All would agree, I suspect, that we have to reckon with the 'Julian effect'. The facts of Ursicinus' Gallic command are for ever blinded from view in the bright light of Julian's advent as Caesar at the end of 355, and the avowedly propagandist tone in which Ammianus describes the descent of this heaven-sent saviour to rescue the hard-pressed Gauls.[39] Where the rhetoric of Libanius went so far as to complain of the generals 'sleeping' (Ursicinus presumably included) at the time of Julian's arrival on the scene,[40] Ammianus preferred a retreat into silence about his commander's activities to avoid any upstaging of the Caesar. John Drinkwater has recently offered a realistic appraisal of Ursicinus' limited room for manoeuvre as far as his military dealings went in the wake of Silvanus' downfall;[41] but what of the political role of the general who had just nipped rebellion in the bud? 'We may surely assume', writes John Matthews, 'that the general had some contribution to make to the broader aspects of the restoration of loyalty to the Gallic provinces', in the context of supposing that Ursicinus, with Ammianus at his side, will have actively headed the tracking down and punishment of Silvanus' remaining adherents.[42] The completion of the security mission on which they had been sent would seem to demand nothing less. Ammianus' silence is given even sharper point by the intriguing possibility that he and his commander may have acted in concert with the *tartareus delator* himself, Paul, in bringing to book the last of the usurper's supporters. Ammianus may even have been present in person, Matthews suggests, at the investigation and torture (before 'civilian and military' judges) of Silvanus' attendant Proculus, an incident to which he brings an especial vividness of description (15.6.1–3).[43] The historian had already suffered a bout of evasive embarrassment over Ursicinus' (and his own?) share in Gallus' unsavoury trials: little wonder that he opted not even to mention any collaboration in Gaul with the 'Chain', the court *notarius* who in the rest of the *History* embodies all the hated features of Constantius' suspicious regime, and whose eventual execution by burning (along with Apodemius) he would hail as one of the more judicially satisfying outcomes of Julian's Chalcedon tribunal (22.3.11). Ammianus the historian had good reason to disguise the fact that Ammianus the *protector* had once kept such bad company in the service of the state.

At the outset of describing the mission to Gaul Ammianus had been keen to emphasize the risks of failure for himself and his fellow *protectores* on the staff of Ursicinus. We can now see that it may not only have been the thought of sudden death at the hands of mutinous soldiers at Cologne that concentrated the minds of Ammianus and his colleagues: for failure to stamp out the rebellion would equally have stirred the wrath of the imperial government on whose security they were engaged – only shortly before, he had recounted the fate of two other *protectores domestici* who had paid the penalty for a lapse of vigilance in delivering an alleged plotter to trial, and who would have been executed but for the intercession of Arbitio (15.3.10–11). The thought that, if events had turned out other than they did, Ammianus' own fate might have come to hang on the word of Arbitio into those perilously 'wide-open ears' of the emperor might well have encouraged him to collaborate readily with the likes of Paul.

The spectre of Ammianus thus enmeshed in the invidious machinery of state security and imperial protection points up the sense of slipperiness and shifting perspective which bedevils this Silvanus narrative: there is no one clear-cut version of events in which Ammianus allows his readers to take refuge and to 'pigeon-hole' his verdict. In the course of the above analysis I have identified three distinct vantage-points, moving (as it were) from the outside in: the conventional critic of the tyrannical regime of Constantius, the close observer of court and consistory reacting to unfolding events, and the unquestioning servant of the government's bidding. All three poses have variously influenced the telling of the tale, and give it the multidimensional character which I have attempted to explore. Everyone knows that the relationship of the historian's craft to the reality of the world he is describing is a complex one,[44] and Ammianus' treatment of the rebellion of Silvanus is clearly no exception.

Notes

1 See, e.g., R. Martin, 'Ammien Marcellin ou la servitude militaire', in R. Chevallier (ed.), *Colloque Histoire et Historiographie, Clio*, Paris 1980, 203–13.
2 J.F. Drinkwater, 'Silvanus, Ursicinus and Ammianus: Fact or Fiction?', in C. Deroux (ed.), *Studies in Latin Literature and Roman History* VII (Collection Latomus 227), Brussels 1994, 568–76.
3 So Martin, 'Ammien Marcellin', following J. Fontaine in seeing Ammianus as 'historien romantique'. On the historian's literary artifice, cf. F. Paschoud, ' "Se non è vero, è ben trovato": tradition littéraire et vérité historique chez Ammien Marcellin', *Chiron* 19 (1989), 37–54; *contra* N.J.E. Austin, 'In Support of Ammianus' Veracity', *Historia* 22 (1973), 331–5.
4 Julian, *Or.* 1.48c ff., 2.98c ff. (98c, 'which happened, one may say, yesterday or the day before'); Aurelius Victor, *De Caes.* 42.14–16. Cf. also Mamertinus (*Pan. Lat.* 3(11), Jan. 362), 13.3, for Silvanus and Nepotianus as recent examples of usurpers.
5 For the decline of the Trier mint in this period, see K.-J. Gilles, 'Die Aufstände des Poemenius (353) und Silvanus (355) und ihre Auswirkungen auf die Trierer Münzprägung', *Trierer Zeitschrift* 52 (1989), 377–86.
6 For the Aquileia rebellion, see Amm. Marc. 21.11; for Trier: 15.6.4.
7 Drinkwater, 'Silvanus, Ursicinus and Ammianus', 576.
8 Libanius, *Or.* 18.31.
9 So Julian's *Ep. ad Ath.* 273d (cf. 274c).
10 Mamertinus, *Pan. Lat.* 3.4.1–2; cf. Libanius, *Or.* 18.34–5 (it was Julian's own claim, *Ep. ad Ath.* 278d–279b). For a somewhat less devastated state of affairs in reality, see now J.F. Drinkwater, 'Julian and the Franks and Valentinian I and the Alamanni: Ammianus on Romano-German Relations', *Francia* 24 (1997), 1–15.
11 On the nature of Ammianus' account of the regime of Constantius, see J.F. Matthews, *The Roman Empire of Ammianus*, London 1989, ch. 3; R.C. Blockley, *Ammianus Marcellinus. A Study of his Historiography and Political Thought* (Collection Latomus 141), Brussels 1975, 38–41.

12 14.5.2 (*animus eius angustus et tener*); 15.2.2, 3.5; 16.7.1; 18.3.6, 4.4; 22.11.5 (*patulae aures*); 19.12.5 (combination of both).
13 On the inflated style of the late Roman ruler and his court, see now C. Kelly, 'Emperors, Government and Bureaucracy', in *CAH* XIII (1998), ch. 5; with Matthews, *The Roman Empire of Ammianus*, chs 11–12, and classic pieces by R. Macmullen: 'Roman Bureaucratese', *Traditio* 18 (1962), 364–78; 'Some Pictures in Ammianus Marcellinus', *The Art Bulletin* 46 (1964), 435–55 (both repr. in his *Changes in the Roman Empire: Essays in the Ordinary*, Princeton 1990); *Corruption and the Decline of Rome*, New Haven 1988, ch. 2 ('Power Effective'). For an instance, see Amm. Marc. 15.1.3 (on Constantius' mode of address).
14 On late Roman 'theatricality', recalling Gibbon's famous 'splendid theatre', see Macmullen, 'Some Pictures in Ammianus', *passim*.
15 On the (not necessarily critical) connotations of *cothurnus*, see J. den Boeft, D. den Hengst and H.C. Teitler, *Philological and Historical Commentary on Ammianus Marcellinus XXI*, Groningen 1991, 243.
16 *PLRE* I, 94–5; for the context of military rivalries around Constantius, see R.C. Blockley, 'Constantius II and his Generals', in C. Deroux (ed.), *Studies in Latin Literature and Roman History* II (Collection Latomus 168), Brussels 1980, 467–86.
17 For some speculation about the true role of Apodemius in the whole affair, see D.C. Nutt, 'Silvanus and the Emperor Constantius II', *Antichthon* 7 (1973), 80–9.
18 Amm. Marc. 14.5.8, 15.3.4.
19 On Ammianus' fondness for moralizing *exempla*, see Blockley, *Ammianus Marcellinus*, 157–67, with appendix F.
20 For Constantius as *medius princeps*, see 14.9.2, 21.16.8 (cf. Eutropius, *Brev.* 10.7.1 on the later stages of Constantine's rule, '*mediis comparandus*').
21 On the ceremony of *adoratio*, see Matthews, *The Roman Empire of Ammianus*, 244–6. The rank of *protectores domestici* entitled them to this privilege: *Cod.Theod.* 6.24.4.
22 Amm. Marc. 16.8.8; cf. 14.9.7, for another incident involving the political sensitivities surrounding purple garments.
23 See Matthews, *The Roman Empire of Ammianus*, 266–9.
24 For a brief survey of the increasing prominence of barbarian officers in the Roman high command, see J.H.W.G. Liebeschuetz, *Barbarians and Bishops*, Oxford 1990, 7–10; on Franks in particular, K.F. Stroheker, 'Zur Rolle der Heermeister fränkischer Abstammung im späten vierten Jahrhundert', *Historia* 4 (1955), 314–30 (= Stroheker, *Germanentum und Spätantike*, Zurich 1965, 9–29).
25 Examples at 14.10.7–8, 29.4.7. For Ammianus' general view of barbarians, see A. Demandt, *Zeitkritik und Geschichtsbild im Werk Ammians* (diss. Marburg), Bonn 1965, 31–8.
26 On Laniogaesus, see E. Galletier and J. Fontaine, *Ammien Marcellin, Histoire I*, Paris 1968, 246, n. 202; for Silvanus' action at Mursa, see Amm. Marc. 15.5.33; Julian, *Or.* 1.48b, 2.97c; Aurelius Victor, *De Caes.* 42.15.
27 So G. Sabbah, *La méthode d'Ammien Marcellin. Recherches sur la construction du discours historique dans les Res Gestae*, Paris 1978, 225–6.
28 The paradox is noted by Martin, 'Ammien Marcellin' (see n. 1 above).
29 Ammianus' treatment of Ursicinus' involvement with Gallus was discussed by E.A. Thompson, *The Historical Work of Ammianus Marcellinus*, Cambridge 1947 (repr. Groningen 1969), 42–3; cf. Matthews, *The Roman Empire of Ammianus*, 34–5.
30 Thompson, *The Historical Work of Ammianus Marcellinus*, 45.
31 The view of Sabbah, *La méthode d'Ammien Marcellin*, 182–3.
32 15.8.6, 17.5.13; cf. R. Seager, *Ammianus Marcellinus. Seven Studies in his Language and Thought*, Columbia 1986, 120. For remarks on the vocabulary of 'tyranny' in relation to usurpers, see A. Wardman, 'Usurpers and Internal Conflicts in the Fourth Century AD', *Historia* 33 (1984), 220–37 and now V. Neri, 'L'usurpatore come tiranno nel lessico politico della tarda antichità', in F. Paschoud and J. Szidat (eds), *Usurpationen in der Spätanike* (Historia Einzelschriften 111), Stuttgart 1997.

33 As reflected in panegyrics of Constantius: Julian, *Or.* 1.48c, 2.98c–d.
34 See esp. 19.12.17, on the legitimate ruler's right to protection; cf. Matthews, *The Roman Empire of Ammianus*, 201–3, 250–2.
35 26.6.1. For Ammianus' demolition of the claims of Procopius, see Matthews, *The Roman Empire of Ammianus*, 191ff. Ursicinus' accusers at court laid the same charge against him: 18.4.2. More material was available to the historian against Silvanus if he had chosen to use it, to judge from Julian on 'women's purple' (*Or.* 1.48c, 2.98d).
36 A.D. Momigliano, 'The Lonely Historian Ammianus Marcellinus', in his *Essays in Ancient and Modern Historiography*, Oxford 1977, 127–40, at 128.
37 Cf. 16.2.8 for Ursicinus' remaining in Gaul; for the technicalities of his position (on secondment from his eastern post), see E. Frézouls, 'La mission du "magister equitum" Ursicin en Gaule (355–357) d'après Ammien Marcellin', in M. Renard (ed.), *Hommages à Albert Grenier* II, Brussels 1962, 673–88.
38 Frézouls, 'La mission du "magister equitum" Ursicin en Gaule (355–357)', 685–8, attempting to exonerate Ursicinus; cf. Thompson, *The Historical Work of Ammianus Marcellinus*, 45–7.
39 For Ammianus' Julianic panegyric (explicit at 16.1.3) see esp. 15.8.21 (his entry into Vienne seen by the assembled population as *communium remedium aerumnarum*).
40 Libanius, *Or.* 18.42.
41 Drinkwater, 'Julian and the Franks', 3–9.
42 Matthews, *The Roman Empire of Ammianus*, 81–3.
43 This assumes that the interrogation took place in Gaul; although Paul may have escorted his 'victims' to the imperial court then in Milan (cf. the procedure followed with the round-up of Magnentius' supporters, 14.5.8: see Drinkwater, 'Julian and the Franks', 6). Note the contrasting emphasis of Julian's panegyrics on Constantius' exercise of clemency towards Silvanus' supporters (see above, n. 4).
44 For a recent discussion in relation to Ammianus, see J. Szidat, 'Ammian und die historische Realität', in J. den Boeft, D. den Hengst and H.C. Teitler (eds), *Cognitio Gestorum. The Historiographic Art of Ammianus Marcellinus*, Amsterdam 1992, 107–16.

6

AMMIANUS AND THE EUNUCHS

Shaun Tougher

It is a well-known fact that eunuchs became a heavy presence at the imperial Roman court in late antiquity, some attaining significant power in the service of the emperor. In this chapter I wish to reassert the evidence of Ammianus Marcellinus which is witness to the eunuch presence at court, but I will also suggest that the nature and depth of Ammianus' interest in this subject has not been recognized sufficiently.[1] Our historian discusses the origin of eunuchs, their nature, their character, their roles, their political influence as individuals and as a group, and uses them as a tool for political criticism, reflecting particularly on Constantius II and his court, but also on the decline of the Roman empire.

The increasing presence of eunuchs at the Roman court is generally linked with the emperor Diocletian (284–305), whose reign is said to have witnessed an 'orientalization' of the Roman emperor and his court. This aspect of late antiquity has attracted the attention of ancient historians, most notably Keith Hopkins, who produced a classic study accounting for the phenomenon of the powerful court eunuchs.[2] There is certainly no shortage of fourth-century texts attesting to the development of the eunuch presence at court and the power of eunuchs as individuals and as a group. For instance Lactantius remarks on the power of the court eunuchs and their crucial importance for Diocletian and his palace;[3] the *Historia Augusta* devotes much space to eunuchs, and nails its colours to the mast by expressing gladness that an emperor has dispensed with the services of eunuchs at the court;[4] whilst Claudian in two invectives attacks the eunuch Eutropius, so powerful a figure at the eastern court.[5]

Ammianus is very much at home with these fourth-century commentators. The surviving part of his history in fact has a substantial contribution to make to the picture of the powerful court eunuchs of late antiquity, irrespective of its bias. In particular Ammianus relates details concerning the chamberlains (*cubicularii*), Grand (*praepositus sacri cubiculi*) or otherwise, who were generally eunuchs in the later Roman period.[6] He conveys something of their functions and blend of delegated and *de facto* power.

The prime case is that of Eusebius,[7] Grand Chamberlain to Constantius II, whose vital role in the service of the emperor, but also his influence with the emperor as well as his peers, is made emphatically clear. When a plot to kill the praetorian prefect Rufinus (uncle of the Caesar Gallus) is altered, it is Eusebius who is sent to Châlon (Cabyllona) to quell the rowdy soldiers with gold (14.10.3–5). When it was a question of the Caesar Gallus himself Eusebius was one of those who opposed the plan to bring him to Milan and execute him, identifying Ursicinus as a figure of far graver concern (14.11.1–3). Thus Ursicinus was summoned to Milan first. When Gallus was apprehended on his journey from Antioch and taken to a place near Pola in Istria, it was Eusebius who visited and questioned him, prior to his execution (14.11.20–1). Then when Gallus' adherents had to be dealt with Eusebius was sent, with Arbitio, to Aquileia to try the eastern military personnel and court functionaries in question (15.3.1–3). The extent of Eusebius' *de facto* influence is also stressed by Ammianus. He relates that courtiers were keen to secure the favour of the influential Eusebius (18.4.3). Arbitio and Florentius, heads of the inquiry into the fall of Amida, failed to blame it on the newly appointed Master of Cavalry Sabinianus since they feared the reaction of the eunuch (20.2.2–3). Upon the death of Constantius Eusebius was among the leading courtiers who discussed what course of action to take regarding the succession (21.15.4). Finally, when Ammianus comes to the fate of Eusebius, condemned to death at the trials at Chalcedon at the start of Julian's reign, he reflects on the degree of power that Eusebius had acquired in his career (22.3.12).

Another chamberlain whose role and influence Ammianus describes is Eutherius. Eutherius had served Constans (who failed to heed his good advice, remarks Ammianus), but it was his time as Grand Chamberlain to Julian in Gaul which concerns Ammianus most (16.7). Eutherius was sent to Milan to defend the Caesar Julian against the smears of Marcellus, the Master of Cavalry and Infantry in Gaul, who was alleging that Julian had designs on power. Later Eutherius was chosen for another mission to Constantius, in the aftermath of Julian's acclamation as Augustus in Paris (20.8.19). With Pentadius he was to deliver two letters from Julian to Constantius.[8] The two envoys were entrusted with Julian's interests. Of Eutherius Ammianus also remarks that he would sometimes criticize Julian's Asiatic manners (16.7.6).

Another named Grand Chamberlain is Gorgonius,[9] who served Caesar Gallus in Antioch, and again Ammianus conveys the notion of the influence of such eunuchs. After the execution of Gallus Gorgonius was exempted from punishment even though he had admitted that he had participated in Gallus' crimes, and had sometimes inspired them (15.2.10).

Heliodorus is a further Grand Chamberlain named by Ammianus, playing a key role in the trials at Antioch during the reign of Valens (29.2.6–7). Ammianus notes that in his capacity as chamberlain (*cubiculariis officiis praepositus*) Heliodorus 'constantly and openly visited the women's apartments'.[10] However, in this case there are doubts as to whether Heliodorus was a eunuch.[11]

In the course of his narrative Ammianus also refers to chamberlains generally. Owing to the intervention of the chamberlains a case against Arbitio during the reign of Constantius was dropped (16.6.3). Eusebius uses his chamberlains to poison Constantius' mind against Ursicinus (18.4.4). Julian believes that Constantius will have heard about his acclamation in Paris not only from the notary Decentius but from the chamberlains who had been in Gaul to supply him with his income (20.8.4). During a campaign of Valentinian against the Alamanni the chamberlain who carried the emperor's helmet disappeared together with the helmet, never to be seen again (27.10.11). When Valentinian suffered the paroxysm which led to his death, the chamberlains ensured that a group of witnesses was gathered around his bed (30.6.4).

Beyond these mentions of chamberlains Ammianus refers to a general eunuch presence at court.[12] When officials of Constantius advise bringing Ursicinus to Milan as well as Gallus they were 'supported by the other royal eunuchs' (14.11.3). Gorgonius, the chamberlain of Gallus, evaded punishment due to the agency of the eunuchs (15.2.10). The eunuchs (as well as Eusebius) were instrumental in turning Constantius against Ursicinus (18.4.2–4). The influence of the court eunuchs surfaces again in the reign of Valens, when this emperor was persuaded not to sit as a judge; prominent among those who influenced Valens was the praetorian prefect Modestus whom Ammianus presents as an agent of the court eunuchs (30.4.2). Finally one of the versions of the fate of Valens at the battle of Adrianople in 378 reveals the presence of eunuchs with the emperor at his fiery death (31.13.14).

Ammianus' information concerning eunuchs is, however, not solely restricted to their roles and influence within the imperial court, for he also builds up a striking picture of their history and nature. He attributes the initial creation of eunuchs to the Assyrian queen Semiramis (14.6.17). Another key point in the history of eunuchs (as far as the Roman empire was concerned) that Ammianus comments on is the edict of Domitian by which this emperor had forbidden the castration of boys within the Roman empire (18.4.5). Ammianus states that if Domitian had not issued this decree the empire would have been swarming with eunuchs.

Ammianus' discussion of the career of the chamberlain Eutherius usefully illustrates the origin of those eunuchs who found roles within the Roman empire, and the receptive market for eunuchs that existed (16.7). He records that Eutherius was originally born of free parents in Armenia, but was captured and castrated as a boy and sold to Roman merchants, and thus ended up serving in the palace of Constantine the Great. Ammianus makes it clear that imperial service was not the only consumer of eunuchs, for they could be found in Rome in the households of the rich (14.6.17).

Ammianus also comments on the nature and character of eunuchs. He found eunuchs unnatural. He accuses Semiramis, the first creator of eunuchs, of 'doing violence, as it were, to nature and wresting her from her intended course' (14.6.17). Ammianus stresses the unnatural quality of eunuchs by dwelling on their physical peculiarities. They are 'mutilated', and are 'sallow and disfigured'. This even gives rise to a comparison with the Huns; Ammianus notes that the Huns slashed the faces of their children at birth, with the result that the scars prevented the growth of facial hair and 'they grow old without beards and without any beauty, like eunuchs' (31.2.2). Ammianus also remarks on the shrill quality of the eunuch voice (21.16.16). Another physical peculiarity mentioned is that eunuchs alone are immune to the noxious and stinking gas that emerges from a cleft in the earth at Hierapolis in Phrygia (23.6.18).[13]

Personality traits arising from the eunuch condition are identified by Ammianus. Discussing the enmity that the eunuchs held for Ursicinus the historian comments that such men 'are always cruel and sour', and are attached to wealth as they can have no children (18.5.4). He characterizes eunuchs who have retired from imperial service as looking for bolt-holes in which they can hide from those who have suffered at their hands (16.7.7). The prefect of the Armenians, Cylaces, is described as being good at 'cajoling like a woman' because he was a eunuch (27.12.6).

All of this information is of course couched in the deeply antipathetic language of a male 'aristocratic' elite.[14] Ammianus declares that it is because of his disgust with the eunuchs found in the entourages of the Roman élite, and eunuchs in general, that he takes pleasure in praising the usually reviled Domitian for his anti-castration edict, and remarks that it is bad enough to have to tolerate the small number of eunuchs that can legally exist. As for the female Frankenstein who created eunuchs in the first place Ammianus asserts that anyone who saw the troops of eunuchs in Rome 'would curse the memory of that queen Semiramis of old' (14.6.17).[15] Ammianus' famous eulogy of the chamberlain Eutherius (16.7.4) of course only reinforces the idea that all other eunuchs are beyond the pale; the historian states that 'if a Numa Pompilius or a Socrates should give any good report of a eunuch, and should back their statements by a solemn oath, they would be charged with having departed from the truth'.[16]

Thus Ammianus provides us with striking comment both on eunuchs who were politically significant in imperial circles, and on eunuchs in general – their history, condition and character. Whilst it has been recognized that Ammianus does have a significant contribution to make to the picture of the increasing prominence of eunuchs at court in late antiquity, I would suggest that the extent and the depth of his interest in eunuchs generally has not been appreciated, and deserves to be accounted for. Simply, why is Ammianus so keen on the subject?

It could be argued that we are merely witnessing the influence of Tacitus, an inheritance Ammianus seems to acknowledge given the decision of this self-professed Greek to write in Latin and to start his history with the emperor Nerva, where Tacitus had broken off. Certainly eunuchs are to be found in Tacitus,[17] but more significant here are his remarks on the imperial freedmen. The reign of Claudius is particularly marked by this phenomenon, and the names of Narcissus, Pallas and Callistus are infamous.[18] Tacitus describes the power that these men held; Narcissus was able to order the execution of Messalina in the name of the emperor (*Ann.* 11.37), whilst Pallas is said to be the virtual controller of the empire (*Ann.* 13.14). Thus we have a familiar image of imperial aides of servile origin who exercise power through influence with the emperor and who look to their own interests. Tacitus also emphasizes the personal wealth and the greed of these elite ex-slaves (e.g. *Ann.* 13.1, 14.65). However it seems to me that these parallels that can be drawn between Tacitus' treatment of freedmen and Ammianus' treatment of court eunuchs are historical rather than literary:[19] it is the similarity of the historical phenomenon and the response of a member of the male 'aristocratic' élite to it rather than intentional echoing that is found in Ammianus.[20] In fact the most striking parallels are to be found in the work of a contemporary of Ammianus; in Claudian's first invective on Eutropius of 399 we find the initial creation of eunuchs ascribed to Semiramis, and also the story of the fate of Pompey in Egypt (Claudian, *In Eutr.* I. 339–42 (Semiramis); 480–3 (Pompey); see also p. 71 below).

A simpler explanation of Ammianus' interest in eunuchs is that as a historian of his times he had identified the developing phenomenon of the powerful court eunuchs, and felt this to be a subject deserving of his attention and the attention of posterity. However, I would argue that simple historical observation, like the influence of Tacitus, does not seem sufficient to account for the impassioned tone detectable in Ammianus' writings on eunuchs, general and specific. Would mere observation of this phenomenon have led him to unroll 'many records of the past', hunting to find a eunuch with whom he could compare that paragon Eutherius (16.7.8)? There is a personal angle here.[21] No doubt part of this personal interest is due to Ammianus' experiences in Rome. It is his negative reaction to the lifestyles of the rich of that city that led him to curse Semiramis, the originator of the eunuch condition. Further, Ammianus tells us that Eutherius passed his retirement in Rome, and this eunuch with the formidable memory has been nominated as an informant of the historian when he was in that city.[22] Having a eunuch as an appreciated contact may have caused Ammianus to have been more aware of the presence of the castrated male in late Roman society, though hardly more sensitive to the condition.

Another dimension to Ammianus' interest is revealed by his account of the experiences of his two great heroes, Ursicinus and Julian, at the court of Constantius II. Ammianus relates that Ursicinus had several confrontations with the court, which are mainly accounted for by the influence of the court eunuchs in general and of Eusebius in particular.[23] Ursicinus was recalled from the East in 354 on the advice of Eusebius, amongst others (14.11.2), who pointed to his ambition. The court eunuchs then accused him of grooming his sons for power, and aggravating Gallus on purpose (14.11.3). It is notable that when Ursicinus came to Milan at this time he was accompanied by Ammianus. Ursicinus was however restored to favour with his crucial role in the crushing of Silvanus' bid for power (15.5), and in 357 he was sent back east (16.10.21). However the courtiers, instigated by the eunuchs, continually warned Constantius about Ursicinus (18.4.2), and Eusebius too through his chamberlains slandered Ursicinus to Constantius, motivated by the fact that Ursicinus did not seek his influence, and would not give him his house in Antioch (18.4.3–4). Thus Ursicinus was recalled once more, but was ordered back again before having reached the West (18.6). In the aftermath of the fall of Amida in 359 Ursicinus yet again found himself in trouble at court; the inquiry led by Florentius and Arbitio did not blame the fall on the inactivity of Sabinianus, fearing to offend Eusebius, and Ursicinus found himself forced to resign and retire into private life (20.2).

Like Ursicinus, Julian found himself in trouble at court in the aftermath of the fall and death of Gallus (15.2.7–8), though Ammianus does not spell out a specific eunuch element to his problems, referring generally to defamers and flatterers. Again when Constantius contemplates making Julian Caesar, those who oppose his plan are not named, but are referred to in general terms as the emperor's 'intimates' (15.8.2); Eusebius was surely reckoned amongst these.[24] Julian's successes as Caesar also incited slander of him at Constantius' court, though once more the slanderers are left as a generic group of courtiers and flatterers (16.12.67–8; 17.11.1). Evidence of Eusebius' specific opposition to Julian is implied with the reference to his guilty conscience in the wake of the death of Constantius and the approach of Julian (21.15.4). The fact that the chamberlain was condemned to death at the trials at Chalcedon (22.3.12) seems telling, even if others wanted Eusebius dead too.

However, Ammianus is not just concerned with the histories of his heroes, but also with the very nature of the imperial court of Constantius II, and indeed the character of this emperor,[25] though this in turn feeds back into his idealization of Julian;[26] in short, Ammianus exploits the subject of eunuchs as an element of his political criticism. Slander, greed, flattery, suspicion and despotism appear as the hallmarks of Constantius' court, characteristics not unconnected with eunuchs.[27] Ammianus notes that the phenomenon of slander and accusation in the hope of thus securing the property and wealth of the accused was prevalent at Constantius' court, and that 'the leading men of every rank were inflamed with a boundless eagerness for riches, without consideration for justice or right' (16.8.13). Ammianus specifically names four such leading men, one of whom is the Grand Chamberlain

Eusebius.[28] At the time of the fall of Gallus Ammianus comments that 'the love of gain' of the court eunuchs 'was growing beyond mortal limits' (14.11.3). The eunuch Eusebius was the man whose particular favour at court was sought, for he had the ear of the emperor (18.4.3). This pernicious influence with the emperor reflects not just on the influencers but on the influenced: it is the suspicion and timidity of Constantius, his 'too receptive ears', that are exploited so ruthlessly by the courtiers and court eunuchs (see also 14.11). Ursicinus himself is recorded as having condemned the emperor as being in thrall to the eunuchs (20.2.4), and when Ammianus presents his summation of the character of Constantius he opines that he was excessively influenced not only by his wives and certain court officials, but also by his eunuchs (21.16.16).[29] The solution to this corrupt and despotic court comes of course in the form of Julian, whose purge Ammianus describes (22.4). It is indicative that in the account of Ammianus Julian's reign is free from the evil of flattery, a subject that Ammianus persistently refers to throughout his history and which is an obvious indicator for him of the quality of an emperor and his reign.[30] Significantly flattery resurfaces immediately after the death of Julian at the start of Jovian's reign (25.7.10).

The impression that Ammianus connects eunuchs primarily with Constantius and his reign to create a negative effect is confirmed when one considers the attention paid to eunuchs and the treatment of them by Ammianus throughout the course of his history. As Blockley comments, 'Ammianus ... mentions eunuchs almost exclusively during his narrative on the reign of Constantius'.[31] The most significant comments on eunuchs come in Books 14 (14.6.17) and 16 (16.7.4–10), with recurring references to the court eunuchs up to the deaths of Constantius and Eusebius. After this Ammianus' interest seems less intense. When the eunuch Cylaces figures in the account of relations between Armenia, Rome and Persia (27.12) Ammianus makes little of this eunuch angle, though one might have thought that there was ample scope for it. The influence of the court eunuchs does feature in the reign of Valens, for they worked through the praetorian prefect Modestus to persuade the emperor not to sit as a judge. Despite this comment Ammianus' interest is focused squarely on the practice of advocacy, and he also drops the explicit eunuch dimension, stating that the judges and advocates 'sold their decisions of the cases of poorer people to officers in the army, or to powerful men within the palace' (30.4.2). The specific target of his attack is no longer the eunuchs but the leading soldiers, which reflects Ammianus' identification of the military élite as the key problem for the empire upon the accession of Valentinian (27.9.4; see also 26.6). Thus the eunuch issue was one that Ammianus particularly linked with the reign of Constantius, and this is where his most pointed comments upon eunuchs are located. It is highly revealing of Ammianus' motivations that the duo of the bad emperor and the bad eunuch, Constantius and Eusebius, is mirrored by the equal and opposite pairing of Julian and Eutherius, the good emperor and the good eunuch. This positive/negative mirror image, and the issue of the influence of the eunuchs, emphasizes the very nature of Ammianus' history, for its focus is the figure of Julian and his reign, to which Constantius and his reign were the vital and contrasting precursors.

To sum up, Ammianus Marcellinus is a historian who conveys the phenomenon of powerful court eunuchs in late antiquity, but his interest and deployment of information go further than this. Not only does he impart something of the history and condition of eunuchs in general, he also exploits the eunuchs theme as a strand of his political criticism of the condition of the Roman empire and in particular of Constantius II and his reign. This in turn reflects upon Julian and his reign, as well as upon the fate of Ursicinus.

It is useful to cite finally the comments of Ammianus upon two subjects, Pompey the Great and the Gothic disaster, which are particularly telling. Like Julian and Ursicinus, Pompey was a hero of Ammianus. For our historian there was no one 'more valiant or circumspect with regard to his country' than Pompey (17.11.4); he was also a man whose fate, says Ammianus, was to be 'butchered in Egypt to give the eunuchs pleasure' (14.11.32). Considering the Gothic disaster, Ammianus comments that Rome had suffered disasters before, but had always managed to recover. He explains that this was 'because the temperance of old times was not yet infected by the effeminacy of a more licentious mode of life, and did not crave extravagant feasts or shameful gains' (31.5.14).[32]

In the mind of Ammianus, eunuchs had an emphatic part to play in the decline of Rome, and the destruction of its heroes.

Notes

1 For a general account of Ammianus on eunuchs see P. Guyot, *Eunuchen als Sklaven und Freigelassene in der griechisch-römischen Antike*, Stuttgart 1980, 164–6; J.F. Matthews, *The Roman Empire of Ammianus*, London 1989, 274–7; P.C. Francis, 'Eunuchs and the Roman Imperial Court', unpubl. MA thesis, University College Dublin 1993, 107–12.

2 K. Hopkins, *Conquerors and Slaves*, Cambridge 1978, 172–96. See also Guyot, *Eunuchen als Sklaven und Freigelassene*, 130–76, and O. Patterson, *Slavery and Social Death*, Cambridge (Mass.)/London 1982, 317–24. More recent contributors to the field are Francis, 'Eunuchs'; H. Scholten, *Der Eunuch in Kaisernähe* (Prismata V), Frankfurt am Main, Berlin, Berne, New York, Paris and Vienna 1995; D. Schlinkert, 'Der Hofeunuch in der Spätantike: Ein gefährlicher Außenseiter?', *Hermes* 122 (1994), 342–59 (who emphasizes Hopkins' highlighting of the dependency of the court eunuch on the emperor and his role as a counterpoise to the court nobility), and his appendix on the *praepositus sacri cubiculi* in his *Ordo senatoribus und nobilitas. Die Konstitution des Senatsadels in der Spätantike* (Hermes Einzelschriften 72), Stuttgart 1996, 237–84. See also W. Stevenson, 'The Rise of Eunuchs in Greco-Roman Antiquity', *Journal of the History of Sexuality* 5 (1995), 495–511.

3 Lactantius, *De mort. pers.* 15.2.

4 See A. Cameron, 'Eunuchs in the "Historia Augusta"', *Latomus* 24 (1965), 155–8.

5 See J. Long, *Claudian's In Eutropium. Or, How, When, and Why to Slander a Eunuch*, Chapel Hill and London 1996.

6 See for example J.E. Dunlap, *The Office of the Grand Chamberlain in the Later Roman and Byzantine Empire*, New York 1924, 205; Guyot, *Eunuchen als Sklaven und Freigelassene*, 143; Francis, 'Eunuchs', 64; also Scholten, *Der Eunuch in Kaisernähe*, 65.

7 Schlinkert, 'Der Hofeunuch in der Spätantike', makes Eusebius the prototype for his study of the court eunuch's function and relationship with his master the emperor and the court nobility.

8 One diplomatic and concerning Julian's conditions for sharing power, but the other more reproachful.

9 On Gorgonius see for instance Scholten, *Der Eunuch in Kaisernähe*, 213; Dunlap, *The Office of the Grand Chamberlain*, 309.

10 For convenience direct quotations are taken from the revised edition of J.C. Rolfe's translation of Ammianus Marcellinus, 3 vols, London and Cambridge (Mass.), 1935–9 (various reprints).

11 For problems see Scholten, *Der Eunuch in Kaisernähe*, 216–17, who states that Heliodorus is not a eunuch and is from Antioch.

12 Separate from the blanket group of 'courtiers' he so often mentions, though eunuchs could be found amongst the courtiers. On the connection between courtiers and eunuchs see Francis, 'Eunuchs', 109.

13 See also Cassius Dio 68.27.3 (who says he was there), and Pliny, *HN* 2.208, who says that it is the priest of Cybele/Magna Mater who is unaffected, which is rather different from saying that all eunuchs are unaffected.

14 For a contrasting attitude see P. Boulhol and I. Cochelin, 'La rehabilitation de l'eunuque dans l'hagiographie antique (IVe–VIe siècles)', *Studi di Antichità Christiana* 48 (1992), 49–76.

15 Note the appearance of Semiramis again at 28.4.9.

16 See the comment of T.E.J. Wiedemann, 'Between Men and Beasts: Barbarians in Ammianus Marcellinus', in I.S. Moxon, J.D. Smart and A.J. Woodman (eds), *Past Perspectives. Studies in Greek and Roman Historical Writing*, Cambridge 1986, 189–201, at 197.

17 For example Tacitus, *Ann.* 4.8 and 4.10 (the eunuch Lygdus); 12.66 (the eunuch Halotus); 14.59 (the eunuch Pelago).

18 See for instance A.M. Duff, *Freedmen in the Early Roman Empire*, Oxford 1928, 176–8.

19 Certainly neither Matthews nor Guyot points to a literary borrowing from Tacitus for Ammianus' treatment of the court eunuchs. Of course Tacitus is not complete, nor is Ammianus, though the latter's chapters on Rome and Eutherius suggest that these are the first times he has reflected on eunuchs. Further, Ammianus may have wanted to pick up where the last great Latin historian ended, but this does not mean he has a particular empathy with that historian. C.W. Fornara, 'Studies in Ammianus Marcellinus II: Ammianus' Knowledge and Use of Greek and Latin Literature', *Historia* 41 (1992), 420–38, has argued that the heritage of Latin historiography shaped Ammianus' history rather than that of Greek historiography, but it is to the figures of Cicero and Sallust that he looks more than to Tacitus. See also the comments of T.D. Barnes, 'Literary Convention, Nostalgia and Reality in Ammianus Marcellinus', in G. Clarke et al. (eds), *Reading the Past in Late Antiquity*, Rushcutters Bay 1990, 59–92, at 64. Ammianus' idealization of Pompey as a loyal patriot certainly has nothing in common with Tacitus' view of Pompey as 'more devious than Marius and Sulla in his quest for domination, but no better': R. Seager, *Pompey. A Political Biography*, Oxford 1979, 185.

20 It is perhaps telling that the late antique historian Zosimus believed that the freedmen of Claudius were eunuchs; see Guyot, *Eunuchen als Sklaven und Freigelassene*, 122 and n.4.

21 Note Matthews' identification of the personal motive forces for the writing of Ammianus' history, his own experiences and the figure of Julian: 'Ammianus' Historical Evolution', in B. Croke and A. Emmett (eds), *History and Historians in Late Antiquity*, Sydney 1983, 30–41; 'Ammianus Marcellinus', in T.J. Luce (ed.), *Ancient Writers: Greece and Rome* II, New York 1982, 1117–38.

22 For example Matthews, *The Roman Empire of Ammianus*, 25.
23 E.A. Thompson, *The Historical Work of Ammianus Marcellinus*, Cambridge 1947 (repr. Groningen 1969), 54 comments that

> We hear a great deal of the machinations of the court eunuchs against Ursicinus and we cannot but admire the vigour and power of Ammianus' language in describing them; yet is it not a little surprising that, although he turns aside no less than seven times to inveigh against them, they never succeeded in bringing anything upon the head of their intended victim except promotion, honour and opportunity? If we bear all this in mind, we may be sure that we are dealing here with the least satisfactory part of Ammianus' narrative.

Thompson (p. 55) then argues that Ammianus is relating Ursicinus' version of events, who felt aggrieved that he had 'suffered from the same lack of public recognition as Julian'.

24 It does seem odd that in the case of Julian Ammianus does not spell out a specific eunuch opposition. Perhaps he sought to suggest the general weight of opposition to Julian at Constantius' court. Julian himself blamed Eusebius for his bad relations with Constantius: *Ep. ad Ath.* 274a; and see the comments of Schlinkert, 'Der Hofeunuch in der Spätantike', 354–5.
25 R.C. Blockley, *Ammianus Marcellinus. A Study of his Historiography and Political Thought* (Collection Latomus 141), Brussels 1975, 33, comments that 'The Emperor . . . figures largely in Ammianus' thought and he is central to the historian's critique of the imperial system . . . To Ammianus a cruel regime means a cruel Emperor.' On Ammianus' portrait of Constantius see *ibid.*, 38–41, 48–52, and the contribution of Michael Whitby in this volume (chapter 7).
26 On the contrast between Constantius and Julian in Ammianus see Blockley, *Ammianus Marcellinus*, 49–50.
27 Blockley, *ibid.*, 142, comments: 'Though corruption is described in all branches of the bureaucracy, as a group the eunuch chamberlains are the most vilified.'
28 Elsewhere Eusebius is also described as 'unjust and cruel' (15.3.2).
29 See 16.8 and 19.12 for courtiers, flattery and despotism in general. Ammianus provides no evidence for the influence Constantius' wives exerted on their husband.
30 On flattery see R. Seager, *Ammianus Marcellinus. Seven Studies in his Language and Thought*, Columbia 1986, 97–104. Seager notes the lack of effect the flatterers have, which seems to reinforce the notion that Ammianus is using the theme symbolically.
31 Blockley, *Ammianus Marcellinus*, 142–3.
32 For Ammianus on the decline of the Roman empire see *ibid.*, 137–56, and also Barnes, 'Literary Convention, Nostalgia and Reality', 84, who highlights this passage too.

Part II

IMAGES OF EMPERORS

7

IMAGES OF CONSTANTIUS

Michael Whitby

Ammianus' obituary notice of Constantius (21.16) provides a typically incisive verdict on that emperor's character and qualities: although he is accorded a fair amount of praise, the overall impression is unfavourable, partly because of the relative length of the positive and negative parts, partly because the commendation is often qualified whereas the criticism is more rhetorically developed.[1] Ammianus' attachment to Ursicinus meant that he was a jaundiced observer of events such as Constantius' grand entry into Rome in 357 or the persecution of Magnentius' followers (16.10; 14.5), which contribute to his assessment of the emperor. Naturally, though, he professed objectivity, and contrasted his judgement with the reputation which Constantius strove to achieve: 'he made a special effort to be considered just and merciful' (21.16.11).

Part of this effort is evident in the panegyrics which survive from Constantius' reign by the Greek orators Libanius and Themistius and the future emperor Julian,[2] and it is the intention of this chapter to compare their positive assessment with that of Ammianus. His views, however prejudiced, represent criticisms which Constantius and his panegyricists will have believed they had to tackle, and conversely these Greek panegyrics sustained an image which supporters of Julian had to undermine. This can be inferred from the speech of thanks to Julian delivered in January 362 by Claudius Mamertinus in front of the Constantinopolitan senate, most of whom will have owed their status, directly or indirectly, to Constantius' patronage: Mamertinus, speaking in Latin, referred to the power of Greek eloquence, which could 'exalt beyond their due the accomplishments of all your rulers', and had 'expanded glorious deeds to meet your abundance of words'.[3] Ammianus was familiar with this speech,[4] and arguably also with some of the rhetorical themes to which Mamertinus was responding. There was considerable interaction between the various orators: Julian sent Libanius a copy of his first speech, and was himself influenced by the first two speeches of Themistius; Libanius and Themistius corresponded and were probably aware of each other's encomiastic strategies; Themistius' third speech may reveal awareness of Julian's first speech.[5]

77

Constantius' achievements presented a challenge to panegyricists, but a more basic problem was the devalued currency of the genre: as Julian observed, 'the genre of panegyric has already come to incur grave suspicion on account of those who have embarked on it improperly, and it is now held to be base flattery rather than a true testimony to noble deeds' (*Or.* 1.4c). Menander Rhetor's advice about inventing material reflects the expectations of composers, recipients and audiences, who were all thoroughly familiar with the conventions into which life had to be breathed.[6] Orators had to establish their own legitimacy, and various strategies were adopted in the corpus of Latin panegyrics to create the persona of honest commentator. A common approach was to contrast the speaker's personal inadequacy with the honorand's exceptional qualities and achievements (e.g. *Pan. Lat.* 6.1; 12.1), but frequent use meant that this gambit had to be reformulated. Libanius attempted this by alluding, in an extended deployment of the theme of the speaker's inadequacy (*Or.* 59.5–9), to its status as a cliché: 'Now it is the custom of those embarking on a speech of praise to criticize their own powers as being greatly deficient ... But even if this had not been said by anyone in the past ...' Orator and listeners colluded in playing the same game; thus, when historical comparisons are introduced, it is with specific allusion to the audience's expectations that the honorand will be shown superior to Alexander (*Or.* 59.53).

Libanius also drew upon his intellectual repute by stating that philosophers, like farmers, had a duty to offer the fruits of their labours to the emperors, though he did not develop the possibilities of a claim to special philosophical status (*Or.* 59.2). By contrast, in his first speech to Constantius, delivered at Ankara in 347,[7] Themistius highlighted his independent pose as a philosopher, for whom truth was all important and who alone could testify to virtue (*Or.* 1.1a; 3d); a decade later, when acting as envoy for the Constantinopolitan senate, he presented himself as a man who must speak the truth, one who was delivering a decree passed by Philosophy (*Or.* 3.44d–45a). Devaluation of oratory was counteracted by the assumption of a guise more widely associated with the truth, and Themistius donned the persona which would serve him in his dealings with emperors for the next thirty-five years.[8] This pose had been exploited by Dio Chrysostom in his dealings with Trajan: Dio stressed the contrast of truth and frankness against flattery and guile, and presented himself as a man whose philosophical training and standing as a true friend to the emperor ensured that he must speak the truth (*Ors.* 1.15, 33; 2.2, 12–25; 4.5–9).[9] The influence of Dio and other Second Sophistic orators on Themistius has been noted, albeit somewhat tentatively.[10] The philosophical approach naturally appealed to Julian, who began his first speech for Constantius by distinguishing himself from orators, for whom flattery is permissible, and poets whose Muse gives them abundant licence to invent (*Or.* 1.1d–2c); Julian claimed independence by asserting a different literary background, clearly philosophy though this is not explicitly stated, and proclaimed that he would only express views which could be referred to the standard of virtue and philosophy (*Or.* 1.3c–4b); he could provide true and hence effective praise (*Or.* 1.23a).[11]

Inevitably, rhetorical deployment soon devalued this approach, and the philosophical stance itself had to be defended.[12] Themistius alluded to criticism that philosophers have assimilated themselves to rhetoricians (*Or.* 4.62a), and on various occasions felt obliged to discuss the role of philosophers in society.[13] Julian subsequently wrote to Themistius that he ought not to flatter and deceive (*Ep. ad Them.* 254b), actions commonly associated with rhetoric.[14] Mamertinus praised the rehabilitation of philosophy under Julian, who 'not only freed Philosophy from condemnation, which not long ago was suspect and not only despoiled of honours but accused and arraigned' (*Pan. Lat.* 3.23.4); Themistius responded by celebrating the restoration of philosophy under Jovian (*Or.* 5.63c). The central issue in these exchanges was, most probably, Themistius' philosophical presentation of himself as honest spokesman for Constantius, a role which ensured that his relations with Julian were strained.[15] The contentious reputation of Constantius and that of his chief spin-doctor were interlinked.

A key issue in packaging Constantius can be subsumed under the heading of justice. For Ammianus, Constantius' fierce investigation of conspiracies, when he displayed more eagerness than humanity, surpassed the savagery and cruelty of the notorious trio of Roman tyrants, Caligula, Domitian and Commodus (21.16.8); the comparison at once locates Constantius beyond all limits of acceptable imperial behaviour.[16] In spite of occasional leniency, Constantius' bitterness, angry suspicions, and a harsh distrustful nature characterized by deadly enmity to justice quite overshadowed the efforts he made to be considered just and merciful.[17] Ammianus had used similar language to emphasize the emperor's vindictive anger in the narrative of the suppression of Magnentius' followers (14.5.4–5); here, though, flattering courtiers are also blamed for increasing the cruelty which became more extreme as his reign progressed. Imperial anger and rage are also mentioned by ecclesiastical historians, especially in Constantius' dealings with Church Councils and bishops who opposed his heretical designs (Sozomen, *Hist. Eccl.* 4.19.1; Theodoret, *Hist. Eccl.* 2.27); his repeated disputes with Athanasius of Alexandria provoke much comment, naturally unfavourable since Athanasius emerged as the doctrinal victor so that his writings, especially the *History of the Arians*, shaped the historical record. The judicial rigidity noted by Ammianus (14.5.5) is also evident in the debate with Pope Liberius: 'The sentence which has once been passed ought not to be revoked' (Theodoret, *Hist. Eccl.* 2.16). But imperial wrath was not confined to doctrinal matters, being mentioned also in the context of rioting in Constantinople (Sozomen, *Hist. Eccl.* 3.7.5; 4.21.6).

The evidence for Constantius' harshness was undoubtedly improved after his death, but it was still a reputation that had to be countered during his life since mildness and mercy were important imperial virtues.[18] Constantius proclaimed 'the *philanthropia* of our gentleness' in writing to Athanasius to grant him permission to return to Alexandria, while Cyril of Jerusalem, eager to consolidate imperial favour, referred to 'your customary *philanthropia* for the holy churches'.[19] Libanius presented Constantius as trained by his father in the practice of justice,[20] which involved the distinction between the times for anger and mildness, or between tyranny and *basileia* (*Or.* 59.36); his rule was noted for kindliness and generosity, for the renunciation of anger towards enemies and an absence of executions (*Or.* 59.85, 97); composure, self-control and mercy were among the qualities praised in Libanius' concluding summary of Constantius' character (*Or.* 59.122). This is the central theme for Themistius' first speech, which sets out to praise the *philanthropos basileus*, of whom Constantius is the current manifestation: *philanthropia* is the virtue which overcomes anger (*Or.* 1.4d), and Constantius manifests this through self-control (*Or.* 1.6a), mildness (*Or.* 1.16a), preference for honours over punishment (*Or.* 1.13c), avoidance of the death penalty and tempering of harsh written laws (*Or.* 1.14b–15a).[21] These two speeches from the mid-340s antedated the major internal challenges to Constantius' rule: for Libanius the only incident to be confronted was the family purge after Constantine's death, which is presented as proof of the government's stability – the empire remained on an even keel, even if there was some trouble and the heirs had to use their hands to retain what they had been granted (*Or.* 59.48). This was the massacre which prompted Ammianus' comparison of Constantius to the classic trio of imperial tyrants (21.16.8).

Imperial rivals were a sensitive issue, since Constantius had to cope with his brother Constans and then confront a succession of challengers who ranged from well-established co-rulers to potential threats (Magnentius, Vetranio, Silvanus, Gallus, Barbatio); although Magnentius and Gallus could be portrayed as harsh and unjust,[22] the suppression of usurpations occasioned the full display of Constantius' own judicial savagery. Themistius' second speech (late 355), which presents Constantius as a philosopher-king,[23] had to tackle the question of tyranny: the emperor's mildness and philanthropy justified his appellation of philosopher (*Or.* 2.31d–32d), which was also confirmed by the fact that God had granted him success (*Or.* 2.38b); he was born to be king, not a dinner-party emperor (*Or.* 2.36a: referring to Magnentius' elevation); he overcame one usurper (Vetranio) through words and allowed him to live, while the other (Magnentius) took his own life (*Or.* 2.37a–b, 38b). The bloodless success over the elderly Vetranio was deployed again in the speech which Themistius delivered at Rome in 357 on behalf of the Constantinopolitan senate (*Or.* 3.45b–46a). Focus on the leaders' fate obscured the fierce revenge exacted on the followers: thus Constantius could remain a mild and moderate ruler who pursued philosophy (*Or.* 3.44b–46c).[24]

The justice of Constantius, and its display in the context of usurpations, were sensitive issues for Julian: most of his family had been eliminated in 337, his brother Gallus succumbed in 354, and his own position as co-ruler was likely to arouse suspicions, however much Themistius might stress the philosophic compatibility of the imperial pair (*Or.* 2.39d–40b). Julian alluded to fraternal rivalries, but praised Constantius because he had avoided exacerbating these (*Or.* 1.18c–d, 19a–20b); 'in some cases, forced as you were by the critical state of affairs, you could not, in spite of your wishes, prevent others from going astray' (*Or.* 1.17a) – nothing would be gained by disguising Constantius' difficulties, but he faced problems which were not his fault.[25] Constantius was milder than his father Constantine (*Or.* 1.9b). The amnesty offered to Magnentius' followers was a proclamation worthy of imperial generosity (*Or.* 1.38b; cf. 2.58b),[26] he was never made arrogant by prosperity or success (*Or.* 1.45d), he showed mercy even when angry, removed harshness from vengeance, proved himself a good legislator and guardian of the laws, enforcing them without being involved in their harshness (*Or.* 2.88b–89b); above all he remained moderate and controlled (*Or.* 2.101b–d). The Vetranio affair was a prime example of his preference for conciliation, with rhetoric employed to win over the rebel's support and comfortable retirement provided for the unsuccessful old man (*Or.* 1.31c–d; *Or.* 2.77c); even the suppression of Silvanus' rebellion is presented as an occasion for kindness and mercy (*Or.* 2.99a–b). When praising the empress Eusebia Julian referred to Constantius' natural propensity to mercy (*Or.* 3.114c), though also remarking that Eusebia provided encouragement.[27]

These western usurpers dominate Julian's account of Constantius' military achievements. Thus the defence of Nisibis in 350 is incorporated into the praise of his careful preparations for confronting Magnentius (*Or.* 1.26d–27a) – a clever way to introduce a signal reverse for the Persian king, Shapur, for which it was difficult for Constantius to claim personal credit. Vetranio was the simpler of the challengers: he demonstrated Constantius' imperturbability in the face of an extra threat, the power of his oratory, and his nobility and generosity once successful. Magnentius was different, since there was bloody campaigning to be presented. One tactic was to assert that it was wrong to call the conflict a civil war (*Or.* 1.42a), a reinterpretation which could be justified on the grounds that it was waged to avenge the laws, *politeia*, and slaughter of numerous citizens, and to prevent further murders and arrests: Magnentius was a genuine barbarian (*Or.* 1.33c–d; *Or.* 2.95c), which suited his reliance on barbarian allies (*Or.* 1.34d; *Or.* 2.56c).[28] Once the contest had been redefined in this way as a struggle between Roman order and barbarian mayhem, Constantius' military achievements could be lauded, with his opponents' ferocity and determination increasing his praise. This was a sensitive and subtle representation of events, though it might also have had benefits for Julian himself, since he was now the ruler primarily responsible for opposing the bellicose tribes which Constantius had overcome when they served Magnentius.

Ammianus (21.16.15) contrasted Constantius' foreign failures with the pride he took from victories in civil wars, and the panegyrics do pay more attention to the latter than the former. The lack of external victories is clear in Aurelius Victor's favourable portrait of Constantius' achievements:[29] Julian's successes in Gaul reflected Constantius' good fortune and planning, a Persian attack was withstood, and a king was appointed for the Sarmatians (*De Caes.* 42.17–21), scarcely an impressive tally for twenty-three years of campaigning. Themistius asserted that the proximity of the virtuous Constantius secured the destruction of the Persian king (*Or.* 1.12b), but the brevity of the passage suggests that there was a shortage of appropriate material. Only Libanius focused at length on an external conflict, the battle at Singara in 344 which Eutropius (*Brev.* 10.10) described as an occasion when Constantius 'lost a certain victory through the headstrong bravery of the soldiers'. Libanius did his best with this awkward event, stressing Constantius' intelligent strategy and tactics, and arguing that the troops' failure to obey Constantius' orders merely highlighted the quality of his leadership: 'the more one finds fault with them, the more one increases the emperor's reputation' (*Or.* 59.99–120; quote from 108). Julian adapted Libanius' sophistic presentation of Constantius' achievement at Singara (*Or.* 1.22d–25b), but his treatment of Magnentius' suppression is about three times longer, an example of the focus on internal victories which Ammianus criticizes.

Constantius' education was another sensitive area. Ammianus noted his pretensions to learning, which did not result in commensurate achievements even in the versification to which he turned after failing in rhetoric (21.16.4; part of the positive assessment of Constantius). Libanius asserted that emperors needed a double education, both for the practice of administration and for the shrewd argument and vigorous rhetoric which would permit the achievements to be presented graciously; Constantius and Constans both possessed the skill in words appropriate for Romans (*Or.* 59.33–4), in addition to a thorough training in government. Constantius' appropriate verbal skill is compatible with an absence of formal training, whose deficiency Libanius subsequently asserted (*Or.* 62.8–9, 12–14). The efficacy of Constantius' rhetoric could be defended through his success in winning over Vetranio's troops (Julian, *Or.* 1.31c–d; cf. Victor, *De Caes.* 42.4); in his lost Book 13 Ammianus had presumably advanced an alternative explanation, in which bribery or superior force were perhaps decisive. Themistius was keen to present Constantius as a fellow philosopher, especially in his second speech, but he defines philosophy in relation to actions rather than knowledge,[30] thereby evading the question of the success of his schooling; Constantius' enthusiasm for education and philosophy (*Or.* 3.46c) does not demonstrate that he had received a good education. Julian followed Libanius in treating education as the acquisition of both skills and experience (*Or.* 1.11c–d), though with decided emphasis on the practical side. When Julian alludes to Constantius' wisdom, he again emphasizes actions which provided practical demonstration of a quality 'which it is by no means easy to praise as it deserves' (*Or.* 1.47a). Julian may here be gracefully sliding over a weakness.

Taxation was another difficult area: Ammianus condemned Constantius' lack of attention to provincial problems which led to harsh taxation (21.16.17). The issue was of personal concern to Julian, since one of his major differences with the emperor would be over the need for superindictions in Gaul; Julian was to pride himself on his ability to reduce the tax levy. Libanius and Themistius are quiet on the subject, although when praising Valens two decades later Themistius referred to the remorseless increase in tax burdens over the previous generation (*Or.* 8.112–13). Julian confronted the issue when discussing Constantius' preparations for conflict with Persia: a period of reduced burdens had to end, but whereas the Athenians had more than doubled their tribute Constantius was 'content, I understand, with the original revenues, except in cases where, for a short time, and to meet an emergency, it was necessary that the people should find their services to the state more expensive' (*Or.* 1.21c–d); it was all in the interests of ensuring proper supplies for the troops. Such equivocation might seem out of place in a panegyric, but Julian exploited the awkwardness to uphold his stance as honest reporter: his narrative preferred truth in every case, and so was true praise rather than fiction (*Or.* 1.23a).

Another potentially difficult issue was the role of courtiers: Ammianus criticized the influence on Constantius of wives and eunuchs (21.16.16; cf. 14.5.4), and regarded Julian as one of the victims of a cabal of courtiers (16.12.67);[31] Julian alleged that Gallus was destroyed to please Constantius' eunuch chamberlain (*Ep. ad Ath.* 272d).[32] Libanius commented on Constantius' affection for close friends, whom he chose slowly but thereafter remained attached to (*Or.* 59.122);[33] this theme is developed by Themistius who noted the especial importance to the philanthropic king of friends and his concern that they should suffer no harm (*Or.* 1.17b–18a).[34] Julian followed Themistius' sentiments quite closely, though more briefly (*Or.* 1.46b), but in his second speech he developed a rather different angle by complimenting the good king on his ability to select good associates (*Or.* 2.91b–d); in the panegyric to Eusebia he naturally praised her influence on Constantius (*Or.* 3.114c–116a). Ammianus praised Constantius for his determination to maintain a proper separation between civil and military authorities (21.16.2–3), but the coda to Aurelius Victor focused on the poor quality of Constantius' officials and subordinates, caused in part by the emperor's inadequate attention to appointments (*De Caes.* 42.24–5). Friends and agents were another area where Constantius' reputation was contested.[35]

Constantius was sensitive about his imperial image, and received praise from Ammianus for his concern for imperial majesty, his great and lofty spirit which disdained popular favour, his prudent and temperate lifestyle, and proper public behaviour (21.16.1, 5). Ceremonial displays, such as the grand procession through Rome in 357, could propagate this image but it also had to be spread more widely around the Roman world, especially among the literate upper classes, whose favour, particularly in the flourishing cities of the eastern empire, was essential for Constantius' regime. This raises the issue of what the orators were attempting to achieve through their speeches, whether the content is straight flattery, a cynical presentation of the desired imperial image,[36] whether there is a hidden agenda with the flattery intended to make the honorand responsive to the speaker's policies and requests,[37] or whether praise of virtues served as tactful exhortation to emperors to make the statements true.[38] There is likely to be some truth in each of these approaches, and different orators will have had different priorities at different times, but recent commentators on Themistius, for example, seem too generous in asserting his independence.[39]

But to start with Libanius. It is clear that he received instructions, either a direct imperial commission or strong hint: 'When I was still contemplating the matter the injunction confronted me and my intention and the request coincided' (Or. 59.4). Some of the speech's contents are extremely defensive, for example the explanation of Constantine's presents of iron to Shapur: the emperor saw through Persian deception, but thought that praise for victory would be even greater if the enemy were properly equipped (Or. 59.67).[40] Constantius' performance at Singara required careful treatment. Such commissioned praise might serve as the sweetening for diverse requests, but it is difficult to see what Libanius wanted in this speech. Constantius might try harder to display the qualities with which he is credited, such as composure, accessibility, self-control, mercy, prudence, affection for friends: these are mentioned, but not highlighted in the speech, and, if Libanius had a hidden agenda, it was so well concealed that it might have escaped the notice of its target.

In the case of Themistius, one could argue that his aim was to encourage successive emperors to approximate to his philosophic ideal;[41] for Constantius this would have involved greater self-control, avoidance of anger, and general mildness. But it would be wrong to focus on the persona of wise adviser adopted by Themistius, without considering the benefits which Constantius derived from these panegyrics and for which he handsomely rewarded Themistius: rapid elevation to leadership of the senate, and the statue in Constantinople with its verse inscription.[42] Ammianus noted Constantius' special efforts to be considered just and merciful, i.e. philanthropic (21.16.11), and the match between Constantius' agenda and Themistius' presentation is close: protestations that he is a free and impartial witness who honestly attests what he admires and knows (Or. 3.44c–d), or the assertion that he presents a collective view on Constantius (Or. 1.4a), are too defensive to be trusted.[43]

Julian's position was more complex, since he was a prominent participant in the imperial game as well as a commentator: he had received the maximum reward that Constantius was going to offer, whereas Libanius and Themistius could benefit from imperial patronage. His speeches in elevated Greek are likely to have had a restricted audience in the western part of the empire where he was based, so that he was probably addressing a different constituency, in particular Constantius' court.[44] As Libanius observed, after receiving a copy of Julian's first speech, his Caesar's oratory demonstrated to Constantius that there was absolutely nothing to be regretted in his choice of co-ruler.[45] In both speeches to Constantius Julian's primary focus was the emperor's virtues and achievements, things already known to the audience (*Or.* 2.94a) but which had not yet secured a worthy record (*Or.* 1.2d). However, in each case he switches to Constantius' qualities, his loftier attributes (*Or.* 2.75a–b), and in these latter sections there might be scope for hints about a better presentation of conduct.[46] It depends whether an individual in Julian's delicate position would have risked attempting to alter Constantius' imperial image, even subtly, or indulging in irony which might be detected; a straight demonstration of loyalty, which was Libanius' interpretation of the first speech, might seem more plausible. That Constantius did not match the image of Julian's ideal emperor, or live up to the Homeric parallels, does not prove that Julian was parodying his imperial pretensions by deploying these literary conceits.[47] Contemporaries had to be careful, but Ammianus, writing a generation later, could afford to be ironical:[48] Ammianus probably knew some of these panegyrics, or recalled their general thrust, and deliberately undercut their favourable presentation of Constantius.[49]

Notes

1 For discussion of the obituaries, see J.F. Matthews, *The Roman Empire of Ammianus*, London 1989, 238–42; detailed commentary on 21.16 in Joachim Szidat, *Historischer Kommentar zu Ammianus Marcellinus Buch XX–XXI*, Teil III (Historia Einzelschriften 89), Stuttgart 1996, 193–239.

2 Translation of Libanius' *Or.* 59 in Samuel N.C. Lieu and Dominic Montserrat, *From Constantine to Julian, Pagan and Byzantine Views*, London 1996, 164–205; Themistius' *Orations* 1 and 3 are to be included in the forthcoming translation of selected speeches in the series 'Translated Texts for Historians' by David Moncur and Peter Heather (Liverpool 1999); Julian's *Orations* 1 and 2 in W.C. Wright, *Julian* I (Loeb), Cambridge (Mass.) 1913.

3 *Pan. Lat.* 3.8.1; translation from C.E.V. Nixon and Barbara Saylor Rodgers, *In Praise of Later Roman Emperors. The Panegyrici Latini*, Berkeley 1994, 406. Nixon and Rodgers comment (406 n. 53) that the sentiment is an ancient commonplace, but it also had immediate relevance to the assembly of Constantius' place-men to whom Mamertinus was describing Julian's virtues.

4 G. Sabbah, *La méthode d'Ammien Marcellin. Recherches sur la construction du discours historique dans les Res Gestae*, Paris 1978, 321–3; Szidat, *Historischer Kommentar*, 91.

5 Libanius, *Ep.* 369 (Foerster) refers to Julian's first speech to Constantius (no. 30 in A.F. Norman, Loeb, Cambridge (Mass.) 1969, I. 444–51); C. Gladis, *De Themistii, Libanii, Iuliani in Constantium orationibus*, Breslau 1907; John Vanderspoel, *Themistius and the Imperial Court. Oratory, Civic Duty and Paideia from Constantius to Theodosius*, Ann Arbor 1995, 77 n. 29, suggested that Libanius composed summaries for a collection of Themistius' speeches in *c.* 357.

6 Menander, *Or.* 80.10–82.14 (Russell and Wilson), to commemorate the nativity of an honorand.

7 O. Ballériaux, 'La Date du ΠΕΡΙ ΨΙΛΑΝΘΡΩΠΟΣ Ἡ ΚΩΝΣΤΑΝΤΙΟΣ (Discours 1) de Thémistios', *Byzantion* 66 (1996), 319–34.
8 With this exploitation of philosophy, one could compare the trajectory of party political broadcasts: commercial advertising creates greater slickness until the smooth image threatens to backfire, and prompts a return to a gritty realism, which is just as carefully prepared as the previous gloss. See P. Heather, 'Themistius: A Political Philosopher', in Mary Whitby (ed.), *The Propaganda of Power. The Role of Panegyric in Late Antiquity*, Leiden 1998, 125–50, 127–30.
9 See D. Konstan, 'Friendship and Monarchy: Dio of Prusa's Third Oration on Kingship', *Symbolae Osloenses* 72 (1997), 124–43.
10 By Vanderspoel, *Themistius*, 7–10, who understates Themistius' deliberate manipulation of this convenient model; the influence is strongest in Themistius' early speeches, when he was constructing his own public character. See now Heather, 'Themistius', 129.
11 Cf. Julian, *Or.* 3.101 (panegyric of Eusebia) for a similar sentiment.
12 In his *De Regno* Synesius emphasized the importance to the ruler of honest friends (11), as much as of philosophy (1, 29); in this he adapted a different aspect of Dio's inheritance (e.g. Dio, *Or.* 1.28–32); see further Konstan, 'Friendship and Monarchy'.
13 *Orations* 21, 23, 26, 28, 29. Vanderspoel, *Themistius*, 108–10, 230–40, dates all five speeches to Constantius' reign: he regards the key issue as Themistius' political philosophy, with opponents objecting to its exposition in imperial panegyrics which they were obliged to attend. Undoubtedly there were intellectual differences, but in the harsh competition at court an attack on Themistius' carefully crafted persona as philosopher was a challenge to his influence, and also an indirect commentary on his presentation of Constantius.
14 The Loeb translation interprets this more broadly: 'you as a philosopher ought not . . .'; philosophical probity may well have been in Julian's mind, but he does not make that specific point.
15 L.J. Daly, '"In a Borderland": Themistius' Ambivalence towards Julian', *Byzantinische Zeitschrift* 73 (1980), 1–11; G. Dagron, 'L'empire romain d'Orient au IVème siècle et les traditions politiques de l'hellenisme: le témoinage de Thémistios', *Travaux et Mémoires* 3 (1968), 230–5; Vanderspoel, *Themistius*, 122–34, though regarding the disagreement between Julian and Themistius as primarily academic, about approaches to Hellenism; T. Brauch, 'Themistius and the Emperor Julian', *Byzantion* 63 (1993), 79–115, fails to argue away all the evidence for tension.
16 Szidat, *Historischer Kommentar*, 208–12; Matthews, *The Roman Empire of Ammianus*, 241.
17 Cf. Julian, *Ep. ad Ath.* 270c–d, which sarcastically challenges Constantius' reputation for *philanthropia*; 281b for Constantius' anger.
18 R. Seager, 'Some Imperial Virtues in the Latin Prose Panegyrics, the Demands of Propaganda and the Dynamics of Literary Composition', *Papers of the Liverpool Latin Seminar, Fourth Volume 1983*, Liverpool 1984, 129–65 (references to *clementia* are scattered through this analysis); cf. also Nixon and Rodgers, *In Praise of Later Roman Emperors*, 21–6; L.J. Daly, 'The Mandarin and the Barbarian: The Response of Themistius to the Gothic Challenge', *Historia* 21 (1972), 351–79, at 354–5.
19 Athanasius, *Apol. c. Ar.* 51.2; Cyril's letter is published by E. Bihain, 'L'épître de Cyrille de Jérusalem à Constance sur la vision de la croix (*BHG* 413)', *Byzantion* 43 (1973), 264–96. Athanasius addressed the emperor six times as 'your *philanthropia*', and once as 'most *philanthropos* Augustus' in his *Apology to Constantius*; ed. J.M. Szymusiak, *Sources chrétiennes* 56 (1958), 181.
20 Cf. Julian, *Or.* 1.14a: he has been taught to be governed by nature and law.
21 Vanderspoel, *Themistius*, 78–83; Dagron, 'L'empire romain', 129–32; Daly, 'The Mandarin and the Barbarian', 355–60.
22 Even Julian, *Ep. ad Ath.* 272c admitted his brother's cruelty.

23 Vanderspoel, *Themistius*, 91–4.
24 Cf. Aurelius Victor, *De Caes.* 42.2, 'He alone, since the birth of the empire, achieved glory through his powers of speech and clemency', a judgement based on the success over Vetranio; significantly Victor passes quickly over the bloody battles against Magnentius and ignores the suppression of his followers.
25 After his own elevation, Julian naturally exploited these 'family problems' to castigate Constantius; *Ep. ad Ath.* 270c–271a.
26 The amnesty, proclaimed at Lyons on 6 September 353, did not cover criminals, who were to be executed; *Cod. Theod.* 9.38.2.
27 On this speech see S. Tougher, 'In Praise of an Empress: Julian's Speech of Thanks to Eusebia', in Mary Whitby (ed.), *The Propaganda of Power. The Role of Panegyric in Late Antiquity*, Leiden 1998, 105–23.
28 Themistius had introduced this theme, but did not develop it so fully (*Or.* 2.43a–b).
29 Cf. Eutropius, *Brev.* 10.15 for another neutral statement of the external/internal contrast.
30 Compare Plutarch's treatment of Alexander the Great in *On the Fortune of Alexander*, a text which probably influenced Themistius.
31 Julian, *Ep. ad Ath.* 283c; Matthews, *The Roman Empire of Ammianus*, 274.
32 Mamertinus (*Pan. Lat.* 3.25.3) complimented Julian on choosing virtuous friends, in contrast to several predecessors.
33 Contrast Libanius, *Or.* 62.9, 11 for a posthumous attack on Constantius' associates.
34 For the general theme, see Konstan, 'Friendship and Monarchy'.
35 Another contentious issue, Constantius' involvement in doctrinal controversies (Amm. Marc. 21.16.18), is not confronted in the panegyrics; naturally, there is plenty of criticism on this score in the orthodox church historians and Athanasius of Alexandria.
36 P. Heather and J. Matthews, *The Goths in the Fourth Century*, Liverpool 1991, 15–18.
37 Vanderspoel, *Themistius*, 5; Daly, 'The Mandarin and the Barbarian'; Dagron, 'L'empire romain', 100–8; P. Brown, *Power and Persuasion in Late Antiquity. Towards a Christian Empire*, Madison (Wisc.) 1992, 68.
38 Vanderspoel, *Themistius*, 83.
39 *Ibid.*, e.g. 94, tends towards a charitable assessment, though on occasions he accepts that Themistius was an imperial spokesman.
40 Cf. H.-U. Wiemer, 'Libanius on Constantine', *CQ* 44 (1994), 511–22; discussion of *Oration* 59 at 512–15.
41 Julian, *Ep. ad Them.* 254b–c, adopted a modest pose by asserting that he interpreted Themistius' praise as exhortation to virtue.
42 Libanius, *Ep.* 66.5–6 (Foerster = Loeb 52) asks for a copy of the verses.
43 See Heather, 'Themistius', in Whitby (ed.), *The Propaganda of Power*; contrast Vanderspoel, *Themistius*, 4, who accepts Themistius' accounts of his rhetorical purpose.
44 This is the accepted interpretation in modern scholarship: G.W. Bowersock, *Julian the Apostate*, London 1978, 37; P. Athanassiadi, *Julian, an Intellectual Biography*, London 1992, 61.
45 Libanius, *Ep.* 369.6 (Foerster = Loeb 30); Bowersock, *Julian*, 37; Athanassiadi, *Julian*, 60–1.
46 A contrast is sometimes drawn between the two speeches to Constantius (Athanassiadi, *Julian*, 63–6; F. Curta, 'Atticism, Homer, Neoplatonism and Fürstenspiegel: Julian's Second Panegyric on Constantius', *GRBS* 36 (1995), 177–211), with the second speech becoming a manifesto for Julian's own views. But the fact that Julian's depiction of the ideal emperor can be linked to his own behaviour as ruler does not prove that he was proclaiming his own political manifesto in his speech. The opening passage on the quarrel between Agamemnon and Achilles may allude to the relationship of Constantius and Julian, but Achilles' behaviour is explicitly criticized, and Julian is certainly not threatening to abandon his campaigning; *contra* Curta, 'Atticism, Homer, Neoplatonism'.

47 *Contra*, Curta, 'Atticism, Homer, Neoplatonism'. Curta's analysis is interesting, but misguided; it ignores the impact that content has on literary presentation, and the danger in airing views that might be misinterpreted at Constantius' suspicious court (especially if Julian is represented in the initial figure of Achilles, who should have tolerated Agamemnon's behaviour).

48 Cf. the post-mortem criticisms of Constantius in Mamertinus and Aurelius Victor, who chose to end the *De Caesaribus* with a 'brief note of truth' (42.24–5), both referred to above.

49 Sabbah, *La méthode*, 348–66, argues that Ammianus was influenced to some extent by Themistius' philosophy and presentation of emperors, and that in particular he reacted against Themistius' favourable portrayal of Valens (*ibid.*, 359–61). Sabbah does not discuss the panegyrics of Constantius.

8

TELLING TALES

Ammianus' narrative of the Persian expedition of Julian

Rowland Smith

> I shall describe [the achievements of Julian] one by one in progressive order, deploying all the resources of my modest talent, if they will suffice. What I shall narrate will come close to the category of panegyric, yet it is not made up of eloquent deceit, but is a wholly truthful account, based on clear evidence...
> (Amm. Marc. 16.1.2–4)

> What wish is enacted, what desire is gratified, by the fantasy that real events are properly represented when they can be shown to possess the formal coherence of a story?
> (Hayden White[1])

Running intermittently at first, then increasingly sustainedly, Ammianus' narrative of the career of Julian spans ten of the eighteen extant books of the *Res Gestae*.[2] Even allowing for punctuating digressions within the stretches of text at issue, no other emperor is granted such lengthy treatment in the work as it survives. How much space was allotted to Constantine's thirty-year reign in the lost earlier books we cannot know; but given that the starting-point of Ammianus' work was AD 96, the scale of treatment is unlikely to have matched that devoted to Julian's much briefer career. In one sense or another, Ammianus' narrative of Julian plainly must count as the centre-piece of the entire work.

I shall focus on the culminating segment of this narrative: Julian's Persian campaign of 363. Ammianus himself served on this expedition, and his account of its aims and execution has been closely studied by late Roman historians. My concern here, though, is not with the historical adequacy of Ammianus' account; and the significance of his personal experiences and observations as a participant will figure only tangentially. The subject is rather the story of the campaign presented in the *Res Gestae*: I wish to discuss certain features and tendencies of the narrative, and to ask how they affect the story's shape and tone. I am committed to no theory that would bar recourse to 'the author' over and above 'the text', but the focus in what follows is largely internalized within Books 23–5 of the *Res Gestae*, and Ammianus' name will often serve simply as convenient shorthand to refer to a narrative voice embedded in a stretch of text.

Our text narrates the progress and failure of a massive military expedition. Picking up with the army's departure from Antioch and the crossing of the Euphrates into Mesopotamia (23.2.1–7), the narrative runs largely – though not quite entirely[3] – in a simple time-line into Book 25, and the sorry outcome: Julian's death, and the army's humiliating retreat back to Antioch. Within the *Res Gestae* this narrative is clearly pivotal, conjoining two major themes of the preceding books: on the one hand, fighting against Persians, which has had a prominent place in the narrative of Julian's predecessor Constantius – and which cannot but have been similarly prominent in the lost books of a work that began with Trajan and proceeded to review the third century; on the other, the career of Julian – a story which Ammianus has earlier declared must appear almost an exercise in panegyric (16.1.3).

Panegyric is not the only literary mode invoked. Opening his account of Julian's campaigns in the West, Ammianus had echoed the *Aeneid* – 'Greater the story that opens before me; greater the task I now attempt' (15.9.1; cf. Virgil, *Aen.* 7.44) – and within the larger narrative a near-epic aura attaches to the story of the Persian expedition. The grandeur of theme, signalled by lengthy punctuating excursuses which constitute a good quarter of the stretch of text in question,[4] is implicit too in the way the narrative closes: Book 25 does not merely end, it ends with a 'sense of an ending'[5] – an heroic figure lost, and the chance he had represented for Rome's empire gone for good. The account of Julian's fatal wounding slides into a philosophic deathbed scene, then into a laudatory obituary of one 'truly to be numbered among the heroic spirits' for his 'glorious deeds and innate majesty' (25.4.1–16). When the narrative of Book 25 resumes, it sets up a pygmy to Julian in the shape of Jovian, his 'shameful' acceptance of harsh peace terms, and his dispiriting retreat through Mesopotamia. Near the Book's end, in stark contrast, Julian makes a last, posthumous appearance, as a corpse transported for burial at Tarsus. To perpetuate the memory of his grandeur and achievements, we read, he should have been interred not by Cydnus' banks, but beside the Tiber as it skirts the tombs of deified emperors of old (25.10.4): such is Ammianus' farewell to the Apostate. A closure of some kind is implicit, and on one view the end of Book 25 concluded the entire *Res Gestae* in its first version.[6] On any view, it comprised a narrative climax: Ammianus would begin Book 26 with a new preface to usher in 'the more recent record' – the story, that is, of the empire after Julian.

Against all this, however, one can set a common impression that the obituary's elevation of Julian as an idealized bundle of virtues is uncomfortable, and undercut by the obituarist's granting that Julian had his faults. In the obituary's structure these criticisms are made *sotto voce*, but for many readers they cut deep, and not least because the faults seem foreshadowed in actions of Julian recounted in the preceding narrative – actions sometimes explicitly criticized, moreover, at the point of narration, and on grounds readily accessible to human standards of judgement (I exclude for the moment, as a special case, remarks appealing to the mysteries of 'divine will' as the measure of judgement). A striking instance in our portion of the narrative is the order Julian gave outside Ctesiphon for the burning of the Roman supply and transport fleet on the Euphrates (24.7.4). The narrator not only reports but openly endorses the soldiers' dismay and complaints; he judges that the fleet was 'needlessly' and 'rashly' lost (24.7.6–8), and he underlines his verdict with a subversive echo of the Virgilian tag that had prefaced Julian's *res magnae* in the West; again he evokes the seventh book of the *Aeneid*, but now in much less happy lines: it was as if Bellona herself, he says, had lit the 'fatal torch' (*funesta face*) that did for the ships (24.7.4; cf. *Aen.* 7.319ff.: *Bellona . . . face . . . funestae . . . taedae*).

In brief, then, we have a narrative which Ammianus predicts, as he begins, must be a virtual panegyric, but which itself seems at times to subvert both the narrator's opening declaration and the obituarist's closing praises. And even if we set aside explicit criticisms voiced in the narrative, the obituary's praises still seem to sit oddly beside the immediately preceding account of what befell an expedition devised to be Julian's crowning glory.

How to reconcile this glaring import of the narrative – that Julian's plan issued in humiliating defeat, and was failing even before his death – with the presentation of Julian as an exemplary emperor and general worthy to stand with Trajan and Marcus Aurelius (16.1.4)? This problem could hardly fail to occur to the author. At one level, his answer is explicit. The obituary, we have said, having instanced Julian's virtues, admits failings, and again gives instances. Responsibility for the Persian disaster, however, is assuredly not among them. The obituary stoutly (if quite unconvincingly, to moderns) denies that charge, rejecting it on two grounds. First, it was not Julian, but Constantine, who had stirred up war with the Persians; here Ammianus directs us to a story recounted in a lost earlier book, the import of which is that Julian had no choice but to tackle Persia. And second, as for the way he did so, his failure was not attributable to any personal shortcomings. A divine will had determined the outcome; Julian would have triumphed spectacularly, we read, 'if only the decrees of heaven had coincided with his plans and splendid deeds' (25.4.26). The sense of strain and special pleading in all this is patent, for on the presentation the *Res Gestae* has offered no emperor was more deserving of divine support than Julian: at his first substantial appearance in the narrative, he is presciently hailed as 'the one who will restore the temples of the gods' (15.8.22), and as he leaves the stage his devotion to ritual sacrifice is judged by the obituarist to be so pronounced as to have seemed excessive. Not that the will of the gods was to be understood by mortals: but readers are human, and for them the puzzle remains disquieting.

It would be wrong, though, to suppose that what we have in the obituary is simply a desperate appeal to the divine injected to counteract a negative impression arising from the narrative of Julian's military failure. The narrative, too – especially our segment of it – makes abundant play with the divine, both as an explanatory mechanism and in various guises as a virtual participant; and abundant play, also, with the figure of the heroic Julian. However one reads the tension in the presentation and evaluation of Julian in the *Res Gestae*, it is not merely a feature of the obituary; it informs the texture of the narrative itself.

To explore this ambiguity, I shall extract from the text two notionally separable and tonally contrasting story-lines – I will call them stories A and B – and consider how they relate and converge within the narrative. Of the two, *Story A* has a more complex narrative texture, and I will discuss it first, and at greater length.

Story A, on this procedure, is the story of an expedition whose nobility the outcome could not tarnish, an epic mission conceived by a surpassingly great emperor. It starts at 22.12.1, with active preparations for the Persian war that Julian's 'exalted mind' had long contemplated as punishment for sixty years of savage depredations. He 'burned with a twofold desire for war': his innate energy demanded military adventure; and he wished to add the title *Parthicus* to his earlier glorious triumphs. The narrator's viewpoint here is wholly commendatory, the protagonist's heroic merits as king and general having been firmly signalled much earlier in the text: at Julian's investiture as Caesar, the soldiers present had joyfully clashed their shields and had 'gazed long into his eyes, at once delightful and awe-inspiring, and at his animated and charming face', hoping to sense what kind of man he would prove to be, 'as if they had read ancient books [of physiognomy]' (15.8.15–16). For Ammianus' own readers an answer to that question is supplied by various devices in the chapters immediately following, some of which I have mentioned already; by the Virgilian tag at the head of the Gallic excursus preceding the narrative of Julian in the West (15.9.1); by the declaration that, to convey the truth, the narrative must be almost a panegyric (16.1.3); by a punctuating chapter on the prince's *virtutes* (16.5); and by the colour of the ensuing narrative itself, in the account of the victory at Strasbourg with which Book 16 culminates – an achievement, we are now told, that Julian naturally wished to match in the East (22.12.2). It is true that the opening of our notional *Story A* tells how some persons doubted from the first the emperor's wisdom in the attempt, but these are *desides et maligni*, detractors of no account whose 'barking' was understandably disregarded by one whose 'greater spirit' had placed him 'beyond others': our hero is as impervious to such backbiting as Hercules had been to the pygmies stuffed in his lion-skin

(22.12.3–4). The comment recalls the opening praises of Julian as Caesar, the statement that 'some law of a better life seems to have attended the young man from cradle to last breath' (16.1.4), and seems to subvert the very possibility of justified criticism of Julian on normal criteria – the consideration, for instance, that those who had warned against the Persian adventure were proved right. In my *Story A*, the test of the expedition is not to be its contingent success or failure, but its nobility of conception and the Homeric grandeur of its leader.

It seems in keeping with this stance that nowhere in the extant narrative is precise mention made of specific military or diplomatic purposes which may have prompted Julian to invade. The motivation remains generalized, expressed in terms of an heroic superabundance of energy and *philotimia* implying something outside any normal frame of reference. A similar effect, one may think, is produced by the absence in Julian's case of a metaphorical motif often used by Ammianus in other settings, the likening of men to animals.[7] Elsewhere in the *Res Gestae* one meets men as snarling dogs, serpents, beasts in the amphitheatre, often with a moral judgement of actions or emotions implicitly conveyed. Nowhere in our narrative are Julian's actions or moods ever so presented: here too, he stands outside the usual frame of judgement.

Later touches in the narrative enhance this impression. At Pirisabora, for instance, the besieged inhabitants pour from the city gates shouting that a saving *genius* had shone forth to them in Julian's shape (24.2.21–2), and when Julian criticizes his generals for inertia at Ctesiphon the deep reason is traced to the emperor's own character, his 'constant ambition to achieve what lay beyond' (*semper ad ulteriora cupiditas*; 24.7.3). The failure to capture Ctesiphon is a major turning-point in the story, and the account of Julian's order at this juncture to destroy the Roman supply fleet discloses an ambiguity in narrative viewpoint to which I shall return later. In my notional *Story A*, however, a hero is allowed to err: the loss of the fleet is not subsequently harped upon as decisive, and up to Ctesiphon, at least, the narrative has disclosed a sequence of successes in the course of which Julian's own actions are repeatedly highlighted for admiration. Speeches that he delivers at key points – the entry into Assyria (23.5.16–25), the siege of Pirisabora (24.3.4) – fire the army with the appropriate rhetoric, and promise that this commander will share their hardships (a promise amply fulfilled as the narrative unfolds: e.g. 24.5.11; 25.2.2). They also give the soldiers a history lesson, and the narrative an evocative context: Julian will emulate the eastern achievements of Lucullus and Pompey, Trajan and Severus, to remove a long-standing threat: Persia will fall as an eastern Carthage 'so that posterity may have material for a glorious account' (23.5.16–18). The effect on the troops boded well, we read, particularly on those who recalled Julian's triumphs in the West (23.5.25); and their mode of applause – shields rattled against legs – recalls the scene at Julian's investiture as Caesar years before

(24.3.8; cf. 15.8.15). So too, Julian's own bravery in the field gets special stress. At Pirisabora, he breaks the defence by leading a daring charge against a city gate in the face of a hail of missiles (24.2.14; cf. 24.5.11). At Maiozamalcha, he is ambushed by ten Persians and personally dispatches one assailant with expert swordplay: 'Let this *facinus pulchrum*', we read, 'be added to the records of the past' (24.4.5).

'After these glories' (24.4.31), the army approaches the environs of Ctesiphon and engages in the first set-piece fight with a sizeable Persian force. At this point the narrator acknowledges a touch of the excessive in Julian's behaviour. Baulked in one engagement, he became enraged and carelessly exposed himself to Persian archers (24.5.6). 'He now hoped for so much from his previously constant good fortune as often to dare things verging on rashness' (24.6.4: *propius temeritatem*) – a plan of attack, for instance, requiring a risky night crossing of a defensive river-channel and a frontal assault on the opposite bank. In the event, though, his 'keen vigour of mind' (24.6.5) brought the manoeuvre off, and the battle was won. The manner of describing the battle has some interest. Against the mail-armoured cavalry and elephants of the enemy, Julian sets out his forces in an 'Homeric arrangement', mixing weak units between lines of choice troops (24.6.9; cf. *Iliad* 4.297ff.). He himself participates actively in the fighting, speeding about to reinforce weak points and spur on stragglers: the Persian line breaks, and soon the whole force is retreating in disorder back into Ctesiphon. Ammianus' closing comment only underlines the Homeric echoes of a battle fought on a plain before a citadel whose defenders flee for refuge within their walls; poets and historians of old, we read, may tell of Hector and Achilles, or of heroes of the ancient Persian Wars, a Sophanes, a Callimachus, a Cynegirus: 'but all agree that on this day the courage of some shone no less bright' (24.6.14).

Plataea, Marathon, Homer's Troy – the elevated parallels mark a wish to monumentalize a campaign in which no full-scale battle was actually ever fought. The Persians had chosen all along to hold back their main army: quite where Shapur's army was, and what he planned, were still unknown – and the narrator is content to leave them so. The engagement on the plain is taken up as the best chance to recount anything much resembling a classic field-battle in the course of the campaign. It is also the narrator's last chance to record a success, for the sequel to this 'Homeric' victory is distinctly anticlimactic: Julian's generals advise against besieging Ctesiphon, and he grudgingly accepts their 'better view' (24.7.1). A lacuna in the text may obscure the narrative tone at this point, but it is striking that Ammianus chooses not to take the moment to amount to what it may in fact have been: a decision to turn back. Rather, he attributes to Julian an alternative, more ambitious plan: to leave the riverlands and advance into the heart of the interior (24.7.3). Only when this proves unworkable does our account disclose a decision to retreat (24.8.2) – and even here, the true import of the decision is left curiously opaque.

From this point on, the narrative takes on darker colours. Topography and the weather enter the picture as menacing forces, and the predominant mood becomes one of uncertainty, 'human wisdom being [now] of no avail' (24.8.4). As the retreat begins at daybreak, a distant cloud of dust is seen: a herd of wild asses, perhaps – or was it what others thought, the elusive Persian army finally arriving (24.8.5–6)? One could not tell: 'the atmosphere', we read, 'remained murky, and we could not make out what we saw through the gloom until the evening. That night was a dark night unrelieved by any starlight, and we passed it as one would in difficult and doubt-filled moments' (24.8.7–25.1.1). At least the doubts are dispelled next morning: the Persian host is now visible in the distance. The retreat becomes increasingly desperate, and soon the best that my notional *Story A* can hope to say of Julian is that 'he nothing common did or mean upon that memorable scene'. That, at least, it achieves, with a death-scene whose echoes pass from the *Iliad* to Plato's *Phaedo*.[8] In the fatal encounter, Julian is riding without his breastplate when he observes and rides into a mêlée. Like Homer, the narrator includes stark details of what happens when a spear hits a body: the missile grazed the emperor's arm, pierced his ribs, and lodged in his liver. He tried to pull it out, cutting his fingers to the bone on the blade, then fell from his horse. Carried to his tent for treatment, he willed himself not to die, determined to return to the fight for his soldiers' sake: the narrator is reminded of Epaminondas at Mantinea (25.3.6–8). Only when his strength is plainly gone does he lie still, accepting death philosophically as a gift from the gods 'to whom I am akin', and rejoicing that it came in battle. His dying words declare the well-being of his subjects to have been his guiding aim, and comfort his weeping friends with a Neoplatonist's picture of a soul returning to its celestial home (25.3.15ff.). The obituary immediately follows.

I have spoken of my *Story A* as monumentalizing and epicizing, a story of tragic glory recorded for posterity. The Homeric echoes we observed are one device to this end – and the ground had been laid for them almost from Julian's first appearance in the *Res Gestae*, in a detail of his accession as Caesar; entering the royal carriage, he had whispered a line from Homer prophetic of the tragic narrative to come: 'Wrapped in death's purple by all powerful fate' (15.8.17; *Iliad* 5.83). So too, our text is heavy with allusions to historical exempla and events. We have met Epaminondas, and Herodotus' heroes of Marathon; there are many others. Alexander intrudes most clearly within our narrative – he also offers *comparanda* in both the obituary and the opening praises (25.4.15; cf. 16.5.4) – after the capture of Maiozamalcha: Julian forbears to take any of the beautiful captive Persian girls offered to him, and Ammianus duly remembers Alexander's gracious treatment of Darius' women after Issus (24.4.27; cf. Plutarch, *Alex.* 21). But there are other, *sotto voce*, prompts: it would be hard not to recall Alexander in the talk of Julian's *semper ad ulteriora cupiditas* (24.7.3) and of the siege-assaults he personally led (24.2.15, 6.6, 6.11); and the Homeric line the newly appointed Caesar Julian whispers had supposedly been uttered by Alexander at his own accession (Athenaeus, *Deipn.* 540a). Again, generals from Rome's past haunt Julian's campaign, and not only in the speeches he is given. One name was irresistible: out of care for his army, Julian would leave his bed to work at dead of night 'after the fashion of Julius Caesar' (Amm. Marc. 25.2.3). More often, though, like Alexander, the Roman precedents invoked make an eastern connection. One of the earliest rings a mournfully prescient bell, as the expedition passes Carrhae, 'famed for the calamity of Marcus Crassus' (23.3.1); but there are past successes to remember too. At Cercusium, Julian enters a fortress 'which Diocletian had encircled with lofty walls and towers' (23.5.2); later, he will visit the deserted ruins of Coche, 'destroyed in earlier days by the emperor Carus' (24.5.3). Passing Zaitha (23.5.7), he sacrifices at the tomb of Gordian, 'whose successful Persian campaigns, and treacherous murder, we have already recounted'.[9]

Trajan is another ghostly presence. Oaths that Julian swears before his troops put the narrator in mind of those of Trajan (24.3.9); at Ozogardana, the expedition gazes on a remnant of past triumph, a tribunal dating from Trajan's reign (24.2.3); near Ctesiphon, it repairs and travels down a canal constructed 250 years earlier, in the course of Trajan's campaign (24.6.1). More recent times yield a living human relic: at Anatha, the expedition is amazed to encounter an octogenarian veteran of the army Galerius had marched into Persia seventy years before. Abandoned by his unit, the man had gone native, settling down to enjoy the locals' polygamous customs: none the less, he said, he had always known he would see a Roman army return and would die in Roman territory (24.1.10). It is a joyful moment for the expedition, but the irony is evident: its commander will die young in Persia. An effect of these vestigial presences is to press a reading of the narrative of Julian's campaign as a reprise of past exploits (and, in the end, past griefs). The past weighs heavily on this narrator – and on his hero, too: Ammianus' Julian himself looks to texts for comparative *exempla*, feeling shame when applauded for an act of personal bravery because it did not match 'what he had read' in Polybius about an exploit of Scipio Aemilianus at Carthage (24.2.16). To have dwelt on what Ammianus does not elucidate – specific strategic or diplomatic objectives of the campaign – would have jarred in this setting: specificity implies limitation. Better to hint that, for a moment, a lost age of imperial Roman power in the East seemed poised to return. And as relics in the text commemorate the days of Trajan and Gordian, so our narrative itself will serve as a memorial to the virtues of Julian: his physical monument at Tarsus, we recall, did not, in Ammianus' view, match the stature of this emperor (25.10.4).

There is another feature of the narrative in *Story A* that cannot but affect the reader's impression of Julian's *res magnae* – the fact that much of it is narrated in the first person. At first sight, the cause may seem obvious:

Ammianus himself served in the campaign, and the very way the 'we' narrative starts invites appeal to his personal experience in this connection: its abrupt first entry (23.5.7), in the course of the march through Mesopotamia, most likely marks the point at which Ammianus' own unit joined the expeditionary force. But that does not exhaust the questions at issue here – no more so than our granting that Luke accompanied Paul on some of his travels would fully explain the resonances of the celebrated 'we' passages in Acts.[10] An author's decision to narrate in the first person is also a literary choice and it generates literary effects and questions, most obviously in connection with narrative point of view, the issue for which Gerard Genette coined the term 'focalization'.[11] In our narrative, for instance, it is 'we' who pass the tomb of Gordian, and 'we' who take the town where the Trajanic tribunal can still be seen; in the course of Book 24, it is 'we' who pass through Assyria and advance in high spirits after the fall of Maiozamalcha. As 'we' go, 'we' witness marvels and *curiosa*: a royal hunting lodge set among paradisal orchards, cypress-groves and vineyards, filled with choice Persian paintings and sculpture (24.6.3); another such 'palace' built in the Roman style (it pleases us, and we let it stand); an enclosed park containing lions, boars and peculiarly savage bears (here, however, 'our' cavalry slaughters the lot); a fertile countryside filled with various crops (24.5.1–2), not to mention palm-trees that take sticky pleasure in sexual intercourse – though girl palms, we learn, can be secretive in love (24.3.12–13).

In this connection Stephen Greenblatt's readings of the *conquistadores*' accounts of the New World come easily to mind. In the *conquistadores*' discourse, Greenblatt argued,[12] the experiencing of marvels is represented in ways that serve the aim of colonial appropriation, and there are touches in our narrative that might be read similarly: the palace built by Persians in Roman architectural style could count as an acknowledgement of Roman cultural superiority, the slaughter at the beast-park as an assertion of Roman power to tame barbarian frenzy. So too, the huge excursus on the Persian empire and its peoples in Book 23 contains criticisms based on cultural stereotypes that might justify a Persian war; and Ammianus' Julian makes the same patriotic appeal to cultural difference when addressing his troops, balancing it with promises that would certainly warm a *conquistador*'s heart: Persia is a *natio molestissima* that must be destroyed (23.5.19, 21), but there is the prospect of wealth in abundance by and by, 'if only you keep trust with the god and me' (24.3.6). Greenblatt himself, however, found in antique discourse a case of 'tolerance' of cultural difference to contrast with his New World texts, in the shape of Herodotus;[13] and in Ammianus' narrative of Julian's expedition the accounts of *curiosa* read much more, overall, like a Herodotus than a Columbus or a Bernal Diaz: the predominant message conveyed is wonder at the 'otherness' of what is encountered. The excursus in Book 23 has already at times worked to similar effect, pointing to a race of men who have a single arched eyebrow across the forehead (23.6.75), to a cleft in the earth exuding a deadly vapour to which eunuchs alone are immune (23.6.17), or to shellfish that copulate with dewdrops scattered from the moon (23.6.85). In Book 24, though, the use of the first-person narrative mode in the accounts of the *curiosa* encountered as 'we' march heightens the effect, eliding the 'impersonal' third-person voice of Ammianus' excursus and his voice as narrator of the expedition. *Curiosa* of the sort a reader might expect to meet – has met – in an ethnographic excursus on Persia are now drawn into the narrative texture itself: in the narrator's company, we follow Julian on a tour through a world where much is strange – and rendered all the stranger, perhaps, by ghostly relics of an earlier Roman presence there.

Our narrative is only *partly* recounted in the first person. Where Julian himself is the immediate object in view, the narrating 'we' notably keeps its distance: the form of expression here is 'Julian did *x*', never 'we saw/were amazed to see Julian do *x*'; and when Julian communicates and interacts, he does so with 'the soldiers' or a similar third party, not with 'us'. But it is not simply that the grammatical form of the narrative is consistently cast in the third person at these points; the issue is rather the broader question of the implicit point of view. Third-person narrative is in itself no bar to focalization, and internal focalization is certainly sometimes at play in Ammianus' narrative of Julian: nowhere more tellingly, perhaps, than at its start, in the gaze of the troops who stare at Julian's 'beautiful yet awe-inspiring' face in an effort to 'read' the character of their new Caesar (15.8.16); there, we are surely nudged to view Julian through the soldiers' eyes, and to share their impulse to grasp an enigma. And of course the narrator can give the stage to Julian himself, by granting him direct speech – and it is another expression of his privileged status in this narrative that he alone is granted this throughout the campaign. In the main, none the less (instances are too numerous to need illustration), Julian's doings are recounted in the classic 'non-focalized' style of an 'omniscient', 'impersonal' narrator with privileged access to the subject's emotions and intentions.

In consequence, our text produces a shifting pattern of first- and third-person narrative. Quite what the shifts contribute to the overall point of view from which the narrative is recounted is a question that deserves more attention than I can give it here, but a basic distinction drawn by Genette is clearly relevant. Genette insisted that in assessing point of view one must separate questions about 'mood' (questions, that is, about which character's point of view orients the narrative perspective) from questions of 'voice' (the question of who is narrating). On both counts, the employment of a first- or third-person mode of narration may be tangential in itself, a merely grammatical choice: as we have just noted, focalization can generate 'mood' in first- and third-person modes alike; and in any narrative, whatever its formal grammatical mode, the narrator is in *some* sense an invariant 'first-person' presence.[14] In so far as the grammatical person of the narrative in our text informs its point of view, then, what is important is not so much the mere fact that this or that part of the narrative is first or third person, but rather the effects that the shifts between the two modes produce.

One such effect is perhaps to enhance the narrative's immediacy as a spectacle unrolling before our, the readers', eyes: are we not drawn to assimilate the 'impersonal' third-person narrating voice with the participating first-person narrator, and to read even sections ostensibly 'impersonally' narrated through the gaze of a narrative 'we' that repeatedly punctuates them? One can certainly illustrate such an effect operating in miniature within a single scene. Consider the transitions between the first and third persons at the critical moment of retreat with which Ammianus so artfully closes Book 24 and opens Book 25, the point when a dust cloud obscures the view and gives way to a starless night (24.8.6–25.1.2): 'Some insisted' (*firmabant*) that the Persians had intercepted 'us' (*nobis*); 'the soldiers having been halted' (an ablative absolute), 'we' rested (*quievimus*) in camp; not until evening could 'that which was so dimly seen' (*quod squalidius videbatur*) be made out for what it was; 'we' passed (*exegimus*) a dark and utterly starless night in doubt and fear, 'no one daring to sit down and close his eyes'; when morning came, gleaming weapons 'seen from afar' (*longe prospecti*) 'showed' (*indicabant*) the arrival of the enemy; 'the troops, set alight by the sight, wished to attack' (*visu accensum, properantem congredi militem*), but 'the emperor forbade them'; there was some fighting, nevertheless, between the Persians and 'our' skirmishers. The passage is clearly focalized throughout by a locally placed 'we', even where grammatically third person. The stress on the visual plays its part too, of course, intensifying the narrator's gaze: the passage is a beautiful instance of the visual quality often remarked upon in Ammianus' writing,[15] visual perceptions being played upon to express a state of mind or convey a stimulus to action. Similarly, our narrative can pick on visual details to fix a scene. At 24.6.8, the glittering mail of the tight-packed enemy cavalry dazzles the eyes of the troops facing them; behind them are elephants 'looking like walking hills'. Through whom are we witnessing this scene? The soldiers facing it? Or a narrator within the locally placed 'we' who encamped earlier in the chapter (*consedimus*: 24.6.3)? Or a privileged narrating voice that speaks in both the first and third persons at different points?

Once again, here, the distinction between 'first' and 'third' seems elided. It is a particular moment in the narrative, but I have suggested that the point may have a broader bearing. Julian's own actions, we noted, are narrated in the third person, and seemingly in a classical 'omniscient' and 'impersonal' voice. But those narrative passages are repeatedly punctuated by others narrated by a locally placed 'we', and one effect is arguably to destabilize the 'impersonal' and 'omniscient' voice: are we not often prompted to read the accounts of Julian's own actions from the grammatically unexpressed viewpoint of an observing first person? The status of that narrating 'we', of course, is itself ambiguous. In so far as it is a locally placed observer, it is also an emotionally susceptible (and by no means omniscient) participant in events, shocked by a sudden mishap (24.5.5), marvelling at *curiosa* – or peering apprehensively through a dust-cloud to try to make out the true nature of what is happening. Julian's particular actions are accessible to this observing 'we', but the deep impulses that inform them and the fate they express are a thing apart, as obscure to it as they had earlier been to those who gazed in admiration at Caesar Julian's face. But any narrator, we noted earlier, is in *some* sense an invariant 'first-person' presence in the text, and in ours there is always another potential narrating 'we', an especially privileged observer – the *miles quondam* Ammianus who served on the expedition and later wrote an account of it that fed on personal memory and experience. *This* narrating 'we' has an eyewitness authority, but its vision is freed from the bonds of localized place and time: is not a reader prompted to invest this 'we' with the knowledge and authority of the historian who is composing the *Res Gestae*, and who narrates the reign of Julian in the course of it? And does not that in turn prompt a reading of the narrative that assents to Ammianus' opinion in a crucial connection noticed earlier – the presentation of Julian in the preamble to the whole account of his career as a hero beyond the range of normal human judgement?

That exculpatory vision, however, I attributed not to the narrative as a whole, but to a delimited aspect of it: what I have called *Story A*. It remains to set it against a second notional story-line I proposed to extract from the text: my *Story B*. A comparatively brief treatment suffices: this story has a simpler texture, and its essentials are lucidly laid out in John Matthews' *The Roman Empire of Ammianus*.[16] It is a story standing in stark contrast to *Story A*. Whereas *Story A* commended the campaign as a glorious (albeit a tragic) expression of heroism, and treated criticism of Julian as a kind of impertinence, *Story B* recounts a campaign always doomed to failure, and marked out as such by signs available to Julian from the outset. It provides a kind of counterpoint to *Story A*, undercutting its record of successful sieges and engagements with warnings of what must come. The story's subject matter is communications from the gods in omens and dreams, and its purport is that the expedition is contrary to the will of heaven. Amidst the preparations at Antioch, Apollo's temple at Daphne burns down (22.13.1). On New Year's Day 363 a priest attending Julian at the temple of Genius Romae collapses and dies (23.1.6); from Constantinople, news comes of an earthquake; from Rome, a letter announcing that consultation of the Sibylline Books has elicited a 'clear response': the emperor must not cross the frontier that year (23.1.7).

Julian disregards these warnings and the expedition sets out. As it crosses the Euphrates, another 'baleful portent' intrudes: a giant stack of horse-fodder topples over and kills fifty ostlers (23.2.8). A few days later Julian's own horse, Babylonius, collapses in agony: Julian divines a favourable sign, for

'Babylon is fallen' (23.3.6) – a response more convincing to bystanders than to readers. Next, a delayed message arrives from a trusted intimate, Sallustius, begging Julian to give up a venture that lacks the requisite divine protectors and must end disastrously (23.5.4); it too is ignored. Then, soon after Julian's sacrifice to Gordian at Zaitha, the corpse of a huge lion is presented to the emperor (23.5.8–11). A royal death is foretold: but whose? Julian and his philosopher friends think the Persian king's, but expert Etruscan soothsayers in the entourage think differently: they 'demonstrate' (*ostendebant*) from their books that the sign is prohibitory, and the narrator is explicit that the philosophers were sometimes stubbornly wrong about matters of which they knew little. The same parties dispute again next day over a thunderbolt that has struck a soldier and two horses: the soothsayers judge it 'advisory'; the philosophers entirely dismiss it (23.5.12).

Omens now cease till near the close of Book 24, permitting an epic momentum to attend the successes from Pirisabora to the 'Homeric' victory near Ctesiphon. But immediately after that high-point, when Julian proposes to sacrifice to Mars as a thank-offering, the gods speak again, and most forcefully. Of ten choice bulls, nine collapse before they reach the altar; the tenth bolts, and when finally dispatched shows sinister signs in the entrails. Enraged, Julian swears that he will make no more offerings to Mars – nor did he, the prescient narrator comments (24.6.17), for death would soon overtake him. Two chapters on and the army is in full retreat, with portents coming thick and fast. Long before, Julian had had a dream-vision of Rome's Genius come to his aid: now at night he saw the deity walk sadly from his tent (25.2.3ff.; cf. 20.5.10). He was dismayed, too, by a shooting star, suspecting a hostile sign from Mars. The soothsayers who were summoned urged a pause from all military activity, but they could not persuade the emperor, and not just because he disagreed with their particular interpretation: he was now *omni vaticinandi scientia reluctante*, 'averse to the whole art of divination' (25.2.8). Julian here stands markedly at odds with the Julian the obituary will gently chide as being, like Hadrian, rather too inclined to divination (25.4.17); the ground of criticism now is just the opposite, and the fault is fatal: the next day is the day of Julian's death.

As distinct from the localized 'we' of *Story A*, the narrative voice in these happenings is manifestly knowing and ironic as it recounts the misreadings of omens and the promises Julian undertakes to fulfil after the war (23.5.22). It also makes a plain and persistent criticism: the counsels of Etruscan soothsayers and the Sibylline Books were correct, and Julian repeatedly ignored them. On the face of things, there is a clear inconsistency here with the viewpoint we have ascribed to *Story A*; if it is resolvable, it is only because the criteria of judgement to which the narrator of *Story B* subscribes are not ultimately human: they are rather the criteria of fate or the gods. In *Story B*, the gods virtually become participants in events, warners communicating in the usual ways of gods. The narrator records the signs (once again, one notices the prominence of the visual: they are *visa vel lecta*, things seen in dreams or the sky or the organs of animals and checked in soothsayers' manuals), and makes their import plain from the start: the explanation of the failure of the campaign lies with a divine injunction, and Julian's disregard of it in pursuit of 'more than mortal hopes' (22.9.1). It is against this background that we can best catch the resonance of a passage that we touched on earlier – the burning of the fleet at Ctesiphon on Julian's orders (24.7.4). Ostensibly, Ammianus criticizes a particular strategic decision on common-sense military grounds. But it is highly significant that the criticism follows almost immediately on the point in *Story B* at which the gods show their displeasure most dramatically, and at which the god-loving Julian acts most strikingly out of character: the abortive sacrifice to Mars, and the emperor's angry oath to honour him no more. Such is Julian's mood – it approaches *atê* – when he gives the order to torch the ships, 'as if Bellona herself had lit the fatal flame'. The order, then, is intimately linked with his failure to respect the will of heaven; it marks a point in the narrative at which the voice of *Story B* has come to impinge directly and dramatically on that of *Story A*.

What I have called *Story A* and *Story B* are only notional stories, of course: in the *Res Gestae* they are strands of a larger narrative, and having extracted them we may set them aside. They have provided a convenient means to highlight shifts and contrasts in narrative voice; the placing of what is told in two sliding but complementary planes, human and divine; and the chance that this offered the narrator to present Julian in terms that would put him beyond criticism at one level, while allowing it entry at another (the little shall not judge the great; for the rest, only the divine mind, as read by the narrator, can judge). On this score, construed simply as a story, our narrative could be said to cohere, notwithstanding its shifting voices. But the *Res Gestae* was written by one author, and he intended to write not just narrative, but narrative history. To say his story of Julian coheres is not to say it is coherent history: when a historian points to the divine mind for an explanation, it is quite likely because his own mind is divided or perplexed. The conclusion that Julian, of all men, could be so mistaken about the will of the gods was surely a disturbing one for Ammianus, and a mark of his difficulty in coming to terms in his history with the failure of Julian's reign in general. It is a capital narrative irony, too ironic for this author's taste, and we can see him tempering his own criticisms. For one thing, it is Julian's philosophic friends who are most overtly pitted against the soothsayers in the narrative: in that sense, what Julian is criticized for here is what he is praised for in other contexts in Ammianus – his zeal for philosophy and the company of philosophers. Then again, signs from the gods are in their nature hard to read, as the narrator is quick to observe in recounting the omen of the lion's corpse: he recalls the 'ambiguous truths' of the Delphic oracle, not least in its reply to a previous would-be conqueror of Persia, Croesus (23.5.9). Earlier in the *Res Gestae*, moreover, Ammianus had chosen to include an excursus on divination (21.1.7–14): significantly, it is prompted by a portent sent in a dream to Julian soon after his acclamation as Augustus. The excursus emphasizes both the general validity of the practice, and the difficulty of interpreting a given sign. Interpretation, we are told, is always problematic – but then again, 'if a grammarian makes a mistake, that does not cause us to abandon grammar' (21.1.13). Like those who had gazed intently at Julian's face to 'read' the nature of the man, the diviner must try to apprehend reality from a host of signs. The excursus ends by quoting Cicero: 'The gods give signs . . . if we mistake them, the error lies with the interpretation of men, not the nature of the gods' (*De nat. deorum* 2.12). Mistakes in interpretation, Ammianus avows, are all too human: does he not here look forward to the tragic object lesson soon to be narrated in the fate of the Persian campaign?

On that count – the working of fate – we can notice a last ambiguity in our ambivalent narrative. *Story B*, we have said, insists that Julian and his campaign came to grief because he failed to recognize the will of the gods. But here and there our text hints at another view: that the divine will was more inscrutable than this; that Julian was fated not to recognize it, and so to die in Persia; that an expedition that was fated to fail must also have been fated to occur. A signal is given in the aftermath of Julian's fatal wounding: on learning that the name of the locality where he fell was 'Phrygia' he gave up hope, remembering that an oracle had named Phrygia as his destined place of death (25.3.9). But the notion has already had a more explicit statement much earlier in the narrative, when Julian received the delayed letter from Sallustius counselling against the invasion: he ignored it, 'for no human power or virtue has ever availed to prevent what the order of destiny has ordained' (23.5.5). Julian's disregard of the omens, this passage seems to say, was itself ordained as the channel through which the will of heaven was accomplished. In the narrative that follows, this note is drowned out by the critical presentation of his rejection of the signs, but it is a note that Ammianus chooses to sound loudly again in the obituary; his kinder verdict there is that Julian would indeed have won the title *Parthicus*, 'if only the decrees of heaven had coincided with his plans and splendid deeds' (25.4.26). 'Some law of a better life' had attended Julian from first to last (16.1.4): who could properly blame him if, after a career of unbroken victories, he sought to match in Persia his own past exploits? Certainly no lesser human, the author implies: one might as soon try to justify the ways of God to man.

Notes

1 H. White, *The Content of the Form*, Baltimore 1987, 4, provocative on the epistemological standing of historical narrative; cf. D. Carr, 'Narrative and the Real World', *History & Theory* 25 (1986), 117–31, for a counter-theory.
2 Career as Caesar: 15.8, 16.1–7, 16.11–12, 17.1–3, 17.8–11, 18.1–2; as Augustus: 20.4–5, 20.8–10, 21.1–5, 21.8–12, 22–4 *passim*, 25.1–4.

3 On the doublet of 23.5.4–15 and 24.1.1–5, J. Fontaine, *Ammien Marcellin, Histoire IV (Livres XXIII–XXV)*, 2 vols, Paris 1977, vol. 1, 20–1 and vol. 2 comm. *ad loc.*; J.F. Matthews, *The Roman Empire of Ammianus*, London 1989, 130–1, 178.
4 On the digressions at 23.4.1–14 (siege-artillery) and 23.6.1–88 (Persia), see Fontaine, *Ammien Marcellin*, vol. 1, 54–64; J. den Boeft, J.W. Drijvers, D. den Hengst and H.C. Teitler, *Philological and Historical Commentary on Ammianus Marcellinus XXIII*, Groningen 1998, and the contributions of Den Hengst (chapter 3), Drijvers (chapter 16) and Teitler (chapter 18) in this volume.
5 I quote the title of F. Kermode, *The Sense of an Ending*, London 1966, classic on a topic now intensively studied; see D.H. Roberts et al., *Classical Closure. Reading the End in Greek and Latin Literature*, Princeton 1997.
6 Matthews, *The Roman Empire of Ammianus*, 481 n. 34.
7 R. MacMullen, 'Some Pictures in Ammianus Marcellinus', *The Art Bulletin* 46 (1964), 435–55, at 441–5; repr. in R. MacMullen, *Changes in the Roman Empire: Essays in the Ordinary*, Princeton 1990, 78–106; Matthews, *The Roman Empire of Ammianus*, 258.
8 On the 'Platonic' deathbed scene, Fontaine, *Ammien Marcellin*, vol. 1, 218; G. Scheda, 'Die Todesstunde Kaiser Julians', *Historia* 15 (1966), 380–4, perhaps too sceptical of an authentic element; cf. J. MacManners, *Death and the Enlightenment*, Oxford 1981, 234–69 on eighteenth-century conventions of behaviour at the deathbed.
9 Ammianus here refers to a lost book, and quite what he had said of Gordian's death eludes us, but others had put it down to the intrigues of the emperor Philip, and one tradition had made Philip a crypto-Christian. One might perhaps press Ammianus' comment here to find an echo of the story that Julian was killed by a Christian in the Roman ranks – a story Ammianus certainly knew (25.6.6), but chose not to mention in his account of the fatal skirmish. If so, the text at 23.5.7 is colouring the story it is currently telling by pointing to another, told earlier.
10 E. Haenchen, *The Acts of the Apostles*, Oxford 1971, 81–90, 119–20.
11 G. Genette, *Narrative Discourse*, Oxford 1980, 189–94.
12 S. Greenblatt, *Marvelous Possessions*, Oxford 1991, *passim*, esp. 7–25, 52–85.
13 *Ibid.*, 122–8.
14 Genette, *Narrative Discourse*, 185–98, 243–5.
15 E. Auerbach, *Mimesis. The Representation of Reality in Western Literature*, Princeton 1953, 50–60; MacMullen, 'Some Pictures in Ammianus Marcellinus'.
16 Matthews, *The Roman Empire of Ammianus*, 175–9.

9

AMMIANUS ON JOVIAN

History and literature

Peter Heather

Ammianus' account of the reign of the emperor Jovian (27 June 363–17 February 364) provides an excellent case study of Ammianus' authorial technique. It is itself relatively brief (the last six chapters of Book 25), and focuses strongly on two main subjects: the new emperor's election, and the peace treaty which he subsequently negotiated with the Persians. The reign also receives coverage in a variety of other sources, not least Themistius' fifth *Oration*. The latter provided the starting-point for this chapter,[1] and also suggests a third subject for consideration here: Jovian's religious policies. The range of alternative sources makes it possible to consider not just what Ammianus *actually* wrote, but also what he *might* have written, and hence bring into focus the way in which his skills as a writer were deployed to shape the available raw material.[2]

The election of Jovian

Ammianus' account of Jovian's election is characteristically vivid. Stunned by the death of the former emperor Julian in an ill-judged skirmish with the Persians, the commanders of the now leaderless Roman army met to decide on a successor. Two factions quickly formed, headed on the one hand by the Gallic generals Dagalaifus and Nevitta, whom Julian had brought with him from the West, and, on the other, by two eastern generals, Arintheus and Victor, survivors from the reign of Constantius II. The two factions sought to resolve the deadlock between them by offering the throne to Julian's praetorian prefect, Salutius Secundus, but he refused on the grounds of age. With the council deadlocked, the issue was decided elsewhere, by a few hot-headed soldiers (*tumultuantibus paucis*: later described as camp attendants; 25.5.8), who clothed Jovian in the imperial purple and paraded him through the camp, heralding him as Augustus. This was picked up, not least by subsequently disappointed troops who mistook Jovianus Augustus for Julianus Augustus (25.5.1–6).

This account is not only fuller in circumstantial detail than those available in other sources, but it also disagrees with them. According to Themistius, Jovian was the universal choice of the entire army, not the opportunistic beneficiary of deadlock in high places (*Or.* 5.65b–66c). A similar vision of his election can also be found in the church historians (Socrates, *Hist. Eccl.* 3.22; cf. Sozomen, *Hist. Eccl.* 4.3). A more flattering view of the election is perhaps no more than we might expect to find in these quarters. Themistius was speaking in front of Jovian in celebration of the latter's consulship (1 January 364), and the new emperor was also a Christian, so that none of these sources would be likely to refer to the rather dubious election circumstances reported by Ammianus. More strikingly, however, the same vision of military unanimity is also found in the pagan historical tradition deriving from Eunapius, which had no particular axe to grind on Jovian's behalf (Zosimus 3.30.1).

How should we resolve this disagreement? Because of its greater circumstantial detail, one is instinctively drawn to Ammianus' account. On reflection, however, it becomes clear that Ammianus is, at the very least, not telling the whole truth. As John Matthews has pointed out, Jovian was not such an obscure figure as Ammianus implies. His father, Varronianus, was a guard commander (*comes domesticorum*) of Constantius II, and Jovian himself had escorted the mortal remains of that emperor to their final resting place. This was a mission with a high political profile.[3] Consonant with this is Themistius' claim that Jovian had previously been considered for promotion to the purple on the death of Constantius II in 361 (*Or.* 5.65b). This has generally been discounted as a piece of flattery (not least because Ammianus does not mention it in his account of the transition from Constantius to Julian). It is worth, however, a little reflection. Themistius certainly flattered all the emperors before whom he spoke, and, whatever the circumstances of their election, always claimed that they had been destined by the divinity from birth to rule the empire.[4] The claim that Jovian had already been considered for the purple, however, is of quite a different order of specificity. It was not something Themistius claimed for any of the other emperors he served. The claim was made, moreover, in front of the emperor himself and his court, an audience comprising many of the leading generals and politicians of the day. Some of them (such as Arintheus and Victor) were even survivors from Constantius' regime and would have had substantial knowledge of the political manoeuvres which separated Constantius' death and the eventual acceptance of the usurper Julian as his legitimate successor. In these circumstances, Jovian's prominence and the nature of Themistius' audience suggest that we should take the claim seriously. Ammianus is not very specific about what happened on Constantius' death, but does make it clear that the switch of allegiance to Julian was far from automatic, with other names being canvassed in between (21.15.4–5). It is far from impossible that Jovian's name was one of those considered, however briefly.

Apart from misrepresenting Jovian's importance, whether or not we believe Themistius' claim, Ammianus also omits to tell us how the deadlock in high circles was ultimately resolved. The narrative moves straight from Jovian's *coup d'état* to details of continuing Persian–Roman clashes, without further comment. From subsequent career patterns, however, it is quite clear what must have happened. Arintheus and Victor – like Jovian himself, former adherents of Constantius II – both survived to serve prominently in the new imperial regime. Of the two Gallic generals, however, while Dagalaifus was promoted from *comes domesticorum* to *magister equitum* and again figured prominently under Jovian, Nevitta disappeared from sight and was never heard of again.[5] The two-all deadlock was thus broken by Dagalaifus swapping sides and Nevitta being outmanoeuvred.

The different accounts of Jovian's elevation are consistent with a number of possible historical reconstructions, depending upon where, on the basis of the other sources, one thinks the line between literature and history should be drawn in Ammianus' version. At the far end of the spectrum of possibility stands the 'big lie'. In this case, one would conclude that the other sources are in fact more or less correct in stressing the unanimity of the choice. There never was a minority coup in Jovian's favour, and, after Salutius Secundus demurred, the choice fell on the already prominent Jovian, whom Dagalaifus eventually decided he could support. The only loss involved was Nevitta's retirement. This is perhaps too much of a distortion with which to accuse Ammianus, but, at the very least, if at the other end of the spectrum, he certainly told a lesser lie. By any account, he is guilty of exaggerating Jovian's anonymity, and of omitting to report how Julian's leftover advisers reacted to Jovian's seizure of the purple. Indeed, given that they were all three Constantius' men, it is quite possible that Arintheus or Victor (or both) were involved in pushing forward Jovian as a means, *de facto*, of breaking the deadlock.

Whether one opts for the big lie or the smaller alternative, it is apparent that Ammianus adopted a strategy of subterfuge and omission to influence the nature of his audience's thoughts about Jovian. The direction in which he was attempting to push his audience, indeed, is very clear, both from the account of the election and his other comments elsewhere. For Ammianus, Jovian was not, despite first appearances, a legitimate Roman emperor. For Ammianus, as the election account stresses, Jovian was not properly chosen either for dynastic reasons or by mature deliberation of a properly constituted council of leading military and civilian dignitaries. He was, on the contrary, the beneficiary of a *coup d'état*. Consonant with this, Ammianus later tells us that for a long time his purple imperial robes did not fit properly, because he was too tall (25.10.14). Usurpers in Ammianus always have trouble with their purple clothing, not least Julian's uncle Procopius pathetically waving a piece of purple cloth about in Constantinople.[6] Likewise, crucial ceremonies did not work properly. Jovian's consular celebrations

(1 January 364) were ruined by the howling of his infant son, where, once again, literary invention may have intruded.[7] Or again, Ammianus carefully builds up a sense of Jovian rushing to his doom, a predetermined, if rather mysterious, death on the road to Constantinople.[8] A fated early death merely underlines that, in Ammianus' view, Jovian was never meant to have been emperor in the first place. As Ammianus comments at the moment of election, Jovian was chosen 'as if by the blind decree of fortune' (*his ita caeco quodam iudicio fortunae peractis*; 25.5.8), rather than the protecting divinity of the state. Julian, by contrast, was joined, according to Ammianus, by this divinity on the eve of becoming Augustus in Gaul, and the being left him on the eve of his death (20.5.10; 25.2.3–4). Late Roman state ideology, whether pagan or Christian, claimed divine inspiration underpinned its existence,[9] so this is another way of making the point that Jovian was not a properly legitimate emperor. The same conclusion is also suggested by the comment, put in the mouth of an anonymous wise soldier, that any election should have been delayed until the Persian expeditionary army met up with the second force which had been left behind in the north.[10]

In Ammianus' view, therefore, Jovian was not a legitimate, divinely chosen Roman emperor, but the lucky recipient of a chance promotion. The careful crafting of the election narrative thus comes into focus. For Ammianus, it was crucial both to make Jovian's background as anonymous as possible, and to conceal the working-out of the deadlocked process of political negotiation. It is this overall purpose, indeed, which makes it impossible to be certain of the exact course of Jovian's promotion, despite, or rather because of, the particular circumstantial details Ammianus chose to include (and hence, by implication, to omit). Historical detail has been subordinated to an authorial strategy designed to transmit the essence of what Ammianus wanted his audience to understand about Jovian. All appearances to the contrary notwithstanding (appearances that were clearly accepted by all our other sources, including the pagan Eunapius),[11] Jovian was not for Ammianus a legitimate emperor. Why Ammianus chose to write up Jovian's election in this way becomes clear when a similar examination is conducted of his account of the peace deal the new emperor subsequently negotiated with Persia.

Peace with Persia

Ammianus' account of the peace treaty Jovian negotiated with Persia, immediately after his accession to the throne, is straightforward. The Roman army, still on Persian territory, needed to be brought to safety. According to Ammianus, this could and should have been done either by crossing the river Tigris, as a group of Gauls did without difficulty (25.6.12–15), or by a swift retreat to Roman territory. The province of Corduene, Ammianus notes, was only 100 miles away.[12] In any event, very far from being frightened, the soldiers of the Roman army were in vengeful mood after Julian's death, and the omens foretold that should they march out to battle they would be victorious. That Shapur was, on the contrary, frightened of them, because of the many battles they had won on the advance to and retreat from Ctesiphon, was shown by the fact that it was the Persian who opened peace negotiations (25.7.1–5). Jovian, however, was much more worried about establishing his rule at home than Roman honour abroad. He thus caved in to Persian diplomatic pressure, in order to extract himself quickly, with his army intact, rather than fighting it out as he should have done (25.7.6, 9–14; cf. 25.9.9–11).

Ammianus' reporting of events here is much more obviously problematic than his account of Jovian's accession. Shapur may have opened negotiations, but it was not through fear. The final terms – involving a Roman surrender of five provinces, a series of fortified strongpoints, and the cities of Nisibis and Singara (25.7.9) – demonstrate clearly the extent of his advantage. Sapor presumably calculated that he could make the gains he wanted by negotiation at no further loss to himself, rather than having to risk battle against increasingly desperate Roman opponents.[13]

Ammianus' vision of possible routes of retreat is equally unconvincing. Although the Gauls crossed the Tigris successfully, this was clearly an isolated incident, whose significance Ammianus overstates. When Roman deserters subsequently crossed the river, Persian and Saracen guards, although beaten earlier by the Gauls, killed some and captured the rest (25.8.1). Corduene, likewise, was more like 160 miles away,[14] and Ammianus underestimates the time needed for any retreat. On 1 July, in the face of Persian pressure, the Roman army had managed only 30 *stadia* (= $3\frac{3}{4}$ miles) in an entire day (25.6.9), and had then been prevented by Persian harassment from moving for four days in a row (25.6.11). At that kind of rate, a fighting retreat to Corduene would have taken at least two months.

At the moment negotiations began, moreover, the Roman army had already run out of food (25.2.1; 7.4, 7), and large-scale desertions had begun (25.8.1), so that a fighting retreat of 160 miles was not a serious option. The Romans had repulsed the Persians in any number of tactical engagements during the long march to and from Ctesiphon, but, in strategic terms, they were already beaten. The Persians did not need to risk a major engagement in search of a knock-out military victory, but had merely to delay their opponents until the food ran out. At the moment Jovian came to the throne, the Roman army was far from safety, faced intense Persian pressure and was beginning to starve. The new emperor had no choice but to make the humiliating peace that duly followed, and Ammianus' bluster cannot hide the real situation.

Both the extent of the distortion in Ammianus' account of the Persian peace, and the overall point of it, are clear enough. Julian is Ammianus' hero, not least for his military endeavours.[15] Responsibility for the defeat of the Roman army had therefore to be shifted to another individual, to preserve his favourite's heroic reputation. Jovian was the obvious candidate for the role of scapegoat, and Ammianus duly constructed the narrative to transfer responsibility for military failure to him. For Ammianus, Jovian was too concerned with internal politics to march out and win the victory which, even after his accession, the omens still heralded for him (26.5.1). Exactly the same line, if in slightly less sophisticated form, can be found in the Eunapian tradition, where, again, it is asserted that the Roman army was totally victorious until Jovian took the throne and betrayed Julian's heritage (Zosimus 3.32.1–6: after Eunapius). The overriding need to explain why the reign of the hero Julian ended in defeat required the identification of a suitable villain. Jovian, especially given the brevity of his reign, could not but be cast in this role. Indeed, the need to fit him for it surely underlies Ammianus' presentation of Jovian's accession, where the historian, as we have seen, goes out of his way to emphasize its overall illegitimacy.

Ammianus' construction of the peace deal, like that of his accession, was thus subordinated to the wider role Jovian was required to play in the narrative: getting Julian off the hook. Within this construction, there are some very literary moments. Shapur's supposed fear of the Romans which leads him to open peace negotiations is pure invention. Likewise, one can only have the deepest suspicion of the report that an Antiochene statue of the emperor (C. Galerius Valerius) Maximian, who had originally conquered the provinces returned to Persia in the peace, dropped the orb of power at the moment the peace was signed (25.10.2: although a protestor with a hacksaw is, I suppose, not impossible). I wonder too about the omens telling Jovian he could still win if he marched the army out to battle.

In this case, however, it is not so much – as with the accession narrative – a question of considering the balance between historical reporting and literary invention, as of the historian's basic historical judgement. The only real question here is whether, or to what extent, Ammianus actually believed his own account of events. Ammianus, ideologically committed to the Julianic myth, would certainly have *wanted* to believe in his own reconstruction where the fault lay entirely with Jovian. But did he really believe that victory could still have gone to the Romans, if only Jovian had acted properly? As we have seen, the real strategic situation emerges clearly from many of the details Ammianus records of the Roman retreat, as opposed to his overall judgement upon it. This must make it possible that he was, at least to some degree, aware of the hollowness of his attempts to salvage Julian's reputation.

On the other hand, it probably was just about possible for Ammianus to believe in his own vision. Professionally, he was an aide-de-camp, not a strategic analyst close to central decision-making.[16] It is not unbelievable, therefore, that he might have been misled by his own day-to-day tactical experience, where the Romans seemed consistently to beat the Persians,[17] into mistaking the truly disastrous position in which the Roman army found itself by the time of Julian's death. The kind of parallel which comes to mind is the defeat of the German army in western Europe in 1918. Recently victorious in the East, experience on the ground in spring and summer 1918 seemed to ordinary soldiers to be one of similar success. They were not aware of the logistic crisis building up, nor of the disastrous wastage of reserve manpower, both of which meant that apparent advances belied total defeat. In this instance, the gap between individual experience and overall reality later made possible the myth that the German army had not been defeated in 1918, but 'stabbed in the back' by the politicians. A similar gap between individual experience and strategic reality may likewise have made it possible for Ammianus to believe that Jovian was responsible for the Roman disasters.

This may also help explain a peculiar feature of the propaganda of Jovian's regime. The harsh terms of the peace treaty demonstrated to all that the Persian campaign had resulted in a major Roman reverse. Yet, rather than simply admitting the defeat, and blaming the whole thing on Julian, which would seem the obvious propaganda strategy (and which was the line subsequently taken by the Christian commentators: Socrates, *Hist. Eccl.* 3.22; Gregory Nazianzus, *Or.* 5.15), Jovian's regime chose instead to try to claim the campaign and resulting peace as a victory. This emerges from Themistius' brief comments on the subject, and is confirmed by Jovian's coinage.[18] 'Victory' was, of course, the central and most necessary of imperial virtues,[19] and this would have made it embarrassing for any new regime to start off by admitting defeat. Jovian's regime was also composed of many men who had previously served Julian.[20] The chosen propaganda line also suggests, however, that leading members of the new regime had concluded that it would be too difficult to persuade people that responsibility for the defeat really lay with Julian, when it was Jovian who had actually agreed the peace. One factor in that decision would surely have been the huge military reputation Julian had established for himself in Gaul in the course of inflicting huge defeats on Franks and Alamanni. Another was perhaps the personal experience of the soldiers on the Persian campaign. If, like elements of the German army in 1918, they really did not perceive themselves to have been defeated, this, together with the other factors, might have forced the regime into the line it eventually took.

This final suggestion cannot be proved, obviously enough, and should not be pressed. The overarching point is that, in Ammianus' reconstruction, the narrative of the Persian peace has been subordinated to the greater need of safeguarding Julian's reputation. This may not have involved our author in too conscious a process of lying. His personal experience may well have been of an army that still seemed intact, and he may have lacked sufficient insight to realize that it was on the point of collapse. On the other hand, Ammianus knew well its supply problems. Likewise, Rowland Smith's identification (chapter 8 in this volume) of an underlying ambivalence in Ammianus' account of Julian's whole Persian campaign might also indicate that the historian was not without suspicions of where matters really stood. Ammianus, I suspect, probably did consciously believe that Jovian had betrayed a victory that Julian had left within his grasp, while at the same time entertaining some barely suppressed doubts on the matter. If not deliberately mendacious, Ammianus' account of Jovian's peace, like that of his accession, cannot be understood apart from its role as a counterpoint to the Julianic narrative.

Jovian and religion

The same may also be true, if in a rather different way, of Ammianus' account of Jovian's religious policies. In this case, comparisons, again particularly with Themistius, suggest further thoughts on quite how deliberately constructed a piece of writing the narrative of Jovian is.

Ammianus, in fact, has little to say about the religious stance of Jovian's regime. In the brief obituary which follows Jovian's mysterious death, our historian merely notes that the emperor was a devoted Christian, who paid his religion a reasonable amount of attention (*christianae legis itidem studiosus et non numquam honorificus*; 25.10.14). Other sources fill out this account of Jovian's personal preferences with rather more detail about how they translated into religious policy. According to Socrates, and there is no reason to disbelieve him, the emperor extended and maintained Julian's recall of the pro-Nicene churchmen who had been exiled under Constantius II. He refused, however, to take sides between the different factions, and held some important meetings at Antioch in the autumn of 363 where this position was vigorously asserted.[21]

Much more to the point is the oration given by Themistius to celebrate Jovian's consulship on 1 January 364. This speech includes a lengthy disquisition on the merits of a public policy of religious toleration, one which would not seek to interfere with the private consciences of loyal subjects. Themistius even asserted that God wanted men to approach Him via a number of different routes (*Or.* 5.67b–70c). Themistius' words have usually been taken as a sign that Jovian's regime officially adopted a policy of religious toleration towards traditional Graeco-Roman cults ('pagans'), as Valentinian and Valens were subsequently to do. Such a view can be bolstered by Eunapius' report that certain sophistic philosophers of his own religious persuasion, originally supporters of Julian, continued to find favour under his successor.[22] Vanderspoel has recently argued, however, that traditional understandings of the speech are mistaken. There are no laws, he notes, preserved in the *Theodosian Code* for the period before 1 January 364 (the date of the speech) which indicate that a policy of tolerating pagans had been espoused by Jovian. Part of the speech is also cast in the form of a plea to the emperor, which suggests to Vanderspoel that the policy of toleration it advocates had not been officially adopted. Themistius' statements make it clear that Jovian had already done something to mark himself out as a religious moderate, but these refer, Vanderspoel argues, to no more than his refusal to take a stance in Christian faction. More generally, Vanderspoel suggests that Jovian's irregular election represented a Christian coup against the pagan Julianic establishment, and hence wonders if the emperor's mysterious early death represents the latter's revenge on a Christian upstart.[23]

I am convinced that this reinterpretation is ill-founded. Of the arguments proposed, the lack of a law on religious toleration is perhaps the weakest. Vanderspoel here takes no account of the difficulties of the transmission process separating the original law of the mid-fourth century and *c.* 430 when the Theodosian commissioners went about their business. This was particularly true in the area of religious policy, where the Theodosian run of pro-Christian and overtly anti-pagan legislation from the 390s had in the meantime rendered obsolete previous, milder imperial pronouncements on the subject. Not surprisingly, the latter had tended not to be preserved. Take the case of Jovian's successors: the brothers Valentinian and Valens. We know from Ammianus that they adopted a policy of religious toleration (30.9.5), and it is reflected in one of the items preserved by the Theodosian commissioners (*Cod. Theod.* 9.16.9). This comprises not the emperors' original law of toleration, however, but merely a cross-reference to it in a later pronouncement. The actual law itself did not survive. The lack of a law of toleration from Jovian amounts to no more than a very weak argument from silence.

Themistius' consular celebration speech also contains a whole series of indicative active verbal usages: some in the past tense, some in the present. These make it clear that Jovian had already done something, by January 364, which involved, and continued to involve, active toleration not just of Christian sectaries, but also of non-Christian, traditional Graeco-Roman believers.[24] Nor should Themistius' seeming plea for toleration be taken at face value. The plea is a stance adopted quite often by Themistius in his later speeches, but consideration of the different examples in context demonstrates that it was used by him as a rhetorical device, and should not be read as a straightforward attempt to change imperial policy.[25] Indeed, a comparison of Themistius' fifth *Oration* with those given subsequently to the certainly tolerant Valens would suggest that, if anything, Jovian was the more tolerant. The speech to Jovian employs a much greater freedom of tone in its religious disquisition than Themistius dared to on other occasions. Themistius often identified similarities between elements of traditional Graeco-Roman religion and Christianity, something perfectly acceptable to Christians.[26] One remarkable passage of *Oration* 5, however, refers in one breath to the religions of the 'Syrians' (= Christians), 'Greeks' and 'Egyptians', treating Hellenism and Egyptian mystery cults as more or less equals of Christianity (*Or.* 5.70a). This is not a thought he dared to air on other occasions, and the speech also includes his only reference to Christian infighting.[27]

To my mind, there is no doubt, therefore, that the traditional interpretation of *Oration* 5 is in fact correct. As Eunapius' reference to the honours granted philosophers confirms, the emperor Jovian, though certainly himself a Christian, espoused a policy of religious toleration which included not only a refusal to swing state power behind any particular branch of Christian belief, but also the positive toleration of traditional paganism. Indeed, the whiff of religious freedom so evident in Themistius' speech suggests that, if anyone had a reason to assassinate Jovian, it would have been convinced Christian elements at court, not surviving members of Julian's pagan establishment.[28]

The main point for present purposes, however, is that, once it has been established that Jovian's regime was tolerant of paganism, this offers further insight into how Ammianus chose to construct his narrative of the emperor's brief reign. Elsewhere in the *Res Gestae*, Ammianus' overt stance in religious matters, encompassing all of his explicit statements on the question, is to advocate that emperors should adopt religious toleration as official state policy. Jovian's successors, Valentinian and Valens, are highly commended for doing precisely this.[29] The fact that Ammianus does not even mention that Jovian followed a similar, if not still more tolerant, line towards paganism now becomes rather interesting.

Arguments from omission are inherently weaker than those based on inclusion. It is always possible that a supposedly significant silence represents no more than ignorance. It does not seem at all plausible, however, that the well-connected Ammianus, fully acquainted with other aspects of the regime such as its claims to have won victory in Persia, should have been unaware of the fact that its official religious policy involved tolerating pagans. Much more likely is that Ammianus simply chose to omit this fact because it did not fit the picture of the emperor he was seeking to construct. As we have seen, Ammianus' Jovian simply had to be illegitimate and hopeless, in order to make him a sufficient scapegoat for failings that might otherwise have been ascribed to Julian. Given this agenda, it did not fit in with Ammianus' purposes to have Jovian adopt a religious policy which, in his every explicit statement on the matter, our author advocated as the correct approach.[30]

Conclusion

Overall, Ammianus' account of the emperor Jovian must be seen as a carefully crafted combination of history and literature. The weight of circumstantial historical detail, as ever in Ammianus' text, is striking: certainly much greater than that to be found in the other sources for this reign. Much of it is probably also correct, and, as we have seen in the case of the state of the Roman army at Jovian's accession, the preserved detail sometimes even undermines the interpretative structures Ammianus wished to erect upon it. This does not mean, however, that we are dealing with mere factual reporting.

Inventive literary elements are equally present: the omens portending victory, Shapur's fear of the Romans, the dropping of the orb, the shortness of Jovian's imperial robes, and perhaps even the howling of his son during the consular ceremonies. Omissions are equally well chosen. Failing to report how the emergency council responded to Jovian's appearance in purple adds much to the air of illegitimacy surrounding his accession, and ignoring his religious policy allows Ammianus to escape from the necessity of praising him for a matter of considerable importance.

The fundamental point, of course, is that the narrative construction of Jovian's reign is not a self-standing piece. Ammianus' grander design required Jovian to serve as a counterpoint to his great hero, the emperor Julian. Jovian had to be sufficiently incompetent, and hence illegitimate, for Ammianus to be able to pin upon him the entire blame for the disastrous end to Julian's Persian campaign. The fictive or exaggerated literary elements, together with the omissions, and, no less, the choice of which particular circumstantial details to include, all served to bring out the deeper 'truth' as Ammianus saw it. Jovian was not a properly legitimate emperor and from this sprang wrong choices of policy. It was Jovian's wrong choices, and not any failing on the part of the emperor Julian, which caused the loss of Nisibis and Singara, five satrapies and fifteen forts.

Notes

1 English translation and commentary in P.J. Heather and D. Moncur, *Themistius: Select Orations* (Translated Texts for Historians), Liverpool 1999 (forthcoming), ch. 3.
2 As will become clear, what follows owes much to the perceptive commentary of J.F. Matthews, *The Roman Empire of Ammianus*, London 1989, 183–8.
3 *Ibid.*, 184.
4 My own general view of Themistius' career and significance: P.J. Heather, 'Themistius: A Political Philosopher', in Mary Whitby (ed.), *The Propaganda of Power. The Role of Panegyric in Late Antiquity*, Leiden 1998, 126–50.
5 Arintheus and Victor: *PLRE* I, 102–3, 957–9. Dagalaifus and Nevitta: *PLRE* I, 239, 626–7.
6 Amm. Marc. 26.6.12–20; cf. G. Sabbah, *La méthode d'Ammien Marcellin. Recherches sur la construction du discours historique dans les Res Gestae*, Paris 1978, 362–3; Matthews, *The Roman Empire of Ammianus*, 193–5, 236–7.
7 Amm. Marc. 25.10.11. According to Themistius, the infant Varronianus was 'courageous' and 'imperturbable' during the ceremonies (*Or.* 5.1b). As was pointed out in the conference, the former epithet might indeed imply a certain amount of distress. But Themistius, talking on the day to those present at the ceremony, would have been opening the whole event to ridicule if the child had actually been as distressed as Ammianus implies.
8 Amm. Marc. 25.10.4, 10.12. This picks up and manipulates one of the closing themes of Themistius' *Oration* 5, which portrays Jovian rushing to greet his lover, the city of Constantinople (*Or.* 5.70c–71a).
9 It claimed the empire was a divinely ordained institution created for the absolute good of human beings; see, amongst many others, F. Dvornik, *Early Christian and Byzantine Political Philosophy: Origins and Background*, Washington DC 1966; S. MacCormack, *Art and Ceremony in Late Antiquity*, Berkeley 1983.

10 Amm. Marc. 25.5.3; cf. the comments of J. Fontaine, *Ammien Marcellin, Histoire IV (Livres XXIII–XXV)*, 2 vols, Paris 1977, vol. 2, 246 n. 608.
11 Accepted too by modern commentators: e.g. J. Straub, *Vom Herrscherideal in der Spätantike*, Stuttgart 1964 (2nd edn), 11–14.
12 Matthews, *The Roman Empire of Ammianus*, 186, suggests that Ammianus was thinking that the two fruitless days spent trying to build bridges over the Tigris could have been used for the retreat (25.7.4). Amm. Marc. 25.7.7–8 suggests that he also had in mind the further four days spent in negotiations with the Persians.
13 Cf. Matthews, *The Roman Empire of Ammianus*, 185–6.
14 *Ibid.*, 186.
15 E.g. Julian's action in Gaul and the victorious advance on Ctesiphon. For commentary on Ammianus' account of these, see *ibid.*, chs 6 and 8.
16 See most recently *ibid.*, chs 2 and 18.
17 Amm. Marc. 24.7–25.2 *passim*; especially after the catalogue of success which had marked the advance: 24.1–6.
18 Themistius, *Or.* 5.66a–c; cf. J. Vanderspoel, *Themistius and the Imperial Court. Oratory, Civic Duty, and Paideia from Constantius to Theodosius*, Ann Arbor 1995, 144–6. Coinage: RIC 8, 230–1, 281, 424, 438, 464–75, 533 (*restitutor reipublicae*; *victoria augusti*; *victoria romanorum*). Note too Amm. Marc. 25.8.12 reporting that Jovian pretended that victory had been won in Persia.
19 'Victory' is the theme of M. McCormick, *Eternal Victory. Triumphal Rulership in Late Antiquity, Byzantium and the Early Medieval West*, Cambridge 1986.
20 These included Salutius Secundus, Arintheus, Victor and Dagalaifus (cf. above, pp. 106–7). These are perhaps the four men singled out as present at Jovian's consular celebrations: Themistius, *Or.* 5.67a with comment in Heather and Moncur, *Themistius, ad loc.*
21 Socrates, *Hist. Eccl.* 3.24; cf. T.D. Barnes, *Athanasius and Constantius: Theology and Politics in the Constantinian Empire*, Cambridge (Mass.) 1993, 159–60.
22 Eunapius, *V. Sophist.* 478; cf. A.H.M. Jones, *The Later Roman Empire. A Social Economic and Administrative Survey*, Oxford 1964, 149–50. Socrates, *Hist. Eccl.* 3.24 on the contrary reports that Julian's philosophers were once again expelled and the temples shut. Themistius, *Or.* 5.70b (with comment in Heather and Moncur, *Themistius, ad. loc.*) makes it clear that, like Valentinian and Valens (*Cod. Theod.* 9.16.7 on night-time sacrifice etc.), Jovian defined which elements of traditional religious cult were acceptable, shutting down some but not all. This explains the apparent contradiction.
23 Vanderspoel, *Themistius*, 148–52, identifying pleas for toleration at *Or.* 5.68d–69a, 69c.
24 Themistius, *Or.* 5.67c, 68c, 68d, 69b (three examples). For translation and comment, see Heather and Moncur, *Themistius, ad loc.*
25 See Heather, 'Themistius', in Whitby (ed.), *The Propaganda of Power*. In this case, for instance, Themistius was pleading the value of something that Jovian was already doing, reinforcing, not trying to change, imperial policy.
26 For further comment, see *ibid.*
27 *Or.* 5.70a, 68c–d; as Vanderspoel, *Themistius*, 151–2, notes, this is clearly a reference to the matters related by Socrates, *Hist. Eccl.* 3.24 (see n. 21).
28 Rather than subscribing to a conspiracy theory, however, my own suspicion is that Jovian simply died from accidental carbon monoxide poisoning; cf. Matthews, *The Roman Empire of Ammianus*, 188, citing *Misopogon* 340d–342a on Julian's close brush with a similar fate in Paris.
29 Amm. Marc. 30.9.5; cf. E.D. Hunt, 'Christians and Christianity in Ammianus Marcellinus', *CQ* 35 (1985), 186–200.
30 Jovian's regime in part justified its advocacy of toleration by attacking Julian's partisan support of non-Christian cult: *Or.* 5.70b with comments in Heather and Moncur, *Themistius, ad loc.* This perhaps gave Ammianus a second reason not to refer to it.

10

NEC METU NEC ADULANDI FOEDITATE CONSTRICTA

The image of Valentinian I from Symmachus to Ammianus

Mark Humphries

Introduction

It is Ammianus Marcellinus himself who points to the contrast between panegyrical and historical appraisals of Valentinian I (364–75). At the beginning of his catalogue of this emperor's vices and virtues, he reflects 'that posterity is usually an uncorrupted judge of the past, being constrained neither by fear nor by odious flattery' (*nec metu nec adulandi foeditate constricta*: 30.8.1). The necessary corollary of this is that contemporary opinion is – or may be – influenced by fear and flattery. Moreover, flattery and fear went together as negative reflections of the imperial power. As Ammianus said of Constantius II, 'this fatal fault of cruelty, which in others sometimes grew less with advancing age, in his case became more violent, since a group of flatterers (*cohors adulatorum*) intensified his stubborn resolution' (14.5.5).

This tension between panegyric (the literary embodiment of flattery) and history looms large in Ammianus' final books.[1] At the outset of his narrative of Valentinian's reign, he famously remarks on the dangers of writing a nearly contemporary narrative, and how the omission of apparently trivial details might give offence (26.1.1–2). When he begins his account of the depredations of Valentinian's officials in Rome, Ammianus again casts a nervous eye in the direction of his audience. He talks of the fear (*metus*) which fills him as he approaches a topic which, while it concerns events in the past (*apud veteres*), still has its reverberations in the present (28.1.2). Ammianus is thinking primarily of Rome's senatorial aristocrats, and his attitude towards them is ambivalent. Whereas a few senators, such as L. Aurelius Avianus Symmachus, urban prefect in 364–5, received fulsome praise (27.3.3–4), most of them he denounced as dissipated layabouts.[2] Little wonder, for theirs too was a world in which pernicious adulation flourished, as groups of 'lazy chatterboxes' (*otiosi garruli*) inflated the pride of senators by extolling the beauties of their houses in grossly exaggerated terms.[3] That the tensions between fearful adulation and a duty to the truth should figure so prominently in Ammianus' last books reflects his circumstances at the time of writing, for he was composing and publishing his account in Rome, a city which had suffered badly under Valentinian I.

Taking Ammianus' words as my starting-point, I will explore the relationship between his appraisal of Valentinian's reign and one where the restrictive influence of fear and flattery might seem more apparent, namely that preserved in the three panegyrics penned by the Roman senator Q. Aurelius Symmachus in 369–70.[4] It seems worthwhile to examine this question in detail, paying close attention to the different contexts within which each author wrote. It will emerge that the divergences between the emperor's image in panegyric and history reflect how Symmachus depicted a Valentinian for consumption at the imperial court, while Ammianus' portrait was determined in large measure by the expectations of his Roman audience.

From Trier to Rome: Symmachus and Valentinian I

The relationship between Symmachus and his emperors was a complex one.[5] Whether as *praefectus urbi* or as *princeps senatus*, he had extensive contact with the imperial court, not least in a number of delegations he led in person to successive emperors. Such contacts could be dangerous. In 388, after Theodosius I's victory over the remarkably successful western usurper Magnus Maximus, Symmachus found himself shunned by many of his senatorial colleagues. No wonder, for only a year before Symmachus had delivered a panegyric in Maximus' honour as the representative of the senate, pledging their corporate allegiance to a man who had become effective master of the western provinces. In the wake of Maximus' defeat, the senate was determined to make this expression of loyalty Symmachus' personal crime, not theirs as a group. Yet Theodosius proved indulgent and accepted Symmachus' abject apology, sealed with yet another panegyric.[6]

Symmachus had served as a senatorial ambassador many times before his ill-advised mission to Magnus Maximus. In 369 and 370, he visited Valentinian I's court in Gaul and delivered three panegyrics praising the emperor and his son, Gratian. He was the obvious choice for such a mission: his father, the distinguished aristocrat L. Aurelius Avianus Symmachus, had been senatorial envoy to court several times (*CIL* 6.1698), and from him the younger Symmachus had inherited formidable skills as an orator (Prudentius, *C. Symm.* 1.432–4; Macrobius, *Sat.* 5.1.7). The first two speeches – one (*Or.* 1) on Valentinian, the other (*Or.* 3) on Gratian – were delivered in late February 369.[7] It was an auspicious occasion, since Valentinian was celebrating the beginning of his fifth year as emperor (*quinquennalia*). But it was also a delicate one, in that Symmachus would be called upon to proclaim allegiance to the recent elevation of Gratian: as Ammianus would make clear, this had been a matter of doubtful legality (27.6.16). After delivering his speeches, Symmachus stayed on in Gaul for almost a year, delivering another panegyric before Valentinian (*Or.* 2), this time on the emperor's assumption of his third consulship on 1 January 370. It is clear from his own correspondence and references within the panegyric that Symmachus had been brought on the emperor's tour of inspection along the Rhine frontier in the summer of 369.[8] He also struck up a lasting friendship with Gratian's tutor, the poet Ausonius, who himself accompanied the emperor's entourage that summer.[9]

Why Symmachus remained in Gaul is nowhere stated explicitly. Hagith Sivan suggests that the senator had social networking in mind, and cites his friendship with Ausonius as proof.[10] Yet the emperor too may have had a hand in the decision. If he were shown what the emperor was doing, Symmachus could return to Rome and disseminate an image of Valentinian as a warrior emperor devoted to the empire's defence.[11] Such had been the message Symmachus broadcast in the panegyrics of 369. The senator had enthused about how, thanks to the efforts of Valentinian and his son, the Rhine 'flows from our [Roman] Alps into our [Roman] ocean' (*Or.* 3.9; cf. 2.28). He had been effusive also in his praise of Valentinian's decision, at the outbreak of Procopius' usurpation in 365, to remain on the Rhine frontier, thus following the recommendations of his advisers that he choose the care of his subjects over that of his family (*Or.* 1.14, 17–18). The whole thrust of these panegyrics was to promote the virtues of an emperor whose court was held in military camps on campaign (*Or.* 1.14: *regalis aula sub pellibus*). If Valentinian could keep Symmachus on the Rhine for the campaigning season of 369, he might give the senator a compelling demonstration of how effectively the empire was being defended.[12]

The second panegyric on Valentinian shows the extent of the emperor's success.[13] Symmachus had been treated to spectacles such as the destruction of a barbarian warband (*Or.* 2.10) and the submissive appearance of a Burgundian embassy asking for peace (*Or.* 2.13). He had also witnessed the construction of fortifications which led him to compare Valentinian with Archimedes at Syracuse (*Or.* 2.18). He would be able to return to Rome, then, with impressive proof of Valentinian's prowess as a defender of the imperial frontiers. This was precisely what Valentinian wanted, and Symmachus obligingly told him of the reports he would be able to make: 'I will say to the Roman senate and people, "Send forth the insignia of office (*fasces*) into new provinces, and make ready administrators (*iudices*) for the lands beyond the Rhine!"' (*Or.* 2.31).

It is unimportant to decide to what extent Symmachus' enthusiasm for Valentinian was affected. What is crucial, rather, is to recognize the resonance between Symmachus' orations and other propaganda disseminated by the imperial court. Whether or not the effect was intentional,[14] much the same image of Valentinian's energy emerges from Ausonius' *Mosella*, which refers to joint victories of the emperor and his son (*Mos.* 422). A more significant echo is found in Valentinian's early coinage, much of it issued from the newly reopened Gallic mints of Trier and Lugdunum.[15] The first gold coin struck in Valentinian's reign proclaimed him on its reverse as RESTITUTOR REIPUBLICAE ('restorer of the state') and showed the emperor as a triumphant general, with a military standard in one hand, and in the other a globe upon which stands a figure of Victory crowning him with a wreath. Not long after, another issue was minted proclaiming SECURITAS REIPUBLICAE ('safety of the state'): this was illustrated by a figure, clearly identifiable from his diadem as the emperor, holding a standard and dragging a barbarian captive by the hair.[16]

The images of the emperor projected by the coinage and panegyrics converged on the presentation of Valentinian as an energetic soldier emperor. Effectively, then, Symmachus had given rhetorical voice to Valentinian's own propaganda.[17] While it is impossible to be certain how Symmachus' orations were disseminated after their initial delivery at court, it is probable that the panegyrics on Valentinian and Gratian were circulated to members of the senatorial aristocracy, in much the same way as was his speech of 376 supporting the praetorship of Trygetius (*Or.* 5).[18] In this way, not only did Symmachus expound to Valentinian himself the virtues of his reign, but he would have broadcast this image to the senators of Rome.

Yet like all such expressions of loyalty to a regime, Symmachus' view of Valentinian was subject to revision once the emperor himself was dead. Following the emperor's fatal paroxysm at Brigetio on the Danube frontier in November 375, the senate would have waited tensely to see what policies would be implemented by the new western emperor, Gratian. In a letter to Ausonius, Symmachus described with startling immediacy the mood on 1 January 376 as the senators waited for him to read out the imperial *oratio* in which Gratian outlined his policies.[19] It contained exactly what the senate wanted to hear. Valentinian's Pannonian officials who had terrorized the Roman aristocracy were to be removed from power.[20] The worst of these rogues, Maximinus, who had been *praefectus annonae* and *vicarius urbis* successively between 368 and 371, did not survive long into the new reign, and by mid-376 he had been executed.[21] With a change of regime, then, came a remarkable volte-face in imperial attitudes towards the senate; it was time not only to celebrate, but also to review the image of Valentinian I.

This reversal of imperial policies towards the senate had encouraged many to speak frankly of their complaints about the previous administration. Symmachus himself soon proved an outspoken critic of the old regime, and his former warm enthusiasm for Valentinian was replaced by contempt, albeit a contempt expressed primarily in denigrations of the emperor's officials. Later in 376, in a speech celebrating his father's recent return to the city (*Or.* 4), Symmachus gave full vent to his satisfaction that Valentinian's policies at Rome had been overturned. In a speech that John Matthews has characterized as 'openly political',[22] Symmachus applauded Gratian for rejecting the more unfortunate burdens of his inheritance (*tantum malos iudices quasi hereditatis onera repudiasti*), before proceeding to celebrate the downfall of Maximinus (*Or.* 4.10–11). Yet it is hard to believe that Symmachus' enthusiasm for Gratian was ever more than ephemeral. In turn, perhaps, Gratian would have become the subject of complaint when Symmachus pronounced his panegyric on Magnus Maximus.

Writing Valentinian: Ammianus and Rome

By the time Symmachus was defending himself against the accusations of treason for his panegyric on Maximus, Rome was home to another author. At least since 383/4, Ammianus had been resident there, compiling material for his western narrative of the reigns of Valentinian I and Gratian.[23] It is possible that Symmachus' panegyrics of 369–70 were among the documentary sources he consulted.[24] It is probably significant that Ammianus' evaluation of Valentinian's frontier policies should come in his account of 369, the year when Symmachus accompanied the emperor's entourage in its progress along the Rhine.[25] But the search for explicit lexical similarities between the orations and the *Res Gestae* is a fruitless undertaking, and in their absence it can only be remarked that Ammianus' echoes of Symmachus are faint ones at best.[26]

It is the second panegyric on Valentinian (*Or.* 2) which gives the most detailed information about the nature of the emperor's frontier policies, and a number of distinct parallels can be seen between Symmachus' account and that given by Ammianus. Both authors dwell on the emperor's construction of fortifications along the Rhine, emphasizing how Valentinian's scheme encompassed both banks of the river (*Or.* 2.20, 28, 31; Amm. Marc. 28.2.1, 5). Valentinian's personal role in the construction of these fortifications is also stressed in both accounts (*Or.* 2.18; Amm. Marc. 28.2.1, 4). The negotiations with the Burgundians, which Symmachus had used as a demonstration of how Valentinian had instilled fear in Rome's enemies (*Or.* 2.13), were also narrated by Ammianus (28.5.8–15).

Yet it is precisely events such as the Burgundian embassy's entreaty that reveal the differences between Symmachus' eulogy and Ammianus' attempt at a more critical appraisal. In the panegyric, the Burgundians plead for peace either because they have heard of Valentinian's military prowess or because they could see the roof tiles of Roman fortifications in the distance (*Or.* 2.13). Ammianus, by contrast, describes the event as a complex sequence of diplomatic manoeuvres, some of them showing Valentinian in a duplicitous light. In this account, Valentinian exploited tribal divisions beyond the Rhine, and sought to induce the Burgundians to invade Alamannic territory, promising that he too would launch a campaign against the Alamanni. Yet when the Burgundians began their attack, they discovered that Valentinian, whose army failed to appear, had duped them (Amm. Marc. 28.5.9–13).

A more marked difference is in the nature of Valentinian's character, which in Ammianus comes across as more unstable and impetuous than it does in the panegyrics.[27] For example, in Ammianus' account, Valentinian's reaction to news of the invasions of Pannonia by the Quadi and Sarmatians in 374 wavered between calm good sense and violent passion. On receiving an initial report from the praetorian prefect Petronius Probus, Valentinian read it carefully, 'as became a cautious general' (*ut cunctatorem decuerat ducem*). By the time he read more detailed reports, however, Valentinian's preference was to set out for the Danube immediately (*evolare protinus festinaret*) even though winter, which would have made marching conditions difficult, was close (*quia ... abeunte autumno*). It was only through the strenuous persuasion (*oratum ... et exoratum*) of the best men at court (*omnes per regiam optimates*) that this perilous course of action was avoided and the Danubian campaign was postponed until the following spring (Amm. Marc. 30.3.2–3).

This is strongly reminiscent of the account Ammianus gives of Valentinian's reaction to Procopius' usurpation in 365. Both the revolt and an Alamannic invasion had been reported to Valentinian on the same day (26.5.8). The emperor dispatched his *magister equitum* Dagalaifus to deal with the Alamanni, but his response to the threat of civil war in the East was less confident. When news reached him, he grew anxious and at first seemed determined to march eastwards to deal with the rebel himself (26.5.9–11). As would be the case again in late 374, it was the court advisers who changed the emperor's mind, persuading and beseeching him (*suadentium et orantium*) that he should remain in Gaul (26.5.12). Whatever the strength of Valentinian's convictions in this decision, he frequently reiterated (*replicabat aliquotiens*) that the Alamanni, as enemies of the whole Roman world, were more deserving of his attention than Procopius, who was merely a threat to the ruling dynasty (26.5.13).

As we saw earlier, Valentinian's willingness to be persuaded to remain on the Rhine had been praised by Symmachus (*Or.* 1.14, 17–18). John Drinkwater has argued that Valentinian's decision to put imperial defence before family interests 'might be regarded as a convenient piece of moralizing',[28] and the emperor's frequent reiteration of his motives will have helped to drive the message home. Yet what Symmachus portrayed as an imperial virtue was, in Ammianus' hands, an indicator of Valentinian's shortcomings. The accounts of imperial vacillation in 365 and 374 are instances of the violent and changeable moods which Ammianus so abhors in his emperors,[29] and for which, more than anything else, he criticizes Valentinian I (30.8.2–7). Valentinian's short temper, and the potentially disastrous results to which it could lead, were epitomized in the manner of his death. Confronted by an unrepentant embassy of Quadi, the emperor flew into a rage; then, just as he appeared to calm down, he was struck by his fatal fit of apoplexy (30.6.3).

Valentinian's death was not only regrettable, but in a sense it reflected an abdication of his imperial responsibilities. Ammianus chastised him 'because he forgot that a ruler should avoid all excess, just as he would a precipice' (30.8.2). When Valentinian failed to do this and died in an unnecessary burst of anger, he left the important task of settling affairs in Pannonia unfinished (30.7.10).

The brutality which Ammianus ascribes to Valentinian's character would have sounded familiar to his Roman audience: they had experienced it through the vicious regime of Maximinus. For Ammianus, indeed, it was the unsuitability of certain of Valentinian's ministers that provided the most palpable sign of Valentinian's violent character. While, on the one hand, he certainly states that Valentinian was *scrupulosus* in promoting personnel to high office (30.9.3), he tempers this with a description of the emperor's susceptibility to cruelty and greed: 'he was never found to be content with a mild punishment, but continually ordered bloodthirsty investigations, one after the other' (30.8.3). Such brutality had been apparent nowhere more explicitly than in the very city in which Ammianus was writing and publishing. The prosecutions under Maximinus and his successors Simplicius and Doryphorianus were the subject of one of Ammianus' longest chapters (28.1). Notwithstanding Ammianus' personal opinions of the more dissolute elements among the Roman aristocracy, there can be no doubt that his catalogue of the brutal trials at Rome reflects senatorial opinion.[30] His account of these trials at the beginning of Book 28 ends with a revealing forward glance to the period after Valentinian's death:

> But the final curses of his victims did not sleep. For, as will be told later at the appropriate place, not only did Maximinus, because of his intolerable arrogance, fall victim to the sword under Gratian, but Simplicius was beheaded in Illyricum, and Doryphorianus was charged with a capital crime and thrown into the Tullianum prison.
>
> (28.1.57)

Ammianus could have heard about these events from anyone at Rome, but his narrative resounds with echoes of Symmachus' account of Gratian's repudiation of his burdensome inheritance (*Or.* 4.10).[31]

Yet for all the brutality of his officials, Valentinian I's reign was in one respect a time on which the senatorial aristocracy could look back with some nostalgia. The 380s had seen a concerted imperial assault on a tradition which many senators held dear. In 382 the devoutly Christian Gratian had removed the altar of Victory, before which the senators sacrificed every morning before they began business. At Gratian's death a year later, the senators saw in his young successor Valentinian II an emperor who might be persuaded to return the altar. In a letter written on behalf of the pagan senators who wanted the altar restored, Symmachus now looked back upon

Valentinian I's reign as an age of model toleration: 'from his seat in heaven, that elder emperor [sc. Valentinian I] looks down upon the tears of the priests and believes that he himself is guilty now that the custom which he liberally preserved has been broken' (*Rel.* 3.20). By the time Ammianus was penning his account of Valentinian's reign, such tolerance had gone forever, and emperors such as Theodosius I were becoming more doctrinaire in their religious policies. There is surely a hint of this in Ammianus' reflection that Valentinian

> remained neutral in religious differences, neither troubling anyone in this matter nor ordering him to reverence this or that. Nor did he bend the necks of his subjects by threatening edicts, but left such affairs undisturbed as he found them.
>
> (30.9.5)

As the icy grip of intolerant Christianity increased its hold on Rome, there will have been many who would have heard this and nodded in sad agreement.[32]

Conclusion

While the absence of precise lexical parallels means that any attempt to identify Symmachus as one of Ammianus' sources must be speculative, it does seem that the historian drew on a collective store of memories which shared many of the senator's opinions.[33] Other authors too will have drawn on such material. Valentinian's foul temper, for example, is recorded also by Sulpicius Severus (*Dial.* 2.5.5–10), while his talent for designing fortifications is noted also in the *Epitome de Caesaribus* (45.6). This is enough to warn us against looking to Ammianus' portrayal of Valentinian for the mere rehearsal of topoi of good and bad imperial rule.

Yet there can be no denying that Ammianus' portrait is bounded by the social milieu in which he wrote and published. His depiction of Valentinian allows for his military heroism and religious tolerance, but qualifies eulogy with criticism of the emperor's violent temper and vilification of his agents at Rome. As such, the emperor's image encompasses the full range of opinions expressed about Valentinian by Symmachus. There is the imperial general praised in 369–70; there is also the emperor whose passing was increasingly celebrated by the senate in the course of 376; and finally, there is the emperor whose tolerance in religious affairs could be viewed with nostalgia in the 380s. If Symmachus' opinions can be taken to reflect a broad cross-section of senatorial opinion, then we find in Ammianus a reflection of the shifting perceptions of Valentinian by his aristocratic subjects at Rome.

What is also important in Ammianus' narrative is the *idée fixe* of the atmosphere of fear and adulation which pervades the Valentinianic narrative. It is applied not only to the emperor himself and to his times, but significantly also to the élite of the city in which Ammianus lived when he was writing his account of Valentinian's reign. If Ammianus wrote that his appraisal of Valentinian would be unrestrained by fear and flattery, he qualified his confidence by stating that this *usually* (*solet*) made posterity the better judge (30.8.1). For the groups of flatterers whom Ammianus had to fear were not just those at court; there were also the lazy chatterboxes who inflated senatorial egos. When Ammianus hoped that his narrative could be an impartial judge (*incorrupta spectatrix*) of Valentinian's reign, he knew that the fears and flatteries by which he might be constrained were not simply those of the imperial court. He also had to negotiate the feelings of his audience. A portrait which balanced both positive and negative senatorial opinion was perhaps the most impartial account for which he could hope.[34]

Notes

1 R. Seager, *Ammianus Marcellinus. Seven Studies in his Language and Thought*, Columbia 1986, 97–102.
2 J.F. Matthews, *Western Aristocracies and Imperial Court, AD 364–425*, Oxford 1975, 1–3.
3 Amm. Marc. 28.4.12; cf. S.P. Ellis, 'Power, Architecture and Decor: How the Late Roman Aristocrat appeared to his Guests', in E.K. Gazda (ed.), *Roman Art in the Private Sphere*, Ann Arbor 1991, 117–34.
4 For other treatments see J.F. Drinkwater, 'Julian and the Franks and Valentinian I and the Alamanni: Ammianus on Romano-German Relations', *Francia* 24 (1997), 1–15; F. Paschoud, 'Valentinien travesti, ou: De la malignité d'Ammien', in J. den Boeft, D. den Hengst and H.C. Teitler (eds), *Cognitio Gestorum. The Historiographic Art of Ammianus Marcellinus*, Amsterdam 1992, 67–84; G. Sabbah, *La méthode d'Ammien Marcellin. Recherches sur la construction du discours historique dans les Res Gestae*, Paris 1978, 332–46.
5 J.A. McGeachy, *Quintus Aurelius Symmachus and the Senatorial Aristocracy of the West* (diss.), Chicago 1942, 6–52.
6 Socrates, *Hist. Eccl.* 5. 14. 6; Symmachus, *Epp.* 2.13, 28, 30–2; 8.69; cf. J.F. Matthews, 'Symmachus and his Enemies', in F. Paschoud (ed.), *Colloque genevois sur Symmache*, Paris 1986, 163–75, at 171–3.
7 O. Seeck, *Q. Aurelii Symmachi quae supersunt*, Berlin 1883, ccx–ccxi.
8 Matthews, *Western Aristocracies*, 32–3.
9 G.W. Bowersock, 'Symmachus and Ausonius', in Paschoud (ed.), *Colloque genevois sur Symmache*, 1–14.
10 H. Sivan, *Ausonius of Bordeaux. Genesis of a Gallic Aristocracy*, London 1993, 111–14.
11 J.F. Matthews, *The Roman Empire of Ammianus*, London 1989, 285–6.
12 See J.F. Drinkwater, 'The Germanic Threat on the Rhine Frontier: A Romano-Gallic Artefact?', in R.W. Mathisen and H. Sivan (eds), *Shifting Frontiers in Late Antiquity*, Aldershot 1996, 20–30, on the reality gap between such propaganda and the actual threat posed by the peoples living across the Rhine. See also Drinkwater (chapter 11 in this volume).
13 S. MacCormack, 'Latin Prose Panegyrics', in T. A. Dorey (ed.), *Empire and Aftermath. Silver Latin II*, London 1975, 143–205, at 173–7, outlines how *Oration* 2 is different in character from *Orations* 1 and 3.
14 R.P.H. Green, *The Works of Ausonius*, Oxford 1991, 456–8, is cautious, seeing the poem as being positive in its appraisal of Valentinian without necessarily being panegyrical; Sivan, *Ausonius of Bordeaux*, 106–8, is more sceptical. See now D. Shanzer, 'The Date and

Literary Context of Ausonius' *Mosella*: Valentinian I's Alamannic Campaigns and an Unnamed Office-Holder', *Historia* 47 (1998), 204–33, at 206–16.

15 *RIC* 9: *Valentinian I – Theodosius I*, London 1951, 3, 35.

16 For illustrations see *RIC* 9: *Valentinian I – Theodosius I*, plates iii. 6 (Trier), iv. 17 (Lugdunum).

17 In general, see S. MacCormack, *Art and Ceremony in Late Antiquity*, Berkeley 1981.

18 Matthews, *The Roman Empire of Ammianus*, 285–6, is confident that *Orations* 1–3 were circulated at Rome. On the circulation of *Oration* 5: Seeck, *Q. Aurelii Symmachi quae supersunt*, vi. Similarly, the *Oration* 4 (*Pro Patre*) may have been circulated among Symmachus' friends at Gratian's court in Gaul: Matthews, *Western Aristocracies*, 68. It may also be significant that the manuscript in which the imperial orations are preserved was produced most probably at Rome: E.A. Lowe, *Codices Latini Antiquiores* 1, Oxford 1934, no. 29.

19 Symmachus, *Ep.* 1.13; P. Bruggisser, 'Gloria noui saeculi. Symmache et le siècle de Gratien (*Epist.* 1.13)', *Museum Helveticum* 44 (1987), 134–49.

20 A. Alföldi, *A Conflict of Ideas in the Late Roman Empire. The Clash between the Senate and Valentinian I*, Oxford 1952, 48–95.

21 Matthews, *Western Aristocracies*, 64–9.

22 *Ibid.*, 67–8.

23 Matthews, *The Roman Empire of Ammianus*, 8–13, 20–7.

24 *Ibid.*, 285–6; cf. Sabbah, *La méthode d'Ammien Marcellin*, 332–46.

25 Matthews, *The Roman Empire of Ammianus*, 284.

26 Cf. Sabbah, *La méthode d'Ammien Marcellin*, 339–43.

27 On Valentinian's savagery in Ammianus: Paschoud, 'Valentinien travesti', 77–80.

28 Drinkwater, 'Julian and the Franks', 11.

29 Seager, *Ammianus Marcellinus*, provides the fullest treatment.

30 Matthews, *Western Aristocracies*, 40–1.

31 Cf. Matthews, *The Roman Empire of Ammianus*, 211.

32 I am grateful to John Matthews for raising this point in discussion after my paper.

33 Cf. Paschoud, 'Valentinien travesti', 80–3.

34 This chapter has benefited greatly from the comments of the participants at the Durham conference. I am particularly grateful to John Drinkwater and Daan den Hengst for their generous help subsequently.

11

AMMIANUS, VALENTINIAN AND THE RHINE GERMANS[1]

John Drinkwater

Over the last few years I have become interested in the reliability of Ammianus and the authenticity of the 'Germanic threat' on the Rhine frontier.[2] I have recently pursued both issues in a paper examining Julian's first contacts with the Franks in 355–6, and Valentinian I's early treatment of the Alamanni a decade later.[3] Here I wish to continue the same lines of thinking, concentrating on Valentinian I's later dealings with the Alamanni.

The story of Valentinian's military activities appears to be easily available in Ammianus, complemented by Symmachus, Ausonius and archaeological excavation. Thus, in brief: though Valentinian became emperor in the East in February 364, by the end of the same year he had moved to the West, and by November 365 had established himself in Gaul; here he was continually active in defeating those barbarians (principally, the Alamanni) who threatened the empire from over the Rhine, and in strongly fortifying the Rhenish and upper Danubian frontiers, giving them the strength to survive for another generation.[4] In most accounts, therefore, Valentinian is depicted as the hammer of the Germans, the 'frontier emperor' *par excellence*.[5] The contention of this chapter is that the situation may not have been as simple as it seems. I have already argued this for the period 365–6; here I take up the story from 367 to the end of the reign.

I would make three basic points, the first two of which will be important towards the end of this chapter, and the third I will develop presently. The first is that Ammianus does not provide a comprehensive account of Valentinian's military activities in this period.[6] While it is true that Ammianus 'far surpasses any other source in accuracy, richness of incidental colour and supporting anecdote', this superiority is only relative. His treatment has also been characterized as 'episodic', and 'imprecise, eclectic and anecdotal'.[7] Proof of Ammianus' deficiency is found in comparison between his narrative of the events of 369 and Symmachus' speech in honour of Valentinian's third consulship of 370.[8] Despite the idiosyncrasies of the genre, from Symmachus' panegyric we can reconstruct a fairly coherent narrative of expeditions and building activity on the lower Neckar in 369.[9] Ammianus, on the other hand, offers just a summary of Valentinian's general policy of military construction, supported by two disconnected stories of fort-building in the same region. Ammianus' information, indeed, makes sense only when taken with that of Symmachus. However, such supplementation of Ammianus from other sources is very rarely obtainable. We may assume that there is much that Ammianus does not tell us which we cannot discover from elsewhere. My second point, therefore, is that we have to accept that it is now impossible to reconstruct a precise narrative of events on the Rhine and the upper Danube under Valentinian from 367. Finally, and more positively, I would argue that, using Ammianus and the other sources, we can form a fair impression of the general nature of these activities.

Perhaps the most striking feature of Valentinian's fighting is its localized nature. Despite his ability to command significant concentrations of military might, he embarked on no campaigns deep into the former *Agri Decumates* or beyond: he was no Maximinus Thrax, and no Julian.[10] Valentinian's inclination to stay close to home is evident in Symmachus' account of the 369 campaign, which penetrated only as far as Ladenburg, *c.* 12 km from the Rhine.[11] However, it is also discernible in Ammianus' account, however incomplete, of the years 370–4, where we find Valentinian dealing for the most part with peoples directly bordering on the Rhine.[12] This makes me think that even the major expedition of 368, about which Ammianus supplies the most detail, was similarly limited. It is difficult to determine whether the main thrust of the Roman attack on the Alamanni was north or south of the Main. However, proponents of both views have suggested that, wherever he was, Valentinian advanced relatively far: if north of the Main, to Glauberg, in Oberhessen; if south, to Rottenburg-am-Neckar.[13] However, this does not square with Ammianus' description of an unusually large army, accompanied by important non-combatants (the boy-Augustus, Gratian, presumably with numerous attendants), marching cautiously 'for a few days' (*aliquot diebus emensis*), and then at an even 'gentler pace' (*leniore gressu*), before engaging the enemy at Solicinium (27.10.6–8, 10). The latest estimate of the rate of march of a late imperial army is *c.* 20 km per day;[14] but this is an *average* figure, and Ammianus' account provides good grounds for assuming that Valentinian's force moved at a much slower speed.[15] On this basis, I would say that Rottenburg, *c.* 170 km from Mainz as the crow flies, is out of the question as the location of Solicinium. Glauberg, *c.* 80 km from Mainz, is not impossible, but remains unlikely. My own guess is that Solicinium, like Ladenburg, was located close to the Rhine.

It is also evident that Valentinian encountered no really fearsome enemies on the Rhine. Although Ammianus attempts to suggest that the Alamanni could co-ordinate their actions against Rome, in his narrative they consistently appear as a deeply divided people.[16] In particular, we meet no paramount kings, such as had appeared under Constantius II and Julian (which suggests that this position had come into being in response to politicking Roman emperors). Instead, the scene is filled by regional kings and sub-kings (*reges, regales*), like Rando, Vithicabius and Macrianus, leading groups which occasionally made trouble, but which were usually disinclined to oppose, and indeed for the most part seemed anxious to co-operate with, Rome.[17] Alamannic reluctance to fight was a major feature of the 368 campaign (Amm. Marc. 27.10.7, 9); and Alamannic inclination towards collaboration appears in Symmachus' account of the 369 campaign and in the second of Ammianus' two tales of events in the same year.[18] The latter characteristic of Alamannic behaviour is especially interesting. Worth mentioning, for example, is the way in which the Alamanni settled close to the Rhine, suggesting their positive desire to be neighbours of the empire, and their belief that they would not be regularly subjected to Roman harassment.[19] This attitude was based on experience. Though Ammianus is usually interested only in Roman frustration of Alamannic hopes in this respect, Symmachus shows that the Roman side was not averse to co-operation. This can be seen in his account of Valentinian's 'attack' on an Alamannic village in 369.[20] It is astonishing that this community, which included women and children, was not abandoned by its inhabitants in the face of what, despite Valentinian's efforts at secrecy, must have been an obvious concentration of Roman forces across the Rhine. But all becomes clear when we are told what happened when the Roman attack finally took place, for the villagers were treated with extraordinary consideration: they were not killed in their beds, nor driven from their huts by fire; they were spared, given time to organize themselves, allowed to leave in peace and, according to the latest translation of the text, even permitted to keep their weapons.[21] There is surely good reason to suspect that the whole thing was a set-piece manoeuvre, produced to impress visiting civilian dignitaries, rather than a real assault.[22]

Here is the place to introduce Höckmann's observations about Valentinian's famous trans-Rhenish 'fortified landing-places'.[23] These are small forts, throwing off two parallel walls which run down into a nearby river; the enclosure thus created was intended for the beaching of naval vessels (by this time the light *lusoriae*, in service since the third century).[24] These installations are usually interpreted as bridgeheads – a means of expediting Roman amphibious expeditions.[25] As such they have become a symbol of Valentinianic aggression: 'Valentinian's frontier system included an offensive component.'[26] However, as Höckmann points out, the supposition of such an active role is not supported by the structure of these buildings. The landing- and accommodation-areas are too small for an attacking force; and there are no external gates from which troops might be deployed against an enemy. It appears that, rather than the forts defending the landing-places, the landing-places were there to secure the forts, i.e. to give shelter to ships bringing in materials and replacements. The forts should, therefore, be seen as no more than defended observation posts capable, if the need arose, of being maintained from outside.

I would therefore argue that the threat to the Rhine frontier, and the measures that Valentinian took to counter it, may be interpreted as less important than has traditionally been accepted. If so, what effect might this view have on our understanding of the working of the fourth-century empire, of Valentinian I as one of its rulers, and of Ammianus as its historian?

The empire as a whole can be quickly dealt with. I simply repeat my proposition that throughout the fourth century the real, but relatively minor, 'Germanic threat' on the Rhine frontier was played up to justify the imperial presence, and imperial taxation, in the West.[27] Indeed, it is possible that during this period the talking-up of the Alamannic menace became ever more important for western-based rulers given the rise of Constantinople and renewed pressure from Persia, which might give the East a prior claim on resources.[28] The real danger to the western provinces was not German invasion but Roman civil war, which had among its consequences the encouragement of barbarian raiding over the Rhine.[29]

As far as Valentinian is concerned, I find myself increasingly sympathetic towards the sole major dissenting view in the modern historical estimation of this emperor, that of Otto Seeck.[30] This alternative Valentinian was not a great warrior. He was excessively cautious and secretive; indeed, he could appear rather devious and self-centred. Generally slow-moving and possibly rather lazy, he could spur himself into activity if this was in his interest and could be undertaken on his own terms. The disadvantage of such enthusiasm was that he could become very angry if crossed. This was the man, therefore, who, against the wishes of his supporters, insisted on the appointment of his brother as co-ruler, but who promptly left him to face the Persians and Goths, as he moved to the less threatened but politically more significant West.[31] And this was the man who, when Valens was challenged by Procopius, put self-interest before family ties, and left him to fend for himself. Characteristically, Valentinian left the running of the Alamannic campaigns of 365–6 to his generals.[32] However, he then ran into trouble. By the latter part of 367 Valens had overcome the usurper, and moved on to deal with Procopius' Gothic allies, while Valentinian had only just survived a dangerous illness, which had resulted in the unorthodox proclamation of Gratian as fellow-Augustus. The senior emperor now badly needed to prove his reputation as a general, and to establish his new dynasty.[33] This explains the campaign of 368, which was undertaken for political, not military, purposes. It is hardly surprising that one of its most celebrated incidents was a deed of daring by the emperor in person.[34] On its conclusion, however, I would argue that Valentinian faced a dilemma. He still needed, and wanted, to project himself as a soldier-emperor; and certainly he had no desire to return to the sophisticated civilian society of Italy.[35] It therefore made sense for him to remain on the Rhine. Here, however, in the absence of the stimulus of Roman civil war, Alamanni (and still less, Franks, Saxons and Burgundians) proved ill-matched and unsuitable foes; and, anyway, he was probably disinclined to spend much time in real fighting. The solution was the initiation of his fortification programme, which allowed him to act the peacetime warrior, and also permitted him to indulge his passion for architecture and gadgetry.[36] This programme may be seen as an end in itself, and not necessarily part of a considered defence strategy. In other words, Valentinian was not interested in reconquering the old *Agri Decumates*, or in establishing a 'Verteidigungszone' that would also have the effect of Romanizing the Alamanni.[37] The latter, in fact, were there to be exploited as the emperor saw fit: as the indebted recipients of imperial clemency, or as the wretched victims of imperial intolerance.[38] Indeed, the occasional goading of neighbouring Alamannic communities into revolt was probably useful in maintaining the illusion that this people was a major enemy, requiring the permanent presence of a large (and growing) army and a senior emperor and his court.[39]

And so we return to Ammianus. I believe that Matthews is right in proposing that the preface to Book 26 should not be taken as marking some sort of new beginning to the *Res Gestae*, 'an extension of the original design that had not been intended to go beyond the death of Julian and its immediate sequel'.[40] We have to assume that well before he got down to its final composition, Ammianus had already determined to take his work beyond the extinction of the second Flavian dynasty. However, I am less convinced by Matthews' suggestion that the main stimulus for this was Ammianus' decision to include a detailed account of the revolt of Procopius. Instead I would argue that Ammianus had bigger fish to fry, and that the main attraction for continuing his history was not Procopius but Valens. This fits better with an obvious characteristic of the earlier surviving books, Ammianus' particular interest in those people (usually with Antiochene connections) with whom he had close contact and who, for good or ill, had a direct effect on his life: Gallus, Ursicinus, Constantius II, Julian and Valens.[41] I agree with Matthews that Ammianus' decision to write about events in the East after 364 would have caused problems, since it meant that, for the sake of completeness, he must also cover those in the West. As Matthews says, it must have been the need to research western history that was one of the forces that drove Ammianus to Rome.[42] However, I believe that because Ammianus was fundamentally uninterested in Valentinian, he did not do as good a job of work as he might have done in this respect. In dealing with the main, military, activities of Valentinian, Ammianus drew heavily on official propaganda, consisting of dispatches, panegyrics and, perhaps, even paintings. These would show the ruler in a good light.[43] On the other hand, he cannot have avoided being influenced by the Roman context. Generally, his *History* contains much about the local nobility; and much derived from metropolitan gossip.[44] The bad side of Valentinian, whose poor relationship with the Roman élite is notorious, was easily brought out through the inclusion of stories of his deplorable personal conduct.[45] This somewhat careless approach is the cause of the scrappiness of his account of Valentinian's campaigns, which is where we started.[46] To end, indeed, I would suggest that it may be possible to prove the existence and extent of Ammianus' uneven treatment of Valentinian.

At some time during his sojourn on the Rhine, Valentinian ordered an expedition that took Roman forces to the source of the Danube. Given the customary short range and low intensity of Valentinian's fighting, I think it highly unlikely that, as is generally assumed, this campaign could have been part of those of 368 or 369.[47] It must have been later, perhaps in 370.[48] A very great deal must have been made of this exploit. As is evident from Symmachus' lavish praise of his 'discovery' of the Neckar, Valentinian's Alexander-like advance into 'unknown' territory was another way of justifying his presence on the Rhine;[49] and the reappearance of Roman arms at the Danube source must have been seen as a considerably more memorable event. It can be no accident that we find mention of it in Ausonius' *Mosella* and in two further poems by him, specifically commemorating the achievement.[50] If the Danube expedition caused much official excitement in Trier, it is surely justifiable to assume that similar celebration was ordered in Rome, and recorded and remembered there in close detail. However, when Ammianus came to write his account of Valentinian's military exploits, he ignored the incident. It suited him to pick up enough from imperial propaganda to intimate that Valentinian was an active general because Valentinian's barbarian enemies were those of Julian, and Julian still had to be shown in the best possible light. Otherwise, however, Ammianus was not concerned to present a complete or balanced account of an emperor in whom he was interested really only as the bogeyman of Rome, the employer of the 'good' Count Theodosius, and the brother of Valens.

Appendix 1: Symmachus

Our main source for Valentinian's 369 expedition is Symmachus' second oration; but this is a panegyric, in which we cannot expect to be told the truth.[51] In certain respects, indeed, Symmachus' flattering of his emperor is very obvious, and suits the general line of my argument. Thus, for example, we should not take seriously his brilliant extended conceit that Valentinian's trans-Rhenish strongpoints were new 'cities' (*urbes*, *oppida*, *civitates*; Or. 2.2, 12ff., 18ff.). In the sophisticated concoction of congratulation that was ancient panegyric this image would have established a delicious tension between the speaker and his subject, each knowing that what was being said was false, but each relishing the saying of it.[52] Much more difficult, however, is Symmachus' detailed description of the amphibious assault over the Rhine, the taking of the Alamannic village and the advance to Ladenburg. Instead of stirring tales of imperial daring and of slaughter and victory, like Ammianus' account of Solicinium, we are treated to a fine example of imperial clemency. One must ask why Symmachus focused on incidents which even he, as a civilian, must have been able to recognize as relatively low-key.[53] For here, unlike in his treatment of the 'cities', he must have felt able to rely on factual accuracy to provide an interpretation of events that his audience, in particular the emperor, wanted to hear.[54] What was the message that Valentinian wished his panegyrist to propagate?

The answer could be that the Alamanni were already defeated by Valentinian's efforts to date, i.e. by his military building (*Or.* 2.4, 21f.). The spirit of this people had been broken by his mercy towards them; and they were only too willing to co-operate (*Or.* 2.11f., 15f.). Valentinian's victories were, indeed, peaceful (*Or.* 2.30: *triumfum pacis egisti*). The crucial point here (closely linked in context with the financial benefits of having two emperors; *Or.* 2.31) appears to be that what Valentinian was doing was worthwhile because it saved resources. I would argue that this was an important issue at a time when worries about the size of imperial military spending were very much in the air. Their best-known exponent is, of course, the anonymous author of *De Rebus Bellicis*; but the sentiment is also to be found in the *Historia Augusta* and in the speeches of Themistius.[55] This may possibly be regarded as part of the recognition – realistic, but uncertain and too late – that the 'barbarian threat' was not dangerous enough to justify the amount spent on supposedly countering it. Resources could be saved by the avoidance of fighting; and Valentinian may also have claimed that his building of more compact defence installations required smaller garrisons.[56] Whether such a justification, if made, was practical is, however, another matter: modern experience must cause us to be wary of claims as to the savings to be won from the introduction of new technologies.[57]

Appendix 2: Valentinian I and Britain

It is likely that by the beginning of 367 Valentinian was finalizing plans for a major campaign, to match Valens' successes in the East. This campaign had to be on the Rhine. Although there was trouble in Tripolitania, he will never have contemplated moving to Africa, which had ceased to be a source of military glory under the Republic.[58] By early summer 367, therefore, Valentinian was ready to transfer his headquarters to Trier, but was then diverted by news of disturbance in Britain. He went to the Channel coast, dispatching senior officers to assess the situation on the island. However, he then fell seriously ill; and his illness, by raising the question of succession, resulted in dangerous rivalry at his court (now resident in Amiens). This prompted him, on his recovery, to promote his 8-year-old son, Gratian, Augustus (on 24 August 367). The two then moved to Trier.[59]

For, despite continuing unrest in Britain, Valentinian continued to prepare for a German expedition. For his purposes, Britain was almost as worthless as Africa. The native 'enemies' that it had to offer were little known. Besides, the premature deaths of emperors who had fought there in recent times – Septimius Severus, Constantius I and, perhaps, even Constans – may have made the place one of ill omen. And it is also possible that the British situation had been changed for the worse by Valentinian's illness. The extent, and very nature, of Ammianus' *barbarica conspiratio* – the unholy alliance of Picts, Saxons, Scots and Attacotti that he appears to make responsible for the collapse of Roman Britain in 367 – has recently been much debated, with scholars showing a discernible tendency to discount the 'barbarian' contribution and to propose that the roots of the British disturbances should be sought more in internal unrest, an argument which supports the general thrust of this chapter.[60] In fact, Ammianus informs us that the later stages of these troubles were significantly influenced by a powerful Pannonian, brother-in-law of Valentinian's favourite, Maximinus, exiled to Britain after having been found guilty of a criminal offence, whom he names 'Valentinus'.[61] Ammianus tells us nothing about Valentinus' specific actions or plans. However, Zosimus (4.12.2) says bluntly that he was set upon usurpation and, moreover, calls him 'Valentinian'. If, as Demandt has argued, the latter version of his name is the correct one, it may help us to flesh out the bones of the affair.[62] We may envisage an unscrupulous and disgruntled individual seeking to exploit the uncertainty resulting from barbarian raiding and the excitement caused first by visits by high-ranking imperial officials and then by news of Valentinian's illness. On this argument, the circumstance that he bore the same name as the emperor, and had a common background, will have encouraged him to personate the rightful ruler and seize control of the South-east, the administrative hub of the island. A campaign against a usurper would not have fitted Valentinian I's taste or needs, still less one against a usurper who was not even an honest usurper. Britain, as later Africa, was therefore delegated to Count Theodosius.[63]

Notes

1 I am deeply indebted to Wolf Liebeschuetz and Thomas Wiedemann for reading and commenting on drafts of this chapter.
2 See J.F. Drinkwater, 'Silvanus, Ursicinus and Ammianus Marcellinus: Fact or Fiction?', in C. Deroux (ed.), *Studies in Latin Literature and Roman History VII* (Collection Latomus 227), Brussels 1994, 568–76, and J.F. Drinkwater, 'The "Germanic Threat" on the Rhine Frontier: A Romano-Gallic Artefact?', in R.W. Mathisen and H.S. Sivan (eds), *Shifting Frontiers in Late Antiquity*, Aldershot 1996, 20–30.
3 J.F. Drinkwater, 'Julian and the Franks and Valentinian I and the Alamanni: Ammianus on Romano-German Relations', *Francia* 24 (1997), 1–15.
4 So, for example, A. Nagl, 'Valentinianus I', *RE* VIIA.2 (1948), 2158–2204, at 2176, 2203; A. Piganiol, *L'empire chrétien*, Paris 1972 (2nd edn), 193–5; A. Demandt, *Die Spätantike*, Munich 1989, 111–13; J.F. Matthews, *The Roman Empire of Ammianus*, London 1989, 207.
5 Thus N.H. Baynes, 'The Dynasty of Valentinian and Theodosius the Great', in *Cambridge Medieval History*, vol. 1, Cambridge 1924 (2nd edn), 218–49, at 222; C. Jullian, *Histoire de la Gaule*, vol. 7, Paris 1926 (repr. Brussels 1964), 235; J.F. Matthews, *Western Aristocracies and Imperial Court, AD 364–425*, Oxford 1975, 33.

6 Thus *contra* e.g. H. Sivan, 'Redating Ausonius' *Mosella*', *AJPhil*. 111 (1990), 383–94, at 384.
7 Matthews, *The Roman Empire of Ammianus*, 21, 207; A. Pabst (ed., trans. and comm.), *Quintus Aurelius Symmachus. Reden*, Darmstadt 1989, 307.
8 Amm. Marc. 28.2.1ff.; Symmachus, *Or.* 2 (Pabst, *Symmachus*, 66–90). Cf. Pabst, *Symmachus*, 307. Cf. also the contribution of Humphries in this volume (chapter 10).
9 See p. 129 and Appendix 1.
10 Amm. Marc. 27.10.6 (368); O. Seeck, *Geschichte des Untergangs der antiken Welt*, vol. 5, Berlin 1913, 24.
11 Pabst, *Symmachus*, 333.
12 In the period 370–4, Valentinian's main concern was Macrianus of the Bucinobantes, directly opposite Mainz: Amm. Marc. 29.4.3, 7. The emperor did, of course, operate elsewhere, as in 374, when he was to be found on the upper Rhine before moving to deal with Macrianus for the last time; but Ammianus (30.3.1) indicates that he did not go far from Basel.
13 Glauberg: Demandt, *Spätantike*, 112 and n. 4. Rottenburg: Nagl, 'Valentinianus', 2173; Matthews, *The Roman Empire of Ammianus*, 311.
14 H. Elton, *Warfare in Roman Europe, AD 350–425*, Oxford 1996, 245.
15 At 25.1.10, Ammianus appears to report that in the final stage of the Persian campaign Julian's army advanced only 70 stades (*c.* 13 km) in a day.
16 Implied co-ordination: Amm. Marc. 27.10.3ff. (Alamannic raiding of the north, by Rando, is associated with that in the south, by Vithicabius). See Baden-Württemberg, Archäologisches Landesmuseum, *Die Alamannen*, Stuttgart 1997, 97–8, for the scattered distribution and low population density of early Alamannic settlement.
17 Cf. Matthews, *The Roman Empire of Ammianus*, 314.
18 Symmachus, *Or.* 2.15f. (Alamannic help in moving building materials from Ladenburg to the fort-site at Mannheim–Neckarau); Amm. Marc. 28.2.7ff. (Alamannic desires for peace, rejected by Rome).
19 Amm. Marc. 27.10.7 (368); Symmachus, *Or.* 2.10 (369). Cf. Baden-Württemberg, *Alamannen*, 97 and fig. 83 for the concentration of Alamannic settlements along the middle Rhine, near the confluences of the Main and the Neckar, during the fourth century; see also Baden-Württemberg, *Alamannen*, 86, 103–4 and 108 for the explanation of a similar concentration around Breisach as the result of Alamanni serving as Roman soldiers. Thus, *contra* Pabst, *Symmachus*, 331, it would appear that the Alamanni chose to settle near forts, and not that the forts were built to face concentrations of Alamanni.
20 Symmachus, *Or.* 2.8ff. See also Appendix 1.
21 Pabst, *Symmachus*, 75.
22 Cf. Matthews, *Western Aristocracies*, 32–3, with Drinkwater, 'Germanic Threat', 28 and n. 33.
23 O. Höckmann, 'Römische Schiffsverbände auf dem Ober- und Mittelrhein und die Verteidigung der Rheingrenze in der Spätantike', *Jahrbuch des Römisch–Germanischen Zentralmuseums Mainz* 33 (1986), 369–416, at 399–406.
24 *Ibid.*, 381, 392–3, 396–7 and fig. 13.
25 Pabst, *Symmachus*, 332.
26 J. Lander, *Roman Stone Fortifications. Variation and Change from the First Century AD to the Fourth* (British Archaeological Reports, International Series 206), Oxford 1984, 284.
27 Drinkwater, 'Germanic Threat'. Cf. Baden-Württemberg, *Alamannen*, 95–6, for the absence of significant pressure on the upper German *limes* until the middle of the third century and for the relatively slow rate of Elbe-German (i.e. future Alamannic) immigration into the area of the former *Agri Decumates* immediately thereafter.
28 Cf. Drinkwater, 'Germanic Threat', 28 and n. 35.
29 Cf. J.F. Drinkwater, 'The Usurpers Constantine III (407–411) and Jovinus (411–413)', *Britannia* 29 (1998), 269–98, with Pabst, *Symmachus*, 330 (on the Alamanni as *latrones*).

The contemporary ethnogenesis of the Alamanni (Baden-Württemberg, *Alamannen*, 74) may well have encouraged internal and external shows of strength by local leaders.

30 Seeck, *Geschichte des Untergangs*, 12–14.
31 Drinkwater, 'Julian and the Franks', 10–12.
32 *Ibid.*, 10.
33 Cf. R. Tomlin, 'The Date of the "Barbarian Conspiracy"', *Britannia* 5 (1974), 303–9, at 304; and see Appendix 2.
34 Amm. Marc. 27.10.10f. Cf. M. Mause, *Die Darstellung des Kaisers in der lateinischen Panegyrik* (Palingenesia 50), Stuttgart 1994, 197, on the need for an emperor to be seen as an active soldier.
35 Cf. Amm. Marc. 30.8.10; Nagl, 'Valentinianus', 2191.
36 Nagl, 'Valentinianus', 2203; Matthews, *Western Aristocracies*, 49; T.E.J. Wiedemann, 'Petitioning a Fourth-Century Emperor: The *De Rebus Bellicis*', *Florilegium* 1 (1979), 140–7, at 143–5; Pabst, *Symmachus*, 147–8, 329–38. The sources are Symmachus, *Or.* 2.18ff.; Amm. Marc. 30.9.4; *Epit. de Caes.* 45.6.
37 Pabst, *Symmachus*, 306, 329–55 (esp. 335, 349): correct, I think, in arguing for the first point, but wrong in proposing the other two.
38 Clemency: *ibid.*, 343–5; intolerance: Amm. Marc. 28.2.5ff.
39 Expansion of the army: Nagl, 'Valentinianus', 2192.
40 Matthews, *The Roman Empire of Ammianus*, 204.
41 Drinkwater, 'Julian and the Franks', 14.
42 Matthews, *The Roman Empire of Ammianus*, 20–1.
43 E.g. Valentinian's decision to stay in Gaul in 365; the emperor's daring during the battle of Solicinium; the building of the Neckar fort in 369 (Amm. Marc. 28.2ff.); and perhaps even the dramatic circumstances of the truce with Macrianus (Amm. Marc. 30.3.4ff.).
44 Nagl, 'Valentinianus', 2191; A. Cameron, 'The Roman Friends of Ammianus', *JRS* 54 (1964), 15–28, at 23.
45 E.g. in his treatment of Syagrius: *notarius* in 369, but praetorian prefect of Italy 380–2 and consul in 381 (Amm. Marc. 28.2.9; *PLRE* I, 862f.).
46 Thus *contra* Pabst, *Symmachus*, 307: that this resulted from Ammianus' writing in distant Antioch.
47 Thus e.g. Piganiol, *L'empire chrétien*, 196.
48 See J.F. Drinkwater, 'Re-dating Ausonius' War-Poetry', *AJPhil.* (in press).
49 Symmachus, *Or.* 2.24, 30; Pabst, *Symmachus*, 336.
50 Ausonius, *Mosella* 424; *Epig.* 28, 31 [Peiper] (3, 4 [Green]).
51 On this see most recently Mause, *Darstellung des Kaisers*, and my review of this work in *Francia* 24 (1997), 178–80.
52 Cf. Mause, *Darstellung des Kaisers*, 18, 227.
53 At 2.25 Symmachus appears to defend Valentinian from general criticism of procrastination in his dealings with the Alamanni: Pabst, *Symmachus*, 336–7.
54 Cf. Mause, *Darstellung des Kaisers*, 43–4.
55 *De Reb. Bell.* 5, with E.A. Thompson, *A Roman Reformer and Inventor*, Oxford 1952, 41–4, and Wiedemann, 'Petitioning a Fourth-Century Emperor', 146; Themistius, *Or.* 8.172f./114f., from P. Heather and J.F. Matthews, *The Goths in the Fourth Century*, Liverpool 1991, 15; *Vit. Probi*, 20.3ff. (cf. 14.3f. and 20.2: Probus as Valentinian I?).
56 Cf. Lander, *Roman Stone Fortifications*, 273–5, 291.
57 Cf. Wiedemann, 'Petitioning a Fourth-Century Emperor', 144, for the likely increase in military expenditure occasioned by Valentinian's building programme.
58 Amm. Marc. 27.9.1; Matthews, *The Roman Empire of Ammianus*, 207.
59 For all this I follow Tomlin, 'The Date of the "Barbarian Conspiracy"', 305–7.
60 Amm. Marc. 27.8.1, 26.4.5, 27.8.5. P. Bartholomew, 'Fourth-Century Saxons', *Britannia* 15 (1984), 169–85, at 177, 180–1; W.H.C. Frend, 'Pagans, Christians, and the "Barbarian

Conspiracy" of AD 367 in Britain', *Britannia* 23 (1992), 121–31, at 129; cf. J. Cotterill, 'Saxon Raiding and the Role of the Late Roman Coastal Forts of Britain', *Britannia* 24 (1993), 228–39, at 232.
61 Amm. Marc. 28.3.4ff., 30.7.10.
62 A. Demandt, 'Die Feldzüge des älteren Theodosius', *Hermes* 100 (1972), 81–113, at 90; see also *PLRE* I, 935.
63 See Amm. Marc. 27.8.7ff. for Theodosius' early activity in the South-east, against native insurgents and deserters: cf. Bartholomew, 'Fourth-Century Saxons', 179; Frend, 'Pagans, Christians, and the "Barbarian Conspiracy" of AD 367', 129.

Part III

ROME, THE HISTORIAN AND HIS AUDIENCE

12

AMMIANUS SATIRICUS

Roger Rees

My ambition in this chapter is to consider the nature of the relationship between the *Res Gestae* of Ammianus and the *Satires* of Juvenal, and from that briefly to address issues such as the historian's attitude towards the satirist, to satire in general and its place in historiography, to himself and to the reading public of fourth-century Rome. I focus on the two passages about Roman manners, that is, 14.6.1–26 and 28.4.1–35. Both are classified as digressions with Ammianus' unmistakable expression of a 'return' to his main theme at the end of each – *redeundum ad textum* (14.6.26) and *redeamus ad cetera* (28.4.35). They are reasonably substantial, and each is replete with details about contemporary Roman *mores*. The first begins by viewing Rome's history as the lifecycle of man (14.6.1–6), before proceeding to discuss the faults of the nobles (7–24) and then the city's poor (24–26). A similar distinction between rich and poor articulates the second digression (28.4.6–27 and 28–34). My contention is that these digressions draw on the *Satires* of Juvenal. This claim is not new, but what has been lacking hitherto is a broad-based comparison between the two authors, from which conclusions can be clearly set out and interpretations adopted.[1] A more detailed appreciation of the relationship between the two authors will lead to clearer understanding of this historian's compositional practices.

From as early as the second century the *Satires* were little read. The earliest echoes of Juvenal can be found in the works of the Christian authors Tertullian and Lactantius, but not until the late fourth century was the satirist clearly in vogue.[2] Servius and Ausonius use the *Satires* a great deal, and in what Syme suggests is an oversight in the chronological dissimulation on the part of its author, a few traces of Juvenal are found in the *Historia Augusta* (which is addressed to Diocletian and Constantine).[3] Symmachus and Claudian echo or quote the satirist too.[4] Syme concludes that 'perhaps in the sixties or seventies, somebody discovers Juvenal and brings him on the market';[5] there can be no doubt that the *Satires* were available to Ammianus. Besides, the most compelling evidence comes from a passage discussed later, in which Ammianus himself tells us that the Romans read Juvenal and Marius Maximus.

Below is a series of parallels between Juvenal and Ammianus which differ widely in their nature. They are classified according to four categories – rhetorical trope, subject matter, victim of satire, and lexical echoes.[6] At times, some of these classifications overlap, but the intention is to provide a framework through which the range of parallels between the two texts can be illustrated. Few of these parallels considered in isolation will be universally convincing. Some might appear fortuitous and, therefore, spurious; others the inevitable consequences of satirical treatments of Rome – that is, indicative of generic rather than specific influence. However, when there is a combination of similarities within one pair of parallel passages, the claim that the *Res Gestae* owes a debt to the *Satires* is most convincing. The fact that Ammianus published his work during the renaissance of Juvenal in Rome provides circumstantial corroboration for the claim.

Rhetorical trope

(i) Programmatic statements feature in the early lines of each text, setting out and justifying what is to follow.

Ammianus	*Juvenal*
14.6.2 et quoniam mirari posse quosdam peregrinos existimo, haec lecturos fortisan (si contigerit), quam ob rem cum oratio ad ea monstranda deflexerit quae Romae geruntur, nihil praeter seditiones narratur et tabernas et vililates harum similis alias, summatim causas perstringam, nusquam a veritate sponte propria digressurus. 28.4.1 ad ea strictim exsequenda regrediar	1.30–1 difficile est saturam non scribere. nam quis iniquae / tam patiens urbis? 1.79 facit indignatio versum 1.170–1 experiar quid concedatur in illos / quorum Flaminia tegitur cinis atque Latina

(ii) Contrast between past and present time to emphasize the current state of affairs.

| 14.6.21 illud autem non dubitatur, quod cum esset aliquando virtutum omnium domicilium | 5.110–13 namque et titulis et fascibus olim / maior habebatur donandi gloria. solum / poscimus |

Roma, ingenuos advenas plerique nobilium, ... nunc vero	ut cenes civiliter. hoc face et esto, / esto, ut nunc multi, dives tibi, pauper amicis 11.77–120 haec olim nostri iam luxuriosa senatus / cena fuit ... / at nunc divitibus cenandi nulla voluptas ...

(iii) The use of the second-person singular verb forms in generalizations.

14.6.12 at nunc si ad aliquem bene nummatum tumentemque ideo, honestus advena salutatum introieris primitus, tamquam exoptatus suscipieris ...	5.59–60 quod cum ita sit, tu Gaetulum Ganymedem / respice, cum sities

(iv) Exaggeration.

14.6.17 utque proeliorum periti rectores primo catervas densas opponunt et fortes, deinde leves armaturas, post iaculatores ultimasque subsidiales acies (si fors adegerit) iuvaturas, ita praepositis urbanae familiae suspense digerentibus atque sollicite, quos insignes faciunt virgae dexteris aptatae, velut tessera data castrensi, iuxta vehiculi frontem omne textrinum incedit	3.257–61 nam si procubuit qui saxa Ligustica portat / axis et eversum fudit super agmina montem, / quid superest de corporibus? quis membra, quis ossa / invenit? obtritum vulgi perit omne cadaver / more animae

(v) Conditional clauses to emphasize the patent tastelessness of certain acts and the praise they elicit.

*27.3.5 homo indignanter admodum sustinens, si (etiam cum spueret) non laudaretur, ut id quoque prudenter praeter alios faciens	*3.107–8 laudare paratus, / si bene ructavit, si rectum minxit amicus

(vi) Catalogue

| 28.4.4 namque statuerat ne taberna vinaria ante horam quartam aperiretur, neve aquam vulgarium calefaceret quisquam, vel ad usque praestitutum diei spatium lixae coctam proponerent carnem, vel honestus quidam mandens videretur in publico | 1.22–9 cum tener uxorem ducat spado, Mevia Tuscum / figat aprum et nuda teneat venabula mamma, / patricios omnis opibus cum provocet unus / quo tondente gravis iuveni mihi barba sonabat, / cum pars Niliacae plebis, cum verna Canopi / Crispinus Tyrias umero revocante lacernas / ventilet aestivum digitis sudantibus aurum, / nec sufferre queat maioris pondera gemmae, / difficile est saturam non scribere. |

(vii) Both Juvenal and Ammianus use characters from drama as common currency in their work, as benchmarks against which to judge the people they describe.

| 28.4.27 cumque mutuum illi quid petunt, soccos ut Miconas videbis et Lachetas, cum adiguntur ut reddant, ita coturnatos et turgidos ut Heraclidas illos Cresphontem et Temenum putes. | 6.634–6 fingimus haec altum satura sumente cothurnum / scilicet, et finem egressi legemque priorum / grande Sophocleo carmen bacchamur hiatu? |

Subject matter

(viii) Importance attached to statues.

| 14.6.8 ex his quidam aeternitati se commendari posse per statuas aestimantes, eas ardenter affectant, quasi plus praemii de figmentis aereis sensu carentibus adepturi, quam ex conscientia honeste recteque factorum | 1.128–31 deinde forum iurisque peritus Apollo / atque triumphales, inter quas ausus habere / nescio quis titulos Aegyptius atque Arabarches, / cuius ad effigiem non tantum meiere fas est |

(ix) Importance attached to grand clothing and carriages.

14.6.9 alii summum decus in carruchis solito altioribus, et ambitioso vestium cultu ponentes, sudant sub ponderibus lacernarum 28.4.8 non nullos fulgentes sericis indumentis	3.180 hic ultra vires habitus nitor 3.239–40 turba cedente vehetur / dives et ingenti curret super ora Liburna

(x) The corruption of domestic servants or slaves.

14.6.15 et nomenculatores, adsueti haec et talia venditare, mercede accepta, lucris quosdam et prandiis inserunt subditicios ignobiles et obscuros	6. 'O' 31–3 sed quis custodiat ipsos / custodes, qui nunc lascivae furta puellae / has mercede silent? crimen commune tacetur

(xi) Riding horses (too) fast through the streets of Rome and environs.

14.6.16 quidam per ampla spatia urbis, subversasque silices, sine periculi metu properantes equos velut publicos	1.60–2 dum pervolat axe citato / Flaminiam puer Automedon? nam lora tenebat / ipse, lacernatae cum se iactaret amicae / 8.146–7 praeter maiorum cineres atque ossa volucri / carpento rapitur pinguis Lateranus

(xii) On being followed by domestic slaves through the city – both writers cite cooks.

14.6.17 huic atratum coquinae iungitur ministerium	3.250 sequitur sua quemque culina

(xiii) Legacy-hunting and murder and the central importance of marital status.

14.6.22 vile esse quicquid extra urbis pomerium nascitur aestimant praeter orbos et caelibes 28.4.22 subsident aliqui copiosos homines senes aut iuvenes, orbos vel caelibes, aut etiam uxores habentes seu liberos (nec enim	1.37–8 cum te summoveant qui testamenta merentur / noctibus . . . 1.69–72 occurrit matrona potens, quae molle Calenum / porrectura viro miscet sitiente rubetam / instituitque rudes

hoc titulo discrimen aliquod observatur), ad voluntates condendas allicientes eos praestrigiis miris: qui cum, supremis iudiciis ordinatis, quaedam reliquerint his quibus morem gerendo testati sunt, ilico pereunt, ut id impleri sorte fatorum operante nec putes, nec facile possit aegritudo testari nec funus comitatur his quisquam 28.4.26 parte alia uxor, ut proverbium loquitur vetus, eamdem incudem diu noctuque tundendo, maritum testari compellit, hocque idem ut faciat uxor, urget maritus instanter	melior Lucusta propinquas / per famam et populum nigros efferre maritos 3.128–30 cum praetor lictorem impellat et ire / praecipitem iubeat dudum vigilantibus orbis 5.97–8 instruit ergo focum provincia, sumitur illinc / quod captator emat Laenas, Aurelia vendat 5.140 iucundum et carum sterilis facit uxor amicum 6.620–2 minus ergo nocens erit Agrippinae / boletus, siquidem unius praecordia pressit / ille senis tremulumque caput descendere iussit

(xiv) Circuses.

14.6.25 aut quod est studiorum omnium maximum ab ortu lucis ad vesperam sole fatiscunt vel pluviis, per minutias aurigarum equorumque praecipua vel delicta scrutantes 28.4.29–31 eisque templum et habitaculum et contio et cupitorum spes omnis Circus est Maximus: et videre licet per fora et compita et plateas et conventicula, circulos multos collectos in se controversis iurgiis ferri, aliis aliud (ut fit) defendentibus . . . et ubi neglegentiae tanta est caries, exoptato die equestrium ludorum illucescente, nondum solis puro iubare, effusius omnes festinant praecipites, ut velocitate currus ipsos anteeant certaturos.	3.223 si potes avelli circensibus 10.79–81 nunc se / continet atque duas tantum res anxius optat, / panem et circenses 11.52–3 ille dolor solus patriam fugientibus, illa / maestitia est, caruisse anno circensibus uno. 11.197–8 totam hodie Romam circus capit, et fragor aurem / percutit, eventum viridis quo colligo panni

Victim of satire

(xv) Moral degeneracy of Romans over time.

14.6.3–7	1.87ff., 6.1–27
14.6.10 (alii) ignorantes profecto maiores suos per quos ita magnitudo Romana porrigitur, non divitiis eluxisse, sed per bella saevissima, nec opibus nec victu nec indumentorum vilitate gregariis militibus discrepantes, opposita cuncta superasse virtute.	6.287–92 praestabat castas humilis fortuna, Latinas / quondam, nec vitiis contingi parva sinebant / tecta labor somnique breves et vellere Tusco / vexatae duraeque manus ac proximus urbi / Hannibal et stantes Collina turre mariti. / nunc patimur longae pacis mala 11.77–81, 13.28–30

(xvi) Pride in landholdings. Tone of disapprobation of the excesses.

14.6.10 alii nullo quaerente, vultus severitate assimulata, patrimonia sua in immensum extollunt, cultorum (ut putant) feracium multiplicantes annuos fructus, quae a primo ad ultimum solem se abunde iactitant possidere.	14.140–3 ergo paratur / altera villa tibi, cum rus non sufficit unum, / et proferre libet fines maiorque videtur / et melior vicina seges

(xvii) Patronage and dinner.

14.6.12–13	5 *passim*

(xviii) The lack of interest in learning.

14.6.15 homines enim eruditos et sobrios, ut infaustos et inutiles vitant	2.4–5 indocti primum, quamquam plena omnia gypso / Chrysippi invenias 7 *passim*

(xix) Enormous appetites and excessive dinners.

14.6.16 mensarum enim voragines et varias voluptatum illecebras 28.4.13 poscuntur etiam in conviviis alioquotiens trutinae, ut appositi pisces et volucres ponderentur, et glires 28.4.34 in his plerique distentioribus saginis addicti . . . aulis assistunt	1.137–8 nam de tot pulchris et latis orbibus et tam / antiquis una comedunt patrimonia mensa 4 (Turbot) and 5 (Entertaining clients) *passim* 11.120–9

(xx) Eunuchs

14.6.17 postrema multitudo spadonum a senibus in pueros desinens, obluridi distortaque lineamentorum compage deformes	1.22 cum tener uxorem ducat spado

(xxi) The decline of oratory.

14.6.18 in locum oratoris doctor artium ludicrarum accitur 28.4.2 sed obnubilabat, haec omnia vitium . . . quod citeriorem vitam paene omnem vergentem in luxum, per argumenta scaenica	7.139–40 fidimus eloquio? Ciceroni nemo ducentos / nunc dederit nummos

(xxii) Lyre-players and flautists.

14.6.18 et lyrae ad speciem carpentorum ingentes, tibiaeque et histrionici gestus instrumenta non levia	6.76–7 accipis uxorem de qua citharoedus Echion / aut Glaphyrus fiat pater Ambrosiusque choraules

(xxiii) Women dancing.

14.6.20 et licet, quocumque oculos flexeris, feminas affatim multas spectare cirritas, quibus (si nupsissent) per aetatem ter iam nixus poterat suppetere	11.162–4 fortisan expectes ut Gaditana canoro / incipiant prurire choro plausuque probatae / ad terram tremulo descendant clune puellae

liberorum, ad usque taedium pedibus pavimenta tergentis, iactari volucriter gyris dum exprimunt innumera simulacra, quae finxere fabulae theatrales.	

(xxiv) Drinking.

14.6.25 in tabernis aliqui pernoctant vinariis	8.158 sed cum pervigiles placet instaurare popinas

(xxv) Dicing.

14.6.25 aut pugnaciter aleis certant 28.4.21 quidam ex his (licet rari) aleatorum vocabulum declinantes, ideoque se cupientes appellari potius tesserarios 28.4.29 hi omne quod vivunt, vino et tesseris impendunt et lustris	1.87–8 quando / maior avaritiae patuit sinus? alea quando / hos animos? 11.176 alea turpis 14.4–5 si damnosa senem iuvat alea, ludit et heres / bullatus parvoque eadem movet arma fritillo.

(xxvi) Flatterers.

28.4.12 horum domus otiosi quidam garruli frequentant, variis assentandi figmentis, ad singula ulterioris fortunae verba plaudentes, parasitorum in comoediis facetias affectando	3.41–2 mentiri nescio; librum, / si malus est, nequeo laudare et poscere 3.86–7 quid quod adulandi gens prudentissima laudat / sermonem indocti, faciem deformis amici?

(xxvii) Cruelty to slaves.

28.4.16 ita autem pauci sunt inter eos severi vindices delictorum ut, si aquam calidam tardius attulerit servus, trecentis affligi verberibus iubeatur.	6.479–81 hic frangit ferulas, rubet ille flagello, / hic scutica; sunt quae tortoribus annua praestent. / verberat atque obiter faciem linit, audit amicas. 14.21–2 tunc felix, quotiens aliquis tortore vocato / uritur ardenti duo propter lintea ferro?

Lexical

(xxviii) On being recognized by one's patron.

| 14.6.13 qui sis vel unde *venias* diutius ambigente. *agnitus* vero tandem et ascitus in amicitiam, si te salutandi adsiduitati dederis. | 1.97–9 trepidat ne / suppositus *venias* ac falso nomine poscas: / *agnitus* accipies. |

(xxix) On those who rely on their names, not their behaviour.

| 28.4.7 *praenominum claritudine* quidam (ut putant) in immensum semet extollunt, cum Reburri, et Flavonii et Pagonii Gereonesque appellentur, ac Dalii cum Tarraciis et Ferasiis, aliisque ita decens sonantibus originum *insignibus* multis. | 8.30–2 quis enim generosum dixerit hunc qui / indignus genere et *praeclaro nomine* tantum / *insignis*? |

(xxx) On *ephemerides*, here denoting, it seems, astrological diaries or horoscopes.[7]

| *28.4.24 multi apud eos negantes esse superas potestates in caelo, nec in publicum prodeunt nec prandent nec lavari arbitrantur se cautius posse, antequam *ephemeride* scrupulose sciscitata didicerint. | *6.573–81 in cuius manibus ceu pinguia sucina tritas / cernes *ephemeridas* . . . / aegra licet iaceat, capiendo nulla videtur / aptior hora cibo nisi quam dederit Petosiris. |

This accumulation of parallels in style, content, victim and lexis indicates a thorough and conscious employment of the *Satires* in the composition of Ammianus' Roman digressions. The resulting associative reminiscences recall Juvenal without direct quotation or citation. This effect is in keeping with Ammianus' practice of composition in his use of other authors. Fornara has demonstrated that Ammianus often invokes recollection of Greek and Roman authors and texts without actually quoting or citing them. He argues that the evocation of the three historians Sallust, Livy and Tacitus in the *Res Gestae* is self-conscious and concludes that 'Ammianus intentionally practiced a technique of unannounced adaptation of the major Latin writers, but . . . he did so within certain parameters'; the mosaic effect which results 'is an element of his style which testifies to his artistic aims'.[8] Against this backdrop it seems reasonable to add Juvenal's name to the list of earlier authors whose work is evoked in the *Res Gestae*.

However, unlike the historians Livy and Tacitus (Sallust is named in 15.12.6), Juvenal does get a mention in the *Res Gestae*: 'Some of them hate learning like poison, but read Juvenal and Marius Maximus with avidity. These are only the volumes that they turn over in their idle moments, but why this should be so is not for a man like me to say.'[9]

As mentioned above (p. 141), this reference provides the strongest support for the claim that Ammianus himself could have read Juvenal. That this condemnation appears in one of two passages so indebted to the satirist is a noteworthy paradox. Thompson comments, 'Although [Ammianus] sometimes imitates him, he considered Juvenal a trivial and worthless writer', and Pack states that 'Ammianus does not scruple to borrow an occasional idea from Juvenal, even though he scorns the Roman aristocrats for reading that poet so avidly'; Wallace-Hadrill considers the reference to Juvenal 'remarkable, in view of Ammianus' own debt to him in the Roman digressions', and in a similar vein, Matthews observes that the satirical digression about Rome 'makes his dismissive remark rather surprising'.[10] The paradox demands consideration.

First, it might seem comical. In general, 'Ammianus did not lack for dry humour'.[11] The inclusion of criticism of Juvenal in a passage replete with associative reminiscences of him might be thought to be deliberately ironic, rendering either the criticism or the digression insincere. This would be highly unusual, given that parody is not cited as a function of literary *imitatio* in ancient treatises, although that is not in itself sufficient to discount the possibility. More compelling is the distance which separates Ammianus' two Roman digressions; any humorous charge in the denunciation in Book 28 of those who read Juvenal is considerably weakened by the passing of fourteen books since the first passage so reminiscent of the satirist.

Another possibility concerns the interpretation of Juvenal in the fourth century — clearly an elusive issue. The reference to Juvenal at 28.4.14 could lead us to believe that Ammianus had no quarrel with Juvenal but only with those who read little else. For one further parallel between Juvenal and Ammianus generates the enduring irony that criticism of the prevailing literary taste at Rome is common to both authors — Juvenal's first satire, 'Must I be always a listener only?'[12] condemns the interest in contemporary tragedy and epic, and Ammianus condemns the taste for Juvenal (and Marius Maximus). The importance of taste is fundamental here: Ammianus does not so much criticize Juvenal as those who devote their reading to him — perhaps those who considered the *Satires* of Juvenal not a challenge to their own accepted standards of behaviour, but a justification of them. However, against this, Ammianus closes his brief observation of popular reading tastes with an avowal not to pass judgement. He recognizes the satirist's popularity but in doing so makes no comment on the reasons for his popularity or on the contemporary interpretation of the satirist.[13]

Even so it is difficult to claim that there is not an implicit criticism of Juvenal in this key sentence; there is certainly something in the tone which has convinced all those I have read on the issue that Ammianus is here somehow disparaging Juvenal (and Marius Maximus). Certainly the link between the satirist and those who despise learning like poison damns the satirist by association. The reasons for the condemnation of the satirist must lie in Ammianus' reaction to him, not that of other Romans.

The solution is to be found not only in the similarities between the two texts, but also in their differences. In Juvenal's seventh *Satire*, on the lack of money in literary enterprises, historiography receives particular attention (lines 98–104): there is no profit in it. But this observation, not itself critical of historians, is followed not by reflections on the cultural climate of a society which offers greater reward to town-criers than to historians, but by a ruthless justification of the financial hardships facing *historiarum scriptores*: 'Well, they're a lazy lot, too fond of their couch in the shade.'[14] Whether or not the narrator agrees with this anonymous interlocutor, the sentiment is aired and its validity unchallenged. Ammianus can hardly have approved.[15]

Another important difference between the authors was in nationality. Juvenal was a Roman, writing about life and manners in the city;[16] Ammianus, in these passages also covering Roman life and manners, was, of course, a *Graecus*. Juvenal's *Satires* contain some famously bitter anti-Greek sentiment. The most famous attack on Greeks appears in the third *Satire*.[17] The speaker is one Umbricius who was packing his possessions onto a wagon and leaving Rome to move to Cumae: 'My fellow Romans, I cannot put up with a city of Greeks.'[18] From this, he launches into sixty-five lines of anti-Greek venom. The fact that Umbricius, a Roman, an insider, who wants to leave Rome, makes the Greek community there one of his primary objections to the city, would obviously be distasteful to Ammianus, a Greek, an outsider who was trying to settle inside the city.[19]

For his part, in the digressions about Rome, Ammianus mentions on more than one occasion how unfriendly the native Romans were towards *peregrini*.[20] He writes of the unpleasant hesitation which preceded the extension of an invitation to dinner, or the offer of dole, to a foreigner:

> Moreover, when at suitable intervals preparations are put in hand for a tedious and unwholesome dinner or the distribution of the customary clients' dole, it is a matter of anxious debate whether, except for those who are owed a return of hospitality, anyone from abroad is invited.[21]

Ammianus denounces the broader-scale racism underpinning the expulsion of foreigners from the city during times of food shortage (in 383): 'Lastly, the ultimate disgrace, not long ago, when foreigners were banished in headlong haste from the city because a famine was expected.'[22] Later he remarks on the meagre courtesy shown to foreigners: 'As for strangers, even those to whom they are under an obligation, they think they have done everything that politeness requires if they ask what spa or bath they frequent or where they are putting up.'[23] The urban poor are also charged with such racist motivation: 'they clamour for the expulsion of foreigners from the city, though they have always been dependent on the help of these same foreigners for their livelihood'.[24] Of course there is likely to be an element of aggressive self-defence built into these allegations of Roman xenophobia, rather than what might be termed liberal thinking; nevertheless Ammianus' preoccupations and the sentiments expressed and implied set the ideology of the text far apart from the attitude dramatized in Juvenal's *Satires*.[25]

Briefly to leave aside the question of any relationship with, and attitude to, Juvenal in these passages, what has not been disputed is that the Roman digressions are satirical in character. This orthodoxy is worthy of further consideration. It has long been noted that Christian apologists of the Roman empire incorporated satire in their work as a powerful means of pouring scorn on pagan traditions.[26] However, Ammianus' inclusion of sustained satirical material in his work is, I believe, unparalleled in classical historiography. This idiosyncrasy is revealing of Ammianus' attitude towards history and historiography. When introducing the first of his Roman digressions, Ammianus gives no hint of the satire that is to follow. Rather, he stresses his intention to restrict himself to the truth, *nusquam a veritate sponte propria digressurus* (14.6.2).[27] That satire, a genre characterized in part by its tendency to distort, could be considered an appropriate means of expressing truth, is an extraordinary development in historiography, but one which has been neglected in studies both of Ammianus and of satire. As with, for example, the use of speeches by Thucydides, the degree of licence inherent in satire did not render it unsuitable for inclusion in Ammianus' history. Juvenal's work constitutes one of the most memorable and penetrating attacks on life in the city; to Ammianus, its satirical character did not undermine its claims to veracity.

The parallels between the *Satires* and the *Res Gestae* in Ammianus' two Roman digressions indicate that the historian had read and admired aspects of the *Satires*; echoes of Juvenal's rhetoric, themes, subject matter and diction, and tones, suggest that Ammianus knew Juvenal's work and consciously imitated aspects of his picture of Rome. This associative evocation of Juvenal is consistent with his compositional practice in respect of other authors. As Fornara points out, the taste of such a poetic might strike us as peculiar, but that is our problem, not Ammianus'. But as an historian, Ammianus could object to the denigration of historians in *Satire* 7; and as a Greek in Rome, an outsider inside the city and the system, he was naturally going to be outraged and threatened by the bitter anti-Greek sentiment expressed variously in the *Satires* of Juvenal, an insider, who in Umbricius even had one Roman character willingly move outside the city. But xenophobia and denunciation of literary endeavours are only two of many themes in Juvenal's work; in other respects, Juvenal was very dear to Ammianus, and imitative satire became for him a valid medium through which to describe and criticize Roman *mores*. In this novel enterprise can be seen the wit, learning and passion of the historian, aware of his inheritance but unafraid of change.[28]

Notes

1 Accordingly, there has been little scholarly consensus. There is no entry for Juvenal in G.B.A. Fletcher's 'Stylistic Borrowings and Parallels in Ammianus Marcellinus', *RPh*, 3rd Series 11 (1937), 337–95. With characteristic force, R. Syme states 'Traces of Juvenal have been duly looked for in Ammianus. The search does not prove very renumerative'; 'Ammianus, Juvenal and the HA', in *Ammianus and the Historia Augusta*, Oxford 1968, 84–8, at 84. He cites the three sets of parallel passages indicated by E.A. Thompson in *The Historical Work of Ammianus Marcellinus*, Cambridge 1947 (indicated in the text with an asterisk). However, Syme concedes that

> 'the historian may have derived from the satirist an encouragement to portray with malice the inhabitants of *urbs aeterna*, the poor as well as the rich and pretentious, using the same traditional themes, but enhanced by what he had seen and known.'

(84)

Thompson himself wrote that Ammianus felt driven by what he saw at Rome 'into writing satire which in depth of feeling would almost bear comparison with Juvenal himself' (p. 14). Most recently, P.J. Smith, 'A Note on Ammianus and Juvenal', *LCM* 19 (1994), 23–4, at 23 states that 'there are definite similarities between Ammianus and Juvenal . . . which would lead to a spiritual affinity'. In a sense, what I hope to begin to provide in this chapter is greater rigour in considering the two authors than has been sought previously, when readers have been content to acknowledge in Ammianus a vague 'Juvenalian atmosphere'.

2 G. Highet, *Juvenal the Satirist*, Oxford 1954, 180–90; M. Coffey, *Roman Satire*, London 1976, 145 and bibliography 252–3; Tertullian, *De Pudic.* 1.1; *Ad Marc.* 4.24.12; Lactantius, *Div. Inst.* 3.29.

3 Syme, *Ammianus and the Historia Augusta*, 88. The quotation of Juvenal by Lactantius would just about allow the *Historia Augusta*'s dissimulation to stand, although the survival of the text in North Africa does not signal its popularity elsewhere. More equivocal than Syme is A. Cameron, 'Literary Allusions in the *Historia Augusta*', *Hermes* 92 (1964), 363–77.

4 For Claudian's interest in Juvenal see Highet, *Juvenal*, 188 and 301; for Symmachus', *ibid.*, 298.

5 Syme, *Ammianus and the Historia Augusta*, 87.

6 Neither the parallels nor the classifications are exhaustive.

7 Thompson, *The Historical Work of Ammianus Marcellinus*, 14–15, cites a further parallel from outside the Roman digressions, concerning capital punishment: Amm. Marc. 29.2.18 – Juvenal, *Sat.* 6.221.

8 C.W. Fornara, 'Studies in Ammianus Marcellinus II: Ammianus' Knowledge and Use of Greek and Latin Literature', *Historia* 41 (1992), 420–38, at 438.

9 28.4.14: *quidam detestantes ut venena doctrinas Iuvenalem et Marium Maximum curatiore studio legunt, nulla volumina praeter haec in profundo otio contrectantes, quam ob causam non iudicioli est nostri* (trans. Hamilton).

10 Thompson, *The Historical Work of Ammianus Marcellinus*, 14–15; R. Pack, 'The Roman Digressions of Ammianus Marcellinus', *Transactions and Proceedings of the American Philosophical Association* 84 (1953), 181–89, at 183; A. Wallace-Hadrill, *Ammianus Marcellinus. The Later Roman Empire (A.D. 354–378)*, Harmondsworth 1986, 470; J.F. Matthews,

'Ammianus and the Eternity of Rome', in C. Holdsworth and T.P. Wiseman (eds), *The Inheritance of Historiography 350–900*, Exeter 1986, 17–29, at 20.
11 T.R. Glover, *Life and Letters in the Fourth Century*, Cambridge 1901, 42–3, with examples.
12 Juvenal, *Sat.* 1.1: *semper ego auditor tantum?* (trans. N. Rudd, *The Satires of Juvenal*, Oxford 1991).
13 Cf. Syme, *Ammianus and the Historia Augusta*, 84, on the satirist's popularity: 'The reason is patent. Juvenal brought up and paraded the epic age of luxury and vice.'
14 Juvenal, *Sat.* 7.105: *sed genus ignavum, quod lecto gaudet et umbra* (trans. Rudd).
15 This, despite the fact that as a well-read writer Ammianus surely had strong opinions about what contemporary Latin historiography was and could be; consider, for example, the differences between the *Res Gestae*, the fourth-century breviarists and the *Historia Augusta*.
16 Few reliable details about Juvenal's life survive. See Highet, *Juvenal*, 2–4; Coffey, *Roman Satire*, 119–23.
17 For further anti-Greek sentiment in the *Satires*, see e.g. *Sat.* 6.184–91, 11.147–8.
18 Juvenal, *Sat.* 3.60–1: *non possum ferre, Quirites, Graecam urbem.*
19 This explanation was first suggested by Thompson, *The Historical Work of Ammianus Marcellinus*, 15 and is developed by Smith, 'A Note on Ammianus and Juvenal'.
20 This is despite the fact that Ammianus appears to envisage for himself a readership consisting of Romans and *peregrini* (14.6.2); Pack, 'The Roman Digressions', 182ff.
21 14.6.14: *cum autem commodis intervallata temporibus convivia longa et noxia coeperint apparari vel distributio sollemnium sportularum, anxia deliberatione tractatur, an exceptis his, quibus vicissitudo debetur, peregrinum invitari conveniet*; trans. Hamilton.
22 14.6.19: *postremo ad id indignitatis est ventum, ut, cum peregrini ob formidatam haud ita dudum alimentorum inopiam pellerentur ab urbe praecipites*; trans. Hamilton.
23 28.4.10: *abundare omni cultu humanitatis peregrinum putantes, cuius forte etiam gratia sunt obligati, interrogatum, quibus thermis utatur aut aquis, aut ad quam successerit domum*; trans. Hamilton. This can be contrasted with Roman attitudes in the past, as described by Ammianus in 14.6.21: 'There can be no doubt that formerly, when every good quality found a dwelling in Rome, many of the grandees tried by various acts of kindness to keep among them strangers of good birth' (*illud autem non dubitatur quod cum esset aliquando virtutum omnium domicilium Roma, ingenuos advenas plerique nobilium ... humanitatis multiformibus officiis retentabant*); trans. Hamilton.
24 28.4.32: *peregrinos vociferantur pelli debere, quorum subsidiis semper nisi sunt ac steterunt, et taetris vocibus et absurdis*; trans. Hamilton.
25 Cf. the pejorative sense of *peregrinus* in Juvenal, at *Sat.* 4.127, 6.298, 8.225 and 14.187.
26 E.g. Tertullian, Lactantius, Jerome, Salvian. See A.H. Weston, 'Latin Satirical Writing Subsequent to Juvenal', Yale University Thesis 1915; significantly, there is no entry for Ammianus.
27 Ammianus characterizes his history as *opus veritatem professum* at its close (31.16.9). Cf. M. Grant, *Greek and Roman Historians. Information and Misinformation*, London 1995, 97, who says that Ammianus' 'literary tricks sometimes produce impressions which are not really compatible with truthfulness'. For the question of veracity in Ammianus and historiography in general, see T.D. Barnes, 'Literary Convention, Nostalgia and Reality in Ammianus Marcellinus', in G. Clarke et al. (eds), *Reading the Past in Late Antiquity*, Rushcutters Bay 1990, 59–92, at 82–4; N.J.E. Austin, 'Autobiography and History: Some Later Roman Historians and their Veracity', in B. Croke and A.M. Emmett (eds), *History and Historians in Late Antiquity*, Sydney 1983, 54–65; T.P. Wiseman, 'Classical Historiography', in C. Holdsworth and T.P. Wiseman (eds), *The Inheritance of Historiography 350–900*, Exeter 1986, 1–6.
28 The formal and informal suggestions received at Durham helped to improve this chapter significantly. I extend further thanks to Michael Brown of Newcastle University, who kindly commented upon a later version.

13

A PERSIAN AT ROME

Ammianus and Eunapius, *Frg.* 68

David Woods

It has been well said of Ammianus that 'it is his silences that reveal his apologetical or polemical intentions more than his explicit criticisms of Christianity', and it is my intention here to draw attention to yet another such silence on his part.[1] To begin, however, I must focus on the positive, and demonstrate how Ammianus provides the key to the correct interpretation of that fragment of Eunapius' *History* which has excited more attention than most, his account of the manner in which an anonymous Persian prefect of Rome celebrated an imperial victory over some unidentified barbarians (Eunapius, *Frg.* 68):[2]

> There was a Persian, a prefect in Rome, who reduced the success of the Romans to mockery and laughter ("Ότι Πέρσης ἦν ἐν 'Ρώμῃ ἔπαρχος πρὸς χλευασίαν καὶ γέλωτα τὴν 'Ρωμαϊκὴν παραφέρων εὐτυχίαν). Wishing to offer a representation of what had been done, he assembled many small panels in the middle of the Circus. But all the contents of his paintings were laughable, and he unwittingly mocked his subjects in his presentation. For nowhere did the paintings show or allude to either the bravery of the emperor, or the strength of the soldiers, or anything that was obviously a proper battle. But a hand extended as if from the clouds, and by the hand was inscribed, 'The hand of God driving off the barbarians' (it is shameful but necessary to write this down), and again on the other side, 'The barbarians fleeing God', and other things even more odious and stupid than these, the nonsense of drunken painters.

This fragment has been preserved in a tenth-century source, the *Excerpta de Sententiis* (as *ES* 72), among fragments recording events in and about Constantinople between the autumn of 399, when Gainas allied himself with the rebel Tribigild (*ES* 71 = Eunapius, *Frg.* 67.11), and the summer of 400, when Fravitta was appointed to command the war against Gainas (*ES* 73 = Eunapius, *Frg.* 69.1). Whenever the order of the fragments in this

156

work can be checked, they prove to be in correct chronological sequence, and this is perhaps the only aspect of the problem under discussion here upon which there is general agreement, that Eunapius included his account of the Persian prefect in Rome as part of his larger narrative of events in and about Constantinople during the period 399–400. After this, there is little agreement, as a brief summary of the positions adopted by some of the most recent commentators will quickly reveal.

The first problem concerns the identification of 'Rome'. Does 'Rome' here refer to Rome on the Tiber, or 'New Rome', i.e. Constantinople? Sivan opts for Rome on the Tiber,[3] while Cameron and Long follow a long line of commentators in opting for Constantinople.[4] The answer is important because it affects how we answer the next question also. Who exactly was this 'Persian'? Baldwin has argued that there was no real Persian, that the title was just a nickname, a play by Eunapius on the name of Hesiod's thieving brother, because the official concerned had stolen the credit of victory over the barbarians from the emperor and his army and given it to God instead.[5] Because he believes that the reference is to the prefect of Constantinople, Baldwin identifies him as the Clearchus who is often thought to have held this office in 400.[6] Blockley accepts the explanation of 'Persian' as a nickname, but insists that the reference is to a prefect of Rome. Since he interprets the victory in question as that over the rebellious *comes Africae* Gildo in 398, he then identifies the 'Persian' as Quintilius Laetus, prefect of Rome *c*. 398/9.[7] Sivan also accepts 'Persian' as a nickname, but identifies him as Longinianus, the prefect of Rome *c*. 400/2, mainly because she identifies the relevant victory as that which Stilicho gained over Alaric and his Goths at Pollentia in 402.[8] Finally, Cameron and Long prefer to identify the 'Persian' as an otherwise unknown prefect of Constantinople who held office during the summer of 400, arguing that the evidence that Clearchus held office then is insecure at best.[9] They reject the possibility that 'Persian' was a nickname, preferring to argue either that this prefect was of genuine Persian origin, identifiable as the younger Hormisdas perhaps, or that Perses ('Persian') was a real name even. As for the occasion of the imperial victory, they identify this as the departure of Gainas from Constantinople and the massacre of his remaining Gothic supporters there on 12 July 400.

Despite their obvious differences, the above commentators have all approached this fragment in much the same manner. Hence they have made the same two fundamental errors, although each to a different extent. First, they have all tried to date the relevant victory in or about 400 because *ES* 72 occurs in the middle of a sequence of excerpts all of which refer to Gainas' rebellion 399–400, and the compiler of the *Excerpta* always preserves the correct order of events as present in his original source, Eunapius' *History* here. Those who cannot identify the necessary victory with some event during this exact period 399–400 tend to argue that Eunapius was himself confused, that he found it difficult to combine eastern and western sources, with the result that he misplaced some western events in his narrative, which was chiefly concerned with events in the East.[10] This is their way of explaining why Eunapius apparently described the celebration of the victory at Pollentia in 402, for example, or of the defeat of Gildo in 398, in the midst of his narrative for the period 399–400. This is possible, of course, but it tends to lead people to overlook the alternative. Eunapius sometimes interrupted his narrative with long digressions which could include anecdotes from completely different periods. For example, and to stay with the source of the fragment under discussion here, *ES* 48–51 (= Eunapius, *Frg.* 46.1, 46.4, 47.1–2 respectively), all describe events during the early years of Theodosius I *c.* 379–83, as do *ES* 53–6 (= Eunapius, *Frg.* 48.2–3, 50, 55), but *ES* 52 (= Eunapius, *Frg.* 48.1) describes an event under Nero (54–68). It clearly derives from a moralizing digression on the theme of divine retribution in which a comparison was drawn between an event under Nero and events under Theodosius. So if *ES* 72 represents a similar digression from his main narrative on Eunapius' part, it may refer to almost any period in Roman history. It is not necessary, therefore, to restrict ourselves to personalities and events *c.* 400 when we seek to identify the 'Persian' and the victory which he celebrated.

The second error common to most commentators is that they refuse to admit that *ES* 72 does not necessarily preserve the exact words of Eunapius, and to avoid undue reliance, therefore, on any particular term. Here I find myself in complete agreement with Cameron and Long in their assessment of this fragment:

> It should be noted that the text as given in the *Excerpta* cannot in any case reflect Eunapius's *ipsissima verba* as transmitted. 'Prefect *in* Rome' (ἦν ἐν Ῥώμῃ ἔπαρχος) would be an odd way to refer to the prefect of either Rome or Constantinople, and the construction is abrupt and improbable. It seems clear that the excerptor has at the very least abridged an originally fuller sentence, as often happens at the beginning of an excerpt, possibly substituting something closer to the style of his own day.[11]

They say this because they wish to argue that the excerptor has omitted the word 'New' from an original reference by Eunapius to 'New Rome', or Constantinople. But why stop here? Why be so certain that the excerptor correctly preserves the term which Eunapius had originally used to describe the office held by this 'Persian'? Was he really a prefect (ἔπαρχος) at all?

I will now attempt a fresh interpretation of this fragment by avoiding these two errors. I begin by emphasizing that in order to reach a correct understanding of this fragment, one must constantly test one's assumptions concerning its style and language against the style and language of the rest of the Eunapian corpus. Unfortunately, our knowledge of Eunapius' *History* comes from a variety of sources, principally from that part of his *Historia*

Nova where Zosimus used Eunapius as his main source (2–5.27.1), from the *Excerpta de Sententiis*, and the *Suda*.[12] The result is that we can never be sure whether any particular phrase or term belongs to the author or compiler of one of these sources rather than to Eunapius himself, although the survival of Eunapius' *Vitae Sophistarum* does prove of some assistance in this matter. Yet when a phrase or term is common to all or most of these sources, this surely suggests a dramatically increased possibility, a probability even, that this represents a genuine Eunapian usage. The contrary is also true, that when a phrase or term is absent from all or most of these sources, this suggests that it was absent from the *History* also. In this instance, therefore, it is noteworthy that the known fragments of Eunapius' *History* always refer to Constantinople as such and never as 'New Rome'. The same is true of Eunapius in his *Vitae Sophistarum* also. Hence it is difficult to avoid the conclusion that in the case of *ES* 72 too, 'Rome' means Rome simply, and that the 'Persian' ought to have held his celebrations in Rome, not Constantinople.

We must now establish a time-frame for these celebrations. Given the nature of Eunapian digressions, these may have occurred at almost any point in Roman history. The chief limiting factor here is that the 'hand of God' is a Christian motif, which is why the pagan Eunapius finds it so objectionable.[13] For this reason, the victory of the first Christian emperor Constantine I at the battle of the Milvian Bridge in 312 provides a *terminus post quem* for our investigations. The 'hand of God' appeared on a gold multiple issued by the mint at Constantinople in 330,[14] and on coins issued to commemorate the consecration of the deceased Constantine in 337.[15] As far as we can now tell, it next appeared on a bronze coin issued only by the mint at Sirmium in 364.[16] Later, it appeared on the obverse of *solidi* commemorating the coronation of Arcadius in 383, and again on the obverse of the *solidi*, and the reverse of the bronze coinage, which were issued to commemorate the coronation of Eudoxia as Augusta in 400.[17] It also appeared on the reverse of some *solidi* issued at Ravenna sometime after the death of the emperor Arcadius in 408.[18] Finally, as far as the present note is concerned, it appeared on the reverse of the *solidi* which were issued at Rome in order to celebrate the coronation of Valentinian III in 425.[19] It can be seen, therefore, that Christian emperors availed themselves of this iconographical device from a very early period, and that its appearance on the placards issued by the 'Persian' proves little concerning the identity of the emperor under whom he served.

We are now searching for an occasion, sometime during the period *c.* 312–400, when a 'Persian', a senior figure obviously, attended the celebration in Rome of an imperial victory over barbarians. Other than trivial references to Persians within their own empire, the only two office-holders to whom Eunapius certainly applied this description were Hormisdas, the brother of King Shapur of Persia (309–79) who defected to Rome *c.* 324, and his son of the same name. Zosimus affords some prominence to the elder Hormisdas in his work, particularly during his account of the emperor Julian's Persian expedition in 363.[20] Indeed, the fact that we know nothing more about the elder Hormisdas following this expedition suggests that he died in action, probably during the same engagement which witnessed the fatal wounding of Julian himself and the deaths of several other of his most senior officers. As for the younger Hormisdas, Zosimus records that he fought on the side of Procopius during his rebellion against the emperor Valens in 365–6, and that he led some Gothic recruits to Egypt during the early reign of Theodosius I.[21] Doubtless Eunapius, Zosimus' main source, afforded similar treatment to the two Hormisdases in his work also. Indeed, the *Suda* explicitly attributes to Eunapius a line which clearly refers to the role played by the younger Hormisdas in support of the usurper Procopius.[22] Hence the suggestion by Cameron and Long, as noted already, that the 'Persian' may be identifiable as the younger Hormisdas. But was either Hormisdas ever in Rome? It is noteworthy that the elder Hormisdas features prominently in Ammianus' account of the visit by Constantius II to Rome in 357 as he reports how, when Constantius expressed amazement at the size of the Forum of Trajan, and declared that he would only be able to imitate its equestrian statue, Hormisdas, who was near to him at the time, joked that he would have to order a similar stable to be built also.[23]

The chief factor preventing the identification of our 'Persian' with the elder Hormisdas during the occasion of this visit is that the former is described as 'prefect in Rome' (ἦν ἐν Ῥώμῃ ἔπαρχος). For there can be no doubt that the prefect of Rome in 357 was the senatorial aristocrat Memmius Vitrasius Orfitus.[24] However, there is strong reason to suspect that the excerptor has erred in his description of the 'Persian' as 'prefect in Rome'. The question which needs to be addressed here is, how would Eunapius himself have normally referred to the prefect of Rome (*praefectus urbi*)? There can be little doubt that he would probably have used the term ἔπαρχος to translate the Latin *praefectus*, since this is his preferred usage in his *Vitae Sophistarum*.[25] But ἔπαρχος always governed the genitive, whether in Eunapius' work or elsewhere. The fact that we have 'prefect *in* Rome' rather than 'prefect *of* Rome' is immediately suspicious here, since a prefect *in* Rome was not necessarily the same thing at all as a prefect *of* Rome. It is probable, therefore, that the excerptor has substituted the more specific ἔπαρχος, the term normally used to describe the prefects either of Rome or Constantinople,[26] for a vaguer original term, being misled by the description 'in Rome' to believe that the reference was to the prefect of Rome in particular. In short, he misconstrued the construction of the original sentence, and read the phrase 'in Rome' as part of a title of office rather than as a simple statement of physical fact, that the office-holder really was in Rome. One suspects that this original term had probably been one of those vague terms so beloved of classicizing historians which could be used of a wide variety of officials whether military or civilian, most likely either ἡγεμών or ἄρχων. Hence a ἡγεμών, for example, who happened to be in Rome was misunderstood as the ἡγεμών ἐν Ῥώμῃ and transcribed as the ἔπαρχος ἐν Ῥώμῃ.

So what was Hormisdas' position at the time of his visit to Rome in 357? He must have held a military office of some kind, since Zonaras tells us that Constantius II had appointed him to command a strong cavalry squadron, and we know that he also played an active role as a senior cavalry commander during Julian's Persian expedition in 363.[27] I have suggested elsewhere that he probably commanded the *schola scutariorum clibanariorum*, one of the *scholae palatinae*, the cavalry units which served as the imperial bodyguard, for the greater part of the period *c.* 324–62.[28] This would explain both his easy access to the emperor as revealed by his conversation with Constantius in Rome as reported above, and the mysterious lack of involvement by the commander of this *schola* in the domestic politics of the day which affected the careers of so many of the tribunes of the other *scholae palatinae*. Hence it is my opinion that Hormisdas commanded the *schola scutariorum clibanariorum* during his visit to Rome in 357. It is worth noting, therefore, that the one fragment of Eunapius' *History* which seems to describe the commander of one of these *scholae* refers to him as the ἡγεμών τῶν δορυφόρων.[29] So if Eunapius did refer to Hormisdas by his office, then he probably used the vague ἡγεμών in his case also.

Visually, the *schola scutariorum clibanariorum* was by far the most impressive of the *scholae palatinae*, because of the full armour of both horse and rider.[30] Hence Ammianus singles its members out as he describes Constantius' entry into Rome in 357 (16.10.8). One need not doubt that they played a prominent part in much of the subsequent military ceremony also. It is clear, therefore, that if Hormisdas is to be held responsible for the placement of the small placards in the Circus, then it must be as the head of a body of troops who paraded these about the Circus before setting them in place. The very size of the placards proves that they had originally been designed for use in some such ceremony, since they can hardly have been visible at all to the crowds when finally set along the spine of the Circus.[31] Indeed, such placards seem to have been a traditional feature of triumphal processions.[32] Furthermore, although the wording of our fragment is ambiguous, it does seem to claim that the placards were inscribed on both sides, front and back, which suggests that they had been designed to be read from behind as well as from the front. It is my argument, therefore, that these placards were paraded into and about the Circus by Hormisdas and his men immediately prior to a military display, probably a mock battle similar to that which took place in the Circus Maximus also when the emperor Honorius paid a rare visit to Rome in late 403.[33]

This brings us to the subject of these placards and the identity of the 'barbarians' whose defeat they commemorated. Ammianus characterizes Constantius' visit to Rome as a celebration of his defeat of the usurper Magnentius (350–3), a triumph over Roman blood (16.10.1). Yet Magnentius was a 'barbarian' who enjoyed the support of many other 'barbarians' also, or so it was alleged.[34] So Constantius' defeat of Magnentius and his brother Decentius was easily characterized as a triumph over rebellious 'barbarians'. The turning-point in this civil war came on 28 September 351 when Constantius II defeated Magnentius at the battle of Mursa, and it is noteworthy that it was his armoured cavalry, his *clibanarii*, that finally turned this battle in Constantius' favour.[35] This may well explain why the *schola scutariorum clibanariorum* under Hormisdas were allowed the privilege of bearing the placards depicting the defeat of the 'barbarians' into the Circus. They had played the key role in the defeat of these 'barbarians'. But why the emphasis on the 'hand of God'? Was it merely routine imperial presumption, that God was naturally on the side of the rightful emperor, or was it something more?

There survives a letter by bishop Cyril of Jerusalem to Constantius in which he describes a gigantic luminous cross which had allegedly appeared in the sky over Jerusalem on 7 May 351, and which he interprets as a sign of God's favour towards Constantius.[36] That Constantius would have been receptive to such a tale is revealed by the fact that he spent much of the day of the battle itself in prayer at a martyrial basilica just outside Mursa, and was entirely convinced by Bishop Valens of Mursa when he declared that an angel had revealed Constantius' victory to him.[37] So when in 357 Constantius celebrated his victory over Magnentius, he did so in the conviction that God was on his side and had honoured him with a sign. Hence the prominence afforded the hand of God on the placards which he had paraded about the Circus. These were a direct reference to the sign which had appeared in the sky over Jerusalem on 7 May 351. It did not matter that this might have offended some of the pagan aristocracy at Rome, as it was to offend Eunapius nearly fifty years later even. For his decision to remove the altar of Victory from the senate-house at this time also,[38] a far more direct attack upon the paganism of many of the aristocracy, reveals just how little store Constantius set by their feelings. One suspects even that when, in the speech which he delivered to Constantius at Rome in early 357, Themistius drew a brief parallel between Constantius' defeat of Magnentius and Constantine's defeat of Maxentius, he was merely repeating an important theme in current imperial propaganda, but that as a pagan he was disinclined to dwell on that element which lay at the heart of the parallel, and proved it to imperial satisfaction at least, the sign in the sky.[39]

This brings us to the occasion of Eunapius' digression from his main narrative of events. What was it that led him from a discussion of events at Constantinople in 400 to a description of events at Rome in 357? The connection, it seems to me, is the claim of divine intervention which Christians made on each occasion. According to the ecclesiastical historian Socrates, a number of angels appeared in the form of giant men and deterred Gainas from burning the palace at Constantinople and declaring himself emperor in early July 400.[40] This was alleged to have happened just before Gainas left Constantinople and the Gothic population which remained there was massacred. The form that this massacre took was that many of the Goths sought sanctuary in a church which imperial forces then burned to the ground. Not unexpectedly, devout Christians were greatly offended by this action, as even Zosimus records (5.19.5). This, of course, is why the story of the angelic defence of the imperial palace was invented, to prove that God was on the emperor's side, and that if He did not actually welcome it, then He at least tolerated the burning of a church in this instance. It is clear that imperial officials were eager to argue that God had intervened on their behalf, even if their selfish political motivations were all too apparent to more thoughtful Christians. This, the determination of these officials to claim divine intervention and approval, a claim which even many Christians rejected, was what led Eunapius to digress as he did. For similar allegations by earlier officials also had been no less ill-founded and damaging to the imperial reputation, or so he wished to argue.

To summarize, therefore, the interpretation of Eunapius, *Frg.* 68 is fraught with difficulties, but I believe the interpretation which I have outlined here poses the least number of difficulties. The 'Persian' was indeed a Persian, and when he acted 'in Rome', he really did act at Rome. He was not a prefect (ἔπαρχος), however, but a military officer. The excerptor misconstrued his source, and misled by the reference to Rome, substituted a more precise term (ἔπαρχος) in place of the vaguer term (probably ἡγεμών) of his original source, in the mistaken belief that the reference really was to a prefect of Rome. Fortunately, Ammianus' account of the visit by Constantius II to Rome in 357 provides a clue to the correct interpretation of this fragment, and an alternative to the strained efforts which have been made to identify this 'Persian' with one of the known urban prefects *c.* 400. In brief, our Persian prefect of Rome is none other than the elder Hormisdas, the tribune of the *schola scutariorum clibanariorum*, as he visited Rome in 357 in the company of Constantius II.

We can now return to the silences of Ammianus, in particular to his silence concerning the controversial and unashamedly Christian nature of Constantius' triumphal celebrations in 357. This silence is not very surprising, since he is also silent concerning the controversy over the removal of the statue of Victory from the senate-house. It is all the more striking, though, because of the large amount of space which he does afford to the contemporary decision by Constantius to arrange for the erection of a second obelisk in the Circus Maximus, and because of his emphasis upon the fact that this obelisk had originally been dedicated to the Sun god.[41] So while Ammianus does not directly attest the erection, however temporarily, of Christian placards in the Circus Maximus, one suspects that his emphasis upon the erection of an obelisk dedicated to the Sun god there instead, owes much to his indignation at Constantius' behaviour at this time, including his support for the erection of these placards.[42] In brief, Ammianus was no less angered than Eunapius that Constantius had credited his victories to the support of the God of the Christians rather than to the strength of his soldiers, but he chose to express this anger differently.

Notes

1. T.D. Barnes, 'Ammianus Marcellinus and his World', *CP* 88 (1993), 55–70, at 68.
2. Text and translation (slightly revised) from R.C. Blockley, *The Fragmentary Classicising Historians of the Later Roman Empire*, 2 vols, Liverpool 1981–3, vol. 2, 108–9. All references to the fragments follow Blockley rather than C. Müller, *FHG* IV, Paris 1868.
3. H. Sivan, 'Eunapius and the West: Remarks on *Frg.* 78 (Müller)', *Historia* 40 (1991), 95–104.
4. A. Cameron and J. Long, *Barbarians and Politics at the Court of Arcadius*, Berkeley 1993, 218–23.
5. B. Baldwin, 'Perses: A Mysterious Prefect in Eunapius', *Byzantion* 46 (1976), 5–8.
6. For Clearchus, see *PLRE* I, 213. This identification had been accepted earlier by, e.g., S. Mazzarino, *Stilicone. La crisi imperiale dopo Teodosio*, Rome 1942, 362; A. Chastagnol, *La Préfecture urbaine sous le Bas-Empire*, Paris 1960, 81.
7. Blockley, *Fragmentary Classicising Historians*, vol. 1, 161–2. For Quintilius, see *PLRE* I, 492–3.
8. Sivan, 'Eunapius and the West', 100–1. For Longinianus, see *PLRE* II, 686–7.
9. Cameron and Long, *Barbarians and Politics*, 222.
10. Sivan, 'Eunapius and the West', 102.
11. Cameron and Long, *Barbarians and Politics*, 221.
12. See T.M. Banchich, 'The Historical Fragments of Eunapius of Sardis', unpub. doct. diss. State University of New York 1985 (UMI 8528233), 39–66.
13. See J.D. MacIsaac, 'The Hand of God: A Numismatic Study', *Traditio* 31 (1975), 322–8.
14. *RIC* 7, 576.
15. Eusebius, *Vit. Const.* 4.73. See P. Bruun, 'The Consecration Coins of Constantine the Great', *Arctos* 1 (1954), 19–31.
16. *RIC* 9, 159.
17. *RIC* 10, 241–3, 247–8.
18. *Ibid.*, 331.
19. *Ibid.*, 363.
20. Zosimus 2.27; 3.11, 13, 15, 18, 23, 29; 4.8, 30. See *PLRE* I, 443.
21. Zosimus 4.8, 30. See *PLRE* I, 443.
22. *Suda* M 1048 (= Eunapius, *Frg.* 34.8). It derives from the same passage in Eunapius as Zosimus 4.8.1.
23. Amm. Marc. 16.10.15–16. See R.O. Edbrooke, 'Constantius and Hormisdas in the Forum of Trajan', *Mnemosyne* 28 (1975), 412–17; also A. Cameron, 'Biondo's Ammianus: Constantius and Hormisdas at Rome', *Harvard Studies in Classical Philology* 92 (1989), 423–36.
24. *PLRE* I, 651–2.
25. E.g. he consistently refers to the praetorian prefect as the ἔπαρχος τῆς βασιλικῆς αὐλῆς (*V. Sophist.* 463), or the ἔπαρχος τῆς αὐλῆς (*V. Sophist.* 479), although he does refer to the Augustal prefect of Egypt as the officer ἄρχων τὴν πολιτικὴν ἀρχὴν (*V. Sophist.* 472).
26. Cameron and Long, *Barbarians and Politics*, 220–1.
27. Zonaras 13.5.33; Amm. Marc. 24.1.2, 2.4, 2.11, 5.4.
28. D. Woods, 'Ammianus and Some *Tribuni Scholarum Palatinarum c.* AD 353–64', *CQ* 47 (1997), 269–91, at 289–90.

29 Eunapius, *Frg.* 67.8 (= *Suda* S 793). See D. Woods, 'Subarmachius, Bacurius, and the *Schola Scutariorum Sagittariorum*', *CP* 91 (1996), 365–71.
30 See Julian, *Or.* 1.37d, 2.57c; Heliodorus, *Aeth.* 9.15.5; Claudian, *In Ruf.* 2.359–60.
31 Contrast their size to that of the large placards depicting his victories which the emperor Maximinus (235–8) erected before the senate-house in Rome (Herodian, 7.2.8; SHA, *Max.* 12.10).
32 E.g. Ambrose, *Exp. Ev. Sec. Luc.* 10.109 describes the parading of *excisarum urbium imagines oppidorumque captorum simulacra*.
33 Claudian, *VI. Cons. Hon.* 611–39. See M. Dewar, *Claudian: Panegyricus de Sexto Consulatu Honorii Augusti*, Oxford 1996, 42–3, 400–16.
34 Julian, *Or.* 1.33d–34a, *Or.* 2.56b–c; Themistius, *Or.* 3.43a; Aurelius Victor, *De Caes.* 41.25; *Epit. de Caes.* 42.7; Zosimus, 2.46.3, 54.1.
35 Julian, *Or.* 1.37a, 2.57c–d.
36 See E. Bihain, 'L'épître de Cyrille de Jérusalem à Constance sur la vision de la croix', *Byzantion* 43 (1973), 264–96. Cf. Philostorgius, *Hist. Eccl.* 3.26.
37 Sulpicius Severus, *Chron.* 2.38.5–7.
38 Symmachus, *Rel.* 3.4–6; Ambrose, *Ep.* 17–18.
39 Themistius, *Or.* 3.44b.
40 Socrates, *Hist. Eccl.* 6.6. Cf. Sozomen, *Hist Eccl.* 8.4.
41 Amm. Marc. 16.10.17; 17.4.1–23.
42 See J.F. Matthews, 'The Poetess Proba and Fourth-Century Rome: Questions of Interpretation', in M. Christol et al. (eds), *Institutions, société et vie politique au IVe siècle ap. J.-C.*, Rome 1992, 277–304, at 304 for a similar suggestion that Constantius' tour of the pagan antiquities of Rome 'has been firmly, and perhaps too exclusively, established in the historical record by the famous description of Ammianus', particularly his suggestion that Constantius may well have visited the church neighbouring the Circus Maximus, the *titulus Anastasiae*.

14

SOME CONSTANTINIAN REFERENCES IN AMMIANUS

Brian Warmington

For obvious reasons, Ammianus does not figure largely in the historiography of Constantine, the books which dealt with him having perished. References in the surviving books are so varied in content and significance that it is difficult to form a view of how he felt about that emperor. In general, he is nothing if not judgemental about every leading figure from emperors downwards, but all are his own contemporaries. From our perspective we assume that Constantine was always a controversial emperor and take it that Ammianus must have commented, even obliquely, about his change of religion or about aspects of his administration which might be associated with it. But the Latin epitomators of his own generation are almost entirely discreet about this (and for that matter on the persecution of the Christians by Diocletian and Galerius).

By the time Ammianus was writing the surviving books, most of the historical works from which even today we have to construct our versions of many of Constantine's activities were already in existence – and a mixed bag they are. What we tend to forget is that the focus of all of them is Constantine's rise to power, and to a lesser extent his successful foreign wars – not just the panegyrics but the *Origo Constantini*, the epitomators Aurelius Victor, Eutropius, Festus, the Epitomator of 395, not to mention the Greek Praxagoras; even the Christian polemical work of Lactantius and Eusebius, in the *Ecclesiastical History*, have much of this sort of material, and are all in general agreement about Constantine's military success. In comments about the reign in general, Aurelius Victor is particularly enthusiastic, Eutropius only slightly less so in spite of specific criticisms. They had nothing to say on his change of religion, unless two ambiguous words of Victor count, and are applying to him the same traditional standard of judgement as they had to all the earlier emperors; why should they not? It is instructive to compare what Victor has to say about Diocletian with his chapter on Constantine; both were successful rulers who fulfilled an emperor's primary functions, the defence of the empire and provision of effective administration. This is not what the modern world wants to know about Constantine, but Ammianus would surely not have dissented. It may be disheartening to think that he actually used such slender works as those of Eutropius or the lost *Kaisergeschichte*, at least for Galerius and Diocletian, as did his deplorable contemporary the author of the *Historia Augusta* for earlier emperors, but this was the case.[1] Having decided to concentrate on the history of his own times, he had to adopt the traditional method of following existing sources for the earlier period, and seems to have preferred the Latin tradition made available by his older contemporaries. This at least applied to the reign of Diocletian though it can never be proved that he did not make use of Dio Cassius, Herodian and Dexippus for earlier emperors up to 270. There was of course Eunapius: was he as unsatisfactory as he appears as paraphrased by Zosimus? Later generations, even of Christian writers, mostly church historians, seemed to find no other source for secular events, though that is no guarantee of quality. But when we look at Zosimus on Constantine we find that over two-thirds of what he has to say is the old story, with minor variants, of his rise to power (though not his foreign wars); indeed, his narrative of these events is the fullest we have and reasonably untendentious, with some rhetorical flourishes. Only a few well-known and highly polemical pages, full of errors, confusion and even fantasy, contain specific allegations of the reason for Constantine's change of religion together with other attacks on his character and on fiscal, military and administrative measures.[2] Ammianus was apparently not convinced; on one occasion only do we find him using an apparently tendentious motif drawn from Eunapius, and he seems unlikely to have been more critical of Constantine than the Latin abbreviators. There was also Eusebius' *On the Life of Constantine*, which would presumably have been ignored by Ammianus in the unlikely event of his ever seeing it. But it is worth remembering that later Christians never showed any interest in writing about the first Christian emperor; everyone knows that no one ever attempted to rewrite or improve upon Eusebius' *Ecclesiastical History*, but many fail to notice that the same is true of *On the Life of Constantine*, epitomized a century later by Socrates Scholasticus, followed by a long line of copyists.

There are just over a dozen references to Constantine in Ammianus.[3] Most are unique, occur incidentally in the narrative of later events and do not normally have a comment on Constantine himself. In most cases there is no clue to the source of Ammianus' information but we may suppose he encountered some of it in the course of social intercourse – it related after all to his father's generation – or, perhaps, in meeting the honest eunuch Eutherius of prodigious memory, who had been brought up in the palace of Constantine (16.7.5).

Ammianus' only reference to Constantine's civil wars is phrased in just such a manner as his Latin sources, though in fact it is unique information about Silvanus' father, the Frank Bonitus, who had fought bravely for

Constantine against Licinius, *pro Constantini partibus in bello civili acriter contra Licinianos* (15.5.33). Here Ammianus is seen standing back and using in a neutral manner the traditional language of party strife, but Licinius had, after all, been a legitimate Augustus and co-ruler with Constantine for more than twelve years, a fact also apparent in the epitomators and Zosimus, though played down by Eusebius.

Ammianus noted the coincidence, though only in passing, of the execution of Gallus Caesar near Pola where, so he understands, Constantine's son Crispus met his end (14.11.20). The word *peremptum* for the latter event looks extremely bland; at the time Ammianus was writing, the story of an alleged connection with Fausta was in the process of full and varied elaboration in anti-Constantinian polemic and was certainly reported in Eunapius.[4] Various theories have been constructed on the basis of what look like anecdotes of court scandal from a tendentious source at least sixty years after the event. But in 360 Aurelius Victor had written that Constantine killed his son for unknown reasons and a decade later Eutropius added Fausta to Constantine's victims, but with no elaboration.[5] We can never know whether Ammianus followed the cautious Latins or Eunapius on this matter when he wrote on Constantine in an earlier book, but he is not elaborating here when he reports what looks like new information.

Responsibility for the dynastic murders of 337 following the death of Constantine was a disputed topic following Julianic polemic against Constantius, and Ammianus doubtless had a view on it, though he avoids saying anything on two occasions when he had the opportunity. The wife of Gallus Caesar, as cruel as her husband according to the historian, had previously been married off by her father Constantine to king Hannibalianus, son of Constantine's half-brother.[6] Both father and son had perished in 337. Ammianus could hardly have expected his hearers to know that a son-in-law of Constantine had uniquely been called *rex* unless he had previously explained this in connection with the start of the Persian War. His wife, though fully described, has to wait seven further sections before her name, Constantia, is given, which leads to the same conclusion. Again, the circumstances of the death in 337 of Gallus' father Julius Constantius are not mentioned when Ammianus describes his noble parentage (14.11.27).

A judgement of the historian which is often quoted runs: 'Constantine was the first to whet the appetite of his staff, but it was Constantius who crammed them with the marrow of the provinces.'[7] The main target here is of course Constantius, but what does the criticism of Constantine amount to? Leaving aside the meaningless cliché *primus omnium*, the specific charge is that he condoned the greed of his closest entourage. This, however, had been regretfully admitted as a stain on his hero's reputation by Eusebius, writing only a couple of years after the emperor's death.[8] The chief culprits were apparently the praetorian prefect Fl. Ablabius (also attacked by Eunapius in the *Lives of the Sophists* as being responsible for the death of the philosopher

Sopater) and the shadowy Flavius Optatus, known in no administrative office but the earliest *patricius* of the Constantinian type and a close adviser of the emperor.[9] Both had been victims associated with the dynastic murders of 337, possibly because they were too closely associated with the Caesar Delmatius, but in any case easy to blame after the event for corruption. Given the admission by Eusebius, the historian's comment is not a tendentious one. Eutropius (10.7), indeed, had regarded Constantine's favours to his *amici* favourably.

The name of Constantine also occurs in the context of the transport of an obelisk from Egypt on the orders of Constantius and its erection in Rome in 358 (17.4.13). According to Ammianus the project had been initiated by Constantine and the obelisk transported as far as Alexandria by the time of his death. This directly contradicts an inscription copied off the base of the obelisk in Renaissance times which said that Constantine had originally intended it for Constantinople. It has recently been argued that the historian was right, the dedicatory inscription being intended to flatter the senate, with whom Constantine is said to have been on bad terms, and show that Constantius favoured Rome above its rival in the East.[10] Given the general acceptance of falsehoods in panegyrics, the occurrence of one in an inscription of this sort can hardly be rejected out of hand. Actually, there is little good evidence for bad feelings between the senate and Constantine; more to the point, he is known to have taken important works of art from the Greek world to beautify his new city,[11] so why not an obelisk as well? The arguments, and there are others, are not conclusive. However, we note that although Ammianus suggests the influence of flatterers who urged Constantius to complete the undertaking, he has nothing to say to the discredit of Constantine as its originator, even if the religious consideration is, as Matthews says,[12] more likely to be his own than the emperor's.

There are two references to Persian affairs which Ammianus says he had described in earlier books. One is only indirectly related to Constantine and concerns Hormisdas, a brother of the Persian king (16.10.16). The episode is retailed for us in no less than four other sources – Zosimus, John of Antioch, Zonaras and the *Suda* – with variant details,[13] justifying the comment in the *Suda* that it was well known. The fullest account is in Zosimus and it is assumed that the basic version came ultimately from Eunapius. The gist is that Hormisdas was passed over by the Persian grandees as successor to his father and imprisoned. His wife sent him a file concealed in a fish with which to cut through his shackles, and also arranged for the jailers to be intoxicated by gifts of wine. Three of the sources say he escaped to Constantine (though John of Antioch says Licinius), and the event indeed seems to have occurred *c.* 324. It is notable that even Zosimus is slightly guarded in his report of this romantic tale of a folklore type (with possible Herodotean reference), and it may be that Ammianus' use of the bland word *discessum* to describe Hormisdas' departure from Persia conceals a more prosaic version

– unless it is ironic. However he did not diasapprove of the prince, who subsequently obtained high military rank under Constantius in Ammianus' time. In any case, the anecdote carried no polemical charge, even in Zosimus.

The other reference is more important and was certainly controversial, being concerned with responsibility for the Persian War and all the disasters stemming from it (25.4.23). The story of the 'lies of Metrodorus' is found only in the late Byzantine compiler Cedrenus,[14] and it has as romantic a flavour as that of the escape of Hormisdas. In brief, the philosopher Metrodorus went to India to study with the Brahmins. He got access to the temples and took away precious stones, and received other jewels from an Indian king as a present to Constantine. When he gave them to the emperor he claimed they were a gift of his own and that there would have been more if they had not been stolen by the Persians on the journey home. Constantine wrote to the King of the Persians demanding the return of the jewels and this provoked them to war. The allegation may well, like the story of Hormisdas, derive from Eunapius and ultimately from Julianic circles – responsibility for the war was much discussed after Julian's death, and indeed he was criticized even as it was undertaken. The charge that Constantine had provoked the twenty-five years of war is made by Ammianus in exculpation of Julian. This is obviously special pleading since it was Julian's reversal of the cautious defensive strategy of Constantius which led to disaster. In fact, Aurelius Victor (39.37) could imply that the ultimate reason was the annexation of Mesopotamia by Diocletian, the demand for its return having led to the recent destructive conflict – a judgement of a Thucydidean type much to the taste of those who look for long-term underlying causes, and showing more sophistication than Ammianus here. Matthews noted a connection between the story of Metrodorus and a common charge against Constantine of desire for cash resources, most obviously in the seizure of temple treasures.[15] Actually the emphasis in criticism of Constantine's fiscal policy is not so much on rapacity as on lavish expenditure,[16] though obviously this is the other side of the same coin. It seems surprising that Ammianus should have put such weight on what (if it ever happened) was presumably one item in the diplomatic exchanges which we know went on up to the outbreak of hostilities. All our other sources, mostly pagan, blame the Persians for the initial outbreak (though admittedly to blame the enemy was ever the Roman way), and regarded Constantine's response as entirely proper, with an implication that it would lead to yet another victory to add to an already impressive run of triumphs over external enemies. We might surmise that a professional soldier who had had a dangerous war was not the best person to judge its causes, especially as his hero came to grief in it.

The stories of Metrodorus and Hormisdas were probably located at the end of Ammianus' treatment of Constantine, since the war began in his final year. Even if we take it that this treatment was rather jejune in comparison with what was to follow, it is comprehensible that Ammianus took some pains to describe the outbreak of the war which bulked so large in the later part of his work, and in his own personal story.

The most frequently quoted reference to Constantine is that in which Julian, in his letter to the senate in 360 justifying his rebellion against Constantius, turned on the emperor's father and called him 'an innovator and a destroyer of hallowed laws and traditions',[17] openly accusing him of being the first to elevate barbarians to the consulate. We should remember that we can never know the exact status of this sentence; Ammianus was obviously paraphrasing a whole letter – but did he personally see the document or read about it in an unknown source? Nor can we be sure if the phrase is really Julian's or by Ammianus himself. The main charge is normally taken to be a reference to Constantine's religion, Matthews for example suggesting that this is offset by the allegation about barbarian consuls. Obviously the phrase has a rhetorical resonance about it, and it could be suggested that Ammianus is being devious, safely attributing to Julian a phrase which his first hearers could relate to Constantine's change of religion, and to some specific legal changes stemming from it. But this is not the run of the text. The innovation and breach with tradition objected to was specifically the creation of barbarian consuls, and Ammianus knew, or thought he knew, who these consuls were, though we do not (in spite of having a complete list of Constantinian ordinary consuls). None of the proposed solutions – Latin names concealing barbarian names, suffect consulships, or *ornamenta consularia* – are provable or without difficulties. Ammianus indeed felt strongly enough to stress Julian's hypocrisy and repeat that his own barbarian appointments, and specifically Nevitta, were inferior in status and usefulness to Rome (21.12.25). Julian's use of this sort of rhetoric (if it was his) in an appeal to senatorial opinion followed a venerable tradition; an obvious example, if Ammianus knew his Tacitus, was his predecessor's paraphrase of extreme senatorial objections to Claudius' proposed Gallic senators.[18] Nor does Julian, as quoted by Ammianus, stand alone in appealing to antiquity in criticism of changes in late Roman administration and law. Zosimus (or was it Eunapius?) said that, in altering the role and status of praetorian prefects, Constantine had 'disturbed the ancient and established magistracies' (2.32) – quite similar to Julian's charge about barbarian consuls, in fact. From a different standpoint, Eusebius says of a minor piece of legislation by Licinius, whom he regarded as a persecutor, that 'he dared to abrogate the ancient and wisely established laws of the Romans'.[19]

The bishop's rhetorical expertise could, however, be turned in the opposite direction in Constantine's favour precisely on the point of honours for barbarians. Constantine 'honoured the noblest among the barbarians with Roman offices of dignity, so that many of them henceforward preferred to continue their residence among us and felt no desire to revisit their native land'.[20] This passage gives some weight to the notion of suffect consulships, or possibly *ornamenta consularia* – occasionally given to non-Roman kings in the past, the last known being by Gallienus. One candidate may be suggested, the unnamed father of Athanaric, who was honoured by Constantine with a public statue outside the senate-house and who had got his son to swear never to enter Roman territory; perhaps he was the man sent as a hostage to Constantine after the Gothic treaty of submission in 334, and son of another Gothic king, Ariaric.[21] High birth and usefulness to Rome could be the reason for honouring him. Of course, this would mean that Julian and, more importantly, Ammianus, ignored the difference between the suffect consulship or the *ornamenta* and the consulship itself. It may be noted that Eusebius, writing about 339, saw no discredit to his hero in writing the approving passage quoted, whereas Ammianus used the words *barbarica vilitas* (unless they were Julian's) when he repeated Julian's charge against Constantine.

The passage concerning Constantine's investigation into the Manichaeans and others deserves longer scrutiny:

> Musonianus succeeded him [i.e. Domitianus] as praetorian prefect in the government of the East. His command of both languages won him a reputation which led to a career of unexpected distinction. Constantine, being in need of an interpreter in the course of his strict investigation into the superstitious doctrines of the Manichaeans and those like them, had Musonianus recommended to him as a suitable person, and appointed him to the post. His skilful discharge of this duty caused the emperor to change his name to Musonianus (he was previously called Strategius), and from this beginning he rose through a number of career posts to the rank of prefect.[22]

Strategius Musonianus, about whom we know a considerable amount, was *Praefectus Praetorio Orientis* from 354 to 358; the anecdote occurs in the context of a passage about his rise to power and his character as an administrator – good on the whole but easily bribable. Ammianus was himself in Antioch as *protector domesticus* on the staff of Ursicinus in 354 and again from 357, and his knowledge of the story could well date from that period, if it did not come from a mutual friend – Musonianus (the name he is always given in Ammianus) was, like the historian, well acquainted with Libanius, who, however, always calls him Strategius, as does the *Codex Theodosianus*.

Constantine, we are told, wanted him to be called Musonianus because of his knowledge of 'both languages'. A similar reference to 'both languages' in the story of the Persian agent Antoninus is discussed by Matthews,[23] who shows that Greek and Latin were meant, which is what we would suppose; the usage goes back at least to the first century. The suggestion that Aramaic might also be implied, because of the language of the earliest Manichaeans, is gratuitous.[24] At the very least, Ammianus could never, in using the phrase before a Roman audience, have expected it to understand that a language other than Greek was meant. Manichaean teaching had been available in Greek when the new heresy, as he described it, was denounced by Eusebius of Caesarea. What might have been available in Latin when the proconsul of Africa reported on it to Diocletian in 302 was presumably not available or not adequate for Constantine.[25] The Epitomator of 395 praised Constantine's personal attention to documents, and we know that though Constantine spoke Greek he had written matter presented to him in Latin; he actually made a highly complimentary remark on the Latin translation of a theological work dedicated to him by Eusebius.[26] If Ammianus' statement that no other suitable translator could be found is true, it indicates how thoroughly Latin the central administration at Nicomedia under Diocletian and Licinius still was. Doubtless a translator of more than usual expertise was required for the cloudy language of the Manichaeans.

The choice of the name Musonianus is at first sight surprising; the formation of the word is from Musonius, and the only candidate of this name must surely be the first-century Stoic Musonius Rufus who taught philosophy in the Socratic manner by dialogue, in both Latin and Greek, writing very little. Should we be surprised that Constantine, essentially an autodidact who lacked formal education, knew of him? Perhaps he heard about him from Sopater, the leading pagan philosopher who frequented the court. We may note that Ammianus, contemptuous elsewhere of the lack of culture in elevated Roman circles, does not feel the need to explain the point of the jest; perhaps he thought that those courtiers whom Theodosius had recently brought with him from the East to Rome, and who Matthews suggests were among Ammianus' first audience, were better educated.

Constantine's joke would work well enough if Musonianus was born a Latin speaker like Musonius Rufus; this assumption is contrary to received opinion, but there seems to be nothing definite against it. Of course, the story may do no more than give an explanation of Strategius' *signum*, but a fragment by a Greek historian normally called *Anonymus post Dionem*, probably depending on Eunapius, says that Constantine made up epithets of an uncomplimentary sort, as *cognomina* of approved emperors (*FHG* IV, 199). Augustus was called a toy of fortune, Trajan a wall plant, Hadrian a paint brush, Marcus Aurelius a buffoon – or so it seems: the Greek writer seems to have made heavy weather of Constantine's Latin. But the Epitomator of 395, who had Eunapius, says that Constantine called Trajan *herba parietaria* because his name appeared so often on public buildings in Rome (*Epit.* 41.13). Since Ammianus attributes the same joke to common talk about Lampadius, Prefect of the City in 365, he either overlooked, or tacitly corrected, the Greek historian (27.3.7). To call the young man, perhaps a *memorialis*, Musonianus may well have been more patronizing than complimentary: as the Epitomator says, Constantine was *irrisor potius quam blandus* (*Epit.* 41.15).

So few are the references in non-Christian authors to Christian heresies and schisms that we have no means of knowing their place in the consciousness of someone like Ammianus. It is clear that he does not condemn Constantine's interest in the Manichaeans and can assume his hearers' knowledge of them. Denounced *c.* 300 by Eusebius of Caesarea on the one hand,[27] and proscribed in 302 by Diocletian immediately before he attacked the Christians on the other, they had nevertheless spread rapidly. That there were plenty of Manichaeans in a cosmopolitan city like Antioch, so close to Mesopotamia, must be certain, and a letter of Libanius on their behalf exists.[28] The earliest text, dated to 372, in the *Codex Theodosianus* condemning any heresy or schism by name relates to them. More significant, perhaps, for Ammianus was the fact that the years 381–3, years in which Matthews dates the beginning of the final stage of the composition of his history, saw three detailed laws issued by Theodosius at Constantinople condemning the Manichaeans and outlining severe measures to be taken against them. It was presumably also known that wealthy Spaniards had very recently fallen victim under Magnus Maximus to charges which might have included Manichaeism, an episode important enough to be discreetly alluded to by Pacatus in his panegyric on Theodosius delivered in Rome in 389.[29] Ammianus could thus refer in 391 to the dynamic and evangelistic movement with converts of high social rank, lately the subject of imperial legislation, with no need to explain. An alert hearer could, if he wished, contrast an investigation into Manichaean doctrine by Constantine, which apparently had no follow-up, with the current severe repression. But this does not imply that either Ammianus or his hearers, whether Christian or pagan, disapproved of an investigation into such a *superstitio*.

But what about 'and those like them'? Did Ammianus have a view on what Christian heresies were similar to Manichaeism, or is he just dismissing in a cavalier way other groups which Constantine had investigated? An area of total ignorance for us is the extent to which any pagan like Ammianus had an interest in the detail of Christian divisions of the time. What did he make, if indeed he was aware of them, of the distinctions in theology, obscure to all but a few Christians themselves, between the orthodox and those whom Athanasius taught the world to call Arians? The latter had, after all, been the dominant voice of Christianity in the East for much of Ammianus' lifetime, though we would not know it from his references to Christians. He had of course ascribed to Julian knowledge that no wild beasts were such enemies to mankind as Christians were to one another (22.5.4); yet his account of such a notorious episode as the murder of George, bishop of Alexandria, is not used to exemplify this.

We happen to know from Eusebius that in 325 or 326 Constantine condemned five heretical and schismatic groups – Novatians, Valentinians, Marcionites, Paulians and Montanists;[30] Manichaeans are not named. Only two of these, the Valentinians, a gnostic heresy from the second century, and perhaps the Marcionites, might be regarded, by us at least, as having some similarities with the Manichaeans. But what were Valentinians and Marcionites to Ammianus? If we assume that he knew of them as an Antiochene born, we might still ask if his Roman audience would have made the connection from so casual an allusion. The possibility cannot be rejected out of hand; if it was the case it might indicate a greater interest in doctrinal issues, among Christian senators at least, than is usually assumed. It is likely that Constantine's edict soon ceased to be enforced (it was not included in the *Codex Theodosianus*) but that some knowledge of it survived, for recall by Ammianus. The historian in any case used the word *superstitio*, i.e. bad religion,[31] of these other heretics as he did of Manichaeans, and most Christians among his hearers would have agreed.

It is reasonably certain that Constantine did not proceed against the Manichaeans; Eusebius had denounced them as a dangerous new heresy in his *Ecclesiastical History*, and in his *Life of Constantine* would certainly have mentioned with approval any action taken against them, as he did the edict against the five named groups. We might suppose that following the edict of general toleration issued in late 324 soon after the defeat of Licinius, primarily for the assurance of pagans, the Manichaeans sought to confirm that it applied to them, especially since they, like the Christians, had been the object of persecution by Diocletian, and won their point. Diocletian is said by some to have regarded the Manichaeans as a Persian 'fifth column' threatening the Roman empire,[32] but this is an unconvincing modern construct; to abuse as Persian any novelty coming from the East as his edict does had been a rhetorical commonplace for centuries. We know that an appeal was made by the Novatians following the edict of 325 or 326, who convinced the emperor of the justice of their case and were excluded from its operation. It seems that Constantine, who appears to have drawn the list of the five condemned groups from Lactantius,[33] investigated the Manichaeans on a separate basis and took no action against them. Ammianus, who criticized Constantius' involvement in theological questions, had nothing to say against Constantine for investigating Manichaean doctrines personally. No such personal investigation is attributed to Diocletian, who simply took on board what the Proconsul of Africa had reported – just like Trajan and Pliny on the Christians, in fact. If we follow Ammianus we may observe that Constantine did not turn to one of the ecclesiastics who are said (on slender grounds) to have been influential with him, but to a young man, perhaps a *memorialis*, who was recommended to him, doubtless in the normal way of patronage.

As for Musonianus' further career, we know that shortly after his activity as a translator he was at Antioch with the rank of *comes*, though still only *perfectissimus*, reporting to the emperor on the divisions and disorders in the Christian church there.[34] We next hear of him in another Christian context, supervising the assemblage of eastern bishops at the Council of Serdica in 343, to the disgust of Athanasius who abusively calls him a *paidagogos* in his relationship with the bishops who condemned him.[35] This of course was the largest of those Church Councils to which Constantius was addicted, so Ammianus says, to the ruin of the *cursus publicus* as bishops were transported hither and thither. To the secular historian such activity in the interests of an emperor's policy in church affairs probably had no part in an official's career; hence his ultimate advancement to the prefecture on the strength of a translator's job in early life could be considered surprising.

In conclusion, there seems to be an odd coincidence in a later reference in Ammianus to Musonianus. We read that it was at his suggestion that the pagan philosopher Eustathius was included in a high-level embassy to Shapur in 358, 'as a master of the art of persuasion' (*ut opifex suadendi*, 17.5.15). Eunapius gives an account of Eustathius in the *Lives of the Sophists*, exaggerating in an absurd fashion his powers of persuasion over the king, which are said to have failed only because of the malign influence of the Magi (*V. Sophist.* 465–6). He too made a point of emphasizing that Eustathius was included because of the promptings of others (unnamed) who subsequently obtained high office and imperial favour. Ammianus, having been at Antioch at the time, presumably did not need Eunapius on this point, and in any case we do not know if this story about Eustathius occurred in Eunapius' history. It looks as though both authors were struck by the inclusion of the philosopher among ambassadors who were certainly of higher status than was usual, and far outranked a mere philosopher.

Notes

1 R. Syme, *Ammianus and the Historia Augusta*, Oxford 1968, 105 (Ammianus); 48, 108, 166, 177, 215 (SHA). The references in Ammianus are 14.11.10, cf. Eutropius, *Brev.* 9.24; Amm. Marc. 15.5.18, cf. Eutropius, *Brev.* 9.26; Amm. Marc. 16.10.3, cf. Eutropius, *Brev.* 9.25.
2 Zosimus 2.29–38. For an effort to make something of these passages, see F. Paschoud, *Cinque études sur Zosime*, Paris 1975.
3 Discussed briefly by J.F. Matthews, *The Roman Empire of Ammianus*, London 1989, 447ff.
4 Zosimus 2.29; *Epit.* 41.11–12; later writers are all apparently derivative. For some analysis, see P. Guthrie, 'The Execution of Crispus', *Phoenix* 20 (1966), 325–31.
5 Aurelius Victor, *De Caes.* 41.11; Eutropius, *Brev.* 10.6.3.
6 Amm. Marc. 14.1.2: *Hanniballiano regi fratris filio antehac Constantinus iunxerat pater*.
7 Amm. Marc. 16.8.12: *proximorum fauces aperuit primus omnium Constantinus, sed eos medullis provinciarum saginavit Constantius*; trans. Hamilton.
8 *Vit. Const.* 4.54; cf. 4.29, 30.
9 Libanius, *Or.* 42.23; Eunapius, *V. Sophist.* 463–4 (Ablabius); Libanius, *Or.* 42.26–7 (Optatus); B.H. Warmington, 'Eusebius and the Governance of Constantine', forthcoming. For their careers, see entries in T.D. Barnes, *The New Empire of Diocletian and Constantine*, Cambridge (Mass.) 1982.
10 G. Fowden, 'Nicagoras of Athens and the Lateran Obelisk', *JHS* 107 (1987), 51–7.
11 Eusebius, *Vit. Const.* 3.54; Zosimus 2.31.
12 Matthews, *The Roman Empire of Ammianus*, 450.
13 Zosimus 2.27.1–4; John of Antioch, *frg.* 178 = *FHG* IV, 605; Zonaras 13.5.25–33; *Suda*, *s.v.* Marsyas.
14 Cedrenus 295a. See B.H. Warmington, 'Ammianus Marcellinus and the Lies of Metrodorus', *CQ* 31 (1981), 464–8; G. Fowden, 'The Last Days of Constantine: Oppositional Versions and their Influence', *JRS* 84 (1994), 146–53.
15 Matthews, *The Roman Empire of Ammianus*, 135.

16 Aurelius Victor, *De Caes.* 40.14; *Epit. de Caes.* 41.16; Zosimus 2.38. Eusebius, *Vit. Const.* 1.43, interpreted this aspect of Constantine's reign as liberality, an imperial virtue.
17 Amm. Marc. 21.10.8: *novator turbatorque priscarum legum et moris antiquitus recepti*; trans. Hamilton.
18 Tacitus, *Ann.* 11.23; the words *coetus alienigenarum* ascribed to the senate compare nicely with Ammianus' *barbarica vilitas*.
19 τοὺς παλαιοὺς Ῥωμαίων εὖ καὶ σοφῶς κειμένους νόμους περιγράψαι τολμήσας: Eusebius, *Hist. Eccl.* 10.8.12, repeated in *Vit. Const.* 1.55.
20 ἐτίμα δὲ καὶ Ῥωμαϊκοῖς ἀξιώμασι τοὺς ἐν αὐτοῖς διαφανεστέρους, ὥστ' ἤδη πλείους τὴν ἐνταῦθα στέργειν διατριβήν, ἐπανόδου τῆς εἰς τὰ οἰκεῖα λήθην πεποιημένους: Eusebius, *Vit. Const.* 4.7.
21 Themistius, *Or.* 15.191a (statue); Amm. Marc. 27.5.6 (Athanaric's oath); *Origo Constantini* 31 (Ariaric and his son).
22 15.13.1–2:

> Musonianus eius successor orientem praetoriani regebat potestate praefecti, facundia sermonis utriusque clarus, unde sublimius quam sperabatur eluxit. Constantinus enim, cum limatius superstitionum quaereret sectas Manichaeorum et similium, nec interpres inveniretur idoneus, hunc sibi commendatum ut sufficientem elegit; quem, officio functum perite, Musonianum voluit appellari, ante Strategium dictitatum, et ex eo percursis honorum gradibus multis, ascendit ad praefecturam.
>
> (trans. Hamilton, revised)

23 Matthews, *The Roman Empire of Ammianus*, 70.
24 J.W. Drijvers, 'Ammianus Marcellinus 15.13.1–2: Some Observations on the Career and Bilingualism of Strategius Musonianus', *CQ* 46 (1996), 532–7, with unconvincing arguments.
25 Diocletian's Edict in *Mos. et Rom. leg. collatio* 15.3. For the date, see Barnes, *New Empire*, 169. On Manichaeans in general, see S.N.C. Lieu, *Manichaeism in the Later Roman Empire and Medieval China. A Historical Survey*, Tübingen 1992.
26 *Epit. de Caes.* 41.14; Eusebius, *Vit. Const.* 3.13 (Constantine speaking Greek), 4.35 (Latin translation).
27 Eusebius, *Hist. Eccl.* 7.31. I accept the view of T.D. Barnes, 'The Editions of Eusebius' Ecclesiastical History', *GRBS* 21 (1980), 191–201, that Eusebius had completed Books 1–7 by *c.* 300, at any rate before the outbreak of persecution in 303.
28 Libanius, *Ep.* 1344, ed. Förster.
29 *Cod. Theod.* 16.5.3 (372), 16.5.7 (381), 16.5.9 (382), 16.5.11 (383); Pacatus, *Pan.* 29.1ff. See now C.E.V. Nixon and B.S. Rodgers, *In Praise of Later Roman Emperors. The Panegyrici Latini*, Berkeley 1993, 487–90, with full bibliography.
30 *Vit. Const.* 3.64. The *terminus ante quem* is 28 September 326 when the successful appeal of the Novatians is recorded; *Cod. Theod.* 16.5.2. No text of their earlier condemnation is included in the Code, perhaps a testimony to the importance of the schism at Constantinople when it was compiled.
31 On the implications of this word, see M.R. Salzman, 'Superstitio in the Codex Theodosianus and the Persecution of Pagans', *Vig. Christ.* 41 (1987), 172–88.
32 See Lieu, *Manichaeism*, 121–5, and Drijvers, 'Ammianus Marcellinus', 533–4; P. Brown, *Augustine of Hippo*, London 1967, 46, had used the same phrase but saw Christianity as the target. The pages by T.D. Barnes in *Constantine and Eusebius*, Cambridge (Mass.) 1981, 19–21, on Diocletian's religious motivation in both persecutions are brief but exemplary.
33 See Lactantius, *Div. Inst.* 4.30; B.H. Warmington, 'Did Constantine Have "Religious Advisers"?', *Studia Patristica* 19 (1988), 117–29.
34 Eusebius, *Vit. Const.* 3.62. The chronology of Musonianus' career suggested by Drijvers, 'Ammianus Marcellinus', rests on some doubtful hypotheses.
35 Athanasius, *Hist. Ar.* 15, *Apol. c. Ar.* 36 (without the epithet).

15

TEMPLUM MUNDI TOTIUS

Ammianus and a religious ideal of Rome[1]

Thomas Harrison

'Ammianus was not writing a religious history . . . The "high places" where true history was accustomed to run (26.1.1) were of a secular, not a religious nature.'[2] John Matthews is not alone in this view. Though there are some notable exceptions – David Hunt for one has referred to the *Res Gestae* as 'pervaded by the religiosity of omens and fate'[3] and Guy Sabbah to Ammianus as 'profondément imbu de religiosité païenne'[4] – Matthews' judgement represents a consensus of opinion both on Ammianus and, to an extent, on the whole tradition of ancient historiography.[5]

This is not the place in which to launch an all-out assault on the idea of the secular nature of classical historiography. (It is enough for now to state my personal conviction that such a vision is rooted as much in wishful thinking as in reality.) In the case of Ammianus, however, this picture of a resolute reluctance to contaminate a secular model of history does not tally with the evidence of his work. Ammianus never in the surviving books makes any programmatic statement of his exclusion of the divine. His reference to the 'high places' in which 'true history was accustomed to run', in Matthews' elegant paraphrase, comes in the context of an attack against those who would have him delve into trifling details, in his own words

> those who cry out as if wronged if one has failed to mention what an emperor has said at table, or left out the reason why the common soldiers were led before the standards for punishment, or because in an ample account of regions one ought not to have been silent about some insignificant facts.
> (26.1.1)

He fails to include marvels or omens among his list of trivia. We are thrown back then on the evidence of his work as a whole, and we must judge his attitudes (in so far as we can) by his practice rather than by any credo.

One of the most striking features of the *Res Gestae* is the sheer density of omens or dreams fulfilled, portentous references to the consent of the supreme numen. Such first impressions may be misleading. How are we to distinguish deep-rooted beliefs from formulae? Matthews, for one, concentrates on Ammianus' extended explorations of divination, astrology and mathematics, or of *daimones* or guardian spirits. The remainder, arguably the greatest number, of the religious references in the *Res Gestae* – most notably the 'allusions to the gods, fate and Fortune with which Ammianus equips his narrative' – may, he concedes, be 'in general terms relevant to his attitudes' but

> it will often be difficult to show that a god or a goddess (Mars, say, or Bellona), or an allusion to fate or Fortune, is more than a technical device useful, for example, in transition from one subject to another or to convey the enormity, or unexpectedness, of the events by which the Romans were confronted, but not implying any significant theological or philosophical reflection.[6]

Matthews' words are guarded. I hope then that I will be forgiven for picking over them in some detail.

Matthews allows first for the possibility that one might, in certain cases and with difficulty, be able to show that such allusions are more than a mere technical device; that they may have some general bearing on Ammianus' attitudes. He also then immediately introduces exceptions. The first is Ammianus' account of the Persian campaign of Julian, described, Matthews says, 'as being determined by fate'. Here, however, 'Ammianus is presenting in their true historical light aspects of the religious views of Julian, as relevant to the events in which they were involved.'[7] Second, Matthews introduces the exception that Fortuna can 'in certain contexts ... acquire a purposive, even a moral role'. The example he gives, however – the passage from Book 14 in which Ammianus portrays Fortuna as the daughter of Nemesis or Adrasteia – is 'an unusually elaborate passage, worked up, by rhetorical as much as by philosophic means, to suit the particularly intense sequence of tragic narrative, moral reflection and historical parallels with which Ammianus concludes his Book 14.' The moral dimension of Fortuna is little more than the product of a momentary rhetorical exuberance. Both exceptions, in other words, really are not exceptions at all. Matthews concludes his digression by reiterating his original point: 'In the great majority of cases, fate, Fortune and the gods function in Ammianus as part of the normal equipment of a historian writing in the classical manner.'

I have a number of difficulties here. First, we might observe the curiosity that, in parallel to the tradition of secular history (not enunciated, in fairness, by John Matthews) another tradition exists, one in which 'the gods, fate and Fortune' are central, if only as a matter of style.[8] Behind this lurks a greater problem. We are in danger, surely, of falling victim to what Peter Rhodes has described neatly as the 'topos-fallacy', the assumption that a rhetorical topos or a literary formula is no more than a topos or formula.[9]

Now, of course, the problems of distinguishing the formulaic from the *merely* formulaic are particularly acute in the case of a consciously classicizing historian like Ammianus. Clearly Ammianus must be judged to have been capable of speaking in a number of different idioms, even of writing in a self-consciously old-fashioned idiom. What is more open to argument, however, is the presumption that any one idiom is necessarily more or less characteristic of the writer's purpose than another. As Denis Feeney has put it in another context, 'the challenge is to put the right adverb in front of the word "literary": not "merely" but "distinctively"'; otherwise we are in danger of 'shutting off areas of meaning in the later text'.[10] To put it another way, is Ammianus' classicizing only a matter of style? Rather, surely, it is central to his purpose in writing. As Tim Barnes has written, Ammianus' allusions 'are not mere ornaments . . . He intended his *Res Gestae* to sum up the whole of Greco-Roman historiography.'[11]

Another problem with this picture of religion in the *Res Gestae* is its demand that a belief, or a statement implying belief, must pass muster philosophically before it is accepted as 'religion'.[12] References to fate may say something about Ammianus the literary artist, but they imply no 'significant theological or philosophical reflection'. Matthews makes a similar judgement on the question of the Neoplatonic background to Ammianus' digression on divination, that it 'does not betray a complete mastery of the actual philosophical issues that were involved'; and on Ammianus' apparent misunderstanding of a passage of Cicero, again he comments that 'one may ponder the reason for this, but one possibility is that Ammianus' procedure is more literary than philosophical'.[13] Simply put, because an idea is half-digested or inconsistent, must it therefore be purely literary? Why can Ammianus' digression again not be learned, literary *and* reflect – and, doubtless, in so doing, distort – his own beliefs or preconceptions? Why, moreover, should we discount allusions to fate in characterizing Ammianus simply because they imply no 'significant theological reflection'? Is Ammianus' religious position no more than the sum of philosophical influences upon him?[14]

It might be argued in reply that such references and allusions serve no explanatory purpose in Ammianus' narrative or, in Matthews' phrase (in discussion), that they are not 'load-bearing'. Herodotus' gods have likewise been described as an 'umbrella under which men operated in the way that men do' or, most colourfully, compared by Keith Hopkins to Byzantine court eunuchs, 'convenient personal pegs to hang historical causes on'.[15] Clearly, however, our conception of what is or is not 'load-bearing', our view of what constitutes a respectable explanation, need not be the same as that of Ammianus. Whether or not such passing references to fate or Fortune 'explain anything' is in fact immaterial if our goal is to uncover the patterns of Ammianus' thought. And when we look at such passing references alongside his more self-conscious 'philosophical' digressions, the impression – as R.L. Rike has shown, for example, in the case of the supreme divinity or *numen*

– is that Ammianus' digressions and narrative tally nicely.[16] Ammianus' manner of switching from speaking of a vague, depersonalized divinity or numen to a polytheistic world of more clearly individuated deities is something that, far from revealing him as a closet monotheist, he has in common with any number of ancient writers.[17]

As a system of explanation Ammianus' beliefs are arguably very serviceable. His remarks concerning omens, oracles and dreams, to take one example, show all the hallmarks – in particular the stress on the importance of right interpretation – of the need to prove that divination works, that oracles or dreams are capable of fulfilment.[18] His criticisms of Julian's excessive interest in divination, that both the ignorant and the learned alike were allowed to consult the 'oracles and entrails that sometimes disclose the future', or that no limits or prescribed rules were applied (22.12.6–8), may appear to reflect a degree of scepticism concerning divination, but are in fact typical of the kind of 'let-out clause' or 'block to falsifiability' used by believers in divination in many ages: oracles and entrails do not always disclose the future; some forms of divination, those practised by the ignorant, do not work. These can very easily be used as explanations for the non-fulfilment of prophecies. In short, what may seem initially to be inconsistencies, blemishes on an ideal philosophical religion, may turn out to serve an important role in maintaining belief in the face of experience: they may be tokens of the life rather than the artificiality of Ammianus' religion.[19]

Rather than dwelling on this question of the authenticity of belief, in the remaining pages I will proceed on the basis that Ammianus can be taken at face value, that religion is as central and pervasive in the *Res Gestae* as it at first appears. I do not only mean the religious question *par excellence*, that of Ammianus' attitude to Christianity. Though it is central to modern discussions (and though there are significant differences of opinion as to the degree of Ammianus' underlying hostility towards Christianity), David Hunt, John Matthews and others have shown well how Christianity is marginalized in Ammianus' narrative.[20] Rather I shall be operating with a definition of religion that embraces both Christianity and paganism.

I begin with the fate of individuals, and with the most prominent individual in the *Res Gestae*, Julian. Expressions of the fated nature of Julian's life do not appear only in the mouths of characters: Julian (20.5.4), Constantius (15.8.9), Julian's troops (16.12.13), or the blind old woman who, on hearing that the Caesar had entered Vienne, commented that 'he would repair the temples of the gods' (15.8.22). They also occur in the words of the author, both in passing remarks such as that he would have perished at the hands of flatterers had it not been for Eusebia befriending him *adspiratione superni numinis* (15.2.8), and through a number of more explicit comments, most prominently in his obituary: Julian's success had been so conspicuous that he had 'seemed to ride on the shoulders of destiny'; 'if the decrees of heaven had been in accord with his plans and his splendid deeds', he would have been victorious (25.4.14, 26; cf. 16.1.4). Ammianus' account of the numerous omens and consultations that take place on the Persian campaign again does not suggest detachment. He talks of omens as trustworthy, or as indicating 'what came to pass' (23.1.5–7), and at one point slips into the first-person plural (24.8.4):

> and since human wisdom availed nothing, after long wavering and hesitation we built altars and slew victims, in order to learn the purpose of the gods, whether they advised us to return through Assyria or to march slowly along the foot of the mountains . . . ; but on inspection of organs it was announced that neither course would suit the signs.[21]

Of course, Ammianus' narrative of the Persian campaign is infinitely more varied and more complex in its presentation than simply a personal statement of faith. Although to see in his account an indictment of Julian's 'religious policy' would be an extreme oversimplification, there is surely a level at which his account serves as a commentary on the proper response to omens and prophecy;[22] but at the same time Julian's death is also presented as a tragic outcome from which there was no escape. What is unquestionable, however, is Ammianus' engagement, both in the question of the proper role and interpretation of divination, and emotionally in Julian's tragic story.

Though the emphasis on the fated nature of Julian's death is clearly greater and more nuanced than that of any other figure, Julian is not exceptional. 'Could anyone', Matthews asks,

> read of the departure from Constantius of his guardian spirit without recalling the appearance to Julian in the previous book (20.5.10) of the 'genius publicus', bidding him seize the opportunity that was about to present itself to him? The theme of Book 21 is the rise of Julian and decline of Constantius, not forgetting the divine indications that made the outcome clear to both protagonists. This theme is in the broader sense the setting of the two philosophical digressions . . . It would be perverse to deny the relevance of both digressions, and not only that on divination, to the philosophical tastes of Julian.[23]

By assimilating the death of Constantius to the destiny of Julian, Matthews harnesses Constantius' decline and the omens that accompany it to the 'philosophical tastes' of Julian. Julian is clearly centre-stage. However, to deny (by implication, at least) the relevance of *Ammianus'* philosophical tastes or religious presuppositions is surely equally perverse. Moreover, though indeed it is only in Book 21 that Constantius' (tragic?) blindness becomes complete – with his assertion of his knowledge of future events (21.6.3) and his confident prediction of Julian's imminent punishment (21.13.13) – we may trace the ups and downs of his conceit as far back as Book 15.[24]

More importantly, other figures too follow similar career paths. Gallus leaves Antioch 'under the lead of an unpropitious destiny' (*numine laevo ductante*, 14.11.12). Just as Constantius had been misled by flatterers and his own conceit into supposing that there was nothing that 'a good fortune so nearly celestial could not overcome' (15.8.2; cf. 16.12.68), just as fate led Julian to ignore or misinterpret repeated clear signs of his impending death (despite his former caution with regard to omens[25]), so Gallus also failed to understand his position, but entered Constantinople 'as if in the height of prosperity and security' (14.11.12). Gallus too had premonitions of his death (14.11.17), 'his senses ... wounded by frightful spectres that shrieked about him' as he was seized and thrown to the claws of the furies by the 'throngs of those whom he had slain'.[26] His death is then presented as 'ordained ... by the sad decree of fate' (14.11.19) and – together with the subsequent deaths of those who had lured him to his end – as evidence of the watchfulness of the *superni numinis aequitas* (14.11.23–34):

> Accordingly his hands were bound, after the fashion of some guilty robber, and he was beheaded. Then his face and head were mutilated, and the man who a little while before had been a terror to cities and provinces was left a disfigured corpse. But the justice of the heavenly power was everywhere watchful; for not only did his cruel deeds prove the ruin of Gallus, but not long afterwards a painful death overtook both of those whose false blandishments and perjuries led him, guilty though he was, into the snares of destruction. Of these Scudilo, because of an abscess of the liver, vomited up his lungs and so died; Barbatio, who for a long time had invented false accusations against Gallus, charged by the whispers of certain men of aiming higher than the mastership of the infantry, was found guilty and by an unwept end made atonement to the shades of the Caesar whom he had treacherously done to death.[27]

Many of the same ingredients can be traced again in the accounts of other prominent individuals: Jovian, Valentinian, Procopius, Gratian, Valens.[28] We have the same emphasis on predestination, on omens of impending death, the false confidence of those who are blind to their fate, the stubborn resistance of prophecy. It is not only great men who are susceptible to such fates: Scudilo and Barbitio too are vulnerable to divine vengeance. The theme of the reversal of fortune also can be seen in a number of brief anecdotes, introduced in passing: for example, that of Leo who aspired to the prefecture 'in order to fall from a greater height' (30.5.10), or Salia, taken out of prison to be given a fresh hearing only to fall dead as he was putting on his shoe (29.1.26).[29] These passing references are obviously not the result of theological reflection, but they are no less significant for this; they show almost a reflex attraction to anecdotes illustrative of the mutability of fortune.

Such narrative patterns may imply certain presuppositions concerning the divine, but it is important to state that they do not suggest a rigid template imposed upon events. The sympathy felt for Gratian or Julian determines that their careers are in their different ways seen as thwarted by a cruel fate (27.6.15), while Gallus' death fits without difficulty into the pattern of divine retribution. Such discrepancies are hardly surprising, nor are they any sign of a lack of authenticity in Ammianus' implied beliefs: it is precisely the coexistence of two apparently contradictory explanations of human misfortune, one moral and the other amoral, that allows for the belief in the possibility of divine participation in history to be maintained.[30]

The fates of emperor and empire are intertwined. This is not only because the virtues of the emperor, moral and practical, are essential for the maintenance of the empire. Julian's arrival in Vienne inspired the confidence of the crowd, because they imagined that 'some helpful *genius*' had shone upon their condition (15.8.21). The spirit who delivers the ultimatum to Julian on the night before his proclamation as Augustus takes the form – significantly – of the *genius publicus* (20.5.10). It is no accident that some individuals appear lucky and others do not. 'It was common knowledge that propitious fortune had failed [Theodosius] in none of his undertakings' (28.3.7). It was equally common knowledge that Constantius was only successful (and properly vigilant) in civil wars; this was a belief not only voiced by Ammianus (21.16.15), but ascribed to Constantius' own army (14.10.16), to Julian (21.1–2), to Constantius himself – it is at one stage his only consoling thought (21.13.6; cf. 20.11.32) – and presented subliminally in a whole range of contexts,[31] most colourfully in the anecdote of Constantius' discovery of the news of Gallus' death, with Gallus' shoes 'brought and laid before him as if they were the spoils of a slain Parthian king' (15.1.2–3). This is not only an indictment of Constantius' view of civil conflicts but a comment on the nature of his fortune: hence the irony of the assurances of Constantius' flatterers that 'whatever was done anywhere in the world was due to his favourable auspices' (16.12.68).

Just as there is a link between the fortunes of emperor and empire, so there is also a link between the fortune of the empire and that of the city of Rome.[32] That the city's fortune is divinely ordained is shown by the story of the famine that occurred during the prefecture of Tertullus (19.10). Grain ships were held at sea, and Tertullus was faced with an angry mob. By holding out his sons to the crowd, protesting that they too would endure the same fate, and offering to give them up into their power, he managed to bring the people to a state of calm submission to fortune.

> And presently by the will of the divine power that gave increase to Rome from its cradle and promised that it would last forever, while Tertullus was sacrificing in the temple of Castor and Pollux at Ostia, a calm smoothed the sea, the wind changed to a gentle southern breeze, and the ships

entered the harbour under full sail and again crammed the storehouses with grain.

(19.10.4)

The conclusion is implicit that the change in weather was in response to Tertullus' cult action.[33] The line between the physical definition of the city of Rome and the abstract definition of Rome as empire seems to collapse here. The city is the symbolic embodiment of the empire as a whole – as Ammianus says in justification of Constantius' transferral of the obelisk to Rome, the 'temple of the whole world' (17.4.13).[34]

The story of Tertullus' saving of the city of Rome from famine might even perhaps be taken as a model for the restoration of the fortunes of the empire, as reflecting a sense that the proper propitiation of the gods will ensure their continued favour. Ammianus is curiously inscrutable on Julian's reopening of the temples (22.5.2) – perhaps due to the closure of temples contemporary with his writing – but in other contexts he is more forthright. He gives his explicit approval of the separation by Praetextatus of sacred buildings from private houses in obedience to 'ancient laws' (27.9.10). And he appears – to judge from the portent of an infant born in Antioch 'with two heads, two sets of teeth, a beard, four eyes and two very small ears' (19.12.19) – to express regret that such ill-omens are no longer properly expiated:

> This misshapen birth foretold that the state was turning into a deformed condition. Portents of this kind often see the light, as indications of the outcome of various affairs; but as they are no longer expiated by public rites, as they were in the time of our forefathers, they pass by unheard of and unknown.
>
> (19.12.20)

As François Paschoud has observed, Ammianus omits to say that the failure to expiate such omens might have serious consequences, or that expiation might annul the fulfilment of a portent.[35] Such standards of proof are perhaps unreasonably high, however. Ammianus appears to take for granted the validity of such omens. His point, moreover, is to insist on their continued occurrence in his own day against those who believe otherwise.

The support of the divinity for Rome is not always a simple matter of *quid pro quo*. The celestial power may check the progress of the Goths at the walls of Constantinople (31.16.4–7) – though in part, ironically, through the display of even more barbaric behaviour by the Saracens – but it also, for instance, drove Shapur to new extremes of self-confidence in his attacks on Roman territory. Rome is constantly buffeted in Ammianus' view by new storms (14.1.1, 2.1, 15.5.1): whether they are truly external threats or – like the deeds of Gallus – internal, they are always envisaged as outside phenomena acting upon something fundamentally unchanging. The disaster at Adrianople is presented by Ammianus as part of a series of setbacks to Rome, a worse misfortune than any defeat except Cannae (31.13.19). However, despite occasional warning sounds that perhaps the conditions for recovery are no longer in place – the idea, for example, that the city of Rome is no longer the 'domicile of all virtues', thus undermining the idea of the eternal pact of Virtue and Fortune with which the Roman digression of Book 14 begins (31.5.14)[36] – Rome may totter but she does not fall. The description of the *Res Gestae* as an 'unrelieved chronicle of despair' or the judgement of Auerbach that Ammianus' 'manner of writing history nowhere displays anything redeeming, anything that points to a better future' both fail to observe some constant causes of hope in Ammianus' view of Rome.[37]

The problems that beset Rome – even when in fact they form part of a longer series – tend always to be short-term and manageable. Gallus is lured to the court of Constantius by the hope of greater rewards, 'that the Commonwealth should not be divided ... but that each to the extent of his powers should lend it aid when it was tottering, doubtless referring to the devastation of Gaul' (14.11.9). When the problem of Gaul is dealt with, it is implied, the Commonwealth will be back on its feet. Julian, of course, subsequently did deal with the problem of Gaul, only to be forced, like a harried world policeman, to rush to the next crisis (cf. 15.8.2, 16.12.31). Remedy for Rome's problems is also to be found in the qualities and initiative of individuals, not only emperors but also their advisers. The qualities required in those on whom it falls to manage such crises reflect the fatalistic model of the rise and fall of Rome's fortunes.[38] The proper Roman commander should be cautious, though not timorous (14.9.2). Sometimes, retreat is sensible (14.2.17). He remains placid in the face of the greatest dangers, like Julian laughing at the Alamanni with a calm resolution at the presumption of the savages (16.12.3) or Leontius scanning the crowds of Rome as they raged about him like serpents (15.7.4). Sometimes, paradoxically, rather than show caution, he must throw it to the winds, as when Julian, after declaring war on Constantius, 'unhesitatingly committed himself to whatever Fortune might offer' (21.5.13). The adviser (or the royal woman) should calm and moderate the emperor rather than inflame him with excessive anger (14.5.7, 16.7.6, 30.5.5); he should also, of course, pick his moment opportunely (14.1.10; cf. 29.1.8). He must withstand torture (14.9.5–7; 15.2.3, 6.2). The virtues demanded are, in other words, to acknowledge at all times the variability of Fortune. That very awareness can itself, it seems, protect you from the worst excesses of Fortune. Ammianus, Ursicinus and their colleagues maintain a steady nerve during the Silvanus affair because they are aware that there will be an upturn just as there had been a downturn (15.5.23). Silvanus, on the other hand, is lured to his end by deceptive omens employed precisely to boost his sense of the security of his fortune so that 'he might be caught off his guard by anything hostile' (15.5.25).

The capacity to be trapped by your own self-confidence, though it applies to a number of other Romans – most notably Gallus – is also a particular characteristic of barbarians. The Alamanni and other northern peoples seem to swing from a wild confidence to an attitude of abject surrender to Roman might. Shapur also generally fumes and blasts, as when his garment is torn by a lance and he 'raged as if against the sacrilegious violators of a temple' (19.1.6). There is no trace of any barbarian showing an awareness of the mutability of fortune.[39] It is with the opposition of barbarian and Roman that I will end: the characterization of barbarians is also carried out in significant part through their religion.[40] Foreign religious customs are sometimes placed in stark opposition to Roman customs; on other occasions they are compared as if equivalent (19.2.6).[41] At one extreme, you have the negative model of the Huns, bound by no reverence for superstition or religion (31.2.11);[42] then the Scordisci who sacrifice men to Bellona and Mars (27.4.4), the Taurians to Diana (22.8.34). At the other pole, the Druids (15.9.8), Egyptians (22.16.20), the Brahmins (28.1.13) or the Magi (23.6.33–4) are presented as the privileged inheritors of religious wisdom. Barbarians can also be assimilated through religion, as the example of King Cottius shows. Cottius had come to an accommodation with Octavian and subsequently built roads across the Alps. 'His shades were devoutly venerated for a double reason: because he had ruled his subjects with a just government, and when admitted to alliance with the Roman state, procured eternal peace for his nation' (15.10.7). Religious assimilation mirrors political.

Ammianus was no religious zealot. Unlike Eunapius of Sardis and other such shrill pagan voices,[43] his criticisms of Christian innovation are muted, framed within the diplomatic formula that Christian and pagan worship were roads that led to the same destination (in Symmachus' analogy[44]), that Christians and pagans were both worshippers of the 'perpetual *numen*' (27.3.15).[45] Unlike also those Christian historians, beginning with Eusebius, who, in Momigliano's phrase, 'cut history into two parts',[46] preferring the affairs of the Church to the conventional topics of war and high politics, religious and political preoccupations were for Ammianus one and the same: a proper religious posture was inseparable from the goal of the restoration of Rome. Ammianus' treatment of Christianity is often viewed in terms of exclusion, of marginalization, as if Ammianus saw his task as to protect an antique historiographical model (and the model of Rome that his style of history embodied) from contamination by the contemporary. Arguably a more positive formulation is required. In keeping with the ideal of the restoration of Rome, he attempted to integrate, to absorb, the religious issues of his day into the traditional model of 'Great Historiography'[47] of which he was the inheritor. In so doing, his outlook may perhaps have been characteristic of a breed of paganism that has been under-represented: one that had not yet learnt to call itself by that, or any, name[48] – that did not know how to shout back.

Notes

1. My thanks to Mark Humphries, Jill Harries and Theresa Urbainczyk for comments on a draft, to Peter Heather for initial inspiration, to Michael Whitby and Roger Rees for encouragement and reassurance, but above all to John Matthews for his magnanimity and kindness in response to my original paper. All translations are (with small changes) from J.C. Rolfe's Loeb edition.
2. J.F. Matthews, *The Roman Empire of Ammianus*, London 1989, 425.
3. E.D. Hunt, 'Christians and Christianity in Ammianus Marcellinus', *CQ* 35 (1985), 186–200, at 187.
4. G. Sabbah, *La méthode d'Ammien Marcellin. Recherches sur la construction du discours historique dans les Res Gestae*, Paris 1978, 548.
5. See e.g. the range of views expressed by R.C. Blockley, *Ammianus Marcellinus. A Study of his Historiography and Political Thought* (Collection Latomus 141), Brussels 1975, 5, 70, 105, 122, 176.
6. Matthews, *The Roman Empire of Ammianus*, 427.
7. Cf. Sabbah, *La méthode d'Ammien Marcellin*, 202.
8. Or in the guise of 'moral preconceptions': Blockley, *Ammianus Marcellinus*, 27.
9. P.J. Rhodes, 'In Defence of the Greek Historians', *G&R* 41 (1994), 156–71.
10. D. Feeney, *Literature and Religion at Rome*, Cambridge 1998, 41, 25 (quoting Richard Hunter).
11. T.D. Barnes, 'Literary Convention, Nostalgia and Reality in Ammianus Marcellinus', in G. Clarke et al. (eds), *Reading the Past in Late Antiquity*, Rushcutters Bay 1990, 59–92, at 72. See also esp. C.W. Fornara, 'Studies in Ammianus Marcellinus II: Ammianus' Knowledge and Use of Greek and Latin Literature', *Historia* 41 (1992), 422–38, at 438; R.L. Rike, *Apex Omnium. Religion in the Res Gestae of Ammianus*, Berkeley 1987, 9.
12. Rike, *Apex Omnium*, 6.
13. Matthews, *The Roman Empire of Ammianus*, 430.
14. P.M. Camus, *Ammien Marcellin, témoin des courants culturels et réligieux à la fin du IVe siècle*, Paris 1967, 148.
15. W.G. Forrest, 'Motivation in Herodotos', *International History Review* 1 (1979), 311–22, at 312; K. Hopkins, *Conquerors and Slaves*, Cambridge 1978, 173.
16. Rike, *Apex Omnium*, ch. 1.
17. Feeney, *Literature and Religion*, 91.
18. For Ammianus' belief in divination, see Blockley, *Ammianus Marcellinus*, 174; J.H.W.G. Liebeschuetz, 'Ammianus, Julian and Divination', in M. Wissemann (ed.), *Roma Renascens. Festschrift I. Opelt*, Frankfurt am Main 1988, 198–213.
19. For inconsistency in religion, see esp. H.S. Versnel, *Inconsistencies in Greek and Roman Religion*, vol. 1, Leiden 1990, 1–38. The inconsistency of Ammianus' religious thought is a commonplace; see, most recently, P. Siniscalco, 'Le sacré et l'expérience de l'histoire: Ammien Marcellin et Paul Orose', *Bulletin de l'Association Guillaume Budé* (1989), 355–66, at 359; J. Amat, 'Ammien Marcellin at la Justice Immanente (14, 11, 20–34)', in *De Tertullien aux Mozarabes. Mélanges J. Fontaine*, vol. 1, Paris 1992, 267–79, at 278–9; contrast Barnes, 'Literary Convention', 72.
20. Hunt, 'Christians and Christianity'; Matthews, *The Roman Empire of Ammianus*, 435–51; see also A. Cameron and A. Cameron, 'Christianity and Tradition in the Historiography of the Late Empire', *CQ* 14 (1964), 316–28; V. Neri, *Ammiano e il cristianesimo. Religione e politica nelle 'Res Gestae' di Ammiano Marcellino* (Studi di Storia Antica 11), Bologna 1985, and his 'Ammianus' Definition of Christianity as *absoluta et simplex religio*', in J. den Boeft, D. den Hengst and H.C. Teitler (eds), *Cognitio Gestorum. The Historiographic Art of Ammianus Marcellinus*, Amsterdam 1992, 59–65.
21. Cf. Barnes, 'Literary Convention', 74. For the different senses of *fortuna*, see C.P.T. Naudé, 'Fortuna in Ammianus Marcellinus', *Acta Classica* 7 (1964), 70–89; M.-A. Marié,

'Virtus et Fortuna chez Ammien Marcellin', *REL* 67 (1989), 179–90; for fate, see W. Seyfarth, 'Ammianus und das Fatum', *Klio* 43 (1965), 291–306.
22 Cf. Rike, *Apex Omnium*, 61; Liebeschuetz, 'Ammianus, Julian and Divination'.
23 Matthews, *The Roman Empire of Ammianus*, 434–5.
24 E.g. 15.5.18, 15.5.35, 15.8.2, 16.12.68–70, 19.12.16. Similarly portents predate Book 21: 19.12.19–20.
25 As when he had feared that a double lobe on a liver might be a 'fiction conformable to his desire' (22.1.1).
26 Cf. Rike, *Apex Omnium*, 18–19, comparing Valens (31.1.3).
27 Contrast Blockley's (*Ammianus Marcellinus*, 19, 22) curiously anaemic description of Gallus' death as shaped by 'non-objective factors, especially moral preconceptions and literary considerations', and as a 'punishment for evil'.
28 Jovian: 25.5.8, 25.7.5, 25.8.3, 25.10.1–2, 25.10.11–12, 25.10.16–17; Valentinian: 26.1.7, 26.2.9, 30.5.15–19, 30.6.6; Procopius: 26.6.15–18, 26.7.17, 26.8.13, 26.9.9. 26.10.15–19; Gratian: 27.6.15, 31.10.11, 31.10.18; Valens: 29.1, 31.1, 31.14.8; Theodosius: 28.3.7, 29.5.40. For the clothes of Jovian as presaging his death see Marié, 'Virtus et Fortuna', 184; for Gratian, see Sabbah, *La méthode d'Ammien Marcellin*, 493.
29 Cf. 19.9.3, 21.9.7–8, 21.16.20–21, 28.1.57, 28.6.27.
30 Cf. F. Paschoud, 'Justice et providence chez Ammien Marcellin', in *Hestíasis. Studi di tarda antichità offerti a S. Calderone*, Messina 1986, 139–61, 158–61.
31 Cf. 16.10.1–2, 16.10.6, 15.2.2.
32 For this *urbs–orbis* theme, see esp. J.F. Matthews, 'Ammianus and the Eternity of Rome', in C. Holdsworth and T.P. Wiseman (eds), *The Inheritance of Historiography 350–900*, Exeter 1986, 17–29, 20–1; for Constantius' obelisk, see Rike, *Apex Omnium*, 98–100.
33 Cf. Paschoud, 'Justice et providence', 142.
34 Cf. 16.10.15, 22.16.12, 25.10.5.
35 Paschoud, 'Justice et providence', 142; cf. Liebeschuetz, 'Ammianus, Julian and Divination', 201.
36 Cf. Matthews, 'Ammianus and the Eternity of Rome', 21–4.
37 Blockley, *Ammianus Marcellinus*, 103; E. Auerbach, *Mimesis. The Representation of Reality in Western Literature*, Princeton 1953, 60.
38 Cf. Blockley, *Ammianus Marcellinus*, 146, for the 'good official'; Camus, *Ammien Marcellin*, ch. 6 for 'physionomie morale'.
39 Cf. Matthews' observation ('Ammianus and the Eternity of Rome', 22) that in Rome alone did the emperor fail to control the outcome of horse-races (Amm. Marc. 16.10.14), 'a sort of physical enactment of the concept of perfect liberty'.
40 See esp. Rike, *Apex Omnium*, ch. 5; for barbarians more generally, T.E.J. Wiedemann, 'Between Men and Beasts: Barbarians in Ammianus Marcellinus', in I.S. Moxon, J.D. Smart and A.J. Woodman (eds), *Past Perspectives. Studies in Greek and Roman Historical Writing*, Cambridge 1986, 189–201.
41 See e.g. 17.12.21, 19.1.11, 19.2.1–3, 23.3.2, 23.6.6, 24.1.9, 24.2.21, 31.2.4, 31.2.23–4, 31.7.4, 31.9.5.
42 See A.D. Momigliano, *Essays in Ancient and Modern Historiography*, Oxford 1977, 148.
43 *Ibid.*, 120–1, 148–50.
44 Symmachus, *Rel.* 3.10; for context, see P. Courcelle, 'Anti-Christian Arguments and Christian Platonism: from Arnobius to St. Ambrose', in A.D. Momigliano (ed.), *The Conflict between Paganism and Christianity in the Fourth Century*, Oxford 1963, 151–92; J.F. Matthews, 'Symmachus and the Oriental Cults', *JRS* 63 (1973), 175–95.
45 On this phrase, see esp. Hunt, 'Christians and Christianity', 191. Cf. Momigliano, *Essays in Ancient and Modern Historiography*, 120 ('what matters is *virtus*, not paganism or Christianity'); J.J. O'Donnell, 'The Demise of Paganism', *Traditio* 35 (1979), 45–88, at 55–8.

46 A.D. Momigliano, *The Classical Foundations of Modern Historiography*, Berkeley 1990, 139.
47 The term of J. Marincola, *Authority and Tradition in Ancient Historiography*, Cambridge 1997.
48 See the comments on 'religious affiliation' of M. Beard, J. North and S. Price, *Religions of Rome*, 2 vols, Cambridge 1998, vol. 1, pp. 42–3.

Part IV

THE WORLD BEYOND,
PERSIA AND ISAURIA

# 16

AMMIANUS MARCELLINUS' IMAGE OF ARSACES AND EARLY PARTHIAN HISTORY

Jan Willem Drijvers

Ammianus' digressions, especially those on geography and ethnography, have in general received little attention.[1] That the main interest is still focused on Ammianus' historical account becomes most obvious from the latest English translation of Ammianus' work, where all digressions are left out.[2] This lack of interest in the geographical digressions among modern scholars may be explained by Theodor Mommsen's severe judgement of them in his famous article 'Ammians Geographica' of 1881.[3] Mommsen accuses Ammianus of 'scheinhaftes Bescheidwissen', of 'Unkenntnis', of 'das eitle Bemühen um Allwissenheit' and of using empty words to conceal his deficient knowledge. Mommsen's negative opinion was soon generally accepted,[4] as a consequence of which Ammianus' geographical digressions have attracted little notice, in spite of the growing interest in Ammianus and his work over the past decades.

The digression on the Persian provinces comprises the larger part of Book 23 and covers some eighteen pages in the Teubner edition – the rest of the book covers some thirteen pages. The digression is inserted in the description of Julian's Persian campaign, just at the point where the Roman army near Cercusium had entered Persian territory and the emperor had given a speech to encourage his troops for the coming encounters with the Persians. Ammianus himself remarks in the introduction to the digression that affairs had reached a point at which it was appropriate to explain the topography of the Persian kingdom.[5] Thus Ammianus thought it suitable to inform his audience about the geography and ethnography of Persia to provide a better understanding of Julian's campaign.[6] This was at least his formal argument, but a digression also provided the author with the opportunity to show off his knowledge and interests to his readers, as well as to rival his predecessors.[7] Moreover, a historian writing in the classical tradition like Ammianus could not disappoint his readers who expected digressions. Although Ammianus tells us that he will give his information *in excessu celeri*, the digression is on the contrary extremely long, in fact the longest of all in Ammianus' work.[8] Ammianus, however, modifies his words immediately by remarking that complete knowledge demands a fuller account (*quod autem erit paulo prolixior textus, ad scientiam proficiet plenam*). He informs us furthermore that he had gathered his information from written sources (*descriptionibus gentium curiose digestis*), only few of which, according to Ammianus, told the truth, and that even barely (*in quibus aegre vera dixere paucissimi*).[9] I will return to this matter of the sources briefly at the end of this chapter.

The structure of the Persian digression offers no difficulties. It consists of the following items: § 1 author's introduction; §§ 2–9 historical introduction; §§ 10–14 geographical introduction; §§ 15–74 description of the Persian provinces including an excursus on the Magi (§§ 32–6); §§ 75–84 ethnographical description of the Persians; §§ 85–8 excursus on pearls. In the main part of the digression – the description of the Persian provinces – Ammianus applies a systematic pattern. In general he characterizes the geography of each province, discusses the condition of its soil, its fertility or infertility, and, if appropriate, makes some remarks about its inhabitants, its animals and the products of the land. He always mentions cities and rivers, and occasionally refers to mountain ranges.[10] Ammianus does not limit himself to those regions which were (once) under the control of the Persians, but also discusses other parts of the eastern world such as Arabia Felix as well as regions in Central Asia like Serica. Thus he describes not so much the Persian provinces as the whole eastern world known in his day, except for India. In this Ammianus shows himself to be a follower of famous geographers such as Strabo and Ptolemy.[11]

As in the case of the other digressions, the Persian digression has received little attention either from classicists or from orientalists. This chapter focuses on the historical introduction of the digression and especially on those sections which are dedicated to the earliest history of the Parthian reign, to the person of Arsaces and the role he played in founding the Parthian empire. There are two questions which I want to address. First, how Ammianus' information should be estimated from a historical perspective. Is Ammianus' information on Arsaces and the establishment of Parthian rule of importance for reconstructing the history of the early Parthian empire? Second, how far does Ammianus represent the traditional Roman view on Parthia, the Parthians and Parthian history? But before embarking on these matters, I offer a brief summary of the contents of the passage under examination.

According to Ammianus the Persian kingdom was once small and known by various names. After the death of Alexander the Great it took its name from the Parthian Arsaces. The latter won many victories especially over Seleucus Nicator – who is called the successor of Alexander – and drove out the Macedonian garrisons. He brought the neighbouring lands under Parthian rule by force, by regard for justice, or by fear. In the conquered territories

Arsaces built cities and strongholds. Peoples whom the Parthians had first feared were now themselves afraid of the Parthians. Arsaces is described as a brigand chief who had gradually changed for the better. Ammianus presents him as a mild ruler and judge of his subjects. He died a peaceful death in middle age. After his death he was deified and placed among the stars; hence the Persian kings call themselves, and are called, brothers of the Sun and Moon. The veneration of Arsaces is so great that only a man belonging to the Arsacid house can mount the throne.[12] The lifting of a hand against an Arsacid is considered sacrilege.

After having described in a nutshell the history of Arsaces and Parthian beginnings (§§ 2–6), Ammianus switches without notifying his readers in § 7 to an earlier period of Persian history, namely that of the Achaemenids. He refers to the extension of Persian dominion to the Propontis and Thrace, to Cyrus' fatal campaign against the Massagetae, to the expeditions of Darius and Cyrus against Greece, as well as to the wars of Alexander against the Persians. Ammianus concludes his historical introduction by remarking that in the time of the Roman Republic and the Empire the Persians fought wars with the Romans from time to time, which were sometimes won by the Persians, sometimes by the Romans; occasionally the contest ended equally (§ 9).

The modern reader notices immediately, not only that Ammianus distorts chronology by first treating the Arsacid period and thereafter that of the Achaemenids, but also that he does not refer to the shift of power from the Arsacid to the Sassanid dynasty in 224 CE. In his work Ammianus speaks only of *Persae* or *Parthi* and nowhere does he mention the Sassanians. Since he does so consistently, it has been questioned whether Ammianus was aware of the change of power in Persia in 224.[13] However, although as a historian Ammianus probably knew about the takeover by the Sassanids, he omits referring to it because the Romans usually do not distinguish between a Persia ruled by the Arsacids and a Persia ruled by the Sassanid dynasty.[14] Apparently Ammianus considers the Persians as one entity with one history, without making much distinction between Achaemenids and Arsacids and no distinction at all between the Arsacid and Sassanid dynasty.[15]

The historical value of Ammianus' information

Greek and Roman authors provide amazingly little information about the Parthian empire. For an empire which existed for some five centuries, and was the main power in the East and the greatest adversary of Rome for many years, this is astonishing. It is also disappointing since Iranian culture was aways predominantly oral, as a consequence of which no literary sources from the Parthian perspective are available and thus Graeco-Roman writings are our main sources for the history of Parthia. The most important of these are the *Historiae Philippicae* of Pompeius Trogus known through the epitome of Justin, the fragmentarily preserved *Parthika* of Arrian and Strabo's *Geographica*. More information can be gained from Plutarch's *Lives* of Crassus and Mark Antony, from Appian, Cassius Dio and Tacitus on Roman–Parthian relations, from the elder Pliny on the historical geography of Parthia and from Flavius Josephus on Jewish–Parthian relations. Furthermore there are some Chinese sources, Parthian ostraka found in Nisa – and of course other archaeological material.[16] Ammianus is not considered as one of the more informative sources on Parthia and its early history, since he has no abundant information on Arsaces and the beginning of Parthian rule. However, the two other main sources for early Parthian history – Justin's Book 41 and Strabo 11.9.2 (515C) – are not always clear and are at points contradictory. Ammianus may therefore be used as a complementary source, all the more so because he has information which other authors do not have.

The history of the beginning of Parthian rule is problematic and its chronology difficult to unravel. It is generally held that Arsaces and his followers were Parni, nomads belonging to the Scythian tribe of the Dahae. Probably as a consequence of migratory movements among nomads living north of Iran they were forced to move from the Ochus river, east of the Caspian Sea, where they had lived.[17] The Parni went south and entered the Seleucid satrapy Parthava where they settled. We have to think here of the mountain area in the north-east corner of modern Iran and of south Turkmenistan, in particular the region which includes the two mountain ranges Kopet Dagh and Binalud. When exactly the invasion of Arsaces and his followers took place is hard to establish. According to the general opinion Arsaces became leader or king of the Parni in 247 BCE. Thanks to secessional movements against Seleucid domination in the satrapies of Bactria and Parthava, Arsaces and his followers were presented with the opportunity to invade Parthava/Parthia. This is thought to have happened around the year 238 BCE.[18]

Ammianus gives no date for the establishment of Parthian rule. His chronology is very imprecise and even incorrect since he puts the rise of Arsaces and the Parthian empire immediately after the death of Alexander the Great (*Hoc regnum . . . cum apud Babylona Magnum fata rapuissent Alexandrum, in vocabulum Parthi concessit Arsacis*), as if nothing had happened in between.[19] Ammianus is also vague and inaccurate on the chronology of the expansion of Parthian territory. He speaks of Arsaces' glorious and valiant deeds (*multa gloriose et fortiter gesta*), his victory over Seleucus Nicator (*superato Nicatore Seleuco*), the driving-out of Macedonian garrisons (*praesidiisque Macedonum pulsis*), his conquering of neighbouring lands and the establishment of cities, fortified camps and strongholds in Persia (*civitatum et castrorum castellorumque munimentis oppleta Perside*). Ammianus is clearly mistaken when he says that Arsaces was victorious over Seleucus Nicator. This must be Seleucus II Callinicus, who ruled from 246 to 226 BCE, and against whom, as we know from Justin, Arsaces waged war for the secession of Parthia from Seleucid rule.[20]

Ammianus implicitly records that Arsaces during his lifetime conquered a complete empire and established Parthian rule in regions which shortly before were under the control of the Seleucids.[21] Strabo has a similar view. Although he does not explicitly mention Arsaces' conquest of an empire, he is quite clear on Arsaces' establishment of power in Parthia and the loss of control by the Seleucids over eastern parts of their kingdom. This view is also found in modern works.[22] Historians have for a long time thought that Seleucid rule in the eastern parts of Iran was never strong and that in consequence Arsaces could expand his power quickly. However, thanks to new insights we now know that historical reality was different. Arsaces certainly was not the strong military leader Ammianus and other authors want us to believe he was. We may infer this from Strabo (11.9.2, 514C) who mentions the invasion and conquest of Parthia by Arsaces but explicitly adds that Arsaces and his successors at the outset were weak and continually at war with those who had been deprived by them of their dominions; only later did they grow strong and conquer neighbouring territory. Arsaces was not that powerful in terms of military strength, he did not establish Parthian rule quickly and he was not a great threat to Seleucid rule. It took Arsaces considerable effort to get a foothold in Parthia. He was probably able to consolidate his power only in northern Kopet Dagh in Turkmenistan.[23] From there he and the Parthian rulers after him only gradually and slowly extended their power. Arsaces and his immediate successors could very likely be kept under control by the Seleucids. We know of campaigns of Seleucus II Callinicus between the years 231 and 227 BCE against the Parthians which were apparently successful. Strabo records that as a consequence of these expeditions Arsaces fled and withdrew to the country of the Apasiacae.[24] Furthermore, several decades later during the reign of Antiochus the Great the Parthian kings seem to have been vassals of the Seleucids. As vassals they provided the Seleucid king with cavalry and mounted archers and on coins from this period Parthian kings wore satrapal head-dress. Parthian empire-building was therefore a lengthy undertaking with at times major setbacks.[25] Only in the second century BCE during the reigns of the Parthian kings Mithridates I (c. 171–139/8) and Mithridates II (c. 124/3–88/7) did the great conquests take place, a large territory was captured and an empire was founded.

Ammianus' information on the establishment and expansion of Parthian power, like that of other authors, is clearly not in keeping with historical reality. Conquests were of course made, the Seleucids were eventually driven out, cities and strongholds were founded by the Parthians, and an empire was created, but these things did not happen during the lifetime of Arsaces I. However, in Graeco-Roman historiography Arsaces was seen as the founder of the Parthian empire and therefore (not surprisingly) these great deeds were ascribed to him. Since the Romans hardly possessed any information on the history of the expansion of the Parthians this was all the easier to do.

And it became even easier because every Parthian king also bore the name of Arsaces in honour of the founder of the dynasty (Justin, *Epit.* 41.5.6).

Ammianus devotes comparatively extensive attention to Arsaces as he was considered by him and all other authors as the founder of the Parthian empire. According to Ammianus Arsaces was of obscure origin (*obscuro geniti loco*) and had been a brigand chief in his younger days (*latronum inter adulescentiae rudimenta ductoris*).[26] But this robber of obscure origin changed for the better (*paulatim in melius mutato proposito*). He became a mild ruler and judge of his subjects (*temperator oboedientium fuit et arbiter lenis*) and he eventually died peacefully.[27] After Arsaces' death both nobles and commons alike were eager to place him among the stars. Hence Arsaces and also his successors were deified and called brothers of the Sun and Moon (*Solis fratres et Lunae*). Arsaces especially was venerated and worshipped as a god since he was the founder of the empire and the ruling dynasty. Ammianus makes a somewhat unclear comparison with the title of Augustus, implying that the founder of the Roman empire and his successors were also considered divine. But whereas many Roman emperors were indeed deified after their death, there is no real evidence, except for this passage of Ammianus, that the Parthian kings were venerated as gods or were sacrosanct, either in their lifetime or after death. Although these words of Ammianus are believed by some to be proof that the Parthian kings were deified,[28] given the absence of other evidence or even indications with respect to Parthian sacral kingship, Ammianus' information is presumably mistaken. Since Ammianus does not distinguish between Parthians and Sassanians, he attributed the divinity of the Sassanids and the title of *Solis fratres et Lunae* also to the kings of the Arsacid dynasty. As is well known the Sassanid kings were considered, and considered themselves, as gods – compare for instance the *Res Gestae Divi Saporis*. They bore the title of brother of the Sun and Moon and were seen as partners of the stars. Ammianus himself even, referring to a letter of Shapur to Constantius, calls the Sassanid king 'partner with the stars, brother of the Sun and Moon'.[29]

Ammianus presents a picture of Arsaces not only as a godlike king, but also as an ideal ruler. Arsaces is described both as a very capable military leader who was often victorious and as a benevolent civilian ruler who treated his subjects with generosity. We may infer from this that according to Ammianus Arsaces put his people and their welfare before himself. Furthermore he is considered, especially after his death, to have a special relationship with the gods. His godlike nature made his successors divine offspring and therefore the best men for the Parthian throne. Ammianus clearly has a high regard for Arsaces.[30] His picture of the first Parthian king corresponds to the image of the ideal Hellenistic sovereign. Much was written in antiquity on the ideal monarch. He had to have the qualities of a good general; he had to be wise, righteous and faithful to the laws, humane and even philanthropic, magnanimous and merciful. He is the keeper of order and he ought to be like a father to his subjects who concerned himself with their general well-being. Furthermore the sovereign had a special relationship with the gods; he had become ruler through divine will, his victories were proof of divine favour and he showed godly virtues. In short the king was godlike.[31] Though Arsaces is not ascribed all of these qualities, Ammianus' description of him is obviously inspired by this image of the ideal Hellenistic sovereign. In this respect the vocabulary with which Arsaces is characterized is of interest. The terms which Ammianus uses in his description – *tranquillius, temperator, lenis, aequitas, placidus* – are undoubtedly chosen with care to present Arsaces as the good king of Hellenistic tradition.

Ammianus' information thus seems to be of little value for reconstructing the early history of the Parthian empire. Not only does our author make blatant mistakes, as in the case of Arsaces' defeat of Seleucus Nicator, but also his description of the rise of the Parthian empire is not in agreement with what can reasonably be inferred from other sources. Ammianus portrays Arsaces as an ideal Hellenistic ruler and we do not learn anything about the man himself. Furthermore, Ammianus' information on the divinity of the Parthian kings is not corroborated by other evidence. Are we therefore to conclude that there is nothing to learn from Ammianus' passage on Arsaces and the rise of the Parthian empire, and should we blacken Ammianus' reputation as a reliable historian by dismissing the passage as historically unreliable? Is it, in Mommsen's words, only 'scheinhaftes Bescheidwissen'? This would be too rash a conclusion. For Ammianus' information on Arsaces and Parthia must be properly considered in the broader perspective of a historiographical tradition and the literary conventions which governed Roman views on Parthia and the Parthians.

The Roman view on Parthia and the Parthians

For the Romans Parthia was an *alter orbis*. This other world represented everything which was not Roman. Rome's oriental counterpart was amongst other things extremely wealthy and luxurious, was characterized by an effeminate style of life and sexual licentiousness, and was known for the cruelty of its kings who reigned according to the rules of despotism. This image of the oriental world is not exclusively Roman but goes back to Greek times when a stereotyped image of the oriental barbarian was developed. This barbarian is portrayed as the negative embodiment of Graeco-Roman values and ideals, whose social life fails to comply with the norms of Graeco-Roman society.[32] The Romans first came into formal contact with the Parthian Empire in 96 BCE when Sulla established friendly relations with the Parthians. In the first century BCE there were regular encounters, some friendly some hostile, between Rome and Parthia, contacts which continued in the first centuries CE.[33] During the reign of Augustus an ideological concept of the Parthian *alter orbis* was developed, when in 20 BCE the Parthians returned the trophies which they had captured in the defeat of Crassus in 53 BCE. The Roman image of Parthia and the Parthians is greatly influenced by the image which the Greeks had developed of the Persians.[34] This image, which expresses a Roman feeling of superiority towards the Parthians, is reflected in Roman literature as well as in iconography.[35] One aspect of Rome's ideology of Parthia is that no distinction is made between Medes, Persians, Parthians and other orientals. All these peoples east of the Euphrates were considered as one entity with the same habits and ethnographical characteristics.[36]

Once established Rome's ideological image of Parthia did not alter over the centuries. Even when through diplomacy, intelligence, trade and other means of contact more realistic knowledge about Parthia and the Parthians presumably became available in Rome, the persuasiveness of written (literary) language persisted. In general the Romans seem to have known very little about their eastern neighbour. They possessed hardly any information on the administrative, military and socio-economic organization or on the religions of the Parthian empire, and they were certainly badly informed, or at least show no sign of specific knowledge, about Parthia's geography and history.[37]

In the Roman empire no concrete image existed of the topography and geography of the lands east of the Euphrates. Tradition determined the Romans' geographical knowledge of the Parthian empire. This becomes obvious from the works of Strabo and the elder Pliny who wrote most extensively on the geography of the eastern lands. Most of their information is based on earlier writings, such as those of the Alexander historians and of Greeks living in the Parthian empire, like Apollodorus of Artemita. Apparently the Romans did not feel the need to gain more and better geographical and topographical knowledge than that which was handed down by tradition.[38] The information on geography and topography as assembled by Ammianus in his Persian digression is also rooted in this tradition and hardly offers any information which cannot be found in earlier works. Furthermore this tradition suited the ideological image which the Romans had developed of Parthia, since there is a relationship between the image of peoples and their natural surroundings. In the case of the Parthians this becomes obvious from Ammianus' description of their homeland, the former Achaemenid and Seleucid satrapy Parthia south-east of the Caspian Sea. It is described as a land abounding in snow and frost where the inhabitants are savage and take pleasure in war and conflict (23.6.43–4). Parthia was in Roman eyes a geographically marginal and barren land: therefore its inhabitants could only be uncivilized people. Whereas fertile lands, like those around the Mediterranean, were the natural habitat of civilized man.[39]

The Romans' presentation of early Parthian history and the provenance of Arsaces and the Parthians is also determined by tradition and by the image of the Parthians as barbarians. When Rome came into contact with the Parthians and became acquainted with Parthia's military strength, it was forced to recognize the Parthians' formidable power. The rise of this power had to be explained. Graeco-Roman writings developed the view that quite suddenly and unexpectedly the Parthians had risen out of anonymity and insignificance to establish a great empire.[40] The chronology of the Parthian conquests and of empire-building was not clear to the Romans, and probably was of no interest to them. Therefore many victories as well as the establishment of the empire were with hindsight attributed to Arsaces I, who consequently received great admiration in Graeco-Roman sources. As to the provenance of the Parthians, the image was created – which in this case probably has a degree of historical veracity – that they were of Scythian origin.[41] This descent could on the one hand justify the opinion that the Parthians were nomadic barbarians and were thus quite distinct from the Romans, but could on the other explain the Parthian rise to power since the Scythians were considered brave and excellent warriors.

The Roman ideology and inherited prejudice regarding the Parthians admittedly displays some ambivalence. Of course the Romans felt far superior to the Parthians but they also showed admiration for Parthian military power and especially for Arsaces who was the founder of this power. Ammianus displays this same ambivalence. In general he does not deviate from the historiographical tradition and literary convention with regard to the early history of Parthia, the geography of the region and the ethnicity of the Parthians. Great conquests of Seleucid territory and the establishment of an empire are ascribed to Arsaces by Ammianus. His description of the geography of Parthia and the ethnography of its people is much the same as Strabo's and Pliny's (*HN* 6.113). Nowhere does he call the Parthians barbarians, but in this respect too Ammianus keeps to the accepted conventions since no author dared to call them so outright; the Romans apparently had too much respect for the Parthians. However, he does refer to them as of Scythian origin,[42] which in itself constitutes a negative value judgement. He also remarks that Arsaces and his successors were of low and obscure origin.[43] Moreover he describes the Parthians as savage and warlike[44] and as a nation constantly inclined to civil strife.[45] These negative qualities are especially attributed to barbarians. Towards the end of the Persian digression Ammianus presents an ethnographical characterization of the orientals, who of course include the Parthians; here too qualities which are stereotypical for barbarians are mentioned.[46] Ammianus' ambivalence towards the Parthians is also shown in his portrayal of Arsaces. While Ammianus admires Arsaces for his conquests and the establishment of the empire as well as his regard for justice, he also presents him in a negative way by calling him a man of low birth, a former brigand chief and a king who ruled through fear.[47]

As Ammianus himself informs us, the Persian digression is evidently based on written sources (23.6.1: *descriptionibus gentium curiose digestis*). His own observation did not play a role of any importance; Ammianus seeks rather to connect with the prevailing historiographical and literary conventions.

Although there are resemblances with earlier writings on Arsaces and early Parthian history, it is almost impossible to establish which sources Ammianus used, and the attempts which have been made are not satisfactory.[48] As to Ammianus' sources for the historical introduction of the digression no attempts have been made to find out from which writings our author's information is derived.[49] Such attempts will be fruitless since not one of the extant Graeco-Roman writings on Parthia and the Parthians can reasonably be shown to be a source for Ammianus. We should therefore be satisfied with the observation that Ammianus' little excursus on Arsaces and early Parthian history belongs to Roman historiographical tradition and reflects Roman ideology of Parthia and the Parthians.[50] Since this tradition was static no new information on the Parthians and Parthian history can be gained from Ammianus' work.[51] From what he has to say there is therefore more to be learned about the historiographical tradition of which Ammianus evidently wanted his work to be a part, than about historical reality. Although Ammianus thus fails to live up to the expectations of a truthful and complete account raised in the digression's introduction, his approach is none the less understandable and justifiable. His traditional method makes Ammianus neither an ignorant author nor a bad historian: and he hardly deserves Mommsen's severe verdict.

Notes

1 A. Malotet, *De Ammiani Marcellini digressionibus quae ad externas gentes pertinent*, Paris 1898; H. Cicochka, 'Die Konzeption des Exkurses im Geschichtswerk des Ammianus Marcellinus', *Eos* 63 (1975), 329–40; A.M. Emmett, 'The Digressions in the Lost Books of Ammianus Marcellinus', in B. Croke and A.M. Emmett (eds), *History and Historians in Late Antiquity*, Sydney 1983, 42–53; A.M. Emmett, 'Introductions and Conclusions to Digressions in Ammianus Marcellinus', *Museum Philologum Londiniense* 5 (1981), 15–33. On the digression on Persia (23.6), there is J. Signes, 'El Excursus de los Persas de Amiano Marcelino (XXIII, 6)', *Veleia* 7 (1990), 351–75; for the excursus on the Huns (31.2), see C. King, 'The Veracity of Ammianus Marcellinus' Description of the Huns', *AJAH* 12 (1987 [1995]), 77–95; U. Richter, 'Die Funktion der Digressionen im Werk Ammians', *Würzburger Jahrbücher für Altertumswissenschaft*, N.F. 15 (1989), 209–22; M. Caltabiano, 'Il carattere delle digressioni nelle *Res Gestae* di Ammiano Marcellino', in A. Garzya (ed.), *Metodologie della ricerca sulla tarda antichità, Atti del Primo Convegno dell' Associazione di Studi Tardoantichi*, Naples 1989, 289–96; J. F. Matthews, *The Roman Empire of Ammianus*, London 1989, *passim*.
2 W. Hamilton and A. Wallace-Hadrill, *Ammianus Marcellinus. The Later Roman Empire (A.D. 354–378)*, Harmondsworth 1986.
3 Th. Mommsen, 'Ammians Geographica', *Hermes* 16 (1881), 602–36; repr. in Th. Mommsen, *Gesammelte Schriften* 7, Berlin 1909, 393–425. Mommsen's article was written in reply to the more positive paper by V. Gardthausen, *Die geographischen Quellen Ammians*, Jbh. f. class. Philol., Suppl. 6, Leipzig 1873.
4 E.g. M. Schanz, *Geschichte der römischen Literatur* IV, 2nd edn, Munich 1914, 96, who remarks that in his digressions 'der alte Soldat mit seiner mühsam erworbenen Gelehrsamkeit glänzen will und daher manchmal aus seinen Quellen Dinge abschreibt, die er selbst nicht versteht'.

5 23.6.1: *Res adigit huc prolapsa ut in excessu celeri situm monstrare Persidis.*
6 Richter, 'Die Funktion der Digressionen', 210–11; G.A. Sundwall, 'Ammianus Geographicus', *AJPhil.* 117 (1996), 619–43, at 624, who remarks that the content of the digression 'ill-fits the immediate context of the chapter'.
7 See e.g. G. Sabbah, *La méthode d'Ammien Marcellin. Recherches sur la construction du discours historique dans les Res Gestae,* Paris 1978, 525–8.
8 Sundwall, 'Ammianus Geographicus', 627, suggests that the length of Ammianus' digressions, unparalleled in ancient writing, was an innovation in literary tradition. The length of the digressions is, I think, caused rather by Ammianus' desire to 'show off'.
9 This is probably a topos. Ammianus does not in fact offer *scientia plena* nor does he add anything to what was already reported by other authors. A similar kind of formulation can be found in Tacitus, *Agr.* 10 where it is said that a faithful narration of facts on Britain will be presented instead of the legends of earlier writers; however, nothing new is presented.
10 M.F.A. Brok, 'Die Quellen von Ammians Exkurs über Persien', *Mnemosyne* 38 (1975), 47–56, at 51; Sundwall, 'Ammianus Geographicus', 628. See for the general outline of Ammianus' geographical digressions, Gardthausen, *Die geographischen Quellen Ammians*, 512ff.
11 These regions are included because they are described in Book 6 of Ptolemy's *Geographica*, which was an important source for Ammianus. The structure of the digression corresponds with that of Ptolemy and there are also strong resemblances with regard to contents. For the same reason India is excluded; it is not dealt with in Ptolemy's Book 6.
12 The attention given by Ammianus and other Roman authors to the dynastic aspect of Parthian kingship is possibly inspired by the lack of rules for succession in the Roman Empire. For this description of Arsaces, see further, pp. 198–9.
13 A. Chauvot, 'Parthes et Perses dans les sources du IVe siècle', in M. Christol et al. (eds), *Institutions, société et vie politique dans l'empire romain au IVe siècle ap. J.-C.*, Rome 1992, 115–25, esp. 121–2. To explain why Ammianus does not refer to the Sassanians, it has been suggested that Ammianus had used sources from before the change of power, but this suggestion has been rightly rejected by Brok, 'Die Quellen', 50.
14 Several sources mention the change of power, e.g. Herodian 6.2; Cassius Dio 80.3.4; Zosimus 1.18.1.
15 Ammianus says that Julian eagerly wanted to add the surname Parthicus to the record of his victories: *ornamentis illustrium gloriarum inserere Parthici cognomentum ardebat* (22.12.4).
16 For the sources on Parthia and Parthian history, see M.A.R. Colledge, *The Parthians*, London 1967, 17; K. Schippmann, *Grundzüge der parthischen Geschichte*, Darmstadt 1980, 7; J. Wiesehöfer, *Das antike Persien*, Munich and Zurich 1993, 172f.
17 Strabo 11.7.1 (508C), 11.8.2 (515C), 11.9.2 (515C); also Arrian, *Parth.* frg. 1.
18 For discussions on the chronology of these events, see e.g. J. Wolski, 'The Decay of the Iranian Empire of the Seleucids and the Chronology of the Parthian Beginnings', *Berytus* 12 (1956–8), 35–52; E. Will, *Histoire politique du monde hellénistique (323–30 av. J.C.)*, vol. 1, 2nd edn, Nancy 1979, 301ff., esp. the notes; A.D.H. Bivar, 'The Political History of Iran under the Arsacids', *CHI* 3.1 (1983), 21–99, at 28–31; R.N. Frye, *The History of Ancient Iran*, Handbuch der Altertumswissenschaft III.7, Munich 1983, 206ff.; K. Brodersen, 'The Date of the Secession of Parthia from the Seleucid Kingdom', *Historia* 35 (1986), 378–81; J. Wiesehöfer, 'Discordia et Defectio – Dynamis kai Pithanourgia. Die frühen Seleukiden und Iran', in Bernd Funck (ed.), *Hellenismus. Beiträge zur Erforschung von Akkulturation und politischer Ordnung in den Staaten des hellenistischen Zeitalters*, Tübingen 1997, 29–56, 39ff.
19 Julian, *Or.* 1, 17c–d might imply the same with his remark that as soon as Alexander the Great was dead, the Persians (i.e. the Parthians) revolted and successfully opposed the Macedonians.

20 Justin, *Epit.* 41.4.9: *nec multo post cum Seleuco rege, ad defectores persequendos veniente, congressus, victor* [Arsaces] *fuit: quem diem Parthi exinde solemnem, velut initium libertatis, observant* ('Not long afterwards Arsaces was victorious in conflict with King Seleucus who came to attack the rebels; the Parthians commemorate this day as the beginning of their freedom').
21 On Arsaces see e.g. J. Wolksi, 'Arsace Ier, fondateur de l'état parthe', *Acta Iranica* 3 (1974), 159–99.
22 E.g. Will, *Histoire politique*, 301ff.; W. Walbank, *The Hellenistic World*, Brighton 1981, 123.
23 S. Sherwin-White and A. Kuhrt, *From Samarkhand to Sardis. A New Approach to the Seleucid Empire*, London 1993, 88. The removal of the Seleucid satrap of Parthia, Andragoras, as referred to by Justin, *Epit.* 41.4.7, may have been helpful in this respect.
24 11.8.8 (513C); cf., however, Justin, *Epit.* 41.4.9.
25 See Sherwin-White and Kuhrt, *From Samarkhand to Sardis*, 89–90; J. Wiesehöfer, '"Kings of Kings" and "Philhellen": Kingship in Arsacid Iran', in P. Bilde et al. (eds), *Aspects of Hellenistic Kingship*, Aarhus 1996, 55–66, at 58.
26 Cf. Justin, *Epit.* 41.4.6–7: *erat eo tempore Arsaces vir, sicut incertae originis, ita virtutis expertae. hic solitus latrociniis et rapto vivere* ('Arsaces was a man of obscure origin, but of well-tried courage: he was used to living by brigandage and plunder').
27 Whereas Ammianus informs us that Arsaces died in middle age (*medium ipse agens cursum aetatis placida morte decessit*), Justin, *Epit.* 41.5.5 reports that he died at an advanced age (*Arsaces . . . matura senectute decedit*). Arrian, *Parth.* 1.2 says that Arsaces was killed after having governed for only two years.
28 Especially G. Widengren, 'The Sacral Kingship of Iran', in *The Sacral Kingship. Contributions to the Central Theme of the VIIIth International Congress for the History of Religions*, Leiden 1959, 242–57, at 246; G. Widengren, 'Iran, der grosse Gegner Roms: Königsgewalt, Feudalismus, Militärwesen', *ANRW* II 9.1 (1976), 219–306, at 230ff. Although the Parthian kings were considered human beings and not gods, they did have godlike qualities; Wiesehöfer, '"Kings of Kings" and "Philhellen": Kingship in Arsacid Iran', 62.
29 17.5.3: *Rex regum Sapor, particeps siderum, frater Solis et Lunae*. Cf. J. Fontaine, *Ammien Marcellin. Histoire IV (Livres XXIII–XXV)*, 2 vols, Paris 1977, vol. 2, 59 n. 134, who has the unlikely view that the Sassanians took over the solar and astral divinity from the Arsacids.
30 The comparison Ammianus makes between the Parthian king and Augustus enhances this esteem. The Romans had a high regard for the first Parthian king; e.g. Justin, *Epit.* 41.5.5 where Arsaces is compared with Cyrus the Great, Alexander and Romulus.
31 P. Hadot, 'Fürstenspiegel', *RAC* 60 (1970), 568–609.
32 Of the many publications on this subject I mention only the following: F. Hartog, *The Mirror of Herodotus: the Representation of the Other in the Writing of History* (trans. J. Lloyd), Cambridge (Mass.) 1988; E. Hall, *Inventing the Barbarian*, Oxford 1989; Y.A. Dauge, *Le Barbare. Recherches sur la conception romaine de la barbarie et de la civilisation*, Brussels 1981. Esp. for Ammianus: T. Wiedemann, 'Between Men and Beasts: Barbarians in Ammianus Marcellinus', in I.S. Moxon, J.D. Smart and A.J. Woodman (eds), *Past Perspectives: Studies in Greek and Roman Historical Writing*, Cambridge 1986, 189–201.
33 K.-H. Ziegler, *Die Beziehungen zwischen Rom und dem Partherreich. Ein Beitrag zur Geschichte des Völkerrechts*, Wiesbaden 1964; Schippmann, *Grundzüge der parthischen Geschichte*, 33ff.; H. Sonnabend, *Fremdenbild und Politik. Vorstellungen der Römer von Ägypten und dem Partherreich in der späten Republik und frühen Kaiserzeit*, Frankfurt am Main and Bern and New York 1986, 157ff. A view of Roman–Parthian relations from the Parthian perspective is given by D. Kennedy, 'Parthia and Rome: Eastern Perspectives', in D. L. Kennedy (ed.), *The Roman Army in the East*, *JRA* Suppl. 18 (1996), 67–90.
34 Sonnabend, *Fremdenbild und Politik*, 229ff.; A. Spawforth, 'Symbol of Unity? The Persian-Wars Tradition in the Roman Empire', in S. Hornblower (ed.), *Greek Historiography*, Oxford 1994, 233–69.

35 Sonnabend, *Fremdenbild und Politik*, 197ff. and 264ff.; R.M. Schneider, 'Die Faszination des Feindes. Bilder der Parther und des Orients in Rom', in J. Wiesehöfer (ed.), *Das Partherreich und seine Zeugnisse* (Historia Einzelschriften 122), Stuttgart 1998, 95–146.
36 E.g. Pliny, *HN* 6.41 (*Persarum regna, quae nunc Parthorum intelligimus*); Virgil, *Georg.* 5.211; Propertius 3.3.11. See further Schneider, 'Die Faszination des Feindes'. In his orations for Constantius also Julian does not distinguish between Medes, Persians and Parthians; see Chauvot, 'Parthes et Perses', 118ff.
37 Sonnabend, *Fremdenbild und Politik*, 264ff.
38 Sonnabend, *Fremdenbild und Politik*, 272. An exception is to be made for the *Stathmoi Parthikoi* of Isidore of Charax, written during the reign of Augustus. A. Momigliano, *Alien Wisdom. The Limits of Hellenization*, Cambridge 1975, 140–1, is of the opinion that the Romans were interested in knowing the Parthians better. However, the Romans seem to have been sincerely interested only in the practices of the Chaldaeans and the Magi; Sonnabend, *Fremdenbild und Politik*, 291f.
39 This image can for instance also be found in Strabo; see J.W. Drijvers, 'Strabo on Parthia and the Parthians', in J. Wiesehöfer (ed.), *Das Partherreich und seine Zeugnisse* (Historia Einzelschriften 122), Stuttgart 1998, 279–93. For more examples of this kind in the works of Ammianus see Sundwall, 'Ammianus Geographicus', 630–1.
40 Justin, *Epit.* 41.1.3, 7, 8; Strabo 11.9.1 (514C); Curtius 6.2.12; Cass. Dio 40.14.2; see further Sonnabend, *Fremdenbild und Politik*, 274–5.
41 Justin, *Epit.* 41.1.1; Curtius 6.2.14; Strabo 11.9.2 (515C); Arrian, *Parth.* 224, frg. 1; Pliny, *HN* 6.50 remarks that the lifestyle of Parthians and Scythians was the same. Also Sonnabend, *Fremdenbild und Politik*, 276ff.
42 31.2.20: *unde etiam Persae* [i.e. the Parthians], *qui sunt originitus Scythae*. In general Ammianus considers the Persians a most deceitful nation (*fallacissima gens*, 21.13.4) and savage people (*gens asperrima*, 22.12.1) who belong to the other *gentes saevissimae* (26.4.5–6).
43 23.6.2: *Arsacis, obscuro geniti loco*; 23.6.5: *regibus Parthicis abiectis et ignobilibus antea*.
44 23.6.44. Exactly the same is said by Ammianus about the Halani in 31.2.22. More or less the same – love for warfare, no fear of death, contempt for cowardly behaviour – is said of Germans and Gauls; Tacitus, *Germ.* 12, 14; Lucan 1.460–2.
45 23.6.6: ... *civili concertatione, quae assidue apud eos eveniunt*. Strabo 15.3.12 (732C) also refers to Parthian insurrections. In 23.6.83 Ammianus mentions that the Persians were constantly plagued by domestic (and foreign) wars.
46 23.6.75–84. Apart from positive, especially military qualities, Ammianus mentions e.g. their wearing of beards and long, shaggy hair, their sexual licentiousness and polygamy, their effeminacy, their mad and extravagant talking, their luxurious clothing, their cruelty, and their inclination to civil wars.
47 Ammianus' characterization of Arsaces closely tallies with Justin's description (*Epit.* 41.3.9, 4.6–10, 5.1–5) of the first Parthian king. Ammianus does not seem to have a high regard for the other Parthian kings whom he calls *reges ... praetumidi* (23.6.5).
48 Gardthausen, *Die geographischen Quellen Ammians*; Mommsen, 'Ammians Geographica', who mentions Ptolemy as Ammianus' main source; L. Dillemann, 'Ammien Marcellin et les pays de l'Euphrate et du Tigre', *Syria. Revue d'art oriental et d'archéologie* 38 (1961), 87–158, who mentions several sources; cf. Brok, 'Die Quellen', who is doubtful about Ammianus' use of Ptolemy and advocates new research to detect Ammianus' sources. However, Ptolemy must have been directly or indirectly one of Ammianus' sources; see also n. 11 above.
49 It has been cautiously suggested by Fontaine, *Ammien Marcellin*, 58–9 (n. 133 ad 23.6.4) that Ammianus made use of Justin, *Epit.* 41.5 for his characterization of Arsaces. I consider this doubtful.
50 K. Rosen, *Ammianus Marcellinus* (Erträge der Forschung 183), Darmstadt 1982, 85 and Richter, 'Die Funktion der Digressionen', 218, argue that Ammianus had a moral goal

with his Persian digression, namely to hold up a mirror to the Romans' face and to bring to their attention their faults and wrongs by presenting the *virtutes* and *vitia* of the Persians. This may be so, but such an approach misses the broader perspective of the historiographical tradition which is sustained by the digression.

51 I disagree, at least in the case of the Persian digression, with Sundwall, 'Ammianus Geographicus', 625, that 'Ammianus clearly had no interest merely in relating what his sources had to say; rather, he evaluated them so that he might present a more accurate representation to his reader.' I think that Ammianus kept very close to his sources just because he did not want to deviate from tradition. There is also nothing that indicates that Ammianus' personal experience and travels play an important role (cf. *ibid.*, 626), except perhaps for the information in 23.6.21 on the name of Adiabene.

17

PURE RITES

Ammianus Marcellinus on the Magi

Jan den Boeft

Introduction

Res Gestae 23.6 is a long digression on the Persian empire, which is functional inasmuch as it provides the reader with a description of the vast empire the protagonist Julian was now attacking and indeed invading. Within this extensive geographical and ethnographical survey which pictures the enemy's moral and material resources, here and there shorter digressions in the second degree have been inserted.[1] Sections 32–5 contain the most important of these, with a short appendix, so to speak a digression in the third degree, in § 36. A translation of the entire passage seems appropriate. It runs as follows:

> (32) In these parts are the fertile fields of the Magi. Since I have happened on this topic, it will be in place to give a few words of explanation about their principles and activities. The most eminent author of excellent views, Plato, teaches about *magia* that it is *hagistia*, the most untainted worship of the divine. In ages long past many contributions deriving from the secret lore of the Chaldaeans were made to this expertise by the Bactrian Zoroaster and, after him, by the very wise king Hystaspes, the father of Darius. (33) When Hystaspes had confidently made his way into the unknown regions of Upper India, he reached a wooded wilderness, the calm silence of which was in the possession of the lofty intellects of the Brahmins. From their teaching he learned as much as he could gather of the laws governing the cosmic movement and the pure religious rites. He communicated some of what he had learned to the views of the Magi, which they, along with the art of divining the future, hand on to later generations, each by way of their own sons. (34) From that time on for many ages down to the present a large throng, sprung from one and the same lineage, devotes itself to the cult of the gods. They also say, if it is correct to believe them, that a fire fallen from heaven is guarded in their country on ever-burning braziers. According to them a small portion of it used to be carried as a good omen

before the Asiatic kings. (35) In old times the number of this stock was small and the Persian authorities regularly made use of their services in divine worship. It was taboo to approach an altar or to touch a sacrificial victim before one of the Magi poured the preliminary libations after a formal prayer. But they gradually increased in number and became a strong clan with a name of their own; they lived in country residences, which were not protected by strong walls, and were allowed to live in accordance with their own laws. They were honoured out of respect for their religion. (36) From this seed of the Magi, as the ancient records relate, seven men mounted the Persian throne after the death of Cambyses, but they were overthrown by the party of Darius, who had acquired the beginning of his kingship by the neighing of a horse.[2]

This passage figures in the collections of the evidence on the Magi gathered by Clemen and Bidez–Cumont.[3] The specific theory of the last-named scholars has met with considerable scepticism and is now not shared by any expert, yet their collection of material is still an important source of information, specifically illustrating the ideas held concerning Magi in the western world. These ideas were quite divergent. Herodotus is the first author who provides substantial evidence, portraying the Magi primarily as ritual specialists: 'without the presence of a Magus it is unlawful for them to offer sacrifice'.[4] Herodotus' general assessment is not negative, which is worthwhile to note, since derogatory references to the Magi already appear in the fifth century BC. A sort of easy equation of μαγεία and γοητεία developed, which according to Diogenes Laertius was even combated by Aristotle 'in his study of the Magi'.[5] The negative reputation persisted, however, as can be witnessed in a passage of Apuleius' *Apology* in which the defendant deems it necessary to clear away some misunderstandings. He portrays the Magi as primarily ritual experts and appeals to Plato's authority, quoting a passage from the *Alcibiades Maior*.[6] This quotation clinches the matter, since it shows that 'mageia' finds great favour with the immortal gods and that it had originated in the times of Zoroaster. Apuleius, of course, had an axe to grind, but he is by no means the only representative of a far more positive tradition, which was fully alive in the first centuries AD.

Magic in its evil sense was legally banned in the Roman world. One clear example in the *Codex Theodosianus* may suffice:

> If any wizard therefore or person imbued with magical contamination who is called by the custom of the people a magician . . . should be apprehended in my retinue, or in that of the Caesar, he shall not escape punishment and torture by the protection of his high rank.[7]

Magic also occurs more than once in the *Res Gestae*, specifically as an object of legal prosecution. In these cases Ammianus never uses the terms *magus* or *magia*, which is remarkable, since the text just quoted from the *Codex Theodosianus* does not refrain from using these terms beside *maleficus* and *maleficium*. As the relevant lemmata in the *Thesaurus Linguae Latinae* show, *magus* and *magia* were also used in this way by fourth-century authors, mainly those of Christian conviction. Ammianus, however, refers to magic with *artes nefandae* (14.1.2), *noxiae* (28.1.26), *pravae* (28.1.14), *secretae* (23.6.78). The words *magus* and *magia* only occur in the digression which is the subject of this chapter. Implicitly the author thus takes leave from current usage: the Magi have nothing to do with 'magic'. They are not performers of suspicious tricks, but serious priests carrying out their duties with a time-hallowed knowledge and expertise.

Presbyteron kreitton

In order to gain a better understanding of Ammianus' positive assessment it is indispensable to sketch in very brief contours a general predilection for the venerable past which is characteristic of the way of thinking in philosophic and intellectual circles in the first centuries BC. 'Older is better' is the implicit guiding principle: *presbyteron kreitton*, as the title runs of Pilhofer's monograph on the influence of this principle in Christian apologetics.[8] Since much of the wisdom, the lore, the religious rites, etc. in the Graeco-Roman world was deemed to derive from the more ancient sources of the Middle East (in the modern sense of that geographical term), it seemed beneficial to study these sources with serious attention. It is worthwhile to quote one of the clearest testimonia of this conviction, namely a fragment of the second-century philosopher Numenius of Apamea:

> we have to go back in history and combine Plato's statements with the lessons of Pythagoras, and call to witness peoples of renown, introducing their rites, convictions and all the foundations which are in harmony with Plato, which the Brahmins, the Jews, the Magi and the Egyptians have agreed upon.[9]

The idea that non-Greek peoples had access to truth and wisdom which had originated in the venerable past is also voiced by Celsus: 'there is an old *logos* from above, which has always been maintained by the wisest nations and cities and wise men'.[10] Small wonder that the third book of Philostratus' biography of Apollonius of Tyana contains an extensive report of the hero's visit to the Brahmins, and that Plotinus, having mastered Greek philosophy, 'wanted to experience the philosophy cultivated in Persia and the one successfully developed in India'.[11] Wisdom and specifically reliable knowledge of the divine have been preserved in the pure traditions of the eastern world. After all, these people lived 'in purer sunlight' and 'near the gods', as Philostratus says the Indians do.[12]

The heyday of this way of thinking may have been past in Ammianus' time; nevertheless there can be little doubt that the author was quite susceptible to such ideas. This is evident in a passage in the last chapter of Book 22 in which Egypt's long and inspiring traditions in the fields of science and especially religion are sketched:

> But anyone who cares to engage in a brisk review of the multifarious books on knowledge of the divine and the origin of prognostics will find that the source from which learning of this kind has spread throughout the world is Egypt. It was there that men, long before others, discovered various religions in what may be called their cradle, and now carefully preserve the origins of worship in their esoteric scriptures . . . Plato drew on this source, and it was after a visit to Egypt that he achieved his highest flights in language whose sublimity rivalled Jove himself, and served with glory on the field of wisdom.[13]

Small wonder that prominent Greek thinkers travelled to Egypt in order to drink from such pure and rich sources: *ad fontes*! It inspired them to their finest thoughts. Greek culture developed on the basis of Egyptian wisdom. This particular perspective is lacking in the short essay on the Magi, since Ammianus refrains from any explicit reference to the Magi's lore and wisdom as a source of inspiration to the Greek world. Indeed, reports on visits by prominent philosophers or on direct borrowing from the Magi are rather scarce. Porphyry writes in his *Life of Pythagoras* that the great man 'had received his knowledge about the rites of divine worship from the Magi'. Earlier, Valerius Maximus had also made Pythagoras travel to Persia in order to be taught by the Magi's 'scrupulously precise expertise'. This meant his being steeped in astrology.[14] About the Pythagoreans Bidez and Cumont note: 'Ils conservèrent toujours une curiosité particulière pour les croyances des Mages'[15] and we have already seen that Plotinus wanted to travel to Persia to gather the wisdom available there. Moreover, connections with Platonic thought are also hinted at sometimes. Generally speaking, however, relations with the Magi are less prominent in Greek tradition than those with Egypt. For this reason it is not surprising that Ammianus hardly refers to such relations, only introducing Plato's authority.

Some details

It is now time to take a look at some details. Remarkably, the digression is introduced in the most casual way: *quoniam huc incidimus*, 'since I have happened on the subject'. This is one of the flattest phrases in Ammianus' repertoire of introductory formulae. It is also worth mentioning that the report on the Magi occurs within the large central part of the long Persian digression, the part which is devoted to a rapid and, it must be said, somewhat superficial survey of a geographical and ethnographical nature. Generally speaking, this survey is characterized by matter-of-fact information, in contrast to the final part of the digression, which deals with Persian morals in a bird's-eye view. In those sections the author is definitely less objective and stresses the vices in the enemy's society.

Ammianus straightaway mentions an unassailable authority for his interpretation of what *magia* is about. The eulogy with which Plato is characterized is by no means otiose: he is renowned for his 'excellent views',[16] and thus deserves to be called *amplissimus*, like Apollonius of Tyana (23.6.19) and Thucydides (23.6.75).[17] As an equivalent of the loan word *magia* Plato used no less a sacred religious term than ἁγιστεία, a word which Julian uses several times in his *To the Mother of the Gods* for the great goddess' sacred rites. Within the Platonic corpus ἁγιστεία is only attested in *Axiochus* 371d, in an entirely different context.[18] It seems that Ammianus' reference ultimately derives from the passage in the *Alcibiades Maior* quoted by Apuleius, ἁγιστεία being a more devout equivalent of θεῶν θεραπεία, which tallies well with his explanation of the term as *divinorum . . . cultum*. The adjective *incorruptissimus* could be regarded as an attempt to bring out the relation with ἅγιος, but in any case it is not merely ornamental: it stresses the purity of the Magi's ceremonial veneration of the divine, which had not been defiled by any *superstitio*.[19]

The Magi do not perform their rites merely as a time-worn formality prescribed by tradition, but on the basis of *scientia*, systematic knowledge. Apuleius had stressed this too by his *nosse atque scire atque callere*. The original scope of this expertise had not been enriched by novelties of recent times, but in ancient, and therefore authoritative, periods many elements from the secret stores of wisdom of the Chaldaeans had been opportunely introduced by Zoroaster. The Chaldaeans also belong to the peoples renowned for their ancient wisdom. In § 25 of the Persian digression the region where the Chaldaeans live is called 'the foster-mother of the old-time philosophy',[20] a praise which can hardly be surpassed, except by what we hear next. Hystaspes was an eastern king, which could raise suspicion, but in contrast to some less acceptable examples of this type he was a man of great wisdom. His thirst for deeper knowledge gave him the courage to travel deep into India and to consult the very prime of human wisdom, the Brahmins, whose lofty intellects had also impressed Apollonius of Tyana. Possibly, *praecelsus* hints at the Brahmins' art of levitation, to which Ammianus refers in 28.1.13: 'he was bent on copying the Brahmins, who, some say, levitate in the air about their altars'.[21] Be this as it may, Hystaspes made the most of his visit by having himself instructed in astronomy and ritual. Of course, the cultic practice he was taught was blameless and pure. One could not imagine a more genuine religious climate than that in which the Brahmins lived in their solitude, far away from all corrupting influences. Some elements (*aliqua*) of this wonderful world were incorporated in the Magi's religious make-up.[22]

Having sketched the Magi's excellent spiritual pedigree, Ammianus in § 34 dwells on their descent. *Mutatis mutandis* we receive the same message. The Magi's lore had not been tampered with in a wrong sense since its origin in far-off days. The same holds good when it comes to the Magi's lineage. In the course of time they had become a large tribe, a *multitudo*, sharply contrasting with the *numerus exilis* of earlier days. Yet this great number had sprung from one and the same lineage. So the purity of their descent matches the unadulterated character of their lore. They had officiated as ritual experts in the times of the old Persian empire and they had preserved their lore and reputation until the author's time.

Value and intention

Ammianus' short sketch of the Magi and their specific role is well-wrought and internally consistent. It offered contemporary readers the possibility to distinguish these Magi from the *magi* they came across in their Roman world. The latter were tricksters, the former highly respectable religious experts. It is a carefully crafted digression in the second degree, but what is the real value of the information it provides? I am afraid it is of no use to Iranists, adding nothing to what they can ascertain from better-equipped sources.[23] The author has gathered some evidence from presumably Greek and Roman books and he does not seem to have added any *visa* to these *lecta*. There are no signs of any autopsy. Neither will the passage offer anything which might be important for those who are interested in the reputation or rather the reputations of the Magi in the Greek and Roman world. The individual elements in Ammianus' description can all be found in other sources, so that from this viewpoint too the author adds precious little to what can be known in this field.

Would this mean that the digression has no value at all? Is it no more than an obligatory piece in the mosaic of the Persian digression? Most certainly not. When one looks through the available Greek and Roman evidence on the Magi, it soon appears that Ammianus has made a purposeful selection, in which any negative elements are left out. The elements which the author has chosen are combined in a compact identikit in which the Magi are not portrayed as curious or dangerous performers of harmful tricks, but as serious religious specialists carrying out their duties with a knowledge of the divine and a ritual expertise which have sprung from an age-old tradition. In this the author ranges himself on the side of the admirers of alien wisdom, as he had done in the digression on Egypt. The present passage is, however, even more coherent in that it primarily focuses on religion. Moreover, as was already noted above, in contrast to the Egyptian digression Ammianus leaves out any reference to borrowings from the Magi's lore by wise men in the Graeco-Roman world.

This emphasis on the intrinsic value of the Magi's religion reveals the author's personal predilections in the religious sphere. These predilections surface in other passages of the *Res Gestae* too, for example when he acknowledges that Christianity is a *religio absoluta et simplex* (21.16.18), that is to say Christianity in its pure form, or when he calls Julian a *superstitiosus magis quam sacrorum legitimus observator* (25.4.17). The emperor lacked the feeling for the correct ritual rules which are the hallmark of true religion, and he thus fell prey to the excesses which are typical of *superstitio*. The adjective *superstitiosus* only occurs at 25.4.17, where it was necessary to state clearly and honestly what was wrong with the religious practice of a man who, for all his devout respect for the rites of the traditional cults, failed to understand what religion really is about. Such a person is doomed to fall into superstition.

So in religious matters Julian unfortunately is an example of *quod vites*, to use Livy's terms. What did Ammianus regard as a good example, *quod imitere*? As a pagan he could not choose Christianity as such an example, although in principle it compelled some admiration, albeit in a detached way. When collecting the material for the Persian digression, the author came across some stereotyped evidence about the Magi. Selecting from this evidence, he composed a picture of what religion should be: a cult which is carried out by experts by virtue of their reliable knowledge of the divine world, a knowledge which was not spoiled by superstition. The Magi enjoyed great esteem because of men's respect for their religion (*religionis respectu sunt honorati*). That was the author's position too. This was a religion of which 'pure rites' were the quality mark!

To sum up very briefly: the digression on the Magi does not enrich our knowledge of these men or of their reputation in the western world. It summarizes, however, in a quiet manner Ammianus Marcellinus' own idea about religion and that is precisely the value of this small part of the *Res Gestae*.

Notes

1 E.g. § 18–19 on phenomena in Asia Minor which are comparable to the chasm in Assyria, which is described in § 17, and § 85–8 on pearls.
2 This rendering is an adaptation of Rolfe's translation. The Latin text according to Seyfarth's Teubner edition runs as follows:

> (32) In his tractibus Magorum agri sunt fertiles, super quorum secta studiisque, quoniam huc incidimus, pauca conveniet expediri. magian opinionum insignium auctor amplissimus Plato hagistiam esse verbo mystico docet, divinorum incorruptissimum cultum, cuius scientiae saeculis priscis multa ex Chaldaeorum arcanis Bactrianus addidit Zoroastres, deinde Hystaspes rex prudentissimus, Darei pater. (33) qui cum superioris Indiae secreta fidentius penetraret, ad nemorosam quandam venerat solitudinem, cuius tranquillis silentiis praecelsa Brachmanorum ingenia potiuntur, eorumque monitu rationes mundani motus et siderum purosque sacrorum ritus, quantum colligere potuit, eruditus ex his, quae didicit, aliqua sensibus magorum infudit. quae illi cum disciplinis praesentiendi futura per suam quisque progeniem posteris aetatibus tradunt.

(34) ex eo per saecula multa ad praesens una eademque prosapia multitudo creata cultibus deorum dedicatur. feruntque, si iustum est credi, etiam ignem caelitus lapsum apud se sempiternis focibus custodiri, cuius portionem exiguam ut faustam praeisse quondam Asiaticis regibus dicunt. (35) huius originis apud veteres numerus erat exilis eiusque ministeriis Persicae potestates in faciendis rebus divinis sollemniter utebantur. eratque piaculum aras adire vel hostiam contrectare, antequam magus conceptis precationibus libamenta diffunderet praecursoria. verum aucti paulatim in amplitudinem gentis solidae concesserunt et nomen villasque inhabitantes nulla murorum firmitudine communitas et legibus suis uti permissi religionis respectu sunt honorati. (36) ex hoc Magorum semine septem post mortem Cambysis regnum inisse Persidos antiqui memorant libri docentes eos Darei factione oppressos imperitandi initium equino hinnitu sortiti.

3 C. Clemen, *Fontes Historiae Religionis Persicae*, Bonn 1920. J. Bidez and F. Cumont, *Les mages hellénisés. Zoroastre, Ostanès et Hystaspe d'après la tradition grecque*, Tome I: *L'introduction*, Tome II: *Les textes*, Paris 1938.
4 ἄνευ γὰρ δὴ μάγου οὔ σφι νόμος ἐστὶ θυσίας ποιέεσθαι (Hdt. 1.132).
5 ἐν τῷ Μαγικῷ (Diogenes Laertius 1.8).
6 Apuleius, *Apol.* 25:

> Nam si, quod ego apud plurimos lego, Persarum lingua magus est qui nostra sacerdos, quod tandem est crimen, sacerdotem esse et rite nosse atque scire atque callere leges caerimoniarum, fas sacrorum, ius religionum, si quidem magia id est quod Plato interpretatur (viz. in *Alc.* 121e–122a, where μαγεία is defined in these words: ἔστιν δὲ τοῦτο θεῶν θεραπεία.)

7 *... si quis magus vel magicis contaminibus adsuetus, qui maleficus vulgi consuetudine nuncupatur ... in comitatu meo vel Caesaris fuerit deprehensus, praesidio dignitatis cruciatus et tormenta non fugiat* (*Cod. Theod.* 9.16.6, 5 July 358). In the text Pharr's translation is quoted.
8 P. Pilhofer, *Presbyteron Kreitton. Der Altersbeweis der jüdischen und christlichen Apologeten und seine Vorgeschichte*, Tübingen 1990.
9 ... ἐπικαλέσασθαι δὲ τὰ ἔθνη τὰ εὐδοκιμοῦντα, προσφερόμενον αὐτῶν τὰς τελετὰς καὶ τὰ δόγματα τάς τε ἱδρύσεις συντελουμένας Πλάτωνι ὁμολογουμένως, ὁπόσας Βραχμᾶνες καὶ Ἰουδαῖοι καὶ Μάγοι καὶ Αἰγύπτιοι διέθεντο (Numenius *frg*. 1a Des Places).
10 ἔστιν ἀρχαῖος ἄνωθεν λόγος, περὶ ὃν δὴ ἀεὶ καὶ ἔθνη τὰ σοφώτατα καὶ πόλεις καὶ ἄνδρες σοφοὶ κατεγένοντο (Origen, *C. Cels.* 1.14).
11 καὶ τῆς παρὰ τοῖς Πέρσαις ἐπιτηδευομένης πεῖραν λαβεῖν σπεῦσαι καὶ τῆς παρ' Ἰνδοῖς κατορθουμένης (Porphyry, *Plot.* 3).
12 καθαρωτέραις ὁμιλοῦντες ἀκτῖσιν... ἄτε ἀγχίθεοι (Philostratos, *Vit. Apoll.* 6.11).
13 Hamilton's rendering of *Res Gestae* 22.16.19–20 and 22:

> sed si intellegendi divini editionem multiplicem et praesensionum originem mente vegeta quisquam voluerit, replicata per mundum omnem inveniet mathemata huiusmodi ab Aegypto circumlata, ubi primum homines longe ante alios ad varia religionum incunabula, ut dicitur, pervenerunt et initia prima sacrorum caute tuentur condita scriptis arcanis ... ex his fontibus per sublimia gradiens sermonum amplitudine Iovis aemulus Platon visa Aegypto militavit sapientia gloriosa.

14 (τὰ) περὶ δὲ τὰς τῶν θεῶν ἁγιστείας ... παρὰ τῶν Μάγων φασὶ διακοῦσαί τε καὶ λαβεῖν (Porphyry, *Pythag.* 6); *inde ad Persas profectus magorum exactissimae prudentiae se formandum tradidit, a quibus siderum motus cursusque stellarum et uniuscuiusque vim, proprietatem, effectum benignissime demonstratum docili animo sorpsit* (Val. Max. 8.7 ext. 2).
15 Bidez and Cumont, *Les mages hellénisés*, vol. 1, p. 32.

16 As more often in the *Res Gestae*, *opinio* denotes a philosophical or scientific theory.
17 In Plato's case the adjective is especially apt in that it refers to the Greek etymology of his name, which he earned by the breadth (πλατύτης) of his written style.
18 The passage in question is a description of the attractive abode of the blessed in the nether world. Those who have been initiated in the mystery cults even celebrate their holy rites (τὰς ὁσίους ἁγιστείας) there. For a discussion of the origin and the structure of the spurious dialogue see Pseudo-Plato, *Axiochus*, edited and translated by Jackson P. Hershbell, Chico 1981.
19 It should be noted that *hagistia* is an emendation, though a quite plausible one. In his *Apex Omnium*, Rike inexplicably spells the word with a capital H and uses it as an official term to denote the Magi's accomplishments: R.L. Rike, *Apex Omnium. Religion in the Res Gestae of Ammianus*, Berkeley 1987, 72, 93 ('The Persian Hagistia is one of the most favorably presented civilized religions in the *Res gestae*').
20 *altrix philosophiae veteris* (23.6.25).
21 *studebat inter altaria celsius gradientes, ut quidam memorant, imitari Brachmanas* (28.1.13).
22 In passing it deserves to be noted that Bidez and Cumont at first apodictically explained the identity of *qui* at the beginning of § 33 in this way: 'non point Hystaspe, mais le fondateur de la secte des Mages' (i.e. Zoroaster). The various translators of the *Res Gestae* have bowed to their authority, but the structure of the preceding sentence (*deinde Hystaspes*) makes this explanation impossible. It seems a case of the wish being father to the thought. Bidez and Cumont were looking for a Graeco-Roman testimony for Zoroaster's passage to India, for which they had found some late oriental sources. In all fairness it should be said that later on in their great book they recanted with: 'Le *qui*, grammaticalement, devrait se rapporter à Hystaspes.'
23 See the relevant sections in R. Beck, 'Thus Spake not Zarathustra: Zoroastrian Pseudepigrapha of the Greco-Roman World', in M. Boyce and F. Grenet, *A History of Zoroastrianism*, vol. 3, Leiden 1991, 491–565; A. de Jong, *Traditions of the Magi. Zoroastrianism in Greek and Roman Literature*, Leiden 1997.

18

VISA VEL LECTA?

Ammianus on Persia and the Persians

Hans Teitler

In his digression on Persia (23.6) Ammianus Marcellinus relates among other things the following custom of the Persians: 'one seldom sees a Persian stop to pass water' – I quote from Rolfe's translation.[1] When reading Ammianus' words in Latin (*nec stando mingens nec ad requisita naturae secedens facile visitur Persa*, 23.6.79), it will be clear that Rolfe's rendering of *stando mingens* is not quite accurate, for where in his translation do we find Ammianus' *stando*? In his edition for the Collection des Universités de France, Jacques Fontaine renders *stando mingens* with 'uriner debout' and Walter Hamilton in the Penguin Ammianus translates the words thus: 'make water standing'.[2] That is correct, I think. When Ammianus says *stando*, he must mean 'standing' in its literal sense, as opposed to 'squatting' or 'sitting', as women normally do – or rather, as women, to the best of my knowledge, do in modern, western countries, for we all know that in Herodotus' ancient Egypt, for instance, it was the other way around: men passed water sitting down and women did so standing up (Hdt. 2.35.3). Incidentally, some years ago a few radical feminists in Holland, when passing water, imitated the women of ancient Egypt and tried to persuade the other members of their sex to follow this example – in vain, I have been told.

I did not quote § 79 of Ammianus' digression on Persia because of the information it contains, interesting though it is. For the moment I actually do not care what precisely Ammianus' Persians did when they felt the urge to relieve themselves. What interests me in this phrase is not so much the present participle *mingens* or the accompanying gerund *stando*,[3] but the main verb *visitur*.

Ammianus, as of course every reader is well aware, knew large parts of the empire whose history he recorded from personal experience. He also visited some regions beyond the boundaries of the Roman empire, notably some regions of Persia. He used his own experience not only in the main narrative, but also – and that is what now concerns me – in his digressions. For example, in his excursion on the provinces of Thrace in Book 27 he says that a description of Thrace would have been easy, if only earlier writers had performed their task properly; but alas, they did not, and therefore 'it will suffice to set forth what I myself remember seeing'.[4] Or take § 21 of Ammianus' description of Persia in 23.6. In a discussion on the origin of the name Adiabena Ammianus mentions two rivers, the Diabas and the Adiabas, both of which, he adds, 'I, myself, have crossed'.[5]

To return to 23.6.79 with its main verb *visitur*: in view of the examples just given, there is at first sight no need *not* to believe Ammianus, when he suggests that in the case of the Persians passing water he is speaking from personal experience. However, Ammianus' digression on Persia was not merely based on personal observation, as he himself clearly indicates in 23.6.30. There he speaks of a special kind of horse, on which the chiefs of Agropatena were wont to ride, 'as the writers of old say, and as I myself have seen'.[6] A reference to these 'writers of old' as a source for Ammianus' digressions, apart from what he had seen with his own eyes, can also be found in Book 22, in the introduction to the excursus on the Black Sea.[7] There Ammianus uses the famous expression *visa vel lecta* – which is, incidentally, the subtitle of part 2 of John Matthews' *The Roman Empire of Ammianus*.

In 1881 Theodor Mommsen, when discussing the digression on the Black Sea, was rather outspoken about the proportion of Ammianus' own observation (*visa*) as opposed to his reading (*lecta*): 'Von eigenen Wahrnehmungen des Schriftstellers . . . finde ich hier keine Spur.'[8] Matthews is slightly more benevolent, but the essence of his words is the same as that of Mommsen's more blunt pronouncement: 'The digression, like others, bears more traces of what Ammianus had read than of what he had seen.'[9]

More *lecta* than *visa*, then, in Ammianus' excursion on the Black Sea, and in his other digressions as well. I wholeheartedly agree. With this in mind the view I held on 23.6.79 needs some adjustment. As I said earlier, there is at first sight no need not to believe Ammianus, when he suggests, by using the verb *visitur*, that in the case of the Persians passing water he speaks from personal experience. I do not take back those words. But something has to be added. For example, someone who wants to write a commentary on this passage[10] should add that Ammianus perhaps borrowed the words in question from 'a writer of old', for there happens to be a statement of a *scriptor antiquus* on the same subject in a part of his work which is quite famous. I allude, of course, to Herodotus 1.133, where it is said of the ancient Persians: 'no one is allowed to vomit or pass water in the presence of another person' (καί σφι οὐκ ἐμέσαι ἔξεστι, οὐκὶ οὐρῆσαι ἀντίον ἄλλου). We find an echo of Herodotus in Xenophon's *Cyropaedia* 1.2.16: 'it is also disgraceful to be seen going apart either to make water or for anything else of that kind' (αἰσχρὸν δὲ ἐστι καὶ τὸ ἰόντα που φανερὸν γενέσθαι ἢ τοῦ οὐρῆσαι ἕνεκα ἢ καὶ ἄλλου τινὸς τοιούτου). We can also compare another passage of Xenophon (*Cyr.* 8.8.11) and one of Strabo (15.3.16 [733C]). It would seem, therefore, that in 23.6.79 we have an example not only of *visa*, but also of *lecta*.

If this conclusion is correct, does it follow that the hypothetical writer of a commentary on Book 23, after citing the parallels (Herodotus, Xenophon, Strabo), can put aside his pen? I think not. There is still at least one problem to be tackled, although it is very doubtful if a solution can ever be reached. It concerns the identity of the 'writer (or writers) of old' whom Ammianus is supposed to have read. One might at first imagine that this writer is Herodotus, the man whose first book is our oldest authority on the customs of the Persians. The historian of Halicarnassus is only once mentioned by name in a rather corrupt passage in Ammianus' extant work,[11] but, according to Tim Barnes, he has left an imprint on several passages of Ammianus' *Res Gestae*.[12]

In order to come closer to answering the question of the relationship between Ammianus and Herodotus, let us take a look at another section of Ammianus' digression on the customs of the Persians.[13] In 23.6.76 we find on the one hand a close parallel to the corresponding part of Herodotus' *Histories*, but on the other hand some remarkable differences:

> Most Persians are inordinately addicted to the pleasures of sex, and find even a large number of concubines hardly enough to satisfy them; they do not practise pederasty. A man has many or few wives according to his means, and his affections, being divided between a number of objects, are lukewarm. The luxury of an elegant table and especially indulgence in drink they shun like the plague.[14]

First let me state the point they have in common, viz. the Persian habit of polygamy. Herodotus in 1.135 had told the same story about this custom: 'Every man has many wives, and a much greater number of mistresses' (γαμέουσι δὲ ἕκαστος αὐτῶν πολλὰς μὲν κουριδίας γυναῖκας, πόλλῳ δ'ἔτι πλεῦνας παλλακὰς κτῶνται). By the way, we find the same information in Strabo 15.3.17 (733C). Now to the differences, which are two in number. In the first place, Ammianus' remark about pederastic practices, or rather, the lack of these among the Persians (*puerilium stuprorum expertes*), is in striking contrast to an observation by Herodotus, who tells us that the Persians learned pederasty from the Greeks;[15] second, Ammianus' words about Persian drinking habits also differ from what Herodotus wrote. Compare Ammianus' words about the avoidance of excessive drinking (*maximeque potandi aviditatem vitantes ut luem*) with Herodotus' 1.133: 'they are very fond of wine' and 'if an important decision is to be made, they usually discuss the question when they are drunk'.

These are remarkable differences indeed. How can one explain them? As far as I can see, there are two possibilities. In the first place it could be argued that Ammianus' familiarity with Herodotus was not as great as Barnes would have us believe. This argument is in line with the observations of Charles Fornara in the second instalment of his 'Studies in Ammianus Marcellinus'.[16] Incidentally, neither Barnes nor Fornara refers to the passages on pissing, faggotry and boozing which I have chosen to discuss. Although, as Fornara argues, certain references in Ammianus bring Herodotus to mind (the Solon–Croesus story, for example, in 15.5.37), such allusions do not necessarily 'indicate the direct use of Herodotus, for these data had long since become common property'.[17] Fornara has a point here, I think. The possibility that, in cases like that of Solon's meeting with Croesus, Ammianus did not draw direct inspiration from the text of Herodotus, but rather used an intermediate source, cannot be excluded. To apply this to 23.6.76: I think that Fornara could have added the polygamy of the Persians to the examples he cites to illustrate his proposition, for this polygamy was, I presume, 'common property' (to use Fornara's term) – I take Strabo in 15.3.17 (733C), quoted above, as my witness. Let there be no misunderstanding, though. I do not want anyone to believe that it is impossible that Ammianus recalled the Persian custom of keeping several women from his own reading of Herodotus. I merely suggest that it is equally possible that Ammianus found this piece of information elsewhere.

Fornara's argument not only covers the cases in which Ammianus and Herodotus are in agreement. Certain disparities can also be accounted for even better if we assume that Ammianus had used an intermediate source. Two examples may serve to illustrate this. Once again both are taken from the digression on Persia in 23.6.

My first example, borrowed from Fornara, is to be found in 23.6.36. Ammianus there relates the well-known story of the counter-revolution of the future Persian king Darius against the seven (note the number) Magi, who had stolen the kingdom after Cambyses' death:

> From this seed of the Magi, as the ancient records relate, seven men after the death of Cambyses mounted the Persian throne, but (we are told), they were overthrown by the party of Darius, who made himself king by the neighing of a horse.[18]

Herodotus – from whose *Histories* the story is ultimately derived, without doubt – in 3.61.1 had asserted that there were only two Magi who had appropriated the kingdom. As to the number seven, in Herodotus' account of Darius' coup we also come across this same number, but there the word 'seven' gives the total number of the Persian conspirators, not of the Magi (Hdt. 3.71.1, cf. 3.76.1). So much for this difference between Ammianus in 23.6.36 and Herodotus, which, if we follow Fornara, would indicate that Ammianus followed not Herodotus, but some other 'writer of old' – such as Valerius Maximus, perhaps, who, like Ammianus, mentions seven Magi (9.2 ext. 6).

A comparable case (not mentioned by Fornara) is to be found in 23.6.32. Hystaspes, the father of the Darius just referred to, is called 'king' by Ammianus,[19] while Herodotus makes him a 'satrap' (3.70.3). Again, it is attractive to assume that Ammianus, here also, used an intermediate source – Hystaspes' kingship is also found, for example, in Lactantius (*Div. Inst.* 7.15.19).

Thus far, following in Fornara's footsteps, I have argued that Ammianus' familiarity with Herodotus was perhaps not as extensive as some scholars would have us believe. This line of reasoning is one way of explaining the discrepancies between Ammianus and Herodotus in passages which seem ultimately to go back to Herodotus. But it is not the only possibility. One argument against it is that it does not take into consideration the alternative view that Ammianus might have quoted from memory. Quite a few of the quotations of canonical writers found in later authors differ from the text which we nowadays consider authentic – authentic, because it has come down to us via the manuscript tradition. Quoting from memory, apart from sheer carelessness of course, often underlies such alternative readings. Thus, paradoxically, slight disparities like the ones we have encountered can arguably be taken not only as an indication that Ammianus was not very familiar with Herodotus, but also as a sign that Ammianus knew, or at least thought he knew, his Herodotus so well that he relied on memory to borrow from him.

One might object that this is all very well, but that the discrepancy between Herodotus and Ammianus in 23.6.76, with respect to pederasty and drinking, is far greater than the one concerning the number of the Magi and that about the rank of Hystaspes. Yes, indeed it is, and there is more to follow. Ammianus' remark about the avoidance by the Persians of excessive drinking is not only in flat contradiction of Herodotus' statement that the Persians were very fond of wine, but stands alone. Xenophon, Strabo, Plutarch, Athenaeus, Aelian, all agree with Herodotus in stating that the Persians were heavy drinkers.[20] Only Ammianus dissents. This brings me to the second possibility which might explain the differences between Ammianus and Herodotus in passages dealing with the same subject-matter.

Before I speak about this second possibility, it is perhaps opportune to say that Fornara's theory of an intermediate source in cases of 'common property' is, to my mind, less likely here, for the simple reason that Ammianus' remark about Persian drinking, far from being 'common property', is, as I said before, quite unique. All other sources known to us contradict Ammianus' statement. Admittedly, we cannot exclude the possibility that Ammianus had read an author unknown to us who had given the same divergent opinion on the Persian drinking habit as he did, but there is, I think, an alternative to which preference should be given.

The alternative solution to our problem is, it seems to me, to assume that, in his succinct ethnography of the Persians in 23.6, Ammianus combines what he had read (*lecta*) with what he had seen (*visa*). We noticed earlier that, in spite of the proportion of *visa* to *lecta* in the digressions of the *Res Gestae* being very uneven, some traces of what Ammianus had seen can nevertheless be detected. In 23.6.76 there is another example of this combination. When stating that the Persians avoided heavy drinking like the plague, Ammianus presumably spoke from his own experience and implicitly polemized against what he had read somewhere — either in Herodotus or elsewhere. In polemizing against what he had read and in covertly or explicitly correcting the views he had found in the work of his predecessors, Ammianus adhered to the rule which he himself had proclaimed in the opening section of the digression on Persia.[21] Let me quote this programmatic pronouncement in which Ammianus confidently says that he will surpass his predecessors, who, in their descriptions of the peoples living in the Persian empire, had made many errors: 'I read carefully the ethnographic literature, but in very few of these descriptions has the truth been told, and that barely.'

Ammianus' criticism of the fact that his predecessors depart from the truth is implicit more often than not. For example, in 23.6.76 Ammianus does not say in so many words that he is polemizing against a time-honoured but false belief about the Persians' drinking habits. However, for those of his readers who know their classics, the hint is clear. Fortunately, in other cases he is sometimes more explicit, for instance in his rejection of a well-known story in 23.6.82, which can conveniently be used to conclude my argument.

In this story in 23.6.82 Ammianus combats the belief that among the Persians a judge was forced to take his seat on the skin of another who had been condemned to death for injustice: *quod supersidere corio damnati ob iniquitatem iudicis iudex alius cogitabatur*. The passage of course recalls Herodotus to our mind. Every reader is at once reminded of Cambyses' cruel treatment of Sisamnes, the father of Otanes, as related by Herodotus in 5.25.1–2:

> to punish him for taking a bribe and perverting justice, Cambyses had Sisamnes flayed; all of his skin was torn off and cut into strips, and the strips were stretched across the seat which he used to sit on when he gave his judgments. Cambyses then appointed Otanes to replace his father as a judge, and told him not to forget in court what his seat was made of.

> (ὅτι ἐπὶ χρήμασι δίκην ἄδικον ἐδίκασε, σφάξας ἀπέδειρε πᾶσαν τὴν ἀνθρωπέην, σπαδίξας δὲ αὐτοῦ τὸ δέρμα ἱμάντας ἐξ αὐτοῦ ἔταμε καὶ ἐνέτεινε τὸν θρόνον ἐς τὸν ἵζων ἐδίκαζε· ἐντανύσας δὲ ὁ Καμβύσης ἀπέδεξε δικαστὴν εἶναι ... τὸν παῖδα τοῦ Σισάμνεω, ἐντειλάμενός οἱ μεμνῆσθαι ἐν τῷ κατίζων θρόνῳ δικάζει)

Ammianus, however, does not accept the truth of the story. According to him the story was an ancient fiction, or, if such a custom had ever existed, it had long since been abandoned: *aut finxit vetustas aut olim recepta consuetudo cessavit*.

So much for the texts and the facts. Now for some questions. First of all: does the resemblance to Herodotus of the first part of Ammianus 23.6.82 indicate the direct use of Herodotus? The answer is: not necessarily. The anecdote is also handed down to us by Valerius Maximus (6.3 ext. 3), while Diodorus Siculus (15.10.1) tells a similar story (Diodorus changes the scenery, transfers the event to the reign of Artaxerxes and speaks of more than one judge). My second question is: does the rejection by Ammianus of the story as told by Herodotus and others indicate that Ammianus had used some other source which is unknown to us? This possibility cannot be excluded, but in my view it is more likely that Ammianus drew from his own experience and that this passage, like others, is the result of both *lecta* and *visa*.[22]

Notes

1 J.C. Rolfe, *Ammianus Marcellinus*, with an English translation, Loeb Classical Library, 3 vols, London/Cambridge (Mass.) 1935–9 (repr. 1971–2), vol. 2, p. 393.
2 J. Fontaine, *Ammien Marcellin, Histoire IV (Livres XXIII–XXV)*, 2 vols, Paris 1977, vol. 1, p. 121; W. Hamilton and A. Wallace-Hadrill, *Ammianus Marcellinus. The Later Roman Empire (A.D. 354–378)*, Harmondsworth 1986, 264.
3 A. de Jong, *Traditions of the Magi. Zoroastrianism in Greek and Latin Literature*, Leiden 1997, 418–19, draws attention to the fact that the practice of urinating while standing is expressly condemned in several Pahlavi books (e.g. *AWN* 25.3, *MX* 2.39–41, *PhlRDd.* 11.3; cf. A.V. Williams, *The Pahlavi Rivāyat accompanying the Dādestan ī Dēnīg*, 2 vols, Copenhagen 1990, vol. 2, 144.4 for more references).
4 *sufficiet ea, quae vidisse meminimus, expedire* (27.4.2).
5 *in his terris amnes sunt duo perpetui, quos transiimus, Diabas et Adiabas* (23.6.21).
6 *ut scriptores antiqui docent nosque vidimus* (23.6.30).
7 *Appositum est . . . super Thraciarum extimis situque Pontici sinus visa vel lecta quaedam perspicua fide monstrare* (22.8.1). Cf. J. den Boeft, J.W. Drijvers, D. den Hengst and H.C. Teitler, *Philological and Historical Commentary on Ammianus Marcellinus XXII*, Groningen 1995, 88ff.
8 Th. Mommsen, 'Ammians Geographica', *Hermes* 16 (1881), 602–36 (= *Gesammelte Schriften* 7, Berlin 1909, 393–425), 623 n. 1.
9 J.F. Matthews, *The Roman Empire of Ammianus*, London 1989, 14.
10 There is now J. den Boeft, J.W. Drijvers, D. den Hengst and H.C. Teitler, *Philological and Historical Commentary on Ammianus Marcellinus XXIII*, Groningen 1998.
11 *pyramides ad miracula septem provectae, quarum diuturnas surgendi difficultates . . . scriptor Herodotus docet* (22.15.28).
12 T.D. Barnes, 'Literary Convention, Nostalgia and Reality in Ammianus Marcellinus', in G. Clarke et al. (eds), *Reading the Past in Late Antiquity*, Rushcutters Bay 1990, 59–92, at 70–1.
13 Ammianus' report of the customs of the Persians can be called a digression within a digression. It consists of 23.6.75–84, that is, approximately 10 per cent of the whole digression on Persia in the sixth chapter of Book 23.
14 *effusius plerique soluti in venerem aegreque contenti multitudine pelicum puerilium stuprorum expertes pro opibus quisque asciscens matrimonia plura vel pauca, unde apud eos per libidines varias caritas dispersa torpescit, munditias conviviorum et luxum maximeque potandi aviditatem vitantes ut luem* (23.6.76, trans. Hamilton).
15 Herodotus (1.135) is supported by Sextus Empiricus (*Pyr.* 1.152), while Ammianus' pronouncement tallies with a passage in Curtius Rufus (10.1.26).
16 C.W. Fornara, 'Studies in Ammianus Marcellinus II: Ammianus' Knowledge and Use of Greek and Latin Literature', *Historia* 41 (1992), 420–38.

17 *Ibid.*, 422.
18 *ex hoc Magorum semine septem post mortem Cambysis regnum inisse Persidos antiqui memorant libri docentes eos Darei factione oppressos imperitandi initium equino hinnitu sortiti* (23.6.36, trans. Rolfe).
19 *Hystaspes, rex prudentissimus, Darei pater* (23.6.23).
20 References can be found in P. Briant, *Histoire de l'empire perse de Cyrus à Alexandre*, 2 vols, Leiden 1996, vol. 1, 304.
21 *Res adigit huc prolapsa ut in excessu celeri situm monstrare Persidis descriptionibus gentium curiose digestis, in quibus aegre vera dixere paucissimi* (23.6.1).
22 It is a pleasure to acknowledge the help of K.J.F. van de Wetering, who corrected my English.

19

AMMIANUS MARCELLINUS ON ISAURIA

Keith Hopwood

Ammianus' *Res Gestae* deal with so-called barbarian peoples, Vandals, Goths, Persians, Huns and many others. This chapter surveys Ammianus' comments on the Isaurians of southern Asia Minor, those classic 'internal barbarians' of the later Roman Empire. The prevailing ideology is best expressed by the *Historia Augusta*:

> in short, since [the uprising of] Trebellianus, they have been considered as barbarians, for indeed their region, in the midst of Roman territory, is shut in by a new sort of defence, protected by the lie of the land (*locis*), not by men. For they are not handsome in stature, nor endowed with courage, nor drawn up in arms, nor wise in counsel, but they are secure because of this one feature; namely that by living on the heights, they cannot be approached.[1]

This chapter argues that although in many places in his Isaurian 'discourse'[2] Ammianus repeats these stereotypes, he is able to combine them with remarkable *aperçus* on the environment and social structure of Isauria. To elucidate these passages, it is necessary to compare Ammianus' account with other sources (regrettably extremely scanty for the events he describes), with our knowledge of the social structure of Isaurian society and its dynamics, derived from local epigraphic sources, and with our knowledge of the pastoralist/sedentarist balance in the power structure of the city-states.[3] Consequently, this chapter will begin with a brief review of work on Isauria since Rougé's study of 1966.[4]

Rougé was the first to attempt an integration of what was known from epigraphic investigators such as Sterrett, and Swoboda, Keil and Knoll,[5] as well as the most recent historiographical and textual research. It was, however, a rather traditional *explication de texte*, taking little account of that major historical source, the terrain itself. An excellent description of Isauria, including the sites of its more important cities, was available in the form of Davis' account of his travels in Turkey. This account is particularly valuable, as it dates from the late nineteenth century, when traditional forms of agricultural exploitation were still in use.[6] Rougé's work was followed by a series of articles by Sir Ronald Syme, whose comments, although largely relevant to the study of Isauria/Rough Cilicia during the Principate, have much of interest in them.[7]

The 1960s was the greatest period of epigraphic exploration of southern Turkey since the years immediately preceding World War I. These researches were carried out by G.E. Bean and T.B. Mitford on behalf of the Österreichische Akademie der Wissenschaften.[8] Sadly, the authors limited themselves quite austerely to a publication of and commentary on the inscriptions found. They did not describe any 'anepigraphic' site, or comment on buildings without inscriptions in otherwise epigraphically rich sites. This is particularly frustrating, as when the authors do discuss the layout of a site or the topography of its surroundings to elucidate an inscription, they are astonishingly perceptive.[9] Their observations reached partial synthesis in a posthumously published article by Mitford.[10] This corpus of work has vastly added to our understanding of Isaurian society, and represents a huge leap forward which outdates any synthesis published earlier. This work formed the basis for Matthews' penetrating comments on Isauria in his magisterial survey of Ammianus.[11]

Throughout the 1980s I followed in the footsteps of Bean and Mitford (with a brief return in 1993). I was able to relocate their sites (and add some few to their total) in the process of studying the settlement patterns and the means by which this often intractable countryside was controlled by the urban elites.[12]

The topographical aspects of my work have been incorporated into Hild and Hellenkemper's contribution to the *Tabula Imperii Byzantini*,[13] along with extensive fieldwork of their own,[14] and so this contributes decisively to our understanding of late antiquity here. Many sites not described by Bean and Mitford receive a full description and there is an adequate photographic coverage in volume 2.

It is also important to note that a special edition of *Quaderni Storici* was devoted to the history of Cilicia (including Isauria) in 1991, and that our period is well covered by the article by Lewin in that volume.[15]

Historical interest has also returned to Isauria. The constant depiction of Isaurians in the historical sources as bandits/brigands (*latrones*/λῃσταί) has interested social historians of the lower classes of the Roman Empire who, following or rejecting Hobsbawm's pioneering work *Bandits*,[16] have attempted to classify Isaurian activity as proto-nationalism,[17] social banditry, or revolt.[18] These schools have been represented variously by C.E. Minor, myself and B.D. Shaw, whose article 'Bandits in the Roman Empire'[19] radically changed the way in which local insurrections were studied. His later articles must represent the current orthodoxy on Isaurian studies.

Isauria was one of the Diocletianic provinces created in the last decades of the third century AD. It corresponded to one of the eparchies of the earlier province of Cilicia, existing at least from the time of Antoninus Pius.[20] The origins of this division are disputed.[21] The Diocletianic province corresponded to the geographical area of Cilicia Tracheia or Aspera ('Rough' Cilicia). It represents the Taurus Mountains' eastern thrust to the sea, between Coracesium (Alanya) and Seleuceia-on-the-Calycadnus (Silifke). It consequently forms the south-eastern mountain barrier between the Mediterranean coast of Asia Minor and the central Anatolian plateau. The mountains rise to *c*. 5,000 feet, and present a formidable barrier. They are formed of heavily folded limestones, retaining little surface drainage and allowing little arable farming. An exception to this bleak picture is the Calycadnus valley, which broadens out in its middle reaches to provide sufficient land for the cities of the Isaurian Dodecapolis, centred on Germanicopolis, and whose fertility still impressed Davis in the last century.[22] This valley also provides the major route up to the plateau apart from the Cilician Gates to the east. Other, smaller routes existed: from Anemurium, a difficult route rose to Germanicopolis and, ultimately, the plateau. Futher west, a route passes Laertes, and a series of minor sites, κλίματα (districts) of the major cities of the coast, before reaching the plateau near Nea Isaura.[23] The western boundary of Cilicia was the river Melas (Manavgat Çayï), and this valley also, as Ammianus relates (14.2.11), was an important route. These routes led to the high pastures of the Taurus, before descending to the Lycaonian plateau. Here were the summer pastures for the shepherds and flocks of both Lycaonian and coastal cities. On these passes, the delicate agreements between rival pastoral interests were hammered out; here the wild upland shepherds faced the first line of defence of the cities on both sides of the Taurus.[24] The dominant power-brokers were the magistrates and estate- and herd-owners of the major cities. Hence the interest in the extension of control to the upland κλίματα of Cotradis, Bonosus and Banava by Casae in the western lowlands of the region,[25] and Colybrassus' interest in perpetuating memory of its arbitration in high Thouththourbia.[26] Tombstones of the mountain herdsmen, carved in their traditional styles, attest to their spread well down into the hinterland of Selinus/Trajanopolis (modern Gazipasa).[27] The danger of such men allying with dissident peasants was ever-present in this area, and was surely the factor that caused banditry to be 'endemic' in this region.[28]

We can now proceed to examine the accounts of the Isaurians in Ammianus.

Ammianus 14.2: the events of 354

Almost at the start of the extant books of Ammianus, we encounter the Isaurians, in the most extensive account in the *Res Gestae*. They are introduced as fickle fighters, now withdrawing, now raiding (14.2.1). Here Ammianus sets the Isaurians in the form of *latrones*, always engaged in undisciplined warfare.[29] This tradition extends from Livy (8.34.7–1), who has the consul Papirius express the difference between *latrocinium* and *militia*:

When military discipline has been defiled even once, the soldier will not obey his tribune nor the tribune his legate, nor the legate his consul, nor the master of horse his dictator. No one would have respect for men or gods, or for military commands. Soldiers would wander without leave in peace and in war; careless of their military status they would go wherever they wished, idiosyncratically, and they would not distinguish day from night, favourable from unfavourable terrain, but would fight whether ordered to do so or not by their general, and they would not cleave to standards or their posts: it would all be blind and by chance like banditry, not like the solemn and sacred rites of war.

Immediately we realize the nature of the Isaurians: they are styled as feckless bandits. We could, however, as 'common-sense' historians, naively read this passage as a vivid description of the tactics of semi-nomadic herders, ranging more widely and turning more desperately to predation when the pastures are at their leanest. Such misfortunes not only affect the pastoralists: neighbouring farmers might also feel the pinch and make common cause with the pastoralists. The modern critic is therefore caught in a double-bind: Ammianus' description fits both our derived concepts of the portrayal of outsiders in Roman historiography and our ethnographically derived views of rural revolt. This passage may well represent Ammianus setting the scene by means of generally accepted stereotypes; however, an effective stereotype must contain some material that is not wholly contradicted by experience, and so must, at least partially, be *true*.

However, in this case, after the statement concerning the fecklessness of endemic banditry, Ammianus goes on to say that 'they broke out in a serious war' (*ad bella gravia proruperunt*; 14.2.1), providing a transitional passage from the generic activities of the Isaurians to this particular incident. Again we encounter difficulties: as ancient historians, we are professionally tempted to use this phrase as evidence of escalation, for which we can adduce a whole series of comparative studies on popular revolts and suggest that communities have a scaled series of responses to crisis or outrage (what the late E.P. Thompson called a 'moral economy'[30]), only reverting to open revolt when all else has failed. A fine example of this is the Rebecca Riots of South-West Wales as studied by David Jones: here charivari displays were first employed against the hated toll-houses and their owners, before full-scale destruction began.[31] It also lends weight to Hobsbawm's comment that 'at times of crisis, peasants *become* bandits'.[32]

On this occasion, uniquely in classical literature, we are told the causes of a peasant rebellion: some fellow Isaurians had been thrown to wild beasts in the amphitheatre in Iconium. This specificity fits in awkwardly with the generalized account of how bandits normally behave, presented earlier. Indeed, it actually contradicts it, for we were told in the opening section that the Isaurians revolted 'with the encouragement of impunity' (*alente impunitate*, 14.2.1).

Even so, the cause of the rebellion is puzzling: the execution of bandits by exposure to wild beasts was not unusual. It is difficult to see how such execution of bandits was *praeter morem* (14.2.1). The only possible answer is that captured Isaurians were not so treated: that local law enforcement was conceived in a manner as elastic as the local response to difficulties, and that, given the nature of the Isaurian landscape and the known characteristics of Isaurians, mercy would be shown.[33]

After details of the specific grievance which triggered the revolt, we return to generalizations based on literary citation to establish the revolt. By citing Cicero[34] Ammianus gives universal validity to the description of the early stages of a peasant uprising, but also conveniently likens them to beasts, a common appellation of bandits in Roman legal discourse.[35] Here again the passage reverts to the stereotyping of bandits seen earlier, despite the explicit statement earlier of the specific causes of this revolt. This trait, of seeking the generalization rather than the specificity, is seen by Auerbach as a feature of Roman historiography.[36] However, the detailed exposition of the cause of the revolt has to be surrounded by normalization for the behaviour of the rebels by stereotype or citation. This is a severe disjunction for modern readers. It is, in Sinfield's terms, a 'faultline', which occurs when 'the unstable juxtaposition of cultural and military-industrial discourses ... [which] is typical of the uneven and changing relations between economic, political, military, and cultural power' and 'the project of ideology to represent such relations as harmonious and coherent, so effacing contradiction and conflict' contradict each other.[37] We have a similar contradiction in this passage of Ammianus, where what historians might consider the 'nugget' of information sits so uneasily within the rhetorical discourse of power constructed around it.

This picture is further complicated by the next phase of the rebellion, when ships are seized and abortive attempts are made to disrupt the shipping in the Cyprus Strait. This is reminiscent of the Amazons' seizure of ships in Herodotus (4.105–14) and further characterizes the Isaurians as outsiders within the mode of classical discourse.[38]

Thence the rebels moved quickly inland to the northern frontier of Isauria with Lycaonia. This represents a considerable journey across the whole province. It is not, however, an impossible undertaking. Any of the western routes described above would have sufficed to ensure the speedy transit of the insurgents across the area. From the heights, they controlled the passes and closed the roads to prey on travellers.

Again, we must consider what actually occurred here in 354. The seizure of ships is an intrusion into the narrative and, given the Herodotus parallel, might be seen as part of the 'colour' of the scene rather than a historical event. The retreat to the mountains does fit in with previous patterns of revolt in the region, going back to the Hellenistic period. When the elders of Termessus handed over Alcetas to his enemies in the early third century BC against the wishes of the νέοι, the youth threatened to abandon the city and withdraw to the higher pastures.[39] Similarly, the rebels of AD 36 'withdrew into the ridges of mount Taurus'.[40]

Withdrawal seems to have become a formal part of the ritual of rebellion. This initial rejection of peasant responsibilities is just as culpable ideologically (and just as striking!) as Thrasea Paetus' withdrawal from Nero's senate. To withdraw is to refuse to be counted: out on the hills were the masterless men, normally shepherds, but now supplemented by peasants who, like the Cathars of Montaillou, were initiated into the mysteries of the drove-roads.[41]

Once ensconced, the insurgents plundered Lycaonia in the face of the local militia. The Isaurians also wisely held to their uplands and employed the raiding tactics with which the mountain-dwellers intimidate plainsmen. When the insurgents were rash enough to fight on level ground, they were easily beaten by the Roman regulars.

The rebels then headed back into Pamphylia, but were kept east of the Melas/Manavgat Çayï by the Roman forces. This route from Lycaonia to western Rough Cilicia is alluded to in the *Synaxarium Ecclesiae Constantinopolitanae* where a disciple returns with a martyr's relics in record time by this route.[42] In 1982 I observed transhumants taking this very route up to their summer pastures by means of a Seljuk *chaussée* which overlay earlier roads.

At the Melas they paused, unable to find the means to cross. Attacked in the rear by the garrison of Side, they returned by the same route to Laranda in eastern Lycaonia. Finding resistance there, they swung down to eastern Cilicia (by the Calycadnus Valley, at the head of which lies Laranda), to Palaea (located by the *Tabuli Imperii Byzantini* at Tahta Limanï).[43] Here was the supply base for the troops in Isauria. Ammianus informs us of their hunger (14.2.13), for given Cilicia's notorious shortage of agricultural surplus, there would not be much left to forage outside supply bases and well-fortified estate centres which were always a feature of the landscape.[44] Unauthorized movements such as this would be precluded from easy access to such supplies, a policy which seems to have been used later by Valens and Theodosius against the Goths,[45] as well as by Stilicho against Alaric:[46] although its merits seem dubious in the Balkan Peninsula, they are self-evident here. Palaea seems not to have been a major fort: Hild and Hellenkemper notice only a 'kleiner spätrömisch-frühbyzantinischer Siedlungsplatz' by a perennial spring.[47] This small fortress defeated the siegecraft of the insurgents who retired to face the provincial garrison at Seleuceia under the *comes* Castricius. Here, the illegitimate bandits faced the legitimate soldiers of Rome in the shape of *Legiones* I and II Isaurica and I Pontica. The narrative seeks to justify Castricius' repeated unwillingness to fight.[48] His technically superior force was confined within Seleuceia until Nebridius, *comes Orientis*, arrived, whereupon the Isaurians wisely departed.

Ammianus 19.13.1–3: the events of 359

Five years later, the Isaurians again come to the historian's notice. Their recrudescence is likened to that of snakes, and so this hydra-headed people, refreshed by sloughing their skins, return to haunt us. We hear no details of their activities; only the Roman response. The *comes* Lauricius, a man of political skill, is employed to deal with them in default of a military solution. However, we hear from other sources of a 'fort long before seized by rebels' being captured by Lauricius (*CIL* III, 6733).

Such small forts, or towers, are mentioned by the sources from the first to the fifth century AD,[49] and their remains are common in the Cilician countryside. There are many such towers in the east of the area, studied by Mackay.[50] I have argued that these structures were enlarged and refurbished in the Roman period.[51] From the west of our area comes a tower of first-century date, described by its dedicatory inscription as a πύργος, which carries connotations of a fortified storage place.[52] This structure was the centre of the estate of the family of Hermogenes, who were the major family in first-century Cagrae.[53] In the fifth century, such towers become important as power bases and detention centres for Flavius Zeno, minister of Theodosius II, and for the emperor Zeno and his opponent Illous.[54] When Anastasius crushed Isauria at the end of the fifth century, he concentrated on destroying the towers.[55]

The importance of these towers in the literary record and as represented in the surviving monuments must imply a corresponding importance within the structure of Isaurian society. I have argued that they served as centres of protection in an otherwise hostile landscape subject to marauders.[56] These towers can be assigned to individual members of the curial classes in the cities and thus represent the extension of the clientage networks into the countryside. As well as giving the élites a hold over the rural dwellers, they also enabled the countryfolk to be concentrated for the exertion of private power. As such, therefore, they were the material representation of the control of the countryside by the town. Lauricius recognized this in his appropriation of a tower in a particularly sensitive position (*CIL* III, 673339 = *ILS* 740). It may well be that this low-key action, directed against small but valuable targets, fits Ammianus' description of the man as somebody who 'connected many evils by threats rather than by actual severity' (*minis potius quam acerbitate pleraque correxit*; 19.13.2). These low-key operations ensured the quiet of the province for almost a decade.

Ammianus 27.9.6–7: the events of 368

This is the final appearance of the Isaurians in the extant books of Ammianus. The Isaurians have taken to wide-scale plunder in small bands (*globatim per vicina digressi praedones*; 27.9.6), raiding the neighbouring rich plains of Pamphylia and Cilicia Pedias. Here, we are told, lay *oppida* and rich villas.

The latter are now being discovered by chance find and excavation, and the publication of the mosaics by Budde attests to the wealth of these coastal villas in the fourth century.[57]

The first response to this (admittedly low-level) problem was a piece of private enterprise by the *vicarius* of Asia, Musonius, who had previously held a post as a teacher of rhetoric at Athens. Like a true sophist,[58] *deploratis novissime rebus*, and scorning the degeneracy of the regular soldiery, he turned to the municipal *ad hoc* police force, the *diogmitae*.[59] Perhaps this was the nearest approach to the citizen militia of classical Greece, which Publius Herennius Dexippus had attempted to revive in his glorious campaign against the Heruli.[60] However, this time, history repeated itself as tragedy:[61] tipstaff men arrayed as regulars were no match for skilled guerrilla fighters and the sophist was no tactician. His forces were ambushed and annihilated.

The defeat both encouraged the rebels and forced the Roman authorities to respond decisively. Ammianus gives us no clear idea of how the Isaurians were driven back into their mountain lairs: he returns to the stereotype of the Isaurians being easy game on the plain. But then something unprecedented occurs. The Roman forces follow up their victory and bear Roman arms into central Isauria and the insurgents

> by means of a truce, asked for peace to be yielded to them, on the initiative of the Germanicopolitani, whose opinions always had power with them, like the standard-bearer's office in battle. When hostages were given (as was demanded), they remained quiet for a long time, daring nothing aggressive.
> (27.9.7)

We must consider the role of the Germanicopolitani.[62] Ideologically, if the Isaurians are merely bandits, their *signiferi* must be the true ἀρχιληϲταί, the leaders of this anti-army. However linked to the insurgents by the ideology of Ammianus' language, they seem to have been sufficiently detached to broker the cease-fire. I know of no parallel in ancient history to this remarkable stand-off other than the treaty between the slave-rebel Drimakos and Chios in the fourth century BC.[63]

The Isaurians clearly needed an armistice. Why did the Roman forces not follow up their victory? It may be that there was some truth in the stereotype and that the Isaurians were a formidable challenge on their own ground. Certainly if the Roman forces were privy to this discourse about the Isaurians, their morale would be low. Perhaps the Germanicopolitani had a strong argument.

By the fourth century AD, the centre of Isauria had shifted from Nea Isaura (Zengibar Kalesi) on the Lycaonian frontier, to the middle Calycadnus Valley, dominated by Germanicopolis (Ermenek). This fertile valley formed the main lateral route through Isauria. Passes to the north led to the high Taurus, the summer pastures of the Isaurians; to the south lay the passes to the coastal cities. Any movement by rebels would have to pass through the territory of Germanicopolis and the other cities of the Dodecapolis. These cities were the front line of the defence of the cities of the coastal plain. Their position made them natural middlemen.

The strength of the position of the Germanicopolitani went further than this. The spokesmen and bargainers of this group were no doubt the town councillors whose status had in earlier times been bought by lavish donations to the city from wealth derived from their estates.[64] These estates would have had strongly fortified centres where protection was available and strong-arm men might serve as estate-guards or ὀροφυλάκες. This provided a refuge and a pool for rebels, and also a means of controlling them. After a revolt, a rebel without some protection would face a struggle for existence.[65] Laws against harbouring bandits on estates can only make sense in an area where estates depend on violence for protection.[66]

These considerations apply also to those apparently furthest from the reach of curial protection: the shepherds. The very existence of an 'Isaurian' type of tombstone and its distribution throughout the mountains and down the transhumance routes suggest that some shepherds had pretensions to respectability and the means to acquire its trappings. Such men had gained status as ἀρχιποίμενες (head shepherds) from their service to their employers. Their subordinates, too, had hopes of preferment from the landlords of the cities. Masters of both deviant groups, bandits and shepherds, were bound to the elders of Germanicopolis.

The Roman order was also tied to the local élites.[67] They were the power-brokers between the central government and the populations of the empire. Local élites were instantly recognizable and worthy of respect. The Germanicopolitani were visibly the people to negotiate a settlement.

The deal, then, was to the advantage of all the contracting parties. The peace, however, was not long secured. Zosimus (4.20.1–2) informs us of a further revolt in 378. By then, Ammianus' narrative (and, arguably, the Roman state) had more pressing concerns: Adrianople neared.

Within Ammianus' narrative, the Isaurian *logos* is a sideshow. He is not a historian of Isauria, but of the Roman empire. It is possible, however, with a close reading of the text, to elucidate the peculiarities of Isaurian social structure which provide the context for the revolts of the fourth century. Isauria can be considered along with the other provincial interests of Ammianus, as a contribution to our understanding of provincial government in the fourth century.

Notes

1 *SHA, Trig. Tyr.* 26. 6–7. All translations, unless otherwise credited, are my own.
2 Ammianus' historical asides on the Isaurians parallel the treatment given to the Scythians in Herodotus as described by F. Hartog, *The Mirror of Herodotus. The Representation of the*

Other in the Writing of History, Berkeley 1988, although the accounts are considerably shorter. These passages also explicitly contrast their subject with the world of the Roman order, by the distancing device of *ekphrasis* – on which, see A.J. Woodman, *Rhetoric in Classical Historiography*, London 1988.

3 Whose existence could not be guessed from the account of the *Historia Augusta* cited above, but can be inferred from Strabo, Pliny and the Byzantine episcopal lists. Honorifics of these cities have been preserved, and in most cases their sites have been established. A similar blindness to the *polis* in Isauria prevails in Ammianus, except on one crucial occasion (29.7.7).

4 J. Rougé, 'L'Histoire Auguste et l'Isaurie au IVème siècle', *REA* 68 (1966), 282–315.

5 J.R.S. Sterrett, *The Wolfe Expedition to Asia Minor*, Boston 1888; H. Swoboda, J. Keil and F. Knoll, *Denkmäler aus Lykaonien, Pamphylien und Isaurien*, Vienna 1935.

6 E.J. Davis, *Life in Asiatic Turkey*, London 1879, esp. chs XII–XVI.

7 R. Syme, *Ammianus and the Historia Augusta*, Oxford 1968; 'Isauria in Pliny', *AS* 36 (1986), 159–64; 'Isaura and Isauria: Some Problems', in E. Frézouls (ed.), *Sociétés urbaines, sociétés rurales dans l'Asie Mineure et la Syrie hellénistiques et romaines. Actes du colloque organisé à Strasbourg, novembre 1985*, Strasbourg 1987, 131–47; *Anatolica. Studies in Strabo*, ed. by A.R. Birley, Oxford 1995, ch. 20.

8 G.E. Bean and T.B. Mitford, 'Sites Old and New in Rough Cilicia', *AS* 12 (1962), 285–317; *Journeys in Rough Cilicia in 1962 and 1963*, Vienna 1964; *Journeys in Rough Cilicia 1964–1968*, Vienna 1970.

9 For a particularly pertinent example, see Bean and Mitford, *Journeys in Rough Cilicia 1964–1968*, 219ff. on the late Roman defences of Imsi Ören (ancient Philadelphia?).

10 T.B. Mitford, 'Roman Rough Cilicia', *ANRW* II.7.2 (1980), 1230–61; itself drafted after Bean's decease.

11 J.F. Matthews, *The Roman Empire of Ammianus*, London 1989, 355ff.; see particularly p. 533 n. 97. Interestingly, the dust-jacket featured the illustration from the *Notitia Dignitatum* (Bodleian Library, Canon. Misc. 378, fol. 114^v) showing the command of the *comes per Isauriam*: a comment on the centrality of this people so peripheral that they are omitted from the Penguin translation of Ammianus?

12 K.R. Hopwood, 'Policing the Hinterland: Rough Cilicia and Isauria', in S. Mitchell (ed.), *Armies and Frontiers in Roman and Byzantine Anatolia. Proceedings of a Conference Held at University College, Swansea in April 1981*, Oxford 1983, 173–88; 'Policing the River Melas', *Yayla* 5 (1984), 25–9; 'Towers, Territory and Terror: How the East was Held', in P.W. Freeman and D.L. Kennedy (eds), *The Defence of the Roman and Byzantine East: Proceedings of a Colloquium Held at the University of Sheffield in April 1986*, vol. 1, Oxford 1986, 343–56; 'Bandits, Elites and Rural Order', in A. Wallace-Hadrill (ed.), *Patronage in Ancient Society*, London 1989, 171–87; 'Consent and Control: How the Peace was kept in Rough Cilicia', in D.H. French and C.S. Lightfoot (eds), *The Eastern Frontier of the Roman Empire. Proceedings of a Colloquium Held at Ankara in September 1988*, vol. 1, Oxford 1989, 191–201; 'The Indigenous Populations of Rough Cilicia under Roman Rule', *X Türk Tarih Kongresi Ankara, 22–26 Eylül 1986, Kongreye Sunulan Bildiriler*, vol. 1, Ankara 1990, 337–46; 'The Links between the Coastal Cities of Western Rough Cilicia and the Interior during the Roman Period', *De Anatolia Antiqua* 1, Paris 1991, 305–9; 'Who were the Isaurians?', *XI Türk Tarih Kongresi, Ankara, 5–9 Eylül 1990, Kongreye Sunulan Bildiriler*, vol. 1, Ankara 1994, 375–86; 'All that may become a Man: The Bandit in the Ancient Novel', in L. Foxhall and J. Salmon (ed.), *When Men were Men. Masculinity, Power and Identity in Classical Antiquity*, London 1998, 195–204; 'Bandits, between Grandees and the State: The Structure of Order in Roman Rough Cilicia', in K.R. Hopwood (ed.), *Organised Crime in the Ancient World*, London 1999, 177–205.

13 F. Hild and H. Hellenkemper, *Kilikien und Isaurien*, Vienna 1990.

14 F. Hild and H. Hellenkemper, *Neue Forschungen in Isaurien und Kilikien*, Vienna 1986.

15 A. Lewin, 'Banditismo e *Civilitas* nella Cilicia Tracheia Antica e Tardoantica', *Quaderni Storici* 76 (1991), 167–84.
16 E.J. Hobsbawm, *Bandits*, 2nd edn, Harmondsworth 1985.
17 C.E. Minor, 'The Robber Tribes of Isauria', *Ancient World* 2 (1979), 117–27.
18 B.D. Shaw, 'Bandit Highlands and Lowland Peace: The Mountains of Isauria-Cilicia', *JESHO* 33 (1990), 199–233, 237–70.
19 B.D. Shaw, 'Bandits in the Roman Empire', *Past and Present* 105 (1984), 3–51.
20 Syme, *Anatolica*, 218; see also Hopwood, 'Who were the Isaurians?', 375–6.
21 Hopwood, 'Who were the Isaurians?', contra Syme, 'Isauria in Pliny'.
22 Davis, *Life in Asiatic Turkey*, 352–3.
23 On these routes, see now Hopwood, 'The Links between the Coastal Cities', 306.
24 *Ibid.*, 307–8.
25 Bean and Mitford, *Journeys in Rough Cilicia 1964–1968*, 124–5; Hopwood, 'Who were the Isaurians?', 382.
26 Bean and Mitford, *Journeys in Rough Cilicia 1964–1968*, 139–40.
27 Mitford, 'Roman Rough Cilicia', 1249 n. 83 (sadly unlocated).
28 Syme, 'Isaura and Isauria', 115, for the adjective.
29 Hopwood, 'All that may become a Man', 195–7.
30 E.P. Thompson, 'The Moral Economy of the English Crowd in the Eighteenth Century', *Past and Present* 50 (1971), 76–136.
31 D.J.V. Jones, *Rebecca's Children. A Study of Rural Society, Crime and Protest*, Oxford 1990.
32 Hobsbawm, *Bandits*, 99.
33 Lucian, *Icaromenippus* 16.771. On the executions at Iconium, see Hopwood, 'Bandits, between Grandees and the State', 182–3.
34 *Pro Cluentio* 25.67.
35 See Hopwood, 'Bandits, Elites and Rural Order', 180.
36 E. Auerbach, *Mimesis. The Representation of Reality in Western Literature*, Princeton 1953, ch. 2.
37 A. Sinfield, *Faultlines. Cultural Materialism and the Politics of Dissident Reading*, Oxford 1992, 9.
38 E. Hall, *Inventing the Barbarian*, Oxford 1989, 202.
39 Diodorus Siculus 18.44–7.
40 *in iuga Tauri montis abscessit* (Tacitus, *Ann.* 6.41).
41 E. Le Roy Ladurie, *Montaillou. Cathars and Catholics in a French Village 1294–1324*, London 1980, 90.
42 *Propylaeum ad Acta Sanctorum Nov.*, ed. H. Delehaye, Brussels 1902, 814.
43 Hild and Hellenkemper, *Kilikien und Isaurien*, 372.
44 On the control of agricultural surplus in Rough Cilicia, see Hopwood, 'Towers, Territory and Terror'.
45 P.J. Heather, *Goths and Romans, 332–489*, Oxford 1991, 132.
46 A. Cameron, *Claudian. Poetry and Propaganda at the Court of Honorius*, Oxford 1970, 168–70.
47 Hild and Hellenkemper, *Kilikien und Isaurien*, 372 n. 52.
48 For a discussion of this stand-off, see Hopwood, 'Consent and Control', 196–7.
49 Pliny, *HN* 5.94; Amm. Marc. 19.3.2; *CIL* III, 6733; P. Gr. Vindob. 29788c; John of Antioch *frgs.* 206; 214.5; 214.6. For a discussion of Isaurian towers, see Hopwood, 'Towers, Territory and Terror', 346–9.
50 T.S. Mackay, 'Olba in Rough Cilicia', unpub. PhD diss. Bryn Mawr, n.d.
51 Hopwood, 'Towers, Territory and Terror', 346–7.
52 For discussion and references, see *ibid.*, 348.
53 See, for details, Bean and Mitford, *Journeys in Rough Cilicia 1964–1968*, 22–9.
54 John of Antioch, *frg.* 205.2; 214.12.

55 Theophanes, *Chronographia*, AM 5988 (= C. Mango and R. Scott, *The Chronicle of Theophanes Confessor*, Oxford 1997, 211).
56 Hopwood, 'Towers, Territory and Terror'; 'Bandits, Elites and Rural Order', 180–1.
57 L. Budde, *Antike Mosaiken in Kilikien*, Recklinghausen 1972.
58 See E.L. Bowie, 'The Greeks and their Past in the Second Sophistic', *Past and Present* 46 (1970), 3–41.
59 These forces had been used by Marcus Aurelius during his desperate northern wars (SHA, *M. Aur.* 21; cf. *CIG* III, 3831a = Le Bas–Waddington III, 992).
60 F.G.B. Millar, 'P. Herennius Dexippus: the Greek World and the Third Century Invasion', *JRS* 59 (1969), 12–29.
61 K. Marx, *The Eighteenth Brumaire of Louis Napoleon*, in D. Fernbach (ed.), *Marx: Surveys from Exile*, Harmondsworth 1973, 143–249.
62 See further in Hopwood, 'Bandits, between Grandees and the State'.
63 Athenaeus VI, 265b–266f. For discussion see A. Fuks, 'Slave War and Slave Crisis in Chios in the Third Century BC', *Athenaeum* 46 (1968), 102–11.
64 For euergetism, see P. Veyne, *Bread and Circuses. Historical Sociology and Political Pluralism*, Harmondsworth 1990, 10–13.
65 Hence the frequent appearance of bandits in the service of Mafias or estate-owners in the modern world; A. Blok, *The Mafia of a Sicilian Village, 1860–1960*, Oxford 1974. Unsupported bandits seem to have a lifespan of only two or three years: E.J. Hobsbawm, *Primitive Rebels*, Manchester 1959, 19.
66 *Cod. Theod.* 9.21.1; 9.29.2; 7.18.7; *Cod. Just.* 9.39.1–2. For a discussion of these passages, see Hopwood, 'Bandits, between Grandees and the State'.
67 See M.D. Goodman, *The Ruling Class of Judaea. The Origins of the Jewish Revolt against Rome AD 66–70*, Cambridge 1987, for the dire effects of a breakdown in the relationship.

SELECT BIBLIOGRAPHY

The following bibliography is restricted to publications on Ammianus Marcellinus which are mentioned in this volume.

Amat, J., 'Ammien Marcellin et la Justice Immanente (14, 11, 20–34)', in *De Tertullien aux Mozarabes. Mélanges J. Fontaine*, vol. 1, Paris 1992, 267–79.
Ammien Marcellin, Histoire, Texte établi, traduit et annoté par J. Fontaine, E. Galletier, G. Sabbah and M.-A. Marié, vols 1–5, Collection des universités de France publiée sous le patronage de l'Association Guillaume Budé, Paris 1968–96.
Austin, N.J.E., 'In Support of Ammianus' Veracity', *Historia* 22 (1973), 331–5.
Austin, N.J.E., *Ammianus on Warfare: An Investigation into Ammianus' Military Knowledge* (Collection Latomus 165), Brussels 1979.
Barnes, T.D., 'Literary Convention, Nostalgia and Reality in Ammianus Marcellinus', in G. Clarke et al. (eds), *Reading the Past in Late Antiquity*, Rushcutters Bay 1990, 59–92.
Barnes, T.D., 'Ammianus Marcellinus and his World', *CP* 88 (1993), 55–70.
Barnes, T.D., *Ammianus Marcellinus and the Representation of Historical Reality* (Cornell Studies in Classical Philology 56), Ithaca and London 1998.
Bitter, N., *Kampfschilderungen bei Ammianus Marcellinus*, Bonn 1976.
Blockley, R.C., *Ammianus Marcellinus: A Study of his Historiography and Political Thought* (Collection Latomus 141), Brussels 1975.
Blockley, R.C., 'Ammianus Marcellinus on the Persian Invasion of A.D. 359', *Phoenix* 42 (1988), 244–60.
Boeft, J. den, Hengst, D. den and Teitler, H.C., *Philological and Historical Commentary on Ammianus Marcellinus XX, XI*, Groningen 1987–91.
Boeft, J. den, Drijvers, J.W., den Hengst, D. and Teitler, H.C., *Philological and Historical Commentary on Ammianus Marcellinus XXII, XXIII*, Groningen 1995–8.
Boeft, J. den, Hengst, D. den, Teitler, H.C. (eds), *Cognitio Gestorum: The Historiographic Art of Ammianus Marcellinus*, Amsterdam 1992.
Brok, M.F.A., *De Perzische Expeditie van Keizer Julianus volgens Ammianus Marcellinus*, Groningen 1959.
Brok, M.F.A., 'Die Quellen von Ammians Exkurs über Persien', *Mnemosyne* 38 (1975), 47–56.
Brok, M.F.A., 'Bombast oder Kunstfertigkeit? Ammians Beschreibung der *ballista*', *RhM* 120 (1997), 331–45.
Broszinski, H. and Teitler, H.C., 'Einige neuerdings entdeckten Fragmente der Hersfelder Handschrift des Ammianus Marcellinus', *Mnemosyne* 43 (1990), 408–23.

SELECT BIBLIOGRAPHY

Caltabiano, M., 'Il carattere delle digressioni nelle *Res Gestae* di Ammiano Marcellino', in A. Garzya (ed.), *Metodologie della ricerca sulla tarda antichità, Atti del Primo Convegno dell' Associazione di Studi Tardoantichi*, Naples 1989, 289–96.

Cameron, A., 'The Roman friends of Ammianus', *JRS* 54 (1964), 15–28.

Camus, P.M., *Ammien Marcellin: témoin des courants culturels et réligieux à la fin du IVe siècle*, Paris 1967.

Cicochka, H., 'Die Konzeption des Exkurses im Geschichtswerk des Ammianus Marcellinus', *Eos* 63 (1975), 329–40.

Crump, G.A., *Ammianus Marcellinus as a Military Historian* (Historia Einzelschriften 27), Wiesbaden 1975.

De Bonfils, G., *Ammiano Marcellino e l'Imperatore*, Bari 1986.

Demandt, A., *Zeitkritik und Geschichtsbild im Werk Ammians* (diss. Marburg), Bonn 1965.

Dillemann, L., 'Ammien Marcellin et les pays de l'Euphrate et du Tigre', *Syria. Revue d'art oriental et d'archéologie* 38 (1961), 87–158.

Drexler, H., *Ammianstudien* (Spudasmata 31), Hildesheim 1974.

Drijvers, J.W., 'Ammianus Marcellinus 15.13.1–2: some observations on the career and bilingualism of Strategius Musonianus', *CQ* 46 (1996), 532–7.

Drinkwater, J.F., 'Silvanus, Ursicinus and Ammianus Marcellinus: fact or fiction?', in C. Deroux (ed.), *Studies in Latin Literature and Roman History* VII (Collection Latomus 227), Brussels 1994, 568–76.

Drinkwater, J.F., 'Julian and the Franks and Valentinian I and the Alamanni: Ammianus on Romano-German relations', *Francia* 24 (1997), 1–15.

Elliott, T.G., *Ammianus Marcellinus and Fourth-Century History*, Sarasota 1983.

Emmett, A.M., 'Introductions and conclusions to digressions in Ammianus Marcellinus', *Museum Philologum Londiniense* 5 (1981), 15–33.

Emmett, A.M., 'The digressions in the lost books of Ammianus Marcellinus', in B. Croke and A.M. Emmett (eds), *History and Historians in Late Antiquity*, Sydney 1983, 42–53.

Ensslin, W., *Zur Geschichtsschreibung und Weltanschauung des Ammianus Marcellinus* (Klio Beiheft 16), Leipzig 1923.

Fletcher, G.B.A., 'Stylistic borrowings and parallels in Ammianus Marcellinus', *RPh*, 3rd Series 11 (1937), 337–95.

Fontaine, J., 'Ammien Marcellin, historien romantique', *Bulletin de l'Association Guillaume Budé* 28 (1969), 417–35.

Fornara, C.W., 'Julian's Persian expedition in Ammianus and Zosimus', *JHS* 111 (1991), 1–15.

Fornara, C.W., 'Studies in Ammianus Marcellinus I: the letter of Libanius and Ammianus' connection with Antioch', *Historia* 41 (1992), 328–44.

Fornara, C.W., 'Studies in Ammianus Marcellinus II: Ammianus' knowledge and use of Greek and Latin literature', *Historia* 41 (1992), 420–38.

Frézouls, E., 'La mission du "magister equitum" Ursicin en Gaule (355–357) d'après Ammien Marcellin', in M. Renard (ed.), *Hommages à Albert Grenier* II, Brussels 1962, 673–88.

Gardthausen, V., *Die geographischen Quellen Ammians*, Jbh. f. class. Philol., Suppl. 6, Leipzig 1873.

Gimazane, J., *Ammien Marcellin, sa Vie et son Œuvre*, Toulouse 1889.

Hamilton, W. and Wallace-Hadrill, A., *Ammianus Marcellinus: The Later Roman Empire (A.D. 354–378)*, Harmondsworth 1986.

Hunt, E.D., 'Christians and Christianity in Ammianus Marcellinus', *CQ* 35 (1985), 186–200.

Hunt, E.D., 'Christianity in Ammianus Marcellinus revisited', *Studia Patristica* 24 (1993), 108–13.

SELECT BIBLIOGRAPHY

Jonge, P. de, *Sprachlicher und Historischer Kommentar zu Ammianus Marcellinus XIV; Philological and Historical Commentary on Ammianus Marcellinus XV–XIX*, Groningen 1935–82.

King, C., 'The veracity of Ammianus Marcellinus' description of the Huns', *AJAH* 12 (1987[1995]), 77–95.

Liebeschuetz, J.H.W.G., 'Ammianus, Julian and Divination', in M. Wissemann (ed.), *Roma Renascens. Festschrift I. Opelt*, Frankfurt am Main 1988, 198–213.

Mackail, J.W., 'Ammianus Marcellinus', *JRS* 10 (1920), 103–18; repr. in his *Classical Studies*, London 1925, 159–87.

MacMullen, R., 'Some pictures in Ammianus Marcellinus', *The Art Bulletin* 46 (1964), 435–55; repr. in his *Changes in the Roman Empire: Essays in the Ordinary*, Princeton 1990, 78–106.

Marié, M.-A., 'Virtus et Fortuna chez Ammien Marcellin', *REL* 67 (1989), 179–90.

Martin, R., 'Ammien Marcellin ou la servitude militaire', in R. Chevallier (ed.), *Colloque Histoire et Historiographie, Clio*, Paris 1980, 203–13.

Matthews, J.F., 'Ammianus Marcellinus', in T.J. Luce (ed.), *Ancient Writers: Greece and Rome* II, New York 1982, 1117–38.

Matthews, J.F., 'Ammianus' historical evolution', in B. Croke and A. Emmett (eds), *History and Historians in Late Antiquity*, Sydney 1983, 30–41.

Matthews, J.F., 'Ammianus and the eternity of Rome', in C. Holdsworth and T.P. Wiseman (eds), *The Inheritance of Historiography 350–900*, Exeter 1986, 17–29.

Matthews, J.F., 'Ammianus and the eastern frontier: a participant's view', in P. Freeman and D. Kennedy (eds), *The Defence of the Roman and Byzantine East. Proceedings of a Colloquium Held at the University of Sheffield in April 1986*, 2 vols, Oxford 1986, vol. 1, 549–64.

Matthews, J.F., *The Roman Empire of Ammianus*, London 1989.

Matthews, J.F., 'The origin of Ammianus', *CQ* 45 (1994), 252–69.

Momigliano, A.D., 'The lonely historian Ammianus Marcellinus', in his *Essays in Ancient and Modern Historiography*, Oxford 1977, 127–40.

Mommsen, Th., 'Ammians Geographica', *Hermes* 16 (1881), 602–36; repr. in his *Gesammelte Schriften* 7, Berlin 1909, 393–425.

Naudé, C.P.T., 'Fortuna in Ammianus Marcellinus', *Acta Classica* 7 (1964), 70–89.

Neri, V., *Costanzo, Giuliano e l'ideale del Civilis Princeps nelle storie di Ammiano Marcellino* (Studi Bizantini e Slavi 1), Rome 1984.

Neri, V., *Ammiano e il cristianesimo. Religione e politica nelle 'Res Gestae' di Ammiano Marcellino* (Studi di Storia Antica 11), Bologna 1985.

Neri, V., 'Ammianus' definition of Christianity as *absoluta et simplex religio*', in J. den Boeft, D. den Hengst and H.C. Teitler (eds), *Cognitio Gestorum. The Historiographic Art of Ammianus Marcellinus*, Amsterdam 1992, 59–65.

Neumann, K.-G., *Taciteisches im Werk des Ammianus Marcellinus*, Munich 1991.

Pack, R., 'The Roman digressions of Ammianus Marcellinus', *Transactions and Proceedings of the American Philosophical Association* 84 (1953), 181–9.

Paschoud, F., 'Justice et providence chez Ammien Marcellin', in *Hestíasis. Studi di tarda antichità offerti a S. Calderone*, Messina 1986, 139–61.

Paschoud, F., '"Se non è vero, è ben trovato": tradition littéraire et vérité historique chez Ammien Marcellin', *Chiron* 19 (1989), 37–54.

Paschoud, F., 'Valentinien travesti, ou: de la malignité d'Ammien', in J. den Boeft, D. den Hengst and H.C. Teitler (eds), *Cognitio Gestorum. The Historiographic Art of Ammianus Marcellinus*, Amsterdam 1992, 67–84.

Richter, U., 'Die Funktion der Digressionen im Werk Ammians', *Würzburger Jahrbücher für Altertumswissenchaft*, N.F. 15 (1989), 209–22.

Rike, R.L., *Apex Omnium: Religion in the Res Gestae of Ammianus*, Berkeley 1987.

Rolfe, J.C., *Ammianus Marcellinus*, with an English translation, Loeb Classical Library, 3 vols, London and Cambridge (Mass.) 1935–9 (various reprints).

Rosen, K., *Studien zur Darstellungskunst und Glaubwürdigkeit des Ammianus Marcellinus*, Heidelberg 1968 (repr. 1970).

Rosen, K., *Ammianus Marcellinus* (Erträge der Forschung 183), Darmstadt 1982.

Sabbah, G., *La méthode d'Ammien Marcellin. Recherches sur la construction du discours historique dans les Res Gestae*, Paris 1978.

Seager, R., *Ammianus Marcellinus: Seven Studies in his Language and Thought*, Columbia 1986.

Seyfarth, W., 'Der Codex Fuldensis und der Codex E des Ammianus Marcellinus', *Abhandlungen der Deutschen Akademie der Wissenschaften*, Klasse für Sprachen, Literatur und Kunst, 1962.2, Berlin 1962.

Seyfarth, W., 'Ammianus und das Fatum', *Klio* 43 (1965), 291–306.

Seyfarth, W., *Ammiani Marcellini Rerum Gestarum libri qui supersunt*, 2 vols, Berlin 1978.

Signes, J., 'El excursus de los Persas de Amiano Marcelino (XXIII, 6)', *Veleia* 7 (1990), 351–75.

Siniscalco, P., 'Le sacré et l'experience de l'histoire: Ammien Marcellin et Paul Orose', *Bulletin de l'Association Guillaume Budé* (1989), 335–66.

Smith, P.J., 'A note on Ammianus and Juvenal', *LCM* 19 (1994), 23–4.

Sundwall, G.A., 'Ammianus Geographicus', *AJPhil.* 117 (1996), 619–43.

Syme, R., *Ammianus and the Historia Augusta*, Oxford 1968.

Szidat, J., *Historischer Kommentar zu Ammianus Marcellinus Buch XX–XXI* (Historia Einzelschriften 31, 38, 89), Wiesbaden and Stuttgart 1977–96.

Szidat, J., 'Ammian und die historische Realität', in J. den Boeft, D. den Hengst and H.C. Teitler (eds), *Cognitio Gestorum: The Historiographic Art of Ammianus Marcellinus*, Amsterdam 1992, 107–16.

Thompson, E.A., *The Historical Work of Ammianus Marcellinus*, Cambridge 1947 (repr. Groningen 1969).

Warmington, B.H., 'Ammianus Marcellinus and the lies of Metrodorus', *CQ* 31 (1981), 464–8.

Wiedemann, T.E.J., 'Between men and beasts: barbarians in Ammianus Marcellinus', in I.S. Moxon, J.D. Smart and A.J. Woodman (eds), *Past Perspectives. Studies in Greek and Roman Historical Writing*, Cambridge 1986, 189–201.

Woods, D., 'Ammianus and some *Tribuni Scholar Palatinarum c.* A.D. 353–64', *CQ* 47 (1997), 269–91.

INDEX

Abinnaeus (*protector*) 18–19
Ablabius (praetorian prefect) 168
Achaemenids: Ammianus on 195
Aelianus (*dux* of Mesopotamia) 18, 21, 25
Alamanni: co-operation with Rome 128–9
Amida 23–6
animal metaphors 93
Antoninus (defector to Persia) 22, 40, 42, 44, 45
Apodemius (*agens in rebus*) 54–5, 60
Apuleius: on Magi 208, 211
Arbitio (*mag. equitum*) 54
aries 33–4
Arintheus (military commander) 105, 107
Arsaces I 194–202; Ammianus on 194–9
Ausonius 119–20, 132

ballista 24–5, 30–1
bandits 225, 226–8, 231–2
barbarians: Ammianus on 57, 187; Constantine and 171–2; Isaurians as 224; Parthians seen as 200–1
Bezabde 33–4, 35
Bonitus (father of Silvanus) 57, 167–8

Castricius (*comes*) 229
Chaldaeans 211
Christianity: Ammianus's view of 163–4, 173–5, 181, 187; and imperial victory 161–2
Cologne: scene of Silvanus' rebellion 51–2, 59
consistory 56
Constantia (daughter of Constantine) 168
Constantine: Ammianus on 166–76; and barbarians 171–2; Julian on 171–2; and Manichaeans 172–5; other sources on 166–7; and Persia 84, 91, 169–70; and Rome 169
Constantius II: Ammianus on 40–9, 53–7, 69–71, 77–85, 182; and church 79; defeat of Magnentius 161–2; education 82; imperial image 83–4; justice 79–81; and rivals 80–1; taxation 83; wars 23, 81–2
Corduene 108, 109
Crispus Caesar: death of 168
Ctesiphon 91, 93, 94, 109
Cylaces (eunuch) 67
Cyril (bishop of Jerusalem) 162

Dagalaifus (military commander) 105, 107
De Rebus Bellicis: on siege engine 35
Diocletian: court ceremonial 56, 64
diogmitae 231
Diskenes (*notarius*) 24
Domitian: and eunuchs 66, 67
Drinkwater J.F. 51–2, 60, 122

Egypt: source of learning 210
Eunapius: *fr.* 68 156–64; on Constantine 167–8; on Jovian's accession 106, 108; on Jovian's peace with Persia 110; on Jovian's religion 112; sources for his *History* 158–9
eunuchs 64–71
Eutherius (eunuch chamberlain) 65, 66, 67, 68, 167
Eutropius (eunuch chamberlain) 64, 68
Eusebia (wife of Constantius II) 81, 83
Eusebius (eunuch chamberlain) 65
Eusebius (historian of sieges) 35–6
Eusebius, *Life of Constantine* 167
Eustathius (pagan philosopher) 176
exempla: Ammianus's use of 4, 55, 95–6

241

INDEX

fate: in Ammianus 183–4
first-person narrative 96–100
Fornara, C.W. 218–20
fortifications: in Isauria 230; Valentinian's on Rhine 129
Franks: serving Rome 56–7, 167–8

Gainas (military commander) 162–3
Gallus Caesar 58, 65, 80, 83, 183
Gaul: condition of in 350s 52–3, 59–60; taxation 83
Germanicopolis 226, 231–2
Gorgonius (eunuch chamberlain) 65–6
Gratian (emperor) 118–19, 120–1, 123, 133

'hand of God': as coin motif 159
helepolis 34–5
Heliodorus (grand chamberlain) 65–6
Herodotus: Ammianus and 97–8, 218–22, 232 n.2; on Amazons 228; on Magi 208; on passing water 216–17
Homer: echoed in Ammianus 94–5
Hormisdas (elder, Persian prince) 159–61, 163, 169–70
Hormisdas (younger) 159–60
Huns: slashed children's faces 67
Hystaspes: visited India 211; described as king 219–20

imperial: court, 'theatre' of 53–4; purple 56
Iovinianus (ruler of Corduene) 24
Isauria: Ammianus on 226–32; fortified towers in 230; geography of 225–6; recent study of 224–5

Josephus: on *aries* 33; on *helepolis* 34
Jovian (emperor): Ammianus on 105–15; accession 105–8; coinage 111; earlier career 106; peace with Persia 108–11; religion 112–14
Julian: and Alexander 95–6; Ammianus on 52–3, 60, 68–71, 89–103, 110–12, 115, 213; on Constantine 171–2; on Constantius 77–85; death 95; and gods 91–2, 100–3, 181–2; obituary 90–2; Persian campaign 89–103; superstition of 213; and taxation in Gaul 83; and Trajan 96
Juvenal: Ammianus and 141–54

Lampadius (praetorian/urban prefect) 35, 55, 173
Laniogaesus (military tribune) 57
Lauricius (*comes* of Isauria) 230
Libanius: on Constantius 77–85
Livy: Ammianus and 150–1

Magi 207–13, 219
magic, offence of 208–9
Magnentius (usurper) 80–1
Maiozamalcha 35, 94, 97
Malarichus (guard commander) 56
malleolus 35–6
Mamertinus: on Julian 77, 79
Manichaeans 172–5
Matthews, J.F. 5–7, 33, 41, 46, 48, 60, 131, 179–80, 217
Maximinus (*vicarius* of Rome/praetorian prefect) 120, 123, 134
Maximus (usurper) 118
Memorius (*protector*) 20
Metrodorus (philosopher) 170
Modestus (praetorian prefect) 66, 70
Mommsen, Th. 193, 217
Mursa 162
Musonianus *see* Strategius
Musonius (*vicarius* of Asia) 231

Nevitta (*mag. equitum*) 105, 107, 171
Nisibis 109

omens 100–3, 178–9, 185
Optatus (*patricius*) 169
Orfitus (urban prefect) 160

panegyric: genre 78–9; purpose 84–5
Parthia: Ammianus on 194–9; Ammianus's sources for 201–2; Greek and Roman sources on 195–6; Roman view of 199–201
Paul (the 'Chain', *notarius*) 55, 60–1
Persia: Ammianus's digression on 193–4, 208, 210–11, 216–22; Ammianus's experience of 220–2; Constantine and 84, 91; Julian and 89–103; peace with Jovian 108–11
Pirisabora 35, 93, 94
Plato: on Magi 208, 211
Pompey: Ammianus on 71
Procopius (historian): on *aries* 33; on *ballista* 30–1

INDEX

Procopius (usurper) 58, 122, 130, 160
protector: Ammianus as 20–1, 56–7, 60; career and duties of 18–26; *domesticus* 19–20; significance for Ammianus's history 17–18, 23–7

religion: Ammianus's view of 114, 178–87, 212–13
Rome: Ammianus's experience of 21, 68, 117–18, 123, 124–5, 131, 152; Ammianus on embodiment of empire 184–6; and Constantine 169; Constantius' entry into 53, 160–4; digressions in Ammianus 141–54

Sabbah, G. 4, 41, 43, 46–7, 48
Sabinianus (*mag. equitum*) 40, 42, 44, 45, 46, 47, 65
Sallust: Ammianus and 150–1
Salutius Secundus (praetorian prefect) 105
Sassanids: Ammianus on 195; divine kingship of 198
Satire: in Ammianus 153
schola scutariorum clibanariorum: commanded by Hormisdas 161, 163
scorpio (*onager*) 24–5, 31–3
Semiramis 66, 67
Shapur (Sapor) II 20, 21, 40, 42, 43, 44, 81, 109, 159, 176, 198
siege engines 24–5, 29–39; Ammianus on 30, 36
Silvanus (*mag. peditum*) 20, 48–9, 51–61; Ammianus's involvement with 57–61; historicity of his usurpation 51–2
Singara 35, 82, 109
Solicinium 128
Strategius Musonianus (praetorian prefect) 172–3, 175–6
Symmachus (elder, urban prefect) 117–18

Symmachus (younger, urban prefect): and Ammianus 121–4; on Valentinian I 118–25, 127–9, 132–3

Tacitus: Ammianus's debt to 68, 150–1
Tertullus (urban prefect) 184–5
Themistius: on Constantius 77–85, 162; on Jovian's accession 106; on Jovian's religion 112–13
Theodosian Code: laws against heresy 174; laws against magic 208; transmission of 113
Thompson, E.A. 1–2, 40–1, 48

Ursicinus (*mag. equitum/peditum*) 18, 20, 23, 24, 27, 40–9 (movements in 359), 51–2, 54, 56, 57–61 (and Silvanus), 68–9
usurpers: Ammianus on 58–9, 107–8

Valens (emperor): religious toleration 113
Valentinian I: in Ammianus 121–5, 127–32; and Britain 133–4; campaigns against Alamanni 119–21, 127–31; character 122–3; coinage 120; death 122–3; expedition to source of Danube 132; historical reputation 130–1; religious toleration 113, 123–4; and Rome 120–1, 123–4
Vanderspoel, J. 112–13
Varronianus (father of Jovian) 106
Vegetius: on siege engines 35
Verinianus (*protector*) 20, 21, 24
Vetranio (usurper) 80–2
Victor (*mag. equitum*) 105, 107
Vincentius (*protector*) 19
Virgil: in Ammianus 33, 34, 36, 90, 91
Vitruvius: on *aries* 33; on *catapulta* 30–1; on *helepolis* 34–5

Zosimus 159–60, 163, 167, 232